THE SMART GUIDE TO

Sláinte,

Elizabeth Riley Bell

Single Malt Scotch Whisky

BY ELIZABETH RILEY BELL

ILLUSTRATIONS BY TED HARRISON

The Smart Guide To Single Malt Scotch Whisky

Published by

Smart Guide Publications, Inc.
2517 Deer Chase Drive
Norman, OK 73071
www.smartguidepublications.com

For information, address: Smart Guide Publications, Inc. 2517 Deer Creek Drive, Norman, OK 73071

SMART GUIDE and Design are registered trademarks licensed to Smart Guide Publications, Inc.

International Standard Book Number: 978-0-9834421-4-1

Library of Congress Catalog Card Number: 2012933748
11 12 13 14 15 10 9 8 7 6 5 4 3 2 1

Printed in the United States of America

Cover design: Lorna Llewellyn
Copy Editor: Ruth Strother
Back cover design: Joel Friedlander, Eric Gelb, Deon Seifert
Back cover copy: Eric Gelb, Deon Seifert
Illustrations: Ted Harrison
Production: Zoë Lonergan
Indexer: Cory Emberson
V.P./Business Manager: Cathy Barker

ACKNOWLEDGMENTS

At a time when fewer people are doing more work, the people in the whisky industry made time to talk to me and show me their distilleries. For many it was one more thing to do, but they all shared their knowledge and their experience — and did it with grace and generosity. Often, they passed me along to other people, who added to my store of information. To all I am deeply grateful.

Bobby Anderson (Speyburn), Russell Anderson (Highland Park), Raymond Armstrong (Bladnoch), Rachel Barrie (Glenmorangie), Iain Baxter (Inverhouse),Wendy Bennett (Macduff), Jim Beveridge (Diageo), Faye Black (Arran), John Black (Tullibardine), Stephen Bremner, (Tomatin),Tom Bringhurst (SWRI), Jennifer Brophy (Chivas Brothers), Carol Brown (Edrington Group), Andrew Brown (Bunnahabhain), Gordon Bruce (Knockdhu), Stewart Buchanan (BenRiach), Neil Cameron (Glenturret), Gregor Cattanach (Diageo), Ian Chapman (Gordon & MacPhail), Stewart Christine (Royal Brackla), Willie Cochrane (Jura), Graham Coull (Glen Moray), David Cox (Macallan), Ronnie Cox (Glenrothes), William Crilly (Macallan), Keith Cruickshank (Benromach), Peter Currie (Springbank), Francis Cuthbert (Daftmill), Katherine Crisp (Burn Stewart), Diane Dickson, David Doig (Fettercairn, Tamnavulin), Tim Dumenil (Diageo), Anne and Alan Duncan, Kirsty Duncan (Glen Garioch), Olivier Fagnen (SWRI), Douglas Fitchett (Glencadam), Robert Fleming (Tomintoul), Richard Forsyth (Forsyths), Callum Fraser (Deanston), Claire Fraser (Clynelish), Robert Fullarton (Craigellachie), John Glass (Ian Macleod), Jonathan Goldstein (Park Avenue Liquor Shop), Yvonne Granger (Glengoyne), George Grant (Glenfarclas), Kenny Grant (Glen Garioch), Lorraine Grant (Boort Malt), Martin Green (Bonhams), Veronica Gunn, Anna Hall (Glenmorangie), Jill Inglis (Whyte & Mackay), Kai Ivalo (SMWS), Frances Jack (SWRI), Campbell Laing (Arran), Fred Laing (Douglas Laing), Gary Lawton (Boortmalt), Catriona Legg (Diageo), Robert Lincoln (Ailsa Bay), Alistair Longwell (Ardmore), Ed MacAffer (Bowmore), Lillian MacArthur (Bunnahabhain), John MacDonald (Balblair), Polly Macdonald (Glen Spey, Benrinnes), Willie Macdougall (Teaninich), Tricia MacIntyre (Lagavulin, Caol Ila), John MacLellan (Kilchoman), Ian MacMillan (Burn Stewart), Grant MacPherson (Cadenhead), Ian McAlister (Glen Scotia), Christine McCafferty (Diageo), Des McCagherty (Edradour), Alan McConnochie (GlenDronach), Stephen McGinty (McTears), Sandy McIntyre (Glen Elgin, Glenlossie, Mannochmore), Stuart and Heather Martin (Freeloader Motors Ltd.), Ann Miller (Chivas Brothers), Andrew Millsopp (Royal Lochnagar), Carol More (Aberfeldy), Joe Mulacheski (Christmas City Studio), John Peterson (Loch Lomond), John R. Piggott (Strathclyde University, *ret.*), Richard Pike (Bonhams, NY), Jeff Power (Blair Athol), Morag Ralph (Edrington Group), Mark Reynier (Bruichladdich), Dylan F. Richard, Gillian Ritchie (Inverhouse), Brian Robinson (William Grant & Sons), John Ross (William Grant & Sons), Ronnie Routledge

(Glenglassaugh), Scotch Whisky Research Institute (SWRI), Andrew Shand (Speyside), Euan Shand (Duncan Taylor), Kartik Shankar (Tech Support Inc.), Alan Shayne (SMWSA), Derek Sinclair (Inver House), Moyra Sirrell (Inverhouse), Courtney Smith (Chivas Brothers), Vicky Stevens (Laphroaig), Gordon Stuart, Duncan Tait (Knockando), Mark Tayburn (Abhainn Dearg), David Thomson (Annandale), Mike Tough (Oban), Chris Ward (Auchentoshan), Malcolm Waring (Pulteney), Stephen Woodcock (Inchgower), and Robin Van Zelst (Diageo).

Additional thanks and gratitude must go to several people for their long-standing support, encouragement, and advice for many years.

Sheila Birtles (SWRI, *ret.*), Jeanne Fredericks (Jeanne Fredericks Literary Agency), Richard Gordon (formerly SMWS),Ted and Helen Harrison (Jobs and Gates Ltd), Peter and Margaret Nicol (Macallan, *ret.*), Dennis Malcolm (Glen Grant), Ronnie Macdonald (Boortmalt), Charles MacLean (writer), Graham MacWilliam (Edrington Group), Frank McHardy (Springbank), Sibh Megson (formerly SMWS), Hamish Proctor (Glenlivet), Colin Ross (Ben Nevis), Iain Stothard, and Jamie Walker. Deepest thanks and gratitude to R.B.

Although I rely on people and personal interviews for much of my information, I always have at hand a core set of reference books that I value for their depth of coverage on a broad range of whisky topics. I first reach for several books that particularly provide a grounding in the history of an industry and a country that I came to second-hand. These include foundation books like *The Whisky Distilleries of the United Kingdom* by Alfred Barnard, *The Making of Scotch Whisky* by Michael S. Moss and John R. Hume, *Scotch Whisky: Its Past and Present* by David Daiches, the *Scotch Whisky Industry Record* by H. Charles Craig, and *Scotch Whisky: A Liquid History* by Charles MacLean. I am grateful to have nearby, Ingvar Ronde's *Malt Whisky Yearbook* and Charlie MacLean' s *Whiskypedia* and *Malt Whisky*. Diageo made their archives freely available and provided the *DCL History Series* written by Brian Spiller from 1981 to 1983. Both the *A to Z of Whisky* by Gavin D. Smith and *The Whisk(e)y Treasury* by Walter Schobert proved to be an essential reference for whisky terminology. With much appreciation, I thank the Scotch Whisky Research Institute for their willingness to allow the reproduction of their *Flavour Wheel*. And finally, several companies have commissioned monographs about their own distilleries that are not always readily available to the public. Among those I found most helpful were C.S. McBain's *Glen Grant*, Jim Turle's *Glengoyne*, and both *Knockando* and *The Mystery and Magic of Aberlour* by Andrew Langley. Although not a monograph, I appreciated having available Ian Buxton's book, *Glenglassaugh, a Distillery Reborn* .

To former and current distillery managers for sharing their knowledge and experience with generosity, kindness, and good humor.

INTRODUCTION

Many years ago, I traveled to northern England to meet my new in-laws. I fell in love with them, new potatoes, the Eden Valley, and single malt whiskies. I drank blended Scotch in America, but when a landlord in the local pub introduced me to single malts, I knew a very good thing when I tasted it. There was no turning back. In fact, there was a turning toward Scotland because the single malts, let alone information about them, were virtually unknown outside of Scotland.

In this book I hope to introduce single malts by sharing the knowledge and adventures I have experienced since that first taste in a Cumbrian pub. There truly is nothing mystical or elitist about drinking single malts. This book will give you the tools to make some initial choices, the words to describe them, and the confidence to choose the styles of malts that you like to drink.

The distillery profiles in Part 3 will give some color and provide the following details to help you better understand a particular single malt and the place that produces it:

> ➤ A pronunciation key to the name on the label of malt whisky

> ➤ A very brief history

> ➤ Several interesting facts or terms or stories

> ➤ A discussion of the production process and its effect on the flavor profile of the spirit

> ➤ Bottlings offered by the distillery

> ➤ Introductory tasting notes for the general house style at the end of each profile

> ➤ A Distillery Locator; an alphabetical listing by distillery name and accompanying page numbers to help you easily locate the information about any distillery

This is a wonderful time to be sampling, understanding, and exploring single malts because of the recent advances and improvements that have occurred in the whisky industry during the last fifteen years. During this time, the understanding and examination of flavor development and the influence of different types of casks have resulted in distillers pushing the boundaries of whisky-making and exploring new possibilities. And the whisky enthusiast has been the happy recipient of their efforts in the arrival of different styles (not only from one region, but from one distillery), different finishes from different types of casks (a variety of wine, rum, and sherry), and perhaps most significantly an increased attention to quality and consistency. And all of the growing interest, globally, has brought us bottlings from distilleries that never previously offered their whiskies as a single malt.

With just a basic foundation and understanding about single malts, you will be ready to explore some of the variations and subtleties offered by some of the newer or lesser-known bottlings. You can browse this book to choose the information that is of interest or importance to you.

Even if you are presently knowledgeable about single malts, there is a recent and growing world of collectible single malt and whisky auctions, as well as a wider list of bottlings offered by independent bottlers. Whatever your level of information, I hope you take pleasure in knowing that there is always something else to discover about single malts.

My uncle, who taught at the West of Scotland Agricultural College as a grasslands advisor, always pours me a dram of single malt and then asks me to name the distillery that produced it. I know this question is coming every time I share a single malt with him. When I correctly named the distillery of the malt we last shared, he sniffed and grumped, "Well, I don't suppose you can tell me which field of barley it came from." Not only does he make me laugh, but he also serves to remind me I still have things to learn about single malt whisky. It is an enjoyable journey made more pleasant with the company of readers like you.

The Sidebars

You will find three different sidebars scattered throughout the book that will provide interesting facts, additional information, or little-known stories associated with malt whisky and its distilleries.

Whisky Lexicon

Provides definitions of terms used in the whisky world

The Noser Knows

Gives tasting tips or information about flavor development. Each distillery profile ends with a Noser Knows sidebar that contains the tasting notes in an easily accessible location.

The Distillery Cat's Meow

Relates to the history of the whisky industry. Not long ago, most distilleries employed a cat or two to control the rodent population attracted by the easy accessibility to free barley. Some, like the legendary mouser Towser of the Glenturret Distillery, became famous; all were pampered and loved. And I didn't know of any distillery manager who didn't complain about them at the same time they were pouring bowls of cream or fluffing pillows or stoking the fire for them.

 # Buying Single Malt Whisky

---

In This Chapter

➤ Understanding a whisky label

➤ Storing your malts

➤ Spreading the cost

The best way to begin learning about single malts or further your knowledge is to taste and enjoy them. While it is certainly possible to enjoy a single malt whisky on one's own, I have always found an added enjoyment and pleasure in sharing the experience with friends, introducing them to new malts, exchanging opinions, and simply enjoying the malts in good company. Unless I am evaluating whiskies professionally, this is the way I tend to drink malts. Of course, before you can taste and enjoy single malt whiskies, you need to be familiar with the range of choices that single malts offer.

Choosing Single Malt Whiskies—Where to Begin?

Ideally, you have a well-stocked wine and spirits store with a knowledgeable staff available to you. Use their experience and knowledge to ask them to recommend several malt whiskies, and also ask about the flavor profiles of their recommendations. Even if you know very little about single malts, you probably know what you like in the way of flavors, but don't be afraid to take a risk from time to time. If you know you like fruity-flavored whiskies and that is all you ever choose, you'll never expand your experience or knowledge.

More realistically, the wine and spirits store available to you has a limited selection with staff that can offer little guidance. Begin, then, with this book, and choose some whiskies from the flavor profiles. Select different types of single malts, choosing a lightly peated, fruity, and sherried whisky, for example. Arm yourself with several choices and then match them to whatever your local shop has in stock.

One fact works in your favor if you have a local shop with a limited selection: you will generally find that the choices they carry include some of the top name brands—The Macallan, The Glenlivet, Glenmorangie, Glenfiddich, Glen Grant, Cardhu, Glen Moray, Laphroaig, or Highland Park.

On the other hand, the shop owners may have had a visit from the distributor of Diageo's Classic Malt series and may carry selections only from that series—Glenkinchie, Cragganmore, Talisker, Lagavulin, Oban, and Dalwhinnie. Even with a limited selection, any of these malt whiskies would provide a good starting point.

Although it is quite possible to get a poor single malt, it happens with less regularity than it does with wine. Particularly, as you expand your horizons and begin to taste some of the more esoteric bottlings or expressions, you may find some that are less than stellar, but the standard brand names tend to be good.

Reading the Label

Prior to 2009, the labels on bottles of single malt whisky contained very little information and sometimes included outright misleading information. All that changed in 2009, when the Scotch Whisky Association lobbied the Scottish Parliament to pass regulations outlining the production process for whisky, its categories and labeling, the use of distillery names, and the description of geographical regions. Many people feel that this came about because of the confusing labeling used when Cardhu Distillery bottled whisky from two distilleries under the description "pure malt."(See distillery profile of Cardhu.)

The labels and explanations [opposite] provide eleven points and expanded details so that you can thoroughly decipher the information on a label. But there are three major points you should remember, particularly if you are a first-time buyer—the category, the age, and the name.

Categories

First, and most important, be certain that the label carries the description Single Malt Scotch Whisky. This indicates that one single distillery produced all the whisky in the bottle from malted barley. If you want to buy single malt whisky, this is how the bottle should be labeled. The label on other bottles of Scotch whisky may carry other descriptions, including blended malt Scotch whisky, single grain Scotch whisky, blended grain Scotch whisky, or blended Scotch whisky.

READING A WHISKY LABEL

1. *Categories of Scotch whisky:* The Scotch Whisky Regulations of 2009 established that "Single Malt Scotch Whisky means a Scotch whisky produced from only water and malted barley at a single distillery by batch distillation in pot stills". Furthermore, it must be matured in Scotland for a minimum of three years in oak casks.

2. *Region or Locality:* The label may mention a region or locality, but the whisky in the bottle must be entirely distilled in the named region.

3. *Distillery Names:* Most distilleries give their name to the whisky distilled there, but, in the past, some single malt whiskies carried contrived names that "sounded" like distilleries. Now, if a distillery name is used as the brand name, the whisky must be entirely distilled at that place.

4. *Age Statement:* The age of the whisky states the age of the youngest whisky in the bottle. Frequently, the bottle may contain single malts from older casks than the stated age on the bottle.

5. *Distillation or Vintage Year:* Some bottlings of single malt promote a vintage year in which the whisky was distilled. In this case, all the whisky must have been distilled in only the vintage year. Additionally, the label must also state either the year of bottling or an age statement.

6. *Second release:* When a bottling states a vintage year, the number of the release may accompany the year as well because the age of the bottling will usually change. For instance, if a distillery first releases a 1989 vintage bottled in 1999, it is a ten year old whisky. If they then decide to bottle a second release of the 1989 vintage, but bottle it in 2009, it is now a twenty year old whisky.

7. *Alcohol Strength:* Most single malts are bottled at either 40 or 43 percent Alcohol by Volume (ABV). Proof is determined by doubling the percentage—i.e. 80 proof and 86 proof. Some malts carry the designation of cask strength meaning that they are bottled at the alcoholic strength they leave the cask. This will naturally vary, but cask strength bottling always carry a higher ABV, ranging between 50 and 60 percent ABV.

8. *Amount of Whisky in the Bottle:* Whisky bottles, sold in the United States, contain 750ml and whisky bottles, sold in Europe, contain 700ml (or 70cl).

9. *Natural Color:* The Scotch Whisky Regulations permit the use of "plain caramel colouring" to maintain a consistency in color, but many distilleries decline to use artificial coloring.

10. *Unchill-Filtered (Non-Chill Filtered):* Past practice has used a method of lowering the temperature of the whisky, before bottling, in order to remove components that cause the whisky to turn cloudy when water is added. However, many whisky drinkers feel that those components contribute to the flavor and the mouth-feel of the whisky and prefer their whisky without chill-filtering.

11. *Distilled, Matured, and Bottled in Scotland:* All Scotch Whisky must be distilled and matured in Scotland; and, after November 23, 2012, the Scotch Whisky Regulations make "it illegal. . for Single Malt Scotch Whisky to be exported from Scotland other than in a bottle labeled for retail sale."

Whisky Lexicon

The Scotch Whisky Regulations of 2009 (SWR) separated Scotch whisky into categories and defined them as follows:

➤ Single malt Scotch whisky: "Produced from only water and malted barley at a single distillery by batch distillation in pot stills."

➤ Single grain Scotch whisky: "Scotch whisky distilled at a single distillery, but which, in addition to water and malted barley, may also be produced from whole grains of other malted or unmalted cereals." The distillation is also completed in large continuous stills that produce whisky continually rather than in batches. This whisky is cheaper to produce but does not have the nuanced character that a single malt whisky has, and virtually all of it forms the base of blends.

➤ Blended Scotch whisky: The combination of "one or more Single Malt Scotch Whiskies with one or more Single Grain Scotch Whiskies." The number of single malt and single grain whiskies used is much larger than the minimum number of two, with most blends like Cutty Sark, Dewar's, Famous Grouse, Teacher's, White Horse, and J&B, among many others, using several grain whiskies and twenty-five to forty single malts.

➤ Blended malt Scotch whisky: "A blend of two or more Single Malt Scotch Whiskies from different distilleries." This is the category that caused much of the trouble before 2009. In the past, the industry sometimes used the terms *pure malt or vatted malt*, which caused confusion and led consumers to think that they were buying a single malt when they were not.

➤ Blended grain Scotch whisky: "A blend of two or more Single Grain Scotch whiskies from different distilleries."

The Age of Single Malt Whisky

The age listed on a whisky label is the age of the youngest whisky in the bottle. Unless the bottle is from a single cask, the master distiller puts together a bottling of your favorite single malt by marrying whisky from many casks in the distillery warehouse. The whiskies are chosen because they contribute to the desired flavor profile and color for that particular expression. For a 10-year-old malt whisky, the casks of whiskies used in the bottling can be no younger than 10 years old, and the bottling almost always contains casks of older whisky. This is a hidden perk that malt whisky enthusiasts enjoy.

For a vintage whisky (i.e., a malt distilled in a certain year), however, every cask used in the bottling must have been distilled in that particular year. Many people choose a vintage year no longer available in stores and to experience an evening of tasting that probably can't be repeated.

Friends and Families

Once you have had an opportunity to taste a variety of single malts and have acquired knowledge about your preferences, you can build a wish list of malts you would like to own. This provides you with more direction than you perhaps had at the beginning of your education, and provides your close family and friends with an easy gift list.

Enthusiasts who have friends or relatives that travel have an added opportunity to buy expressions of malts that are only available in the retail travel (duty-free) stores. You can make a list of your favorite distilleries and ask your traveler to choose a bottle for you. Whilst you are somewhat at the mercy of their taste, a good bottle of single malt can be much nicer than a T-shirt.

What You Need to Know

The best way to begin learning about single malts or to further your knowledge about them is to taste and enjoy them. The following is a short list of some important points you can take from this chapter:

> ➤ Old whisky is not automatically better; young whisky is good too.

> ➤ Single malt whiskies can carry a premium price, so it is best to store them in a way that will protect their quality.

> ➤ Whisky clubs, whisky bars, and tastings (particularly festivals) allow you to sample single malts, especially the expensive ones, without spending a lot of money.

> ➤ You should develop a wish list for friends and family who "just don't know what to buy for you." It sure beats another scarf!

CHAPTER 2

Preparing a Tasting

In This Chapter

➤ Choosing malt selections

➤ Glasses and pours

➤ Water

The place you decide to hold your tasting should be comfortable with a seating arrangement that encourages camaraderie and easy discussion. Other than finding a room of your own where your guests can relax, you should be certain that there are no strong odors lingering. I'm not so much addressing cooking aromas, but rather smells like fresh paint or new construction.

The room should also have an ambient temperature of about 72 degrees Fahrenheit. In a published study by Dr. Frances Jack of the Scotch Whisky Research Institute (SWRI), she notes, "Nosing of cold samples is not desirable as the overall aroma character is suppressed at lower temperatures. Nosing of warm samples (above standard room temperature) is also undesirable, due to increased pungency and irritation." Her study included a low temperature of 5°C (41°F), and a high temperature of 30°C (86°F). As long as your whisky samples return to room temperature of about 70°F for two hours, a glass of whisky that began as too cold or too warm should have little impact on your tasting.

Identifying Selections and Tasting Notes

I usually place each glass of whisky on a place mat with the identifying name of the malt below the glass. By supplying a place for each glass, it is much easier to indicate a tasting order. You may wish to arrange your samples from the most subtle to the more assertive flavors so that the more robust flavors don't overwhelm the more subtle ones.

Using a place mat also allows each glass to return to a specific identified place. When I am sampling whiskies, I always place the sampled glasses to one side so that I have a clear division between the ones being tasted and the ones waiting to be sampled. But I must admit that unless I specifically and consciously place the finished samples in order, it is much too easy to confuse which glass was sampled first or second when I return to a sample for contrast or comparison.

Some guests also like paper beside each place setting for tasting notes, and others take their enjoyment from the discussion. If you decide to add paper for tasting notes, include the following information:

Standard Information

> ➤ Name of the single malt
> ➤ Regional location of the distillery
> ➤ Age
> ➤ Vintage, if it applies
> ➤ Alcohol by volume (ABV) percentage
> ➤ Single cask bottling, if it applies
> ➤ Non-chill filtered, if it applies
> ➤ Natural color, if it applies

Flavor and Aroma Information

> ➤ Nose
> ➤ Mouthfeel
> ➤ Taste
> ➤ Finish
> ➤ Other remarks

I lil- vide the flavor and aroma information into two columns with one headed Vater," and the second headed "With Water."

ections for Your Tasting

nning your malt whisky education, I suggest that you choose whiskies with profiles and arrange them from the most subtle to the most robust. You can

CHAPTER 3

Tasting and Evaluating

In This Chapter

➤ Water, yes water

➤ Tasting procedures

➤ The SWRI Flavour Wheel

The most important point to remember when tasting single malts is that it should be enjoyable. Ideally, it would be an occasion with good friends, sharing pleasant whiskies, and perhaps acquiring some information and knowledge along the way. At its most basic, tastings should help you understand your preferences for different malt whiskies.

It is also important to remember that sensory evaluation is subjective and everyone brings a certain talent for keenly perceiving certain aromas and flavors above others. So if everyone's contribution is respected and valued, your tasting becomes an evening of the "whole being greater than its parts."

With Water, or Without?

There are those among malt enthusiasts who are hard core purists and will only drink their single malts neat, without water or any dilution at all. This view is valid for part of the tasting technique, but it does not allow a complete appreciation of all the aromas and flavors available.

Whisky Lexicon

Drinking whisky neat indicates that a person drinks their dram as it comes from the bottle without diluting it with water.

You should first try your malt neat because many flavor components are drawn to alcohol and will stay in the solution, without the addition of water. When you add water, some compounds are either hydrophobic (they hate water) or hydrophilic (they love water). If they are hydrophobic, the flavor compounds will rush to escape the water and will come off the diluted malt as wonderful aromas and flavors. Some of the flavors and aromas are best detected without water and others are only discernible with the addition of water. While tasting without water often provides the broad flavor picture, the addition of water can allow the flavor details to come forward.

A member of the tasting panel at Diageo's Global Technical Centre observes, "I find it easier to describe the individual components within a liquid when it is diluted down. You might get spiciness but [with water] it is specifically cinnamon. I can come up with more descriptors when a spirit sample is diluted down, than I can when I am nosing it neat." After paying the price for a single malt, I would hope that you might allow yourself the maximum enjoyment by trying your single malt without water and also with a small drop of water, as well.

The Noser Knows

I have a friend who came to single malts by way of Dublin and who always preferred her malt neat. It had nothing to do with alcoholic strength but rather with mouthfeel. Whenever we had a dram together, she always enjoyed the majority of it without water and then added a bit at the end in order to discern any of the hydrophobic volatiles.

Cask Strength Malts and Water

In addition to considering the components released with water, you must also consider the alcoholic strength of your malt. Most malts are bottled at 40 to 43 percent alcohol by volume (ABV), but some are bottled at cask strength, which is the ABV of the whisky when the cask is emptied. Cask strength malts can range from 50 to 60 percent ABV, clearly higher than most bottled malts. Water needs to be added to cask strength malts for the taster to discern the layers of flavors and aromas. Also, without the addition of water the high alcohol content has the effect of numbing the nose and palate.

Non-Chill Filtered Malts and Water

Prior to World War II, malts weren't filtered, except to remove chunks and bits of char that came off the interior of the casks. But the whisky can become milky looking when the ABV percentage drops into the low 40s, leading people to think they had bad whisky. To prevent the cloudiness, the industry began to chill the whisky and filter out the fatty esters that caused the clouding of the whisky's color. The positive result was a consistently clear whisky, but some people felt that the negative consequence was the loss of flavor that went with the removal of the fatty esters.

Today, many distilleries have returned to the old method of bottling their malts without chill filtering in the belief that the abandonment of this practice has returned some of the flavors to the malt. In fact, the return to non-chill filtering seems to have returned the mouthfeel of the malt rather than adding a significant degree of flavor. But this in itself is important because mouthfeel is part of the tasting experience and adds to the malt's quality and enjoyment.

In considering malts with no-chill filtering, the malt taster should remember two points:

➤ Non-chill filtered malts are usually bottled at a higher ABV so that the whisky does not become cloudy.

➤ The addition of water releases the large flavor molecules from the alcohol solution causing your dram to become cloudy, but this milkiness does not affect the flavors or quality of your dram. It does obviously impact the color, so that will be one of the first things you should consider when tasting a malt sample.

Ice and Malts

Most malt drinkers become faint when people consider putting ice (or a mixer like soda or cola or ginger ale) in a single malt. Dr. John R. Piggott,

The Distillery Cat's Meow

A distillery manager once said to me that once you buy a bottle of single malt, you can drink it any way you want to drink it. And I remember drinking a sample of Glen Grant whisky with very cold water from the distillery garden's creek on a sweltering summer day. Although I would not do this as a rule, the dram was glorious and refreshing in the intense heat. So there is some truth in his statement. But, once again, if you have paid a premium price for a single malt, you may want to avoid the ice and mixer in order to fully savor all it has to offer and to fully enjoy all its aromas and flavors.

retired faculty member from the University of Strathclyde, notes, "Ice reduces the volatility of everything so that it will tend to reduce the flavor by nose, but once you get it into your mouth, unless you swallow it very quickly, then it will warm up."

When I want to add ice to whisky, I usually reserve it for a full-bodied blended Scotch whisky that stands up to the ice and is not as expensive as a single malt.

Finally, some distilleries, like Glenglassaugh, are bottling spirits that are less than three years old and therefore not yet whisky. They are being marketed as spirit drinks that lend themselves well to mixers and making cocktails.

The Noser Knows

Very recently, tasters within the whisky industry have experimented with chilling single malt in the freezer, much as one might treat vodka. One taster found that this "slurpy" concoction allowed some very subtle background notes, including peat, to emerge. I am not certain why this altered state would release additional flavor compounds, but it will be worthwhile watching what information this experiment may provide.

A Tasting Procedure

Now that you have poured your whisky samples and gathered your friends, you will want to look at four aspects of evaluating single malts. These include the color, the nose, the taste, and the finish—both with water and without water.

The Color

It is a good idea to hold the glass to the light and enjoy the myriad hues of a single malt. They range from a light straw color to dark molasses with every variation between the two.

Very generally, the lighter colors tend to come from a bourbon cask and the deeper ruby colors tend to come from a sherry cask. But remember that several malts begin their maturation in bourbon casks and finish with a short time in a sherry cask that will lend a deeper red burgundy cast. Many of the wine finishes also provide a variety of colors; and as more malts are matured in different wine, port, and sherry casks, it might be worthwhile tracking the colors that these casks lend to the malt.

The length of time the malt has matured in casks can also deepen the color. And whether the cask is a first fill or second fill will impact the color intensity depending upon how much of the previous fill leached into the aging spirit.

When you hold a whisky glass to the light, tip the glass so that the whisky coats its side and then runs back down when the glass is held upright. The rivulets that slowly trail down the glass's sides are called legs and indicate the presence of fatty esters. The legs can look viscous and almost creamy and will add to the mouthfeel of the whisky.

The Noser Knows

Professional nosers use cobalt blue glasses when evaluating whiskies so that the color is masked. At first, this seems counterintuitive, but if nosers cannot see the true color of the malt, then they do not bring any presuppositions to the evaluation. By masking the color, nosers cannot assume the types of casks used for aging and therefore do not anticipate the flavors and aromas they will find in the malt.

Nosing

There are five hundred components to whisky, and most of them are detected through nosing. On the other hand, there are only four primary tastes that the tongue can distinguish: sweet, sour, bitter, and salty. Obviously, the nose and the aromas it detects provide a lot of information about the flavor profile of the malt under consideration.

When you approach your first malt sample, the head space above the whisky will contain a lot of the high alcohol volatiles. For this reason, I do not suggest that you put your nose down into the glass as so many pictures show master blenders and distillers doing. There will be plenty of time for that maneuver later. Take your first sniff of the primary whisky aromas near the edge of the glass, and try to evaluate the nose feel. Is it very astringent, is there a lot of alcohol prickliness, are the aromas robust, or are they much more subtle and difficult to describe? Then evaluate the secondary aromas with your nose in the head space where it joins the edge of the glass.

Tasting

Single malt tends to be good sipping whisky, and you would do best to take several sips rather than a gulp. When you take the first sip, you should hold the whisky in your mouth and roll it around a bit. This allows you to appreciate the mouthfeel. The coating may be quite creamy and thick, almost syrupy, or it might be a bit thin and more delicate and light in the mouth. It may also be warming or have an astringent bite. Many of the non-chill filtered malts offer a more complex and interesting and discernable mouthfeel because of the fatty esters that now remain in the malt.

With the first sip, you should also think about the primary flavors that you taste in the front of your mouth. When you take a second sip of your dram, concentrate on the secondary flavors that you can taste in the back of your mouth just before you swallow the whisky.

And finally, after you have swallowed the whisky, you might want to think about the flavors that are left on your palate. What kind of finish did your dram provide? Was it lingering or did it finish quickly? Was the final taste a dry or a sweet finish?

The Noser Knows

Members of evaluation panels often evaluate whisky only by nosing it because of the toll a significant number of samples would take on their physical well-being and also on their evaluations. Instead of actually drinking every dram in front of them, they sometimes borrow a practice from the wine trade and spit. They hold the malt in their mouths and then use a separate cup for spitting, which allows them to taste the whisky and experience the finish without having to face the effects of too many samples. Alternatively, some also dip their small finger into the glass and literally taste a "wee drop."

A Drop of Water

Once you have tasted your malt without water, you should go back and do it all over again, but this time with the addition of bottled water at room temperature. As I mentioned in the section With Water, or Without, there are definite advantages and pleasures derived from adding water to your dram. Evaluation teams usually dilute their samples to about to 23 percent ABV, but I think for the malt enthusiasts tasting at home with friends, this percentage is a bit variable. You should begin by adding a small dollop of bottled water, and then sip your malt and determine if it needs more. If the sample is still very astringent and tastes strongly of intense alcohol, you can add more water. I find that some malts with a high ABV and robust flavors need quite a bit of water because the malt is almost like whisky concentrate. Other malts have delicate and light flavors and require only a small amount of water to enhance the aromas.

The addition of water to your glass releases all those hydrophobic flavor components that rush to leave the solution and occupy the head space. Frequently, sulfur aromas are first to leave the water and can present a rotten egg smell that quickly dissipates. This is often followed by the fruity esters, including aromas of apple, pears, and bananas. But Jim Beveridge, master blender at Diageo, cautions that the more volatile aromas released by water are "like a bit of a time bomb. You need to savor the moment because they do flash off, and you are left with the less volatile [aromas]." But evaluating whisky with water allows you to provide details and further delineate the flavor components you found when evaluating it without water.

You can then continue to consider the taste and finish of your malt with water as well. If you rinse your mouth with regular water from the pitcher on the table, you will better appreciate your next sample of single malt. I also suggest that you leave a bit of your previous dram in the glass and return to it after you have sampled all the evening's choices. Often a whisky has layers of flavors that reveal themselves over the course of the evening; and when you return to a malt that you have previously evaluated, it can offer little surprises of new flavors. This often happens with single cask bottling and complex whiskies. People also like to return to an earlier dram and contrast it with another dram that appears later in the tasting.

I have written about discerning aromas and flavors during a tasting, but you may be perplexed about what kind of flavors a whisky might have. The SWRI has developed an excellent flavor wheel that provides guidelines for delineating the flavor components of whisky and a terminology to describe it.

The SWRI Flavour Wheel

A team of sensory analysts at the SWRI developed the original Flavour Wheel in 1979 for use in laboratory analysis, and it included a number of chemical and technical terms. Later, they revised the terminology to include descriptors that would hold meaning and understanding for most people. Descriptive analysis is the technical description for what most of us do when we are discussing a single malt among ourselves. It is an evaluation that usually contains personal descriptions often based on our own experiences and memories. It is, of course, very subjective.

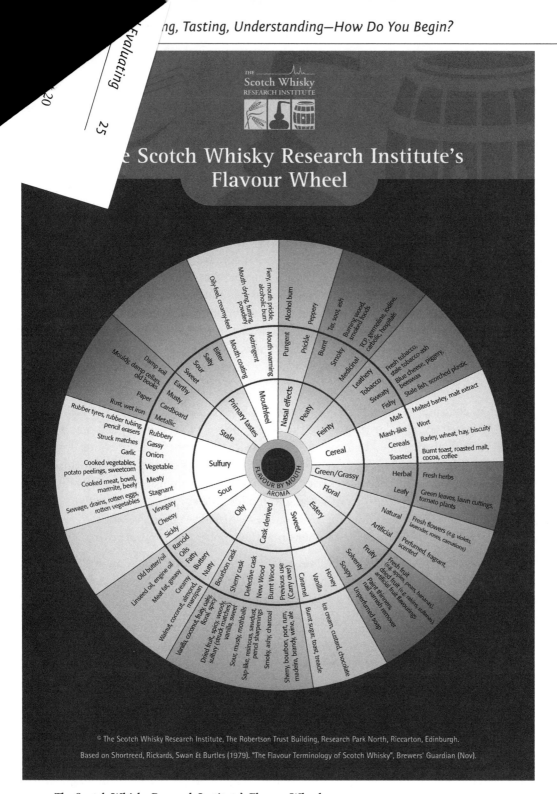

The Scotch Whisky Research Institute's Flavour Wheel

The SWRI Flavour Wheel provides a common and shared terminology that allows all of us to hold a conversation about our favorite malt. The Flavour Wheel also provides guidelines regarding the most common flavors found in whisky. It is a welcome starting point that will take you from general to specific descriptors.

You will want to work from the inside to the outside of the Flavour Wheel as you begin your tasting adventure. The top of the Flavour Wheel begins with three primary categories that you address when you first evaluate a dram of malt whisky—nasal effects, mouthfeel, and primary tastes. The first inner wheel then provides twelve general categories of flavors and aromas common to Scotch whisky. The middle wheel provides examples of the general categories, and the outer wheel contains concrete descriptors of the examples. Through the course of your tasting, you will probably add an outer wheel of your own personal descriptors that provides even more detail and specificity. It is common for people to identify an aroma as spice and then name it specifically as cinnamon, or to identify dried fruits specifically as dates and figs rather than raisins.

Nasal Effects

Nasal effects can include a sharp pungency that makes you pull your head back and occurs more commonly with cask strength malts. It is the result of alcohol burning your nasal passages.

The less assertive version of this is the peppery prickle. One of the reasons we usually recommend adding water to your dram is to tame these aggressive nasal effects, which mask the other aromas.

Mouthfeel

Most drams of malt will have some warming effect because of the alcohol, but it will vary in intensity. Often, cask strength and older malts will have a higher degree of mouth warming that often quiets with the addition of water. Once again, the water will allow you to taste the flavors that the high alcohol content masks.

You may also experience an astringency that comes from the tannin in the wood. It is somewhat like the mouthfeel you experience after drinking multiple cups of strong tea or robust red wine. And the most pleasurable experience is to have a sample of whisky that has a luscious creamy mouth coating that approaches the consistency of syrup or honey.

Primary Tastes and Aromas

The primary tastes are the broad flavors of bitter, sour, and sweet that you first experience when tasting a malt; salty components in whisky are not frequently experienced.

Stale flavors are often quite subtle and are masked by other smells. They tend to be characteristically flat, like wet cardboard.

Sulfury aromas are hydrophobic compounds that flash off quickly. Often they are discernible on the first nose after adding water—and then they are gone. Although some of the descriptors like cooked meat, beef bouillon, and cooked vegetables may not seem appealing in a whisky, they can be acceptable in small quantities, and a sulfury, meaty new-make is sometimes attractive to blenders.

Whisky Lexicon

New-make spirit is the name given to newly distilled spirit as it comes off the stills.

The Noser Knows

When I attended SWRI's sensory evaluation course, we had one colleague who just couldn't detect smoky aromas. If you have tasted any of the smoky Islay whiskies, you know that this aroma is very assertive and is the first component to scream its presence. While the rest of us were working to peel back the layers and find the underlying aromas, he had the flavor profile nailed. Because he couldn't register the smoky phenols, he immediately found all the nuanced and elegant background notes. He was the master of subtleties.

Sour components can provide an acidic tang that is not unattractive, but it can veer toward the off notes of sour cheese or sour dishcloths, as well.

Oily aromas can indicate an off note when they approach rancid smells, but they can also be pleasant when they appear with less intensity as buttery and nutty notes.

Many of the cask-derived components are rather pleasant because they carry the characteristics of the wine or spirit that had previously filled the cask. Typically, bourbon delivers its characteristic vanilla and coconut flavors, whereas sherry offers its distinctive dark fruits and spice notes.

Sweet aromas and flavors usually present notes of bubbling brown sugar, molasses, custards, and honey. It is easy to develop your own more detailed descriptors, like custard specifically moving to crème brûlée, or to combine more than one category, like fruits, brown sugar, and vanilla into a descriptor of pineapple upside-down cake.

Estery usually refers to those compounds that first come off the still at the beginning of the distillery run and include aromas of unscented soaps and nail polish remover. But this category also moves toward the lovely fruity esters that many distillers try to capture. It is easy to expand the fruit descriptor into orchard fruits like apples and pears, tropical fruits like mangos and kiwi, melons, dark fruits like figs and dates, and dried fruits like raisins and apricots. People also combine categories as well, such as baked apples, suggesting a cooked apple and spice component or fruits in syrup, suggesting a combination of sweetness and fruit.

Floral aromas often evoke more robust scented flowers like roses, lavender, lilac, and geraniums. It can also refer to the artificial or dried flower range that includes potpourri.

Green and grassy compounds refer to fresh garden herbs, newly mowed lawns, and the pungent aroma of tomato and geranium leaves.

Cereal aromas can range from the smell of barley or grain to the malt smell and flavor in malted milk balls. It can also suggest oatmeal cooking on the stove, particularly when it boils over. The category extends to include the sweet malty smell in a graham cracker or the aromas associated with roasting malt, coffee, or dark cocoa.

The feinty aromas refer to the compounds that come off the still at the end of the run. Many of these descriptors are off-putting and are not pleasant aromas. But sometimes the feinty character decreases with the maturation in wood, and the leathery component can add some depth to the single malt.

The peaty phenols usually appear toward the end of the middle of the distillery run and at the beginning of the appearance of the feints. These are the smoky aromas that are often associated with peated malt and the Islay malts. But the descriptor of peat or smoke doesn't quite cover the category. The phenol aromas can appear as smoke, as burnt ash, and as a medicinal aroma reminiscent of disinfectants and the hospital.

The SWRI offers an easy and manageable way to begin evaluating single malts. Some of the descriptors for the flavor and aroma categories are immediately attractive (fruits, vanilla, and flowers), and others may appear as less attractive. Some of the compounds can indicate off notes and others may actually provide back notes or complexity depending upon their intensity and combinations with other compounds. Part of the enjoyment of a malt tasting is discovering what combinations work well and what combinations you prefer. I always value the opinions and evaluations of guests and friends because they bring different perspectives, viewpoints, and talents to the tasting.

What You Need to Know

The language surrounding single malt tastings and evaluations can seem daun
Here is a list of the basics to get you started:

> ➤ For a complete tasting experience, taste your malt (particularly cask
> whiskies) without water and with water.

➤ To get the most out of your malt, save ice and mixers for blended Scotch whiskies or spirit drinks.

➤ As you embark on your tasting adventure, refer to the SWRI Flavour Wheel for guidance. Begin with the most general terms and learn to become more specific as you become more experienced.

➤ Add your own descriptors to personalize the malt and connect it to your preferences.

PART TWO

The Whisky-Making Process

The Whisky-Making Process

Considering that single malts have complex and nuanced character, it is surprising that whisky making uses only four ingredients—water, barley, yeast, and peat (an optional choice). In Part 2 we'll examine the importance of these ingredients and how the whisky-making process uses them. Most importantly, you'll learn how different flavors develop during this process and appreciate the skill of the distillers as they create variations. And finally, we'll look at the significant role that the casks, used for maturation, have in forming flavors and complexity.

Because Part 2 examines the origin and development of flavors, it will enhance your understanding of the tasting terminology that you explored in Part 1. After reading Part 2, you will be well on your way to having a deeper appreciation of the individuality of single malts.

CHAPTER 4

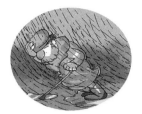

A Distiller's Key Ingredients

> ## In This Chapter
>
> ➤ Basic ingredients
> ➤ Effect of raw materials

Considering the variations and complexity of single malt whisky, it is surprising that the entire whisky-making process begins with only four raw materials—barley, water, yeast, and peat (optional). It is much like shortbread, another of Scotland's products, which is made with only flour, butter, and sugar, resulting in a flavorful and textured cookie. The analogy ends with the simple ingredients because baking good shortbread relies on a consistency in its preparation and a brief storage time. Whisky also relies on a consistent process, but the manner in which the process is manipulated helps to create its variety of flavors. Most significantly, whisky enjoys a long shelf life and improves and matures with time in the cask.

Begin with Water

Distillers are emphatic about using pure water from sources that often originate in the mountains and hills of Scotland. Successful distillation significantly depends on a good water source, and distilleries are careful to protect their water source to ensure its purity. The advertising media make much of the source and purity of each distillery's water and what it adds to the whisky. Generally speaking, distillers prefer soft water, free of minerals; although the people at Glenmorangie, where they use hard water, feel that the minerals add to the flavor and character of the whisky. In fact, the water probably adds very little to the flavor of the final product.

Cool, Clean Water

It is very important that the water used in making whisky is pure, without any contaminants; equally important is the reliability of the water supply. Many people imagine Scotland as a land of continual and abundant rainfall, which is true to a point. Scotland can suffer periods of drought or little rain, however, and some of the water supplies can dry up or produce insufficient amounts of water for production, or the temperature of the water can rise during the summer months, making it too warm for condensing.

The Noser Knows

On hot summer days (yes, Scotland does have a few of them each year) the temperature of the water used to cool the condensers also becomes warmer. Usually, when the hot vapor reaches the cold condenser, it changes into a liquid fairly quickly. If the condensing water is too warm, however, there is not as much difference between the vapors and the cooling water, and the vapors stay in the condenser much longer. It also means that they stay in contact with the copper much longer and consequently run the risk of changing the flavor profile of the spirit.

Traditionally, distilleries close for what is called a silent period during the summer months, and most people associate the closure with vacations and maintenance. But the closures are brought about by the fact that water supplies could dry up or diminish during the warm summer, making this an excellent time to close the distillery for maintenance and provide vacation time as well.

Add Tons of Barley

Particular strains of barley can have an influence on the flavor profile of a whisky, but the effect is slight and somewhat debatable. Barley, however, is the principle ingredient in the making of Scotch whisky; consequently, distillers choose their barley carefully, based on very specific characteristics.

Distillers agree that they want a barley strain that will process easily and produce a high alcohol yield. They look for strains of barley that provide an uncomplicated hot water extraction of sugars from the grain during the mashing process, allowing for a more predictable spirit yield (PSY). The barley should be low in nitrogen, permitting a higher starch content that will begin its conversion into fermentable sugars during the malting process. In order for this conversion to occur, the barley also needs to be high in specific enzymes necessary to effect the change from starch into sugar.

Tom Bringhurst of SWRI remarks, "The making of Scotch whisky must use all natural ingredients and cannot contain any added enzymes or process-aiding materials." It is interesting to note that the Scotch whisky industry has always, and solely, used natural ingredients in their distillations; while other people and institutions have only recently recognized the importance and value of organic and sustainable ingredients.

The Noser Knows

Presently three strains of barley—Optic, Oxbridge, and Concerto—are the most widely used. But the testing and development of high-yield and disease-resistant strains of barley is an ongoing process and as they are developed, they will replace the varieties available today.

Distillery Standards

In their search for the right barley, distillers look for only high-quality spring barley, which produces a higher yield and lower levels of nitrogen than winter barley. To minimize their risk and offer a variety of choices, distilling companies work with plant breeders and farmers who generally grow several strains of barley. The barley undergoes several years of testing and tracking to verify that it can produce a PSY and that it allows a straightforward and easy extraction of its sugars for fermenting. Distillers usually select a blend of different varieties of barley.

Whisky Lexicon

Friability refers to the crumbly factor of the malted barley. Distillery operators adjust their mills to produce the grind they desire based on the barley's degree of friability. Polly Macdonald of Glen Spey Distillery explains that knowing the friability of malted barley is like knowing if she is dealing with a cookie that crumbles or one that is chewy.

A distiller chooses a blend of barley that meets the distillery's standards for moisture content, germination speed, fermentability, PSY, friability, and nitrogen content. Once purchased, the barley goes through the malting process, which begins the conversion of the starch into sugar.

Dry Gently Over Peat and Smoke

Peat is compacted, partially decomposed plant debris found in bogs, and it contributes to the pungent peat-reek (phenols) of malt whisky. Celtic cultures have long used it for fuel, first cutting it into brick shapes, then drying it, and finally using it for heat, or as in the case of distilleries, using it to dry barley.

Peat beds have different types of vegetation growing on them; some support heather, others moss or bracken, depending upon the location of the peat bogs. Distillers believe that the vegetation imparts a slight flavor to the peat and are, therefore, particular about the origin of the peat used in their kilns. But most prefer to use hard peat from older peat bogs that burns more slowly than foggy peat from younger beds that is less compact and contains more moisture.

Whisky Lexicon

Peat is decomposed and compressed plant matter that provided fuel to Scottish households for centuries. It also exists as the fuel to dry barley and to stop its germination. During the distillation process, peat deposits phenol compounds onto the malted barley. These phenols transfer to the spirit during the whisky-making process and produce the smoky and medicinal aromas that define some single malts, particularly the ones from Islay.

Cream 100 Kilos of Yeast

Simply speaking, yeast is a single-celled fungus that metabolizes sugar to produce alcohol and carbon dioxide. In the past, mashmen have used both distiller's yeast and brewer's yeast because they felt the combination provided additional flavor. Today, however, they employ only distiller's yeast, chosen for its flavor production and its ability for maximum sugar-to-alcohol conversion.

Developing Flavors

During fermentation as the yeast feeds on the sugar, it produces only alcohol, carbon dioxide, and esters— serendipitous by-products of the fermentation process.

The esters are the fruity and floral flavors that many distillers want to capture because they are key to the flavor profiles of whiskies like Balblair. Ongoing research suggests that longer fermentation may promote the development of some additional flavors, but then the development of wild or destructive yeast becomes a threat. Fermentation is a process that requires pristine cleanliness and a fine balance between encouraging flavor development and discouraging malign yeast development.

The Noser Knows

Fermentation is one part of the whisky-making process where fragrant floral and fruit esters, ranging from berry to orchard to tropical fruits, can develop. Some distillers want to encourage the development of these desired notes because it suits the required flavor profile of their spirit.

What You Need to Know

➤ Water probably doesn't contribute to the flavors in single malt whiskies, but its purity, availability, and temperature are crucial to the whisky-making process.

➤ The quality of the barley influences the yield of the spirit, not the development of flavor.

CHAPTER 5

Making Whisky: The First Steps

In This Chapter

➤ Preparing for distillation

➤ Making malt, mash, and wash

➤ Tradition and progress in whisky-making

➤ Flavor development

The long-established process for producing distinctive single malt whisky involves several steps: malting, mashing, fermenting, distilling, and maturing. In this chapter we will look at the preparatory steps necessary for distilling. It is in essence a process that results in making beer. After all, whisky-making is basically distilling beer. It is worth noting that the flavor elements, called congeners, are formed in small part during the steps of malting and fermenting.

Whisky Lexicon

Congeners are chemical compounds developed during the whisky-making process that produce the flavors and aromas in both new-make spirit and matured whisky. Their formation tends to occur most commonly during malting, fermenting, and distilling, with the most significant flavor development happening during maturation in oak casks. Master distillers must carefully manipulate and control the congeners' development in order to produce the specific flavor profile for their single malt.

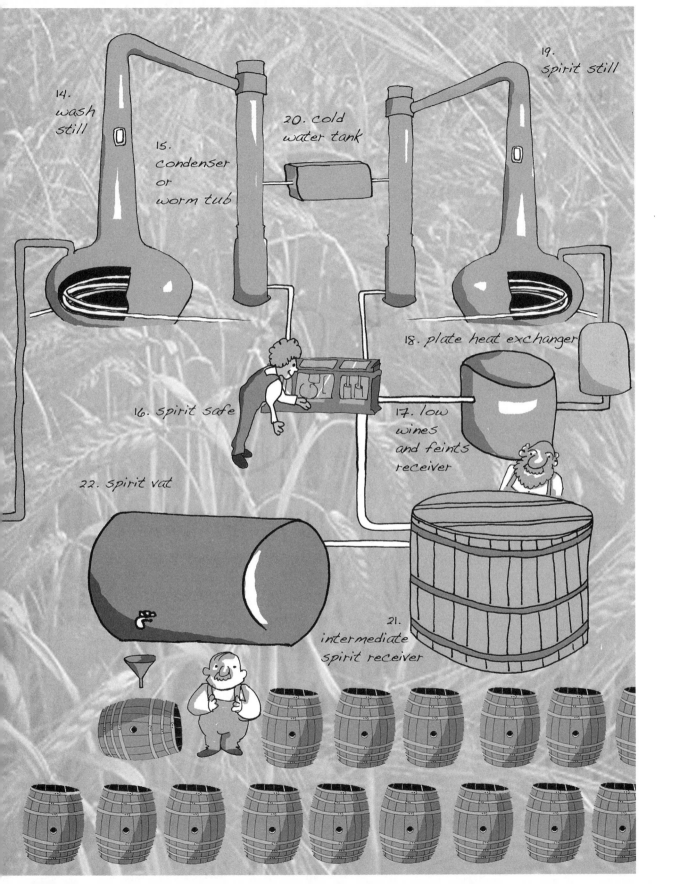

From Malted Barley to Spirit

➤ Upon delivery to the distillery, malted barley is filtered for stones and debris and then stored in the (1) *malt bin*.

➤ Malted barley moves to the (2) *destoner and dust extractor*.

➤ It then passes through the (3) *mill*, which cracks and grinds the malted barley into grist.

➤ The (4) *grist hopper* stores the milled malt until ready for mashing.

➤ Before mashing, the grist moves into the (5) *mashing machine*, where it is mixed with water from the (6) *hot liquor tank* at about 64°C (147°F).

➤ The mixture then pours into the (7) *mash tun*, where three infusions of water increasing in temperature extract the soluble sugars to produce sweet wort.

➤ The wort drains through the perforated floor and into the (8) *underback*.

➤ Before fermentation, the wort passes through a (9) *heat exchanger* to reduce the temperature.

➤ As the liquid travels from the heat exchanger, creamed yeast is injected into the wort line from (10) *refrigerated tanks*.

➤ The wort and yeast fill the (11) *washback*, where fermentation takes place for a minimum of forty-eight hours.

➤ The wort and yeast, now called the wash, then move into the (12) *wash charger* before moving through a (13) *plate heat exchanger*, which uses the heat from the residue of the previous wash distillation (pot ales) to preheat the wash.

➤ Once the temperature of the wash has risen between 65° to 70°C (149° to 158°F), it moves into the (14) *wash still* for its first distillation.

➤ The vapors from the boiling wash rise into the (15) *condensers* or *worm tubs*, where a continual flow of (20) *cold water* through copper pipes or around a copper worm turns the vapor into liquid known as low wines, which pass through the (16) *spirit safe*.

➤ The low wines move into the (17) *low wines and feints receiver* before passing through a (18) second *plate heat exchanger*, which uses the heat from the residue of the previous spirit still distillation (spent lees) to preheat the low wines.

➤ Once the temperature of the low wines has risen between 45° to 55°C (113° to 131°F), it moves into the (19) *spirit still* for the second distillation.

➤ The vapors rise in the still and enter a second condenser or worm tub to return to a liquid, which passes once again through the spirit safe. But the foreshots (heads) and feints (tails) of the distillation return to the (17) *low wines and feints receiver* and the middle cut goes to the (21) *intermediate spirit receiver.*

➤ The new-make spirit passes into the (22) *spirit vat* in the filling room, where it is filled into oak casks for maturation.

Malting Barley

Malting barley involves a process that triggers germination and the production of enzymes that will convert the starch in the kernel to fermentable sugars (even when it is the middle of January). The maltman, or maltster, has the job of making the barley damp and keeping it warm so that it grows roots and produces a green shoot. But before the barley kernel can actually produce a green shoot, the maltster dries the barley over smoky fires and stops the whole process. It is really a case of bait and switch, with the objective of retaining the soluble starch in the barley kernel so that the hot water used during the mashing process can activate other enzymes to convert the starch into sugar.

Enzymes are the Key

The barley kernel consists of an embryo that will produce a green shoot and an endosperm, which contains starch that will provide food for the plant when it germinates. The art of malting consists of tricking the plant into growing and triggering the production of the enzyme cytase, which breaks down the protective barrier around the starch, the food source for the barley. Malting also activates an additional enzyme, diastase, which makes the starch soluble, and amylase, which begins the conversion of starch to sugar. Just as the entire germination process begins, the maltster brings it to an abrupt end by drying the barley in kilns.

Whisky Lexicon

Enzymes truly hold a key position in whisky making. Without enzymes the conversion from starch to sugar just wouldn't happen. Here then is Enzyme 101:

➤ Cytase breaks down the walls of the starch cells in the kernels and makes them accessible.

➤ Diastase makes the starch soluble so that warm water can extract it.

➤ Amylase begins but does not complete the conversion of starch to sugar.

The Malting Floor Heritage

Traditionally, distilleries had their own malting floor and completed all their own malting on-site. To begin the malting process, the maltman steeped the grain for two days—eight hours in water alternating with sixteen hours of being exposed to the air so that the barley would begin to germinate. He then spread the wet barley on large concrete or stone malting floors, where the germination continued.

The barley was constantly turned so that the heat produced by the germination process remained evenly distributed, and the new roots did not tangle and form a sodden clump of grain. Depending on the season and the weather conditions, the malting could take a week or more. Most distillers preferred making their whisky during the cooler months because the temperature was easier to control.

The Distillery Cat's Meow

People who yearn for the romance of traditional floor maltings haven't done the job. In reality, it was tedious, boring, and labor intensive. The continual inhalation of malt dust caused respiratory problems and the endless rhythmic shoveling resulted in a repetitive action injury called monkey shoulder.

In 2005, William Grant & Sons released an expression of blended malt named Monkey Shoulder, which is a blend of three malts produced at their three distilleries: Glenfiddich, Balvenie, and Kininvie.

In order to stop the germination process, the malt was spread thinly on the malting floors so that the root withered and the grain could not develop a green shoot. At this point the barley achieved the designation of green malt, which required drying over slow-burning peat fires in tall kilns distinguished by copper pagoda-shaped chimneys.

One of the keys to successful malting lies in the temperature inside the kiln. If the barley is kilned at a temperature that is too high, the maltster runs the risk of deactivating some of the enzymes necessary to complete the starch-to-sugar conversion. Equally important is that the peat, used as drying fuel, transfers onto the barley and eventually to the whisky, giving it a smoky, medicinal character.

Smoke or No Smoke

The drying process for the barley takes two days, during which the intensity of the peat flavor develops. If the maltman uses peat as the fuel throughout the majority of the drying time, the result will be a very smoky-flavored whisky. But if he uses another fuel during part of the drying time or just places the peat at the edges of the fire, he can reduce these smoky flavors. Usually the intensity of peat-reek is measured in parts per million (ppm), including the following general guidelines:

➤ Lightly peated whisky: < 10 ppm

➤ Medium-peated whisky: 15–25 ppm

➤ Heavily peated whisky: > 30 ppm

The Noser Knows

Single malts that have high levels or high intensities of phenols are described as having peat-reek. Other words used to describe the presence of phenols are smoky, medicinal, or burnt. With a word like *peat*, you can well imagine the amount of wordplay that marketing people use to define and name their products, like Big Peat, a malt offered by Douglas Laing—a blend of Islay's smokiest whiskies.

These peat levels are only guidelines because the SWRI has identified at least eight different compounds responsible for the phenol aromas. Dr. Frances Jack notes that their intensities depend on the "total level of phenolic compounds and the relative proportions in which they are present." Not only does the smokiness of a whisky depend upon the amount of peat used (the ppm), but it also depends on which phenolic compound is responsible for the smoky flavor because different compounds have varying strengths of smokiness.

Maintaining the Tradition

The traditional floor maltings can no longer produce enough malted barley for the volume of malt whisky now being produced. Today, most distilleries submit their recipe to central maltsters, who do the malting for them. Six distilleries, including Laphroaig, Bowmore,

Kilchoman, Balvenie, and Highland Park, still do some floor maltings on-site in order to maintain the institutional profile and to allow visitors to view the traditional process. Springbank, however, is the only distillery to use traditional floor maltings for all the barley used in the production of its single malts.

A distillery may do its own malting if it requires specific malt (i.e., it may wish to distill a whisky with heavily peated malt), or it may wish to distill a limited edition whisky using all local products. The recent interest in agricultural sustainability and sourcing all ingredients locally has led to some new and small distilleries, like Kilchoman on Islay, to generate most of the ingredients for their whisky on their own farm located just beyond the distillery.

Central Maltsters

Because traditional floor malting consumes a great deal of space, time, and energy, and because many of the conditions are extremely variable, central maltsters, large industrial operations, undertake the malting of barley for most distilleries. While central malting seems more mechanical and less romantic, it means that the malting is precise and produces the large amount of malted barley required for the industry. At one time even central maltsters used floor maltings employing manual labor, but they did it on a larger scale than the individual distilleries. Later they used the less labor-intense Saladin boxes and drum maltings that automatically turned the barley after steeping and used pneumatic systems to force air through the germinating barley.

In the 1960s, however, the distilleries significantly expanded production, and by the end of the decade the railway no longer delivered barley and other supplies to the distilleries for malting. It was no longer viable for distilleries to undertake their own maltings. So in order to meet the increased demand, the central maltsters moved to single-vessel malting where the steeping, germinating, and kilning took place in one vessel (SGKV). Today with attention to energy efficiency, the steeping occurs separately in multiple 580-ton steeping tanks.

Preparation

Initially, the distillery submits an order for malted barley with its own specifications, including the barley's moisture and nitrogen content, fermentability, ability to extract the grain's sugar easily and completely, friability, and its PSY. The central maltsters procure the barley from barley merchants who communicate with farmers regarding the amount and types of barley strains they need.

After the barley is harvested, it goes to the central maltster, who checks it for moisture and nitrogen content, and screens it to remove any foreign objects. The barley arrives from farms containing 18 percent moisture, which the maltster reduces to 12 percent by drying the grain. The barley is then stored in large, flat sheds at 25°C (77°F) until it has recovered, which jolts the grain out of its dormancy and makes it ready for germination.

Steeping

The maltmen load the barley into industrial-sized steeping tanks, fill the tanks with water for its first "wet," and then suck air through it during a seventeen-hour air rest. Gary Lawton, Malting Manager at Boortmalt notes, "To initiate germination both oxygen and water have to be supplied to the grain. At the end of the first wet the moisture level will be 33-35% approximately. This large uptake of water means the respiration rate increases . . . producing carbon dioxide and heat [which] must be removed from the grain otherwise it will kill it. We do this by sucking out the carbon dioxide and heat using large fans that run continuously. If air was not drawn through the grain during the air break other compounds can be metabolized in place of oxygen and ultimately can kill the grain." The barley undergoes its second wet, so that its moisture content reaches 45 percent.

Germination

Large elevators then convey the grain into germination and kilning vessels, where the barley is piled almost 2 meters (6.5 feet) deep onto the bed of the containers. Over the course of four to five days, warm air (introduced at 18°C [64°F] and diminishing to 12°C [54°F]) is forced through the moving floor, which completes a slow circuit every four to five hours in order to turn the germinating grain and to keep the sprouting rootlets from tangling. The germination and kilning vessel maintains a sauna-like atmosphere by using moist air to keep the moisture level in the barley at 45 percent. When the acrospire (the green shoot) has grown three-fourths its length inside the husk, it becomes green malt and is ready to be kilned.

The Noser Knows

Maltmen stop the germination of green malt by slowly drying it over peat fires that smoke rather than flame. They burn peat in a large fire grate for two days under an expansive floor of mesh that holds the green malt. It is quite possible for anyone to stand in a kiln ankle deep in drying malt and not feel the fire beneath. The maltman controls the intensity of the phenol compounds by exposing the malt to the smoke for a varying amount of time, rather than by burning a larger amount of peat. He uses peat for only a portion of the two days of the kilning, and uses another fuel to finish the drying. In this way he can increase, decrease, or eliminate the peat-reek depending upon the whisky's flavor profile.

Traditionally, a maltman would say that the grain reached this point when it "chalks your hand," meaning that when he wrote a number or letter on his hand with one of the mealy kernels and it was chalky and crumbly, then the grain was ready for drying, or kilning.

Kilning

When the barley becomes green malt, kilning dries the grain over two days to 4 percent moisture content in order to prevent the kernel from sprouting and to preserve the enzymes necessary for starch conversion during mashing.

Lawton remarks that kilning temperatures "start at around 50°C [122°F] air on until the 'break'—the point at which the air leaving the grain is no longer saturated with moisture. This will stabilize the enzymes the distillers need in the mash tun for their starch conversion." If a distiller orders a malted barley with phenols (peat-reek), the peating occurs just before the break, when the maltster burns the peat in a separate burner and blows the smoke through the grain in the germinating and kilning vessel. Once the maltster completes any required peating and has reached the break, he increases the temperature to 74°C (165°F) to rapidly finish the drying and then begins to recirculate the air back into the warm kiln to reduce energy consumption.

Dressing

After completing the malting and drying of the grain, the malt is "dressed" to remove the withered roots, called malt culms. Samples of the malted barley then undergo a full analysis to specify its components, which include its moisture, color, nitrogen, enzymes, fermentability, PSY, and phenols among several others. Most distillers not only state their specifications, but also choose a spread of malt varieties, and the maltster completes a specific order by blending the different types of malt. He subjects the malt to a final dressing by passing the grain through a malt screen to remove malt dust, roots, husks that have fallen off, and small kernels. He then takes all of the malt culms and the remains from the final screening process and compacts them into pellets for animal feed.

Milling

At the distillery, operators screen the malted barley for debris and store it in large malt bins before passing it through the destoner and dust extractor. As perfunctory as these steps may seem, they are essential to the safe running of a distillery. Any spark from a piece of metal or stone as it passes through the mill could ignite the dust, causing a catastrophe, and people in a distillery consider these steps not only essential, but crucial.

Grinding the Malt into Grist

After dressing the barley, the mashman tips it into the mill, where the first set of rollers cracks the husk and the second set grinds the grain into grist, like coarse flour, in preparation for the mashing process.

The Distillery Cat's Meow

If you visit any distillery in Scotland, you will see a Porteus or a Boby (pronounced Bow-bee) mill in the mill room. They are large metal mills, usually enameled in bright, cheery red or green, and appear to be gently used. Their looks, however, belie their age. Most of these mills date to the 1960s, and many of them were made in the 1920s and 1930s. Quite a few of these mills were bought secondhand, and they are a testament to the quality of their construction. The Porteus and Boby mills just simply do not wear out; consequently, the original manufacturer no longer makes them.

The grist consists of approximately 70 percent grits, 20 percent husks, and 10 percent flour. The friability of the malt, one of the specifications included in a distiller's order, influences how the mill will grind the malt. "Very friable malt may become too fine for some mash tuns and then cause drainage issues. Low friability may make the malt seed difficult to grind to a suitable level," explains Ronnie Macdonald of Boortmalt. The husks, the shell of the barley that contains the peat flavors, forms the bed of the mash through which the sugary

Whisky Lexicon

Despite the sophisticated technology employed in distilleries today, distillery workers still rely upon a very old tool to ascertain if the grist contains the required percentages of flour, husks, and grits. A shoogle (shake) box sits on the shelf of most mill rooms, looking very much like a Victorian lady's glove box. It is usually a rather nicely crafted box with several layers of increasingly fine mesh that evaluates a sample of grist after it's been scooped into the box. The worker gives the box a good shake (hence the name shoogle), and the mesh separates the grist into its three parts and verifies that he has milled the proper balance of flour to grits to husks.

liquid will drain—a percentage of husks that is too high causes the bed to drain too quickly, and a percentage of flour that is too high causes the bed to clog and slow the drainage.

It is worth noting that after milling, the resulting fine white grains in the grits are the sugars that the water will extract, creating sweet water called wort. If one tasted the malted grain at this point, it would taste very much like malted milk balls or the malt used to flavor ice cream sundaes.

Mashing

Next stop is the mashing machine where hot water is added to the grist to create a porridge-like concoction called mash, which is then poured into the mash tun. The grist undergoes three different washes of water in the mash tun so that the enzymes in the grain (alpha and beta amylase) help the soluble starches complete their conversion to the sugar maltose. The combination of water and maltose creates a sugary liquid (sweet wort) that drains through fine holes in the bottom of the mash tun.

The mashman begins the mashing by heating the first water to 64°C (147°F) in order to reactivate the amylase enzymes that have been suspended by the malting process. He then raises the second water temperature to 75°C (167°F) and finishes with the last water at 85°C (185°F). Each increase in water temperature ensures that different fermentable sugars are extracted, guaranteeing a proper balance for successful fermentation. Although some distillers veer from these temperatures, they all use hot water close to these parameters.

Almost 85 percent of the conversion of starch to sugar takes place in the mashing machine with the first water. The mashman must attempt to complete the waters and draining process as rapidly as possible because the enzymes do not like a hot environment. The temperature control is, in itself, a fine balance—if the water is too hot, the desired enzymes die; if the water is not hot enough, the desired sugars are not extracted.

The mashman saves the resulting sweet wort from the first two waters for fermentation in large tanks called *underbacks*. Meanwhile, he diverts the last water, called *sparge*, for the first water of the next mash because it is too low in dissolved sugar. Finally, because of their high protein content, the husks that remain in the mash tun, called *draff*, are dried and used as cattle feed.

Whisky Lexicon

Sweet *wort* is the end product of the mashing process, which completes the conversion of starch to sugar. The sweet wort contains not only sugar, but also vital enzymes.

Mash Tuns

Mash tuns, used in this step of whisky making, can vary in size and material, including functional stainless steel or older cast iron; some have elaborate brass-and-copper covers. Some distillers prefer using a covered mash tun because it creates condensation with the water dropping back into the mash, and because it conserves the heat. In other distilleries,

Whisky Lexicon

Draff is really the malted barley after it has undergone three water baths to extract the sugar. It looks like soggy All-Bran cereal and is very high in protein. The larger distillery companies process it into pellets and sell it to farmers for cattle feed. The smaller distilleries, like Glengoyne, Edradour and GlenDronach, simply have farmers drive to the distillery in a tractor towing a small wagon and park the wagon under a chute through which draff is discharged. The farmer then drives home with his wagon full of steaming draff to feed his cattle.

particularly ones that host large numbers of visitors, the mash tun remains open so that the visitors can gather around it to watch the mashing process and smell the aromas.

Mash looks like cooking oatmeal, and just as a small pot of oatmeal can lump together if it is not stirred, so can the mash but on a much grander, and more costly, scale. In the older traditional distilleries, a rake slowly circles around the mash tun. But this little spiderlike rake either pushes the mash down or lifts it up, and when any major lumping or tangling occurs, workers are needed to clear the mess by hand.

To find a solution, the whisky industry borrowed the better-designed *Lauter tun* from brewers. This much-improved mash tun incorporates a better system of stirrers that tilt up and down, as well as forward and backward. When the mashman drains the wort from the mash, the finely perforated floor of the Lauter tun produces a clearer liquid with most of the solids remaining in the bottom of the mash tun. This modern design allows the use of fine grist and improves the yield and the quality of the sweet wort, which will ferment in washbacks with the addition of yeast.

Fermenting

The Distillery Cat's Meow

Historically, distilling involved hard labor and heavy lifting. Recent European Union (EU) regulations have defined work rules that prevent distillery workers from lifting more than 25 kilograms (55 pounds). Bags of yeast are kept below this limit, usually at 20 kilos (44 pounds) each. These regulations not only ended arduous work practices for the men who generally held distillery positions, but also opened opportunities for women to work on the production side of making whisky.

The distillery operator cools the sweet wort by running it through a *heat exchanger*, lowering the temperature of the liquid and also recapturing the heat. This gift of recaptured energy creates a competition of sorts among distilleries to outdo each other in their creativity of its use, including warming community swimming pools and heating horticultural greenhouses, but more often the reheated water returns to the hot liquor tank to provide hot water for the next mash.

Once the heat exchangers have cooled the wort, it moves toward the washbacks through the wort line where the yeast is added. At one time, distillers used yeast in large containers, which were difficult to manage because of the weight. This took its toll on the physical well-being of the distillery workers. Today, in an effort to reduce the manual labor of handling yeast, most distilleries use a pressed or creamed yeast that is injected into the wort line; others use a dry yeast, which arrives in 20-kilogram (44-pound) bags that mashmen open and tip directly into the mash tun after it has filled with several inches of wort.

The yeast and sweet wort mixture enters the bottom of tall *washbacks*, where fermentation takes place. The washbacks are made of Oregon pine, larch, or stainless steel, and they can be as deep as 18 feet.

Fermentation releases enzymes in the yeast such as *maltase*, which converts the maltose sugar into glucose. It also produces *zymase*, enzymes in the yeast, which promote the conversion of sugar into alcohol and carbon dioxide. During fermentation, the wash gurgles with small bubbles at first, which grow in size and activity. They finally become smaller once again as the activity decreases. During this time, the fermentation can be so active that the washbacks shake, the lids flap open or shut, and the entire brew foams and spits. At one time distilleries employed men to stir the wort with birch switches to keep the foam contained, but today they activate revolving blades, called *switchers*, to prevent the contents from overflowing the washbacks. Other distilleries, like Ardmore, fill the washbacks to a point low enough to accommodate the foam so that they don't need to employ switchers.

Interestingly, if the mashman produces a cloudy wort containing small bits of solids from the malted barley, the wash does not foam. And conversely if he produces a clear wort, the wash will bubble and spit, requiring switchers to control the foam.

The Noser Knows

Occasionally, mashmen resort to the historical practice of hanging a bar of soap into the wash to prevent intense foaming, particularly to manage fermentations that take place over the weekend, when many distillery employees are not working.

After two to three days, the final product becomes *wash* and resembles sour beer in both smell and taste, and has a low alcohol content of about 8 percent. With distillation, this fruity "beer" will become new-make spirit.

Flavor Development

Some discussion swirls around the role fermentation plays in the development of some flavor congeners in the whisky. Mashmen tend to use distiller's yeast, which provides viability and efficiency, but differing opinions exist regarding the temperature of the wort, the length of time for the fermentation, the type of washback used for fermentation, and the overall influence of these variables on fermentation and flavor development.

Temperature is Crucial

Before adding yeast, mashmen must cool the sweet wort in order to avoid killing the yeast with high temperatures. Usually, wort is not cooled below 16°C (61°F) because the yeast simply remains dormant, but mashmen often cool wort within a range of 17°C to 24°C (63°F to 75°F).

When fermentation begins, the yeast multiply in the presence of oxygen and the temperature rises. As the oxygen supply diminishes, the yeast cells begin to convert sugar to alcohol and carbon dioxide, and the activity causes the temperature to continue to rise.

By the time the temperature reaches 34°C (93°F), the sugar levels have dropped, the alcohol levels have risen, and the yeast has died.

If fermentation begins at a lower temperature, the yeast has a longer period of time to deplete the sugar and produce higher levels of alcohol; but if the fermentation begins at a higher temperature, the yeast has less time to reach the critical temperature and finishes *incomplete*, with more unconverted sugar and less alcohol. A slow fermentation can also result in more fruity esters and fewer oily flavors.

The Noser Knows

The temperature of the wort going into the washback depends upon the length of fermentation and the day's ambient temperature. Yeast dies at 34°C (93°F), so a long fermentation requires a lower temperature to provide yeast more time to convert sugar to alcohol; a short fermentation requires a higher temperature because the yeast has less time for the conversion to take place. Similarly, if the day is hot, then the mashman must lower the temperature of the wort; he must raise the temperature if the day is cold.

Length of Fermentation

Most mashmen use an average of 48 hours for the fermentation process; but others, like the people at Isle of Jura Distillery, ferment for 54 hours, and still others, like the people at Springbank Distillery, ferment from 72 to 110 hours because the greater length of time provides more potential for the development of flavor congeners and a more complete fermentation. Additionally, mashmen at distilleries using long fermentations sometimes allow the wash to sit in the washbacks after a complete fermentation to allow the development of *lactobacilli*, which can produce additional flavor compounds or compounds that act as a catalyst to trigger other flavors during distillation.

Washbacks—Wood or Stainless Steel

Distillers use either stainless steel or wooden washbacks, with a very few still fermenting in Corten steel vessels. Those who use Oregon pine or boat-skin larch washbacks believe that the traditional use of wood allows them to better control temperatures and that the wood contains microorganisms that can add to the flavor. Those who use stainless steel vessels believe that the use of modern stainless steel decreases the likelihood of wild yeasts, which compete with good yeasts for the available sugar and produce undesirable flavors. They also contend that the repeated steam cleaning of the wooden washbacks will deplete, over time, any flavor elements that the wood can contribute.

What's Your Flavor Profile?

While fermentation has some influence, it often comes down to the flavor profile each distillery is trying to develop for its whisky. For instance, some distillers want to encourage the formation of esters that provide the fruity flavors in some whiskies; others may want esters to take a secondary role in the flavor profile for their whisky. Some distillers find that they can produce more esters using wort with a high sugar content and a long fermentation. Virtually all distillers, however, try to use fermentation to increase the alcohol yield and try to preserve the flavors in the range they want to see in their specific whisky. Importantly, distillers know that no amount of good distillation in the next step will correct a poor or faulty fermentation.

What You Need to Know

> ➤ Whisky is essentially distilled beer.

> ➤ Enzyme activation during malting and mashing is key to producing high levels of sugar and good fermentation.

> ➤ Smoky flavors and aromas in single malt whisky mainly come from drying green malt over peat fires; estery compounds (fruits and florals) develop during fermentation.

> ➤ Distillers can balance and manipulate the intensity of flavor development during malting and fermentation.

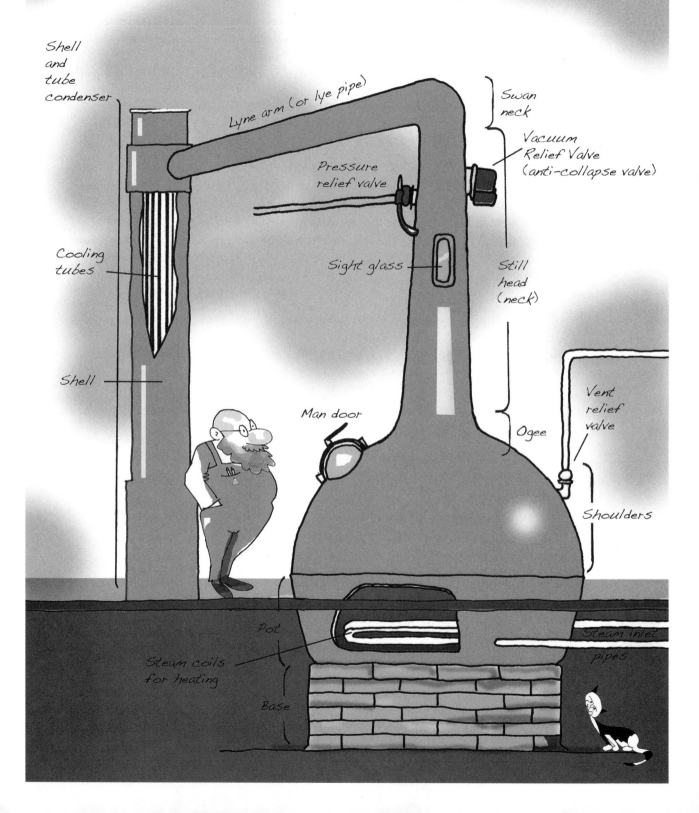

PARTS of a STILL

CHAPTER 6

The Art of Distillation

In This Chapter

➤ Understanding distillation

➤ Examining the variables

➤ Style and body development

➤ The end result

Looking at Basic Distillation

After fermentation, the wash moves to holding tanks (wash chargers) and then to copper pot stills for distillation. The formation of the whisky's character involves a complex interaction between ingredients and processes and develops as it moves from malting through maturation; however, distillation in copper stills plays a role particularly in forming the body and basic style of the spirit.

The First Distillation

A broad view of distillation involves moving the fermented alcohol through a pair of stills—the first named the wash still and the second the low wines, or spirit, still. First, the wash is pumped into the wash still, also called charging the still, and then heated until it boils. A glass porthole (a sight glass) in the head of the still always identifies the wash still. Additionally, a wash still is usually slightly larger than a spirit still with which it is paired. The stillman uses the sight glass to monitor the intensity of the boil and makes sure the distillate doesn't rise above the top of the glass and boil over into the lyne arm. When the froth reaches the bottom of the porthole, he then reduces the heat and maintains a slow simmer so that the distillate bubbles between the top and bottom of the sight glass.

The Distillery Cat's Meow

Before the introduction of the sight glass, the stillman had to swing a ball, attached to the ceiling with a rope, against the head of the still and listen for a dull or hollow sound to determine how far the distillate had risen in the still.

As the wash simmers, the vapor rises to the top of the still and travels through a lyne arm connecting the still to a condenser or to a worm. In the case of the condenser, usually a shell-and-tube design, a bundle of copper tubes containing cool water inside a tall column causes the hot vapor to condense into a liquid; whereas in the case of the worm, the vapor condenses inside a spiraling copper pipe immersed in cold water in a worm tub built outside of the stillroom. Either method turns the steam back into a liquid, designated as low wines, which now is at about 23 percent ABV.

The Second Distillation

The low wines pour through a spirit safe, a brass-and-glass locked case, allowing the stillman to monitor the low wines without touching them. From there, the distillate goes into the low wines and feints receiver to await its second distillation in the next still, called the low wines or spirit still. Any solids, pot ales or burnt ales, left in the wash still after the first distillation are converted into syrup and usually used as cattle feed. A second distillation in the spirit still strengthens and purifies the low wines with the end product now designated as spirit or new-make at generally 68 to 71 percent ABV.

Taking the Cut

Not all of the distilled spirit is considered desirable for casking. During the second distillation, the stillman once again diverts the whisky through a spirit safe, where he carefully monitors the new-make spirit to determine how much he will divert for maturation. Because customs and excise officers lock the safe, the stillman watches the whisky pour into a glass container that resembles a brandy snifter. He divides the distillate into three parts: the foreshots appear first in the spirit run, the middle cut contains the character desired in the new-make spirit, and the feints appear at the end of the run. The stillman determines the beginning of each part and then separates the flow of the spirit into several different receiving tanks by using external handles.

Whisky Lexicon

The first and last part of the distillation run, respectively called the foreshots (also called the heads) and the feints or aftershots (the tails), have too many impurities and are not casked for aging. The center portion of the run, called the middle cut (the heart), is the desirable spirit chosen for maturation.

At the beginning and end of each run, the stillman collects both the foreshots and the feints, returns them to the low wines and feints receiver, and then distills them once again in the spirit still with the next batch of low wines. Mixing the foreshots and feints with a batch of low wines tends to raise the ABV from approximately 23 percent to 30 percent before the entire batch fills, or charges, the spirit still for the second distillation.

The stillman sends the middle cut to the intermediate spirit receiver and then to the spirit vat in the filling room for the addition of water to reduce the new-make spirit to 63.5 percent ABV and to fill the casks for maturation. Once the stillman has diverted all the alcohol into the respective receivers, what remains in the still is called spent lees, and is processed as waste.

Distilling Variables

The broad view of distillation, explained above, requires a more detailed examination of the process in order to fully understand the effects of distillation on the development of whisky flavors. Olivier Fagnen, the resident authority on distillation at the SWRI, notes that several factors, including the number of distillations (double or triple distillation), how the still is operated, the contact between the spirit and the copper of the still, the design of the still, the method of heating the still, the choice of a condenser or worm, and the maintenance of the still, all contribute to the formation of the flavors in each individual whisky. Additionally, the range of the middle cut determines the flavors the new-make spirit will contain —the stillman can move it forward to include different amounts of fruity esters from the foreshots at the beginning of the middle cut, or he can move it back to include varying amounts of feints from the end of the cut. A distiller can manipulate these parameters to influence the body and flavor of the final spirit.

The Spirit Run—Determining the Middle Cut

In order to determine when the stillman begins and ends the middle cut, he brings scientific instruments, time, nature's elements, and experience to the decision. Using a hydrometer to measure the specific gravity, and hence ABV, will help him determine when he will begin and end the cut.

Distilleries maintain a specific alcoholic strength to indicate when the cut begins and another lower strength, as the alcohol diminishes, to indicate when it ends. Often the desired alcoholic strength occurs after a predetermined amount of time has passed, and the decision to make the cut happens when a correlation between the correct passage of time and the correct alcohol strength occurs. The stillman adds distilled water to the spirit to test its purity: the spirit turns cloudy if there are impurities and remains clear if the spirit runs pure.

The Noser Knows

An experienced stillman can detect a faint blue cast if impurities still exist in the spirit, and he will delay the start of the cut until the spirit turns completely clear.

Finding the Heart

The middle cut (the heart) for individual whiskies depends on the flavor profile each distillery desires for its product, and it varies from place to place. The alcohol strength begins high and diminishes as distillation continues—although distillers prefer not to publically discuss their exact middle cut, it can begin high, near 74 percent ABV, and end low, near to 58 percent ABV. It is a procedure that cannot be reduced to a simple formula. Certainly, it involves alcohol strength, time, clarity, and color, but a skilled stillman must use his knowledge and experience to establish the amount of foreshots and feints to include in the middle cut.

While the foreshots and feints contain impurities, they also hold many of the flavor congeners that determine the character of the whisky. Many of the fruit and floral esters reside at the end of the foreshots, and some desired graham cracker-like flavors rest early in the feints. Some whiskies, like Glenlivet and Aberlour, favor more esters; other flavor profiles, like an Ardbeg, call for a greater proportion of feints or phenols (smokiness) that appear at the end of the middle cut. One distillery manager said to me, "If we have ordered peated malt, we'll end our middle cut a bit lower because we want the phenols, particularly if we've paid for them." Whether the stillman begins the middle cut early to include more esters or ends it late to include more feints depends on his judgment and the desired flavor profile for each whisky. There is no hard and fast rule that fits every distillery.

Number of Distillations

Almost all scotch malt whisky distilleries use the distillation process described previously. This process includes double distillation, which involves distilling the fermented wash in two stills. Some distilleries, however, provide a variation on this theme by adding a third, or intermediate, still using a triple distillation process. This technique is more commonly used in Lowland distilleries, like Auchentoshan.

The Noser Knows

Some people mistakenly think that the word *single* in single malt Scotch whisky refers to the number of distillations. There is no such thing as a single distilled malt whisky. Triple distilled malt whisky—yes. Double distilled malt whisky—most definitely. But never single distilled malt whisky.

Triple Distillation

In the triple distillation production, the wash still is run as usual and the low wines are advanced to the intermediate still. The same process continues in the intermediate still, with most of that batch continuing onward to the spirit still; but the feints (the tails) return to the wash still for redistillation with the next batch of incoming wash. After the third distillation is completed in the spirit still, the middle cut is moved to the intermediate spirit receiver for reduction and casking, but the foreshots and feints are returned to the intermediate still for distillation with the next batch of low wines coming from the wash still.

The new-make spirit is lighter and more delicate because most of the foreshot and feint have been removed. Furthermore, the alcohol strength of the middle cut has risen to approximately 81 percent ABV, a higher strength than new-make spirit produced during double distillation. While the alcohol strength is higher at the end of triple distillation, the middle cut, taken from each still becomes smaller.

Two, Two-and-a-Half, Three

The production workers at Springbank Distillery in Campbeltown use both double and triple distillation, and then vary both procedures to use what they identify as two-and-a-half distillations, enabling them to produce three different whiskies on one site. In order to produce the required malts for their blends, they distill Longrow malt whisky using double distillation, and then use triple distillation to produce the lighter, more subtle Hazelburn whisky.

To produce Springbank malt whisky, workers use two-and-a-half distillations by advancing only a percentage of the low wines produced in the wash still to an intermediate still. The remaining percentage of low wines skips the intermediate still and moves directly into the feints receiver, holding the foreshots and feints from the previous run of the spirit still. The spirit from the intermediate still then joins this mixture, and the entire batch undergoes a third distillation in the spirit still. This process removes some of the impurities and raises the alcohol strength of the new-make spirit; but because only a portion of the final distillate undergoes a triple distillation, this procedure is identified as a two-and-a-half distillation. (See Springbank profile.)

Running the Stills

The method the stillman uses to run the still has a notable impact on the distillation. During distillation, the liquid wash boils in the pot of the still. The more volatile components vaporize and move up the head of the still into the lyne arm, and then into the condenser, where the vapor returns to a liquid. But some of the vapors never manage to reach the lyne arm and instead drop back into the still and reboil. This process is called reflux action and is what the stillman tries to achieve when he operates the still.

If the stillman can create more reflux action by maintaining the boil at a slow, steady rate, he allows a greater separation of the volatile components that rise in the vapor and the nonvolatile components that stay behind in the pot. Simmering the distillate instead of vigorously boiling it means that the desirable vapors rise slowly and the undesirable components remain in the bottom of the pot. Generating a greater reflux action also allows the liquid to remain longer in the copper pot, increasing the contact between the distillate and the copper. The idea of reflux action can be likened to trying to reduce a sauce by boiling it down, but in distillation the stillman captures the vapors that we usually allow to evaporate in cooking.

Copper Contact with the Spirit

The role of copper in the distillation process is not unlike the recommendation to use copper bowls to whip egg whites. In the kitchen, the copper in the bowl reacts to stabilize the egg whites and keeps them from forming clumps, rendering the concoction useless. The use of copper's reactive surface to create successful recipes in the kitchen also translates into using it to produce successful distillation.

Once again, Olivier Fagnen notes that because the copper in the pot stills reacts with the distillate to reduce the sulfur notes (the smell of burned matches) and also acts as a catalyst for other reactions, many distillers consider it favorable to keep the spirit exposed to the copper for as long as possible. To this end, some distilleries drag chains, called rummagers, along the inside of the spirit stills, as happens at the Springbank distillery. These rummagers, resembling medieval chain mail, are often used in stills that heat directly from the bottom (like a gas stove top) and serve to prevent the solids from burning on the bottom of the still. Most importantly, the rummagers also expose new copper to the distillate with each turn of the arm.

The size of the still also affects the amount of contact between the distillate and the copper. Smaller stills permit more exposure to the copper, whereas larger stills allow less. And, finally, some of the reasons we like to use copper utensils in our kitchens are the same reasons that distillers like to have copper stills in the stillroom. They are good conductors of heat and are highly malleable, allowing designers a wide variation of shapes.

Designing the Stills

When standing in a stillroom and looking at the large, and sometimes small, copper stills in a range of shapes, it is easy to assume that the design of the stills plays a significant role in the making of the whisky. Actually, the design of the stills plays only a supporting role to the all-important reflux action.

Distillation generates ethyl alcohol, water, and secondary flavor congeners, which help produce the whisky's character. The shape and size of the still helps to determine how much reflux action occurs and primarily influences the body of the spirit. As the distillate boils in the pot, the volatiles with low boiling points rise first into the head of the still; and because there is a small temperature difference between the vapor and the copper neck, the vapor continues to rise and cross into the lyne arm and through to the condenser. The volatiles with higher boiling points require an increased temperature to begin their upward journey into the head, where there is a greater temperature difference between the vapor and the copper sides of the neck. When the hot vapor comes in contact with the cooler copper, the vapor condenses and runs back into the still to reboil and does not cross into the condensers.

Short Ones, Fat Ones, Skinny Ones, Too

Stills come in a range of shapes and sizes. For instance, the stills at the Glenmorangie distillery have long, tapering necks; whereas the ones at the Macallan Distillery have short, thick necks. In long-necked stills, only the lightest vapors reach the head of the still while the rest of the distillate falls back into the still to be redistilled (reflux); however, in short thick-necked stills, heavier flavor elements manage to make their way into the condensers more easily with little reflux action. Furthermore, the shoulders of the onion-shaped still can have a defined round plumpness to it or a gently sloping pear shape, like the stills at Bunnahabhain and Lagavulin distilleries. The onion shape allows little reflux action and creates a heavy-bodied spirit.

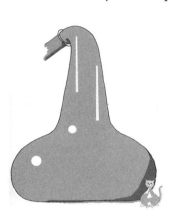

Onion-Shape Still   **Lantern-Shape Still**   **Still with Boil Ball**

The stills can also have a lantern-shape with a sharp-nipped waist or a round boil ball above the pot. Nipped waists, like the lantern-shaped stills at Glenallachie Distillery, initially drive the volatiles upward through the narrow waist, which then condense as they come in contact with the cooler copper in the wide neck. As the distillate returns to the pot of the still, the narrow waist directs the reflux into the center part of the stills where the heat is more intense and the vapors flash back up into the head.

The stills at Balvenie, Glenrothes, and Balmenach distilleries incorporate a boil ball above the pot, allowing more reflux action. As the vapor rises into the ball, it rapidly condenses against the cool copper in the boil ball and falls back into the still—the more pronounced the curve in the boil ball, the more reflux action takes place.

Breaking the Rules

Every family has relatives who decide to go their own way and break all the rules. The whisky world is no different, and a few distilleries have stills that combine design features and also create a few of their own. The stills at Pulteney Distillery incorporate a unique design with a wash still that has an extremely short, flat head that has been cut off. This design significantly increases the reflux because the hot vapors travel a short distance to the cooler flat top of the still and bounce back into the pot. The spirit still has an unusual lyne arm that loops around in an exaggerated U-shape that not only allows greater condensation of the vapors that then return to the pot, but also increases the contact between the distillate and the copper. Cragganmore also employs the flattop design in its spirit still and increases the reflux even further by also incorporating a boil ball.

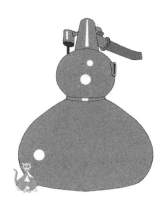

Unique Still at Pulteney Distillery

Variations on a Theme

The lyne arm, the connecting pipe between the still and the condenser, is the final feature of still design. Much thought goes into the design of the still in order to encourage the right amount of desired volatiles to make their way into the condensers and return to liquid spirit. The final link is the lyne arm; and it is more than just a connection pipe—it, too, has its role in defining the body of the spirit.

If the lyne arm at the top of the still is short and angled downward, presenting few impediments, heavier flavor congeners make their way into the condensers and worms, but long lyne pipes angled upward allow only the lighter flavor elements into the condensers. Both Glen Grant and Ardbeg distilleries increase the reflux action by adding purifiers that include a box surrounded by cool water and mounted around part of the lyne arm. When the heavier volatiles enter the cooled purifier, they condense and return to the pot by means of a connecting pipe.

Some distilleries use one shape for the wash still and another for the spirit still; others maintain the same shape for both. At the now-mothballed Glen Keith Distillery, the wash stills incorporated the onion-shape design with gently sloping shoulders resulting in little reflux, but the design of the spirit stills used a boil ball to encourage a greater reflux action during the second distillation. The variation in the still design within one distillery allows the distiller to influence both the amount of reflux that takes place and the place at which the reflux occurs in the distillation process.

If It Ain't Broke, Don't Fix It

Distilleries tend to be adamant about precisely maintaining the design of the stills so that the character of the whisky does not alter. There are stories of stills that were replaced exactly so that even dents and slight imperfections were duplicated. Although some of these stories about dents and nicks may have reached the realm of legend, it is true that altering the shape of the stills will alter the whisky produced in them.

The Distillery Cat's Meow

New stills at the former Caperdonich Distillery offer a cautionary tale about changing the shape of the stills. In the nineteenth century, the Glen Grant Distillery sprawled across both sides of the road in the town of Rothes. The portion on one side was Glen Grant Distillery; the second distillery was known as Glen Grant Number Two.

In 1901, the owners dismantled the second distillery on one side of the road until a rise in whisky sales in the 1960s necessitated more production. At that time, they installed new stills and equipment on the old site of Glen Grant Number Two. Despite using the same water, barley, and mash at both places, the whisky from the new stills was somewhat different than that produced at the old site across the road. Consequently, whisky from the old site was named Glen Grant, but whisky from the new site was Caperdonich.

Heating the Stills

Many whisky-making techniques parallel routines and choices we all make in our kitchens, although the production of whisky happens on a much grander scale and produces a somewhat different product. Both the distiller and the home cook choose copper for its conductivity and its ability to transfer some copper properties to recipes, and the parallel also exists between the choices home cooks make to heat their stoves and distillers make to heat their stills.

Direct or Indirect Firing

A few distilleries, like Glenfiddich, use direct heat, which heats the bottom of the still until it runs hot enough to heat the wash inside the pot (similar to lighting a gas burner on the stove to heat a pan of water). One drawback of direct firing is that it can create hot spots causing burn areas in the pot, but it also generates an unintended consequence that proves beneficial. In order to prevent burning in a direct-fired still, distillers swirl metal rummagers, discussed earlier, along the bottom of the pot. This in turn exposes more of the copper to the distillate, creating a desired reaction between the metal and distillate.

Most distilleries, however, use indirect heat, which heats from within the still using steam coils or pans until the wash runs hot enough to heat the still (similar to using an electric tea kettle to heat the water inside the pot). Many home cooks prefer using a gas stove rather than an electric one because it affords them greater control of the heat, and distillers like this method for the same reasons.

The Distillery Cat's Meow

European Union regulations discourage the direct firing of stills. The combination of an open flame with flammable spirit in the still creates a potentially hazardous situation. Consequently, distilleries like GlenDronach have changed to steam heating and have abandoned direct firing and rummagers.

Some distilleries adamantly defend the method of heating that they use, and others move from one method to another. One distillery may find that changing the method of heating the bottom of the still with a gas fire to heating with steam coils will drastically change the flavor of their whisky; whereas another distillery will find that changing the heating method has little discernible effect on the character of its product.

Springbank Distillery stopped using the direct fire heating system and installed steam coils, but it found that the flavor of the whisky changed. This created a dilemma because direct fire was deemed too slow, but losing the caramelizing that occurred with the direct fire changed the spirit. The resulting solution was to keep both methods so that the stills are now fired by direct fire and steam coils.

On the other hand, Macallan Distillery used direct heat and rummagers and considered this heating process part of its identity; so when it changed to indirect heat, it was a decision not made lightly, and a move not made quickly. The distiller changed a limited number of wash stills to indirect firing and ran them for a year, watching for changes in the new-make spirit before the decision was made to convert all the stills.

Distillers, however, hold one constant objective—to try to maintain an even heat because an uneven heat produces an uneven distillation. Once again, the home kitchen analogy works because when preparing a slow-cooked meal, the chef tries to maintain an even, slow simmer so that the food cooks steadily and regularly without burning.

Cooling Systems—Condensers or Worms

Most distilleries employ vertical column condensers with a shell-and-tube design to return the vapor to liquid, but a few distilleries still use the more traditional method of a copper worm with a diminishing diameter that spirals downward in the worm tub, a tower of cool water built adjacent to the distillery. The shell-and-tube condenser has a columnar shell filled with copper cooling tubes that resemble a bundle of straws. The large bundle of tubes provides a lot of copper, more contact, and produces a lighter whisky. A worm design may appear to use a large amount of copper, but it actually has less contact and generates a heavier whisky.

The distiller also needs to monitor the temperature of the cooling water in the condenser or worm. Increasing the temperature of the water will minimize the temperature difference between the vapor and the copper so that the vapor condenses more slowly and stays in contact with the copper longer. Once again, the distiller tries to maintain a greater exposure of the spirit to the copper in order to reduce the sulfur character and encourage the catalytic action that enhances or diminishes the intensity of other flavor congeners.

Interestingly, a warm summer has a negative effect on whisky-making because it raises the temperature of the cooling water and upsets the balance between the temperature of the vapor and the condenser. Warmer condensing water means that it takes longer for the vapor to condense; it remains in contact with the copper longer and can strip out more of the sulfur compounds, altering the character of the spirit.

The Distillery Cat's Meow

The condenser water can only be cooled to the ambient temperature. On a hot summer's day, production workers have difficulty keeping the water cool enough to condense the vapor in the stills. This goes a long way to understanding why the distillation of Scotch whisky is very much a winter activity. Historically, a farmer had free time during the winter to distill whisky when he wasn't working in the fields, but distillation depended as much on the cool weather of winter as it did on the free time available in winter.

Cleaning and Conditioning the Stills

Once the new-make spirit moves from the spirit still into casks for maturation, the cleaning and maintenance of the stills begins. Like any cooking utensil, the stills require cleaning to remove any deposits that may burn or any film that decreases the copper contact with the distillate. But unlike kitchen utensils, the stills need resting time and air pumped into them to create some oxidation, which makes the copper more reactive. The resting time can work in reverse to avoid oxidation as well. If a distiller wants to retain a sulfury character to its whisky and does not want that flavor stripped by the copper, the workers will often leave the stills closed and quickly recharge them with the next distillation. This ensures that the stills don't oxidize and minimizes the time the distillate interacts with the copper.

Alcoholic Strength and Filling

After the stillman completes the spirit run, he diverts it to the intermediate spirit receiver, a holding tank, and then onward to the spirit vat in the filling room, where the spirit is transferred into casks. When new-make spirit completes its second distillation, it is clear in color, resembling gin or vodka, and is very potent at about 70 percent ABV.

The alcohol strength of new-make spirit varies slightly from distillery to distillery. Reducing it to a standard 63.5 percent ABV serves to standardize reciprocal exchanges among distilleries that trade their distillate for spirit from other distilleries to fulfill their requirements for making their blended whiskies.

Whisky Lexicon

Distillery workers refer to new-make spirit as clearic or spike. Considering the alcohol volume of new-make spirit, perhaps the latter word is the better descriptor.

The Noser Knows

The high point of alcoholic strength demands a lot of attention, and the low point receives virtually none. It is no less important. If whisky, maturing in the cask, falls below 40 percent, it can no longer be bottled as a single malt whisky. This causes some vigilance in distilleries that hold very old casks. If master blenders want an old cask for a memorable and distinctive release, they must closely monitor the alcoholic strength of the whisky—if it comes close to the 40 percent threshold, they may need to release it earlier than intended, or if it falls below 40 percent, then the whisky is only useful in a blend. Below 40 percent ABV, the value of the old whisky disappears.

The standard reduction strength has evolved over time as master blenders observed the correlation between filling strengths of new-make spirit and its maturity. Some distilleries do not reduce their new-make spirit and cask it at the strength it leaves the spirit still, which at first glance warms the accountants' hearts because it means fewer casks needed for aging. But the spirit also matures more slowly and extracts different flavor compounds from the wood. The casking strength very much depends upon the flavor profile the master blender wants in the final product, and some spirits benefit from slower maturation and additional time in the cask, while others do not.

How Much Does it Take?

Being aware of the volumes of ingredients used to produce a final new-make spirit will help you understand the premium placed on the final product, which constitutes a very small percentage of the raw materials used in the whisky-making process.

> ➤ Jura Distillery, for instance, has six malt bins, each holding 30 tons of malted barley, the approximate equivalent of seven truckloads of malted barley.

> ➤ The whisky-making process begins with two mashes that mix a total of 9,000 tons of malted barley and 60,000 liters (15,850 gallons) of water.

> ➤ Two mashes produce 48,300 liters (12,760 gallons) of sweet wort, to which the mashman adds 150 kilos (331 pounds) of creamed yeast to yield 48,000 liters (12,680 gallons) of wash.

> ➤ The distillation of the wash in the first still results in 16,000 liters (4,227 gallons) of low wines, yielding only one third of the wash that first charged the still.

> ➤ The second and final distillation results in 4,000 liters (1,057 gallons) of new-make spirit at 71 percent ABV—a bit more than 8 percent of the wash used at the start of the distilling process.

What You Need to Know

> ➤ A distillery's still design never changes because doing so would change the desired character of the new-make spirit.

> ➤ A distiller, however, can manipulate the number of distillations as well as the operation, heating, cooling, and cleaning of the stills in order to "play different tunes" on one instrument.

➤ Changing the distilling parameters influences the body and style of new-make spirit.

➤ It takes significant amounts of raw materials to produce small amounts of spirit—an important factor to consider when faced with the cost of a single malt whisky.

CHAPTER 7

 # Maturation: The Last Step

In This Chapter

➤ Understanding the aspects of maturation

➤ The importance and effect of oak

➤ Flavor development and casks

In order for spirit to assume the color and rounded tastes that we all associate with Scotch whisky, it must in compliance with the Scotch Whisky Regulations 2009 (SWR), "mature for a period of not less than three years." Although whisky must age for a minimum of three years before the Scottish law considers (or even names) it whisky, the majority of single malt actually ages for much longer than the required time. The length of time spirit spends in the cask can significantly impact the flavor profile of the final product because it has more time to extract flavor components from the wood and more time for evaporation to occur. Once again, choosing the best time for bottling a cask involves determining the moment the spirit has extracted the precise amount of flavor from the cask to produce the desired flavor profile.

The Benefits of Youth and Age

Most core ranges of a distillery's products show a bottling with an age statement between ten and fifteen years. But with a significant improvement in wood policy during the last fifteen years, distillers have successfully bottled whisky at younger ages. At the other end of the spectrum, a glance at the offerings from both distilleries and independent bottlers shows that bottles of older whiskies are available, often at a premium price. Whiskies reach their peak at different ages. Many whiskies benefit considerably from the extra years in the wood;

other whiskies do not. Since *old* does not necessarily mean "better," it is best to sample aged whiskies at a restaurant or a tasting before spending a lot of money. Today, the evaluations of old and expensive whiskies are readily available both in print and online; and, as for any other expensive purchase, they are well worth consulting before buying.

Oak and Only Oak

The importance of maturation in oak casks cannot be overstated because the aging of whiskies in oak accounts for 60 to 80 percent of the flavor development. During maturation, a range of changes occur that Ronnie Cox of Berry Bros. & Rudd has appropriately categorized as "addition, subtraction, and interaction." Reactions occur between the spirit and the wood, adding new dimensions to the flavor development during maturation. The original fill of the cask contributes additional character while off notes evaporate through the wood. And to complicate the understanding of the maturation process, the length of maturation time, the warehousing, the size of the casks, and the number of times the cask has been refilled influence the flavor development.

The Distillery Cat's Meow

A good reason for using white oak casks is that they are waterproof —they don't leak and lose a distiller's investment. The Story of Oak exhibition at Macallan Distillery best explains this characteristic: "Shipbuilders long ago used oak because of its waterproof capabilities. White oak, unlike red oak, has a common feature that allows it to form tyloses, the waterproofing cell structure that forms inside of its moisture channels."

Interaction

Distillers use casks made of American white oak (*Quercus alba*), English, or European, oak (*Quercus robur*), or Sessile oak (*Quercus petraea*). American white oak barrels are usually reused bourbon barrels that undergo charring. English oak and Sessile oak are reused sherry butts that undergo toasting. Specifically, oak wood allows evaporation of undesirable notes and helps a spirit lose its immaturity; additionally, oak provides additional flavors that originate from the wood and from the previous contents of the cask (usually bourbon or sherry). Jim Beveridge's team at Diageo's Global Technical Center, where the company's blending occurs, notes, "American oak tends to impart sweetness to the mature spirit, almost buttery. The European oak again has a sweetness but a different kind of sweetness— more like raisins, sultanas—sometimes described as leathery, tobacco notes. There is a richness there, but a different richness."

The Noser Knows

Because new-make spirit is clear, the oak cask and its previous fill are responsible for the colors we associate with matured whisky. During maturation, the color tends to come early and fast; the flavors and aromas develop over time.

Toasting or Charring

In order to access the flavors in the wood (the woodiness) the coopers, who make the casks, must apply heat to them for maximum flavor extraction. They lightly toast the inside of sherry casks, which release flavors reminiscent of spice, vanilla, and coconut; and fully burn the inside of bourbon casks to create a distinct layer of char. The charring actually delivers more bang for the buck because its benefit is twofold. First, a light layer of toasting rests beneath the layer of char. And second, the actual burning of the cask caramelizes any sugar present and the additional char acts as a filter to extract impurities, most especially sulfur notes.

When master blenders choose casks to mature their new-make spirit, they must carefully consider the effect of the wood on the distillery character of the new-make spirit and strive for the best marriage of complementing (not competing) characteristics. This means that sherry casks are not automatically better than the more available bourbon casks; and first fill casks are not automatically better than second fill casks. Master

Whisky Lexicon

Distillery character, or spirit character, is the flavor profile developed during distillation and is evident in new-make spirit. Maturation develops and enhances this profile over time in the cask, when the whisky takes on its mature character.

blenders truly engage in a balancing flavor act so that the effects of the wood do not mask or overpower a good spirit character created during the distillation process.

Addition and Subtraction

Scottish law also dictates that Scotch whisky can "mature only in oak casks of a capacity not exceeding 700 litres" (SWR, 2009). Once a cask is larger than 700 liters (185 gallons), the proportion of wood surface to spirit ceases to benefit the maturation process—in essence, the cask is too large. Using an oak cask for maturation permits the spirit to breathe— allowing the impurities to evaporate and absorbing air from the surrounding environment.

Generally, evaporation accounts for the loss of 2 percent of the cask's contents each year (the angels' share) for approximately the first twelve years, and then 1 percent afterward. Temperature and humidity are of great importance, and the climate of Scotland may influence the way the whisky matures. In a cool humid environment, like Scotland's, the alcoholic strength of the whisky actually drops during maturation because as the spirit evaporates, the humid air replaces it with moisture.

The Influence of Terroir—Real or Imagined

Because the spirit takes in air from its surrounding environment, much has been made of the influence of the climate and terroir on the flavor of the whisky. The central belt of mainland Scotland boasts acres of warehouses used by distilling companies for the maturation of their whiskies. The need to spread the risk of a catastrophe, like fire, from destroying all of a company's maturing whisky is part of the rationale for warehousing maturing whisky stocks in different locations. But the climate of a particular distilling region cannot affect whisky maturation if it is aged in a totally different environment.

The coastal distilleries on Islay and surrounding islands speak to the possibility of the power of climate in shaping the whisky's character. The Islay whiskies, like Bowmore and Laphroaig, mature in warehouses where the high tides and winter storms batter the distillery warehouses, which carry prominent salt lines on the interior walls. In these instances, a distinctive iodine tang, imparted by the sea, could identify part of the character of Islay whiskies if they are matured in these types of warehouses in coastal locations. Any possible distinctive effect from the environment of the distillery occurs only if the whisky is aged on-site or in the same region.

Warehousing

Traditionally, distilleries aged whisky in dunnage warehouses with earthen floors, where they stacked casks only three high so that the variables of temperature and humidity remained constant. Recently, however, some distilleries have begun maturing whisky in racked warehouses, where casks are stacked eight to ten high, and some in palletized warehouses, where six casks are stacked upright on a pallet.

In racked and palletized warehouses, temperature and humidity vary with the additional height of the building, which can affect the maturation of the whisky depending upon where the cask rests in the warehouse. Studies at the SWRI indicate that an increase in temperature results in greater loss to evaporation but also accounts for an increase in the compounds and the color extracted from the wood. In his book *Malt Whisky* (MITCH, 2006), Charles MacLean explains, "In dunnage warehouses, which are more humid and where there is more air circulation, the volume of whisky in the cask remains high, but its strength declines (by about 4-5 percent ABV in ten years). In racked warehouses, the opposite is true—strength remains high but volume declines."

Size Matters

The size and original fill of the cask can also influence the maturation time and the flavors of the whisky. Maturation of whisky is generally faster in a smaller cask because it exposes the spirit to a greater surface area of wood. People at Kilchoman Distillery release their whisky after three years of maturation, but they use bourbon barrels, which are smaller than hogsheads or butts, to accelerate the maturation time. Laphroaig Distillery also recasks its Quarter Cask single malt whisky into 45-liter (12-gallon) quarter casks for the last six to eight months of maturation so that the interaction between the wood and spirit intensifies.

Wood Finishes

The casks used for whisky maturation previously contained other wines or spirits, but distillers primarily buy used bourbon casks or used sherry casks to age whisky. The last fifteen years, however, have seen an explosion of different finishes for single malts since Glenmorangie distillers triggered this trend with the release of its expression of single malt that had finished its maturation time in port wood casks. Since then, all manner of wine finishes have appeared, including burgundy, sauterne, madeira, and even rum. The choices are incredibly varied and the results are equally interesting.

Bourbon or Sherry

The mainstay choice for maturation casks still remains bourbon and sherry, with bourbon casks constituting over 90 percent of the casks used. American law prohibits the reuse of bourbon casks and does not specify a minimum number of years for aging, which means bourbon casks are available, and they "turn around" quickly. Scottish distilleries buy them and ship them (standing) as whole barrels holding 200 liters (53 gallons), or they break the barrel into numbered staves, tie them together, and ship only the bundles, which are known as shooks. Upon arrival in Scotland, coopers rebuild them with new heads and additional staves into remake hogsheads, also known as dump hogsheads, which increase their capacity to 250 liters (66 gallons).

The Distillery Cat's Meow

Much experimentation has occurred with finishing whisky in different types of casks—wine, rum, port, and the list goes on. Some ideas for finishes are more inventive than others—one in particular was created at the Scotch Malt Whisky Society when it aged some single malts in casks previously used to ferment and age hot pepper mash at McIlhenney's Tabasco® sauce warehouses in Louisiana. You guessed it—the resulting matured whisky "blew off everyone's head." The Scotch Malt Whisky Society did remain inventive, however, and bottled it as hot sauce and accompanied it with suggested recipes (to be followed by some Scotch Malt Whisky Society whiskies, of course.)

Distillers buy sherry butts or puncheons, holding 500 liters (132 gallons), from Spanish bodegas and always ship these casks whole. Some of the distilleries consider the types of casks used for aging to be so important to the character of their whisky that they buy or make European oak casks in Spain, lease them to sherry bodegas for filling, and then claim them after the wine has matured and sold. Although the availability of bourbon casks remains high, some companies own both Scotch and bourbon whisky distilleries, and one distillery supplies casks to the other. Recently, some distilleries, like Macallan, have added another dimension to the sherry cask scenario and have bought American oak casks in the United States and shipped them to Spain to mature sherry for several years before sending them to Scotland so that they use both European and American oak sherry casks.

What Fill, First Fill, Refill

In both reused bourbon and sherry casks, the original fill saturates the wood. When the new-make spirit is added, the original fill leaches into the spirit, adding color and making the whisky rounded and mellow. These casks are refilled several times, but as a result of the present attention to the quality of wood used for aging, distillers now tend to fill their casks once (first fill casks) and reuse them only one more time (second fill casks).

Although it may appear that using a first fill cask would offer an advantage to the flavor of the whisky, distillers often prefer the second (and sometimes a third) fill cask because the first filling can impart too much of the wine or spirit to the whisky. The whisky from first fill casks can be unbalanced because of the overwhelming influence of the original filling, but it truly depends on the intensity of the original fill and the flavor character of the new-make spirit. A new-make spirit, for instance, may not age well in sherry casks, where the full flavors of the sherry might mask the more delicate fruit flavors of a new-make spirit.

After two fills, or after the cask has matured an old vintage whisky for a long time, the benefits in the wood may diminish to a point where the cask is spent and a third filling is then used to mature grain whiskies or whiskies for blending.

Face-Lift

Coopers can regenerate spent casks by igniting the interior of the cask and re-charring it, but it is more of a face-lift than a rebirth. Charring can reactivate flavor compounds, like vanillin (vanilla), that exist because of the heat treatment, but re-charring cannot recreate the compounds that existed in the heartwood. The effect of the original fill (i.e., bourbon) no longer exists in a re-charred cask because the previous use of the casks has extracted all the bourbon that was present in the wood.

Why Use Previously Filled Casks?

The reason for using previously filled casks is probably more historical and practical than anything else. Britain was a major importer of wines at a time when most articles were shipped in casks, and once merchants had sold the wine, there was an abundance of used casks available. Later, when the United States government in the 1930s issued laws prohibiting bourbon casks from being used more than once, a large stock of charred American bourbon barrels became accessible to Scotland's distilleries. This coincided with the Spanish Civil War, which diminished the number of obtainable sherry casks.

The Distillery Cat's Meow

Casks became difficult to obtain directly after World War II, and some whisky was stored in totally legitimate but unconventional casks. One vintage whisky that I tasted from this era was beautifully rounded with strong notes of bittersweet oranges that came from the used marmalade casks in which it had aged.

During the ensuing decades, too many distilleries aged their spirit in any casks available, unless they precisely included a specific type of cask for maturing as part of their product identity. Happily, distillers and researchers have gained an appreciation of the significant role the wood cask plays in the maturation and flavor development of spirit. And the last two decades have seen an intense focus at distilleries on the types of wood used, its quality, and the number of refills, with the ensuing results of better consistency, higher quality, and increased sales of single malt whiskies.

The final flavor profile emerges by dovetailing the flavors formed during the different stages of the whisky-making process, and then allowing it to rest and mature in selected wooden casks. In the cask, the spirit takes on some of the character of the wood and gives up some of its harsher elements to evaporation. The entire process seems to be a combination of chemistry, engineering, tradition, mystery, and myth. But at the end of the day, the final product depends on choosing the different possibilities available during malting, fermenting, distilling, and maturing, and balancing them to create the flavor profile the distillery wishes for its single malt.

What You Need to Know

> ➤ Spirit becomes whisky after it has matured in oak casks for three years. Until its third birthday, it is merely spirit—not whisky.

> ➤ The maturation of new-make spirit in oak casks accounts for 60 to 80 percent of the flavors and aromas in the final single malt whisky.

> ➤ Some whiskies are distilled to mature at a young age; others have a character that benefits from additional years in the cask.

> ➤ The choice of aging in different types of casks does not suggest that one is better than another. Each type of cask adds different flavors and aromas that complement the character of the single malt. Try them all!

The Single Malt Distilleries and their Whiskies

The Single Malt Distilleries and their Whiskies

In chapter 1 you learned how to choose a malt or two, but you're probably still tripping over your tongue when requesting your favorite whiskies at your local liquor store. In Part 3 you will learn the phonetic pronunciations of the distilleries to set you on your way.

The Scotch Whisky Regulations 2009 defines five protected localities—the Highland region, the Lowland region, Speyside, Campbeltown, and Islay. The Highland region lies north of an imaginary line drawn between Greenock in the west and Dundee in the east; the Lowland region falls south of this line. Speyside is a separate region within the Highlands that predominantly clusters around the River Spey. The remaining two regions lie within their own self-contained area—Campbeltown is at the tip of the Mull of Kintyre on the west coast, and the Isle of Islay is an island of the Inner Hebrides off the west coast.

Part 3 provides signposts to guide you through the different distillery regions and explains why some regions, like Speyside, gave its name to a style of whisky. These regional divisions serve to define a geographical area in which specific distilleries can be placed, not to suggest that each region produces a specific style of whisky. You'll quickly learn, however, that all whiskies from one region are not alike and even the various whiskies from one distillery can be different.

With the help of Part 3, you'll understand the styles and variations of whiskies that each distillery produces, and you'll grow to appreciate the role that the equipment and the distiller's skill play in creating different styles. Along the way, we'll talk about the places and people who make whisky.

A Noser Knows sidebar at the end of each distillery profile provides introductory tasting notes to the family profile or house style of the whisky produced at each distillery. A listing of the distillery's bottlings reflects the explosion in the expressions currently offered by the whisky industry. Readers may want to explore Jim Murray's *Whisky Bible* (offered each year) or Serge Valentin's website www.whiskyfun.com, which are both exclusively dedicated to tasting notes for a broad and deep catalog of whisky bottlings.

The profiles include all active distilleries and two that are mothballed, which is the industry's way of saying that they are closed without much indication of reopening. Because some distilleries do reopen when most people had considered them closed permanently, I do not include them in the lost distilleries until they are either dismantled or demolished.

And a final word on works in progress. Three proposed distilleries have acquired designs and planning permissions and are currently engaged in fundraising to finance their projects.

➤ Isle of Barra Distillery: Peter Brown hopes to build Isle of Barra Distillery and return distilling to this Outer Hebrides Island. His plans include sourcing all the raw ingredients locally and using renewable energy resources.

➤ Falkirk Distillery: Rosebank Distillery (now a lost distillery) produced a triple distilled spirit in Falkirk until 1993, and Alan and Fiona Stewart plan to return distilling to Falkirk (situated between Edinburgh and Glasgow) and to produce a spirit that replicates the Rosebank style. Their plans include not only a distillery, but also a business complex that contains a conference facility, retail shops, and a restaurant.

➤ Kingsbarns Distillery: Doug Clement received permission in March 2011 to proceed with his plans to build Kingsbarns Distillery near St. Andrews, famous for its golf and university. St. Andrews has thousands of visitors every year, but no nearby distillery. Clement found the ideal site on the Cambo Estate to build a micro-distillery, retail shops, a restaurant, and a café. Work would also include the restoration of a historic mill and dovecote on the property. He contacted Greg Ramsay, production manager at Nant Distillery in Tasmania, to help shape his ideas, and has Bill Lark, the father of Australian distilling, working as a consultant to the project.

Clement's project is now in the fundraising stage so that he can realize his plans to build a distillery that would supply a spirit that departs from the traditional character of current Lowland whiskies. He hopes to produce a lightly peated whisky with full and robust flavors and a big finish.

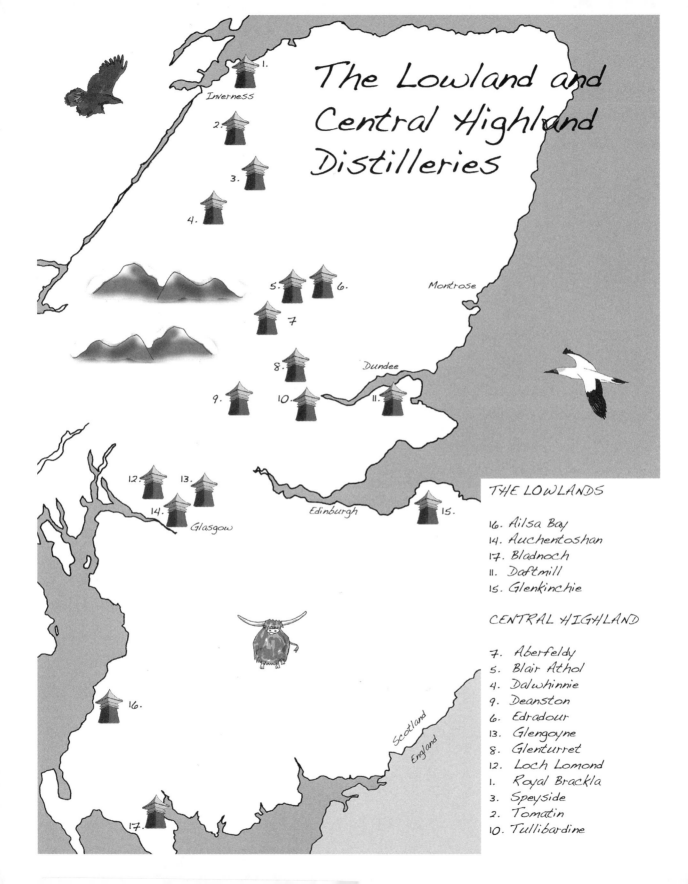

The Lowland and Central Highland Distilleries

THE LOWLANDS

16. Ailsa Bay
14. Auchentoshan
17. Bladnoch
11. Daftmill
15. Glenkinchie

CENTRAL HIGHLAND

7. Aberfeldy
5. Blair Athol
4. Dalwhinnie
9. Deanston
6. Edradour
13. Glengoyne
8. Glenturret
12. Loch Lomond
1. Royal Brackla
3. Speyside
2. Tomatin
10. Tullibardine

CHAPTER 8

The Lowlands

The Lowland region falls below an imaginary line drawn from Greenock to Dundee. It has always supported farms, industry, and large populations that brought the benefits of ready supplies and markets. Traditionally, Lowland distilling has been a business, providing families with their livelihood. It has differed from distilling in the Highlands, where it was one of several farm products and was usually done in the winter months after harvesting. The Lowland distilleries operated in the open and in full view (and easy reach) of the excise man. They paid taxes and licensing fees, and consequently they had to realize a profit.

Triple distillation, and the lighter, cleaner spirit that it produces, became associated with the Lowland malts, and people held the perception that Lowland whiskies lacked the robust flavors and subtle nuances of their Highland cousins. As recently as the 1990s, the Lowland region had only two operating distilleries—Glenkinchie and Auchentoshan—whose bottlings offered the expected delicate Lowland style.

The last decade, however, has seen not only the reopening and building of new distilleries, but also a welcome diversity among them. William Grant & Sons built its mega-distillery at Ailsa Bay with the capability of producing multiple malts and exploring the parameters of whisky making. The other three new distilleries are small, independently owned, and family run. Raymond Armstrong reopened Bladnoch Distillery, Francis Cuthbert recreated a farm distillery at Daftmill, and David Thomson and Teresa Church are presently restoring and rebuilding Annandale Distillery.

The Distillery Cat's Meow

The Lowlands once boasted at least twenty distilleries, but only five currently exist. Annandale will be the region's sixth distillery once it has undergone restoration and reconstruction.

Ailsa Bay Distillery

➤ Pronounced *ALE-zeh bay*

➤ Girvan, Ayrshire KA26 9PT

➤ No website

➤ No visitors center

Ailsa Craig is a volcanic rock that sits off the west coast of Scotland and boasts granite so hard that it is used for curling stones. It is now a protected area under the control of the Royal Society for the Protection of Birds, but enough granite exists on the shores to supply the demand for curling stones for the foreseeable future.

Ailsa Craig lends its name to the Ailsa Bay Malt Distillery, sitting within the massive Girvan grain complex built in 1964 by Charles Gordon of the William Grant & Sons Company. In 2006, the Grant Company decided to develop and enlarge its capacity for producing the correct amount and type of single malt whiskies for use in its blends. Additionally, this would take the pressure off the Grant's single malt distilleries (i.e., Glenfiddich, Balvenie, and Kininvie) to produce malts for blends, reserving its output for the single malt whisky market.

A Malt Distillery Returns to Girvan

The idea of a single malt distillery built as part of the grain distillery was not a new idea to the Grant Company. In 1966 the family built the Ladyburn Distillery in a separate building within the grounds for the same reason they built Ailsa Bay—they needed more malts for their blends. (see chapter 18, *Lost and Hidden Distilleries*). Unlike Ladyburn, which produced one single malt, Ailsa Bay Distillery has the capacity and ability to produce multiple malts.

The Noser Knows

Although William Grant & Sons has stated that it has no intentions of bottling malt whisky from Ailsa Bay as a single malt, collectors may want to watch what happens here. When Prince Charles attended the opening ceremony at the distillery, the company's press release reported the prince filled "one of four casks with new-make Ailsa Bay spirit, which will be laid down in the distillery's warehouse to mature and will be later bottled for the Prince's Trust." The Prince's Trust is a youth charity, and collectors could assume that some whisky from the four casks might appear on the market in the future.

From the Boardroom to the Barrel

In less than a year, the decision to build Ailsa Bay went from the Boardroom to the Barrel, with the first spirit coming off the stills in September 2007. The building already existed and the construction consisted of converting a neutral grain distillery to a malt distillery. From the beginning, Ailsa Bay's design included a natural order from mashing to fermenting to distilling with open and spacious areas beneath the equipment that allows easy access for maintenance.

Fermentation takes place in twelve stainless steel washbacks and produces a high alcohol (11 percent) wash. Eight copper stills rise from the still room floor in two choreographed rows with an unusual octagonal brass spirit safe occupying pride of place in the center of the room. Their design mirrors the stills at Balvenie Distillery with medium-tall necks above a boil ball and slightly angular shoulders, but two of the eight condensers are stainless steel rather than copper.

A Future for Research and Development

The production process at Ailsa Bay allows trial runs and experimentation before any research results are transferred to their smaller malt distilleries. Operators can vary the degree of peating in the malted barley and can change the length of fermentation and the fermentation temperature by activating cooling jackets around the washbacks. Furthermore, the technical director and blender can choose to use a stainless steel condenser, resulting in higher sulfur compounds, which are required in some blended whisky, or using a copper condenser resulting in a lighter, cleaner spirit. And while they cannot alter the shape of the stills and the weight of the whisky it produces, they can vary the speed at which they run the stills in order to produce more or less reflux. Finally, a variety of casks, including first, second, and third fill bourbon casks, sherry casks, and refurbished casks, exist for different aging requirements.

Ailsa Bay Malt Distillery is a far cry from the romantic image of a traditional malt distillery, but it has no pretensions. It exists for its functionality, efficiency, and versatility to produce whatever malts are required for blends and to provide a testing ground for experimentation. It is, however, beautiful in its modernity and sleekness, and in its incorporation of both traditional and contemporary design in the still room.

The Noser Knows

The distillers at Ailsa Bay intended to produce a Speyside-type malt, but they are actually producing several different styles of malt. At present, all of the spirit distilled at Ailsa Bay is reserved for blends, and there are no plans to bottle it as single malt.

Annandale Distillery

(Opening 2013)

> ➤ Pronounced *ANN-en-dale*
> ➤ Northfield, Annan Dumfriesshire DG12 5LL
> ➤ www.annandaledistillery.com
> ➤ Visitors center (proposed)

It took four years for Professor David Thomson and his wife Teresa Church to obtain planning permission to build Annandale Distillery. Construction began on June 27, 2011, but it does not entail the building of a new distillery; rather the original Annandale Distillery, built in the nineteenth century, is being reconstructed. The historically listed buildings remaining on the site are stabilized and undergoing restoration under the watchful eye of Historic Scotland.

Thomson and his wife will restore the mash house and two warehouses but will reconstruct a new tun room and still house in the original mill of the distillery. This involves restoring the buildings to the way they looked between 1890 and 1900 and matching stones and roof slates of the new structures to the existing old ones.

The Distillery Cat's Meow

David Thomson and Teresa Church have designed their distillery logo to reflect their commitment to engage and honor the past. They remark, "When Annandale Distillery opened in 1830, Annan was an established embarkation port for emigrant Scots. As a tribute to these intrepid souls, the 'A' of Annandale is in the image of a billowing sail."

George Donald established the distillery in Annan in 1830 and successfully operated it for more than fifty years with the help of his son. The location at Annan provided him with a good water source not only for the production process, but also for the power to run the distillery. A nearby peat moss, the Cumbrian coal fields, and the Solway Firth provided the peat, the fuel, and the transportation necessary to the successful operation of Annandale.

John Walker & Sons acquired the distillery in 1893 and operated it until 1919. It never completed its plans for expanding the distillery and permanently closed and dismantled it in 1921. "Around 1924 the Robinson Family acquired the freehold of Distillery Farm, including the now-redundant distillery buildings. The maltings, kiln, and mash house were eventually converted into a grain drying plant," and "the bonded warehouses were used for housing cattle." Nearly eighty-five years later, Thomson and Church bought the land and the remaining distillery buildings with the intention of returning them not only to their former use, but also to their former glory.

The Future Becomes the Present

No longer dependent on a gravity-fed water supply to power the distillery, the new Annandale Distillery Company has designed the restored distillery in a straight line with each aspect of the whisky-making process flowing logically from one to the next. The plans include four traditional wooden washbacks and one large 12,000-liter (3,170-gallon) wash still paired with two smaller 4,000-liter (1,057-gallon) spirit stills. David Thomson is quick to note that they will not be doing a triple distillation. Rather, they have consciously chosen two small spirit stills to increase the amount of copper in order to strip the heavy sulfur compounds from the distillate.

The Noser Knows

Today's Lowland whiskies have a distinctive profile that is usually light, clean, and delicate. But this was not always the case. Alfred Barnard's authoritative portraits of Britain's distilleries in 1887 detailed in *The Whisky Distilleries of the United Kingdom* (Birlinn Ltd., 2008), clearly report that both Bladnoch and Annandale distilleries produced a peated spirit. It is conjectured that Johnnie Walker acquired Annandale Distillery in order to secure a smoky malt similar to Islay whiskies for its blends.

Final decisions about the maturation casks will be made by David Thomson and Jim Swan when the first new-make comes off the stills during trial runs. The reconstruction will continue for over a year, from 2011 to 2012, with the first trial runs planned for the end of 2012. All things being equal, the new/old Annandale Distillery will be ready to receive the public sometime in 2013.

The Noser Knows

The proposal for the new-make distillate at Annandale includes plans to produce a smoky phenolic spirit much like the spirit made at the distillery in 1900. In addition to the smoky, peaty expression, it also intends to distill an unpeated version, with a similar profile to the Lowland character of today.

The Next Vision

The five-year vision for Annandale includes a visitors center and an academy to support the "thinking, drinking" philosophy of the owners. It also looks to incorporate the archeological dig that was done by Glasgow University Archaeological Research Division (GUARD). Rather than fill in the excavation, the owners plan to weave the site into the fabric of the place, maintaining the thread to its past.

This is a project worth watching as the distillery and its production take shape because Thomson and Church have done more than restore this distillery. Certainly, they will leave a legacy for future generations by connecting them to their past.

Auchentoshan Distillery

➤ Pronounced *awk-en-TOSH-an*

➤ Near Dalmuir, Clydebank Glasgow G81 4SJ

➤ www.auchentoshan.com

➤ Visitors center

Auchentoshan Distillery ties its identity to the triple distillation that distillers use in the production process. Other distilleries, like Bruichladdich, BenRiach, and Springbank, also use this process but in a more limited capacity. Auchentoshan distillers, however, have used triple distillation consistently for all its production to create its distinctive flavor profile.

Glasgow's Distillery

The name of the distillery means "corner of the field"—an appropriate name since John Bulloch, a corn merchant, bought a portion of the Auchentoshan Estate to build Duntocher Distillery. In 1834, the new owners, John Hart and Alexander Filshie, renamed it Auchintoshan, spelling it slightly differently than it is today. The distillery's history reveals a series of owners over its lifetime of almost two centuries, but its connection to the neighboring city of Glasgow remains constant.

Clydebank Blitz

One of Auchentoshan's strongest bonds with Glasgow occurred during the German bombing of Clydebank's shipyards in World War II. The Clydebank Blitz on March 13 and 14, 1941, destroyed or damaged all but eight houses in the town, and Auchentoshan Distillery did not go untouched. Two nights of German bombing raids destroyed the numbers one, two, and three warehouses at Auchentoshan and unleashed what the *Scotsman* reported as "the equivalent of a million bottles of the golden nectar flowing into a nearby burn that produced a flaming river of whisky stretching to the Clyde." Later, when many of the Lowland distilleries closed and Glasgow experienced a downturn, Auchentoshan persevered, like the city, and moved forward to an improved identity.

The Distillery Cat's Meow

The German bombing of Clydebank in 1941 destroyed three warehouses containing maturing whisky at Auchentoshan Distillery. It is not clear how the management accounted for the three buildings, but the distillery books listed the whisky as "lost through enemy action."

Triple Distillation

Although some people describe Auchentoshan as a breakfast whisky that is especially approachable, particularly to newcomers to malt whiskies, Auchentoshan is really not as simple as this description would suggest. Auchentoshan distillers, indeed, use unpeated barley in the production, making the whisky attractive to people who do not like the smoky assertiveness of Islay whiskies; however, in addition the triple distillation key to the Auchentoshan character creates a delicate body (see chapter 6, *The Art of Distillation*).

During triple distillation, the spirit is processed through three lantern-shaped stills with tall, thick heads in order to increase the reflux action. The continual reboiling of the spirit creates a light and elegant body with some intensity. Additionally, the mashman uses a long fermentation, averaging seventy-five hours over three days, in order to develop the fruity flavors in the wash, which is described as smelling and tasting like apple cider.

More Than a Breakfast Whisky

The Auchentoshan Classic, with no age stated, is aged solely in bourbon casks, but the other bottlings in the core range of twelve and eighteen years use a combination of both bourbon and sherry casks for aging. This practice is slightly altered to produce the 12-year-old Three Wood expression that ages for ten years in bourbon casks and matures another two years in sherry wood—one year in oloroso casks, and then an additional year in Pedro Ximenez casks.

The Noser Knows

The marriage (combining) of whiskies aged in different types of casks helps to create the distinctive Auchentoshan character. The nose begins sweet and fruity, giving rise to citrus in the mouth, complemented by the sweetness of honey and vanilla and a background note of hazelnuts. This is a light-bodied whisky with a short finish. The younger Classic is more delicate with notes of coconut, whereas the spicy and dark fruit notes that appear in the Three Wood and older expressions show the effect of additional years in sherry casks.

Bladnoch Distillery

➤ Pronounced *BLAD-knock*

➤ Bladnoch, Wigtown DG8 9AB

➤ www.bladnochdistillery.co.uk

➤ Visitors center

Bladnoch Distillery's closure in 1993 brought with it the expectation that it would never reopen. So in 2000, its reopening and resumption of production came as a surprise. The fact that it reopened under the leadership of a private individual made it even more remarkable. When Raymond Armstrong saw the distillery property for sale, he regarded it as an investment opportunity and remained untroubled by a restrictive clause in the bill of sale that forbade him from ever distilling on the site.

Bladnoch Distillery is Scotland's most southern distillery and lies among the green farmlands of the low country surrounding Wigtown. An eighteenth-century stone bridge just beyond the distillery's entrance crosses the River Bladnoch, a tidal river that is the distillery's water source. Most of the gray and gold stone buildings date to the distillery's beginnings in the early nineteenth century.

Two brothers, Thomas and Alan McClelland, established Bladnoch in 1818 as an additional agricultural industry on their farm, and operated it until Dunville & Co. Ltd. bought Bladnoch in 1911. The World War I years brought restrictions on distilling, and the resulting loss of profits did not allow any expansion, let alone maintenance on the buildings. The minutes of the Dunville Company show year after year of losses and disintegration of the distillery fabric. In 1937, the minutes record "That the Company be wound up voluntarily." The next sixty years saw a series of owners who dismantled the distillery, refurbished it, and sold it. Finally in 1993, United Distillers & Vintners (UDV) closed and decommissioned the distillery, and Armstrong bought it the following year.

Shortly after purchasing Bladnoch, local people began questioning whether Raymond Armstrong would reopen the distillery. Bladnoch Distillery's charm only served to underscore the growing concern that most of the Lowland distilleries had closed and many were dismantled. In January 1997, Raymond Armstrong approached Dr. Alan Rutherford at UDV to explore the possibility of reopening Bladnoch as a working distillery. Despite the restrictive clause barring any distilling and the concern that some of the equipment had been either removed or disabled, Armstrong received permission to reopen the distillery and began production of new-make spirit in December 2000. He remarked, "I have just enough Irish superstition that I couldn't allow the millennium to pass without one spirit run in the first year of the new century."

The Distillery Cat's Meow

Rather than soaring eagles or stags' heads, the labels for Bladnoch malt depict local sheep and Belted Galloway cattle that are indigenous to the area. At one time the breed was virtually extinct, and the efforts of a local woman, Dame Flora Stuart, established the hearty cattle on the area farms. Armstrong's commitment to portray local animals on his labels has led him to observe that people in the area are grateful that they "didn't have local donkeys."

The distillery still retains its original Boby mill, stainless steel mash tun, and six wooden washbacks. The traditional Bladnoch begins with unpeated malt, but once a year the stillman uses peated malt to distill a different style of spirit. Armstrong observes that "there is no pressure on [the staff] for speed." Consequently, the operators make the fermentation long, run the stills slowly, and take a narrow middle cut. The slow approach results in the development and capture of fruity esters and increases the contact time with the copper.

The stillroom is home to two stills of a similar design—the lyne arm is clearly fixed downward, allowing some heavier flavors to be vaporized, but this feature is balanced with tall, thin necks, a boil ball, and puddled shoulders, which create more reflux and a lighter body. The new spirit is aged mainly in refill bourbon casks and very occasionally sherry casks. The spirit matures in one of the eleven dunnage warehouses on-site.

Because the distillery was not producing spirit for eight years, the bottlings are usually older expressions, distilled before the Armstrong ownership, or younger expressions, distilled by Armstrong's team. Presently, Armstrong bottles whiskies that are 8, 19, and 20 years old, as well as a lightly peated 9-year-old and an 18-year-old from a sherry cask. All of his bottlings reflect a range of alcoholic strengths and use non-chill filtering and natural color. He has structured a program for individuals or groups to buy a cask of new-make spirit, and his website provides an excellent explanation regarding the expenses of evaporation loss, duty owed, and bottling.

Raymond Armstrong saw Bladnoch's prosperity as a success for the industry and for the area. Furthermore, he was convinced that it would make a contribution to the tourism of the region. His satisfaction and achievement appears to come from the knowledge that he has ensured the future of a Lowland malt and connected the distillery to the community that produces it.

The Noser Knows

Bladnoch single malt has a delicate body with citrus flavors of lemon zest and vanilla reminiscent of lemon meringue pies. Subtle grassy notes end with a quick, dry finish. Armstrong finds that the delicate character of the traditional new-make spirit is best suited to refill bourbon casks, and to that end 80 percent of his casks are bourbon barrels from Louisville, Kentucky.

Daftmill Distillery

➤ Pronounced *DAFT-mill*

➤ Cupar, Fife KY15 5RF

➤ www.daftmill.com

➤ Visitors by appointment

➤ +44-1337-830 303

Before visiting Daftmill Distillery, I knew that Francis Cuthbert had built it in 2005 as part of his working farm, but I had not expected the winding lines of beech hedges or the barley growing around the tidy farm buildings. The converted and refurbished stone buildings house the milling, mashing, and fermenting equipment on one side, and a glass-enclosed stillroom with two copper pot stills perched inside, connects the warehouses on the other side. The farm has existed since the Middle Ages, and today it is lovingly and meticulously tended—the entire operation is simply beautiful.

Six generations of the family have farmed here, first as tenants on a nearby farm, and then in the present location as owners, when Cuthbert's father bought the land in 1980. The farm once supported a mill that used the water from the Daft Burn, so called because it appeared to flow uphill—a "daft" idea. Operating the distillery added value to the barley already growing in the farm fields—if the price of grain is too low, the farmer can always use the barley to make whisky.

Much as farmers had historically done, Cuthbert also confines his operation of the distillery to a seasonal calendar. In the spring, the farm demands attention for planting potatoes and barley and newborn calves require his care—no time for distilling exists. The distillery can operate once the crops are in the ground and flourishing, between the end of May and the

The Noser Knows

Cuthbert likes to mill slightly rough grist with more husks, and then pump the completed sweet wort into the underback and back into the mash tun, allowing the wort to filter through the husks an additional time, producing clearer wort for fermentation. As with the mash at Daftmill, the fermentation uses a slight variation at the end of the process: once the fermentation has completed, Cuthbert leaves it to sit another day so that the fruity flavors have additional time to develop.

The Noser Knows

Most of Daftmill's spirit matures in first fill bourbon casks, which add sweet toffee and butterscotch notes to the underlying apple and pear fruitiness. At five years, the whisky has a creamy mouthfeel with a fading of the cereal notes of the new-make spirit and an evolution of other fruit and sweet notes. The remaining spirit matures in sherry casks that, in contrast to the bourbon influence, produce some spicy and dried fruit notes.

end of August. Distilling is suspended from August to October while the crops are harvested, and then begins again in November and continues through February.

Francis Cuthbert's farm supplies his distillery with 50 tons of barley, which he sends to a central maltster for a very lightly peated malting because he lacks the facilities to do it on the farm. All other parts of the process are completed on the farm in a converted farm building that houses bins filled with milled grist, the grain elevator, and the stainless steel mash tun with a copper top.

The two onion-shaped stills have short, thick necks with upward-tilted lyne arms that produce a light and very fruity new-make spirit. As with most distilleries, Cuthbert wastes very little—the heat from the condensers returns to heat the mash water, the farm uses the draff and pot ales. He speaks to the cyclical nature of the distillery farm when he observes, "The draff is fed directly to the cows and the pot ale is spread on the grass, which makes it grow and feeds the cows."

Francis Cuthbert, at present, holds whisky that has aged for seven years but has no plans to bottle it in the near future. He definitely wants to see how the Daftmill whisky continues to mature and how the flavors develop in both sherry and bourbon casks. Francis Cuthbert reflected, "If the whisky is really good, perhaps we'll keep it for ourselves, and if it isn't any good, we'll *have* to keep it for ourselves." The Daftmill whisky has real potential and a bright future, but with the distillery producing only 15,000 to 20,000 liters (3,963 to 5,283 gallons) of alcohol per annum, the bottling (if the Cuthberts decide to share it with the rest of us) could be limited.

Glenkinchie Distillery

➤ Pronounced *glen-KIN-chee*

➤ Pencaitland, Tranent, East Lothian, EH34 5ET

➤ www.malts.com

➤ Visitors center

A trip to Glenkinchie not only furnishes a delightful trip into the rural countryside, but can also include time in the distillery's museum. At a time when companies were modernizing and throwing old equipment and tools onto the scrap heap, Alastair Munro, the distillery manager, salvaged what he saw as the industry's history. One of his refurbished prizes includes a large and impressive model of a distillery that was built for the British Empire Exhibition in 1924. Munro discovered it at Mortlach Distillery and painstakingly reassembled the model. It is significant because of its size and the very clear and detailed diagram of distilling that it offers.

A Model Distilling Village

Glenkinchie Distillery was established in 1837 in the East Lothian region and began life as part of a farm. But the population of Scotland in general and the Lothian region in particular grew significantly, and whisky production expanded with the increasing number of people who demanded it.

In 1898, a group of investors rebuilt Glenkinchie Distillery in Victorian red brick, as a purpose-built distillery with housing, entertainment, education, and shopping all contained in the small industrial village constructed around the distillery. The connection between agriculture and distilling continued at Glenkinchie, however, where the distillery grounds also included three farms, with all activity and employment in the village connected to either the

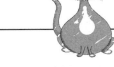

The Distillery Cat's Meow

W.J. McPherson, a distillery manager at Glenkinchie, had a particular interest in the adjoining farms and took great pride in raising prize cattle and competed aggressively in farm shows, including Smithfields in London. At that time, heavy smoke and yellow fog from coal fires continued to plague the city. Animals, both cattle and human, suffered quickly and badly from the effects of the foul air. McPherson's cattle became immediately distressed upon arrival at Smithfields, so McPherson purchased muslin baby diapers, soaked them in Glenkinchie whisky, and draped the muslin over the heads of his cattle. Needless to say, he was the only exhibitor with "beasts" worth showing the next morning and walked away with the farm or the distillery. Until the 1950s the distillery manager's responsibilities included not only the distillery but the farms as well.

The distillery's ties to the farms have loosened over the intervening years, but its connections to whisky-making traditions are still strong at Glenkinchie. Although floor maltings have ended here, it is still possible to see the converted malting barn, as well as the old kiln that was uncovered near the mill room.

The Noser Knows

The Glenkinchie malt is mainly herbal on the nose with aromas of newly mowed lawns and hay followed by some sweet notes. The aromas tend to flatten with water. Herbal notes appear again in the mouth, supported by orchard fruits of apples and pears, and unlike the nose the flavors seem enhanced with water. The malt is soft and round with a gentle dry finish.

Glenkinchie uses wooden washbacks and pot stills whose design at first seems unusual for the delicate lowland whiskies. The lantern-glass stills have tall, thick necks and long, distinctly nipped waists, but the lyne arm is angled steeply downward, allowing some of the heavier flavor components to be condensed in the worm tubs used here. Although the casks are filled elsewhere, a portion of the spirit returns to the distillery for aging on-site in bourbon casks. Diageo bottles its core range at 12 years old because the East Lothian area is relatively drier than many others in Scotland, allowing the whisky to mature more quickly.

Glenkinchie is part of the Distillers Edition range with a 14-year-old malt finished in amontillado casks. The Glenkinchie expressions also include a release in the Managers' Choice range and a distillery exclusive.

What You Need to Know

➤ Lowland malts tend to have a light, dry, and fragrant character, and they don't always develop the complexity of many Highland malts.

➤ Some distilleries, like Glenkinchie, Auchentoshan, and Bladnoch, offer slight variations on the Lowland style by aging or finishing their spirit in different types of casks.

➤ The Annandale Distillery, now undergoing restoration, proposes to produce a peated Lowland malt, like the original Annadale whisky from 1900.

CHAPTER 9

The Central Highlands

Most people associate the Highlands with smuggling because the region provided isolation, glens to hide the stills, and vantage points to see the excise officers. Because the distilling that occurred in the Highlands was done as part of the agricultural life, the whisky developed its own styles. Distillation did not supply the sole or even the primary income for the family, and people made whisky to suit their own tastes. The Highlands region is a large area that contains all the distilleries that simply did not fit into the other four areas. It is not surprising that it has formed its own divisions, including the Northern Highlands, the Western Highlands, the Eastern Highlands, and the Central Highlands.

The Central Highland distilleries stretch along the railway line from Glasgow to Inverness, covering a diverse geographical area that reflects the diverse character of its malts. Several of these distilleries, like Glengoyne and Loch Lomond, lie just slightly north of the dividing line between the Highland and Lowland regions; others have a closer affinity with the Highland distilleries. Some of the distilleries sit outside the city limits of Glasgow, and some rest near Inverness. Loch Lomond has the reputation for producing multiple malts from its odd combination of pot and column stills and remains one of the few distilleries in this region that does not have a visitors center. Because of this region's proximity to Glasgow, Edinburgh, and Perth (all areas that experience a high volume of visitors), most of the Central Highland distilleries offer tours and some, like Tullibardine and Glenturret, also provide restaurant facilities.

Aberfeldy Distillery

➤ Pronounced *ab-er-FELL-dee*

➤ Aberfeldy, Perthshire PH15 2EB

➤ www.dewars.com

➤ Visitors center

Aberfeldy, with its gray stone buildings and curving streets, is one of Scotland's pleasant little towns brimming with activity and offering a variety of stores and small tea shops. It also provides a home to Aberfeldy Distillery. The ten-mile journey to Aberfeldy is quite like driving through New England's countryside in early summer—broad plains rise into hillsides, green trees are in full leaf, and the course of the River Tay defines the fertile valley.

John Dewar and his Sons

When John Dewar opened Aberfeldy Distillery in 1898, he was a long-established and successful wine and spirits merchant in Perth. He ventured into building a distillery solely to secure a supply of single malts for his blends. Instrumental in deciding to build the distillery at Aberfeldy was the supply of good water from the Pitilie Burn, which had served a former distillery on the same site. Additionally, the main railway from Aberfeldy to Perth ran along the edge of the distillery grounds and provided easy access to markets and supplies.

The Aberfeldy Distillery boasts a small distillery engine called a puggie. Many distilleries in the last century had these small railroad engines on the site in order to pull the cars loaded with whisky to the main railroad line. Once the casks had been loaded onto the trains bound for the blenders, the little distillery engine filled with coal and barley and other supplies for the distillery would return with the railroad cars.

The Distillery Cat's Meow

Aberfeldy Distillery, the spiritual home of the Dewar's blends, is clearly marked by a large statue of the familiar Dewar's Highlander, which is the company's trademark used on the White Label blend. Americans gave the statue to the distillery to commemorate the centenary of John Dewar & Sons, and it is positioned to face the nearby hills where John Dewar was born.

John Dewar's sons continued to build his business by successfully opening new markets and extending the Dewar's whisky reputation to a worldwide market. Dewar's distillery merged with other companies to become Distillers Company Ltd., later Scottish Malt Distillers Ltd. When it merged with Grand Metropolitan in 1998, eventually to form Diageo, several of its distilleries, including Aberfeldy, were sold to Bacardi (John Dewar).

The Process

Today, the original water source at Pitilie is still of paramount importance to the distillery. Indeed, people at Aberfeldy are quite proud of the fact that the water used in processing is pure and clear despite the fact that the area around Perthshire continues to grow and develop.

At Aberfeldy, the adjustable Lauter rake stirs the mash, but it is regulated so that it rides above the bed of husks and malt on the bottom of the mash tun without disturbing it. This allows the sweet wort to drain through the bed, filtering it to a clear liquid.

Aberfeldy Distillery uses two stainless steel and eight wooden washbacks for a long fermentation, and it uses traditional plain stills for distillation. The wash stills vary slightly from the spirit stills in that the lyne arm enters the condensers on a slight downward angle, enabling some of the heavier elements to be condensed. The necks, while fairly tall, are somewhat thick, and the shoulders of the stills puddle onto the floor like a melting Hershey's Kiss. This design does not encourage a lot of reflux action but allows more copper contact.

Aberfeldy spirit is aged in used bourbon casks and is used for blending for the Dewar's Scotch whisky brands. The distillery releases two single malt expressions at 12 and 21 years old, although none of it is filled or aged on-site.

Blair Athol Distillery

➤ Pronounced blair-ATH-ole

➤ Pitlochry, Perthshire PH16 5LY

➤ www.discovering-distilleries.com

➤ Visitors center

Blair Athol Distillery experienced a bit of a false start when it was established as the Aldour Distillery in 1798. Robert Robertson and John Stewart took the name from the Allt Dour Burn, which still meanders through the distillery grounds today. The Aldour

The Noser Knows

The long fermentation and clear wort helps to create the orchard fruit flavors in the mature Aberfeldy whisky. An underlying sweetness with a touch of spice complements the fruit character and dry finish.

Distillery closed, but then reopened in 1827 when Robert Robertson expanded it. During the nineteenth century, the distillery continued to operate under several different managers and owners, and it even underwent a second expansion in 1882. Surprisingly, the distillery survived recessions, wars, and Prohibition, but closed its doors in 1932.

Arthur Bell & Sons bought Blair Athol the following year in order to acquire a malt for its blends but did not manage to reopen the distillery until 1949. Blair Athol experienced significant success with the Bell's blended whisky, necessitating the installation of an additional pair of stills in the 1970s in order to increase production. In 1985, Blair Athol came under the control of Guinness (later Diageo), who opened the distillery to the public within two years of acquiring it.

The Distillery Cat's Meow

When Arthur Bell died, the business passed to his sons, Robin Duff and Arthur Kinmond (AK), who established Bell's as a recognized brand in the export trade. AK, in particular, believed in giving back as a local philanthropist. He built 150 model cottages for the poor in the area, and when AK died, his wife turned their home into housing for the elderly.

Given Blair Athol's easy access to major roads and railways and its central location, it has an active and heavily used visitors center. It is indeed a lovely distillery with uncharacteristic red brick buildings festooned with vibrant green Virginia creeper. The Allt Dour Burn continues to meander through the distillery grounds, but with the addition of modern fish ladders to help salmon reach their spawning grounds. Even though the distillery site hearkens to another century, the distillery plant is firmly anchored in the present.

The mash tun is stainless steel and, much like the process in other Diageo plants, it drains continuously as water sprays from the top. Previously, the distillery housed four wooden washbacks, but new stainless steel vessels replaced them in the summer of 2010. The stills incorporate a classic onion-shape with tall, slim heads rising above plump shoulders. All of the new-make spirit is tanked away and filled off-site, and the former filling store is now the reception center. Blenders use almost 98 percent of Blair Athol spirit in Scotch whisky blends, but whisky enthusiasts can experience the Blair Athol single malt as a 12-year-old

Flora and Fauna expression. The shop at the distillery usually offers limited editions and distillery-exclusive bottlings that are frequently cask strength and non-chill filtered.

The Noser Knows

The Blair Athol single malt has a bit of nose prickle to begin but opens to a luscious medium body and a creamy mouthfeel. It is nicely rounded with balanced flavors of dates, figs, and raisins supported by licorice and sweet fudge background notes. The rich flavors on the palate end with a finish that doesn't linger.

Dalwhinnie Distillery

➤ Pronounced *dal-WIN-ee*

➤ Dalwhinnie, Inverness-shire PH9 1AB

➤ www.malts.com

➤ Visitors center

Situated 327 meters (1,073 feet) above sea level, it is not surprising that Dalwhinnie has one of the lowest average temperatures in Scotland, averaging out at 6°C (43°F). It is also not surprising that the meteorological office maintains an official weather station at the distillery. The cooler temperatures at this high distillery, however, work in the whisky's favor because the condensing water remains cold during the summer months and the amount of whisky lost to evaporation during its maturation in oak casks amounts to only 1 percent instead of the usual 2 percent that most distilleries experience. Even on a summer's day the winds are strong and the temperature is decidedly brisk, and one wonders about the motivation to build a distillery in this demanding environment. The reason, of course, was demand, and later it was "location, location, location."

The name *Dalwhinnie* means the "meeting place." It was named as such because it sat at the convergence of the drove roads from the west and the north and was on the way to the southern cattle markets. The residents of Dalwhinnie could offer food and, certainly, whisky for the men who managed the cattle herds. In the 1880s, the opening of the Highland Railway linking Inverness to Southern Scotland made the location of Dalwhinnie even more attractive. Dalwhinnie always seemed to be on a road to somewhere and stood ready to offer refreshment to travelers.

In 1897, several businessmen built the distillery, naming it Strathspey, but they immediately went into liquidation when the whisky industry experienced a recession in 1898. The new owner renamed it the Dalwhinnie Distillery before selling it in the early twentieth century.

The Distillery Cat's Meow

In 1905, American distillers bought the distillery and rumors circulated about an "American" takeover of Scotch whisky. The American states' ratification of the Eighteenth Amendment in 1919 ushered in thirteen years of Prohibition that not only outlawed the manufacture, sale, and transportation of alcohol in the United States, but also ended the American ownership of Dalwhinnie Distillery.

The Noser Knows

The matured Dalwhinnie has a light and shy nose with a trace of fruit, but the nose belies the full fruit taste that develops in the mouth. It has berry fruit flavors, lemon drops, and vanilla beans. It is reminiscent of summer raspberry pies, chocolate, and coffee. The malt has a medium body and a warming finish that doesn't linger long. The 15-year-old bottling has been aged in bourbon casks and the Distillers Edition finishes its maturation with a few additional months in an oloroso sherry cask.

Modernization and Refurbishment

In 1934, a kerosene lantern used to light the distillery fell over and ignited a fire that destroyed all the production side of the distillery. It took four years to rebuild Dalwhinnie. It reopened in time to see the start of World War II, causing its subsequent closing for the duration of the war. In the years following its reopening, the distillery underwent several refurbishments in the 1960s and 1970s that followed similar modernizations in other distilleries. In the mid-1980s, the owners removed the old wooden worm tubs, which altered the character of the whisky significantly enough that they were reinstated in 1996.

Today, the distillery maintains traditional wooden washbacks and, of course, the wooden worm tubs. The two stills have tall, slim heads and lyne arms with a slight downward angle, which allow little reflux and less contact between the spirit and the copper. The use of the worm tubs reduces the copper contact even more and results in a full–bodied, somewhat sulfur new-make character. The last twenty-five years have seen Dalwhinnie whisky emerge as one of the six Classic Malts in Diageo's portfolio. This time period stands in stark contrast to the distillery's first half century when a recession, a fire, and a war seemed to jeopardize its survival and existence.

Deanston Distillery

> ➤ Pronounced as spelled

> ➤ Nr. Doune, Perthshire FK16 6AG

> ➤ www.burnstewartdistillers.com

> ➤ Visitors center

Surprisingly, the Deanston Distillery does not show its age—it appears to be a fine Victorian grande dame, but in reality it is merely a precocious debutante. Private owners established Deanston in 1966 on the much older site of a Victorian cotton mill, originally built in 1785.

The conversion of many of the existing buildings was quite logical since both the cotton mill and the new distillery shared common production needs. Both required a good water supply provided by the River Teith, found immediately adjacent to the site.

At one time, eight water wheels on this river supplied all the power necessary to run the machinery of the mill. In the 1920s, the water wheels underwent conversion to water turbines, which today still supply all the electrical power required by the distillery. Additionally, both industries required cool and damp warehouses, which today constitute one of the more impressive architectural features at Deanston.

Massive vaulted ceilings imprinted with circular ventilation grates support the truly cavernous warehouses. These former weaving sheds, once busy with the activity of the cotton mill, are now quiet with the business of maturing casks of single malt.

The Distillery Cat's Meow

The Deanston warehouses were once used as weaving sheds to process cotton. Because they required a cool and humid environment to keep the cotton from drying out, the eighteenth-century owners planted a turf garden above the ceiling to keep the shed chilled and damp. It was a natural, or green, solution to an earlier problem, but one that has undergone a revival as roof gardens emerge to solve twenty-first century energy problems.

From Cotton to Whisky

In 1972, the founders of Deanston sold the distillery to Invergordon, who operated it until 1982 when the distillery was mothballed because of the recession in the whisky industry. In 1990, Burn Stewart bought Deanston and embarked on extensive refurbishment before beginning production once again.

Even though this is a fairly young distillery, many traditional features are used in the making of whisky here. The distillery houses a cast iron mash tun with no cover to hide the view of hot water cascading into the mash or the workings of the old rake stirring the porridge-like concoction. The clear wort undergoes a long fermentation of eighty hours. These two factors create the fruity profile of the Deanston new-make character.

Deanston's two pairs of stills with boil balls between the slender heads and plump, high shoulders produces a light, delicate whisky that complements its fruity profile. Once the new spirit is distilled, it is placed in first- and second-fill bourbon casks to age in the architectural splendor of the centuries-old warehouses.

Green Whisky

All of Burn Stewart's expressions of Deanston are non-chill filtered and natural colored. The bottlings include a 12-year-old core expression, and most recently a NAS bottling matured in virgin American oak. The plans include releasing a Deanston organic single malt in 2012 or 2013 with a double-digit age statement, probably in the 10- to 12-year-old range. All aspects of its production, from specific barley fields to the casks, will have a traceable organic history.

The Noser Knows

The family profile for Deanston core range malt whisky includes a distinctive fruit character with a honey, graham cracker sweetness and perhaps some crystallized ginger. Callum Fraser, Deanston's distillery manager, notes, "The virgin American oak adds a ginger spiciness" to the core character of the new NAS expression.

Edradour Distillery

➤ Pronounced *ed-rah-DOW-er*

➤ Pitlochry, Perthshire PH16 5JP

➤ www.edradour.com

➤ Visitors center

Located on the edge of Pitlochry, a Victorian spa town, Edradour is one of Scotland's smallest distilleries. The distillery is a tiny cluster of brilliant white buildings with red doors surrounded by carefully tended cottage gardens. In 1825, it began as one of five cooperative distilleries in the valley, so that farmers could malt their excess barley from the previous year's harvest, and then take it along for distillation at the cooperative.

In 1925, William Whiteley, an admirer and customer of Edradour single malt, bought the distillery in order to create his blends, House of Lords and King's Ransom. Whiteley's creations, unfortunately, coincided with American Prohibition, but this obstacle did not prevent him from anchoring ships outside the 12-mile limit and supplying ferries sent by bootleggers and speakeasies.

The distillery experienced several owners during the following decades until Andrew Symington, the founder of Signatory Vintage, an independent bottling company bought it in 2002. When he took possession of the distillery, other than the removal of the floor maltings and the installation of electricity, Edradour was much as it was when Whiteley bought it in 1925.

Passing the Tradition Along

The distillery buildings, looking very much like a miniature village, tumble down a hill with new warehouses and Caledonia Hall, an events center at the top. The former malt barn follows and anchors the production buildings. The middle building houses everything necessary for distillation, including the brightly painted cast iron mash tun, which sits at the lowest level

Whisky Lexicon

The Morton's Refrigerator was a common piece of equipment in dairies and distilleries, where it was used to cool the worts after mashing. All the distilleries have removed them, and the original at Edradour, installed in 1934, remained the last one in use. Recently, when it no longer functioned, Andrew Symington decided to replicate it rather than replace it because of his commitment to maintaining the tradition at Edradour and to pass it along in a better state.

of the distillery. Without the usual cover that is found in most other distilleries, the aromas of mashing combine with all the other smells of fermentation and distillation in the small space.

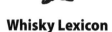

Whisky Lexicon

Purifiers resemble large metal boxes mounted around part of the lyne arm and contain cool water. When the heavier volatiles in the form of vapors enter the part of the lyne arm surrounded by this cool water, they immediately condense, and a long thin connecting pipe returns the liquid spirit to the pot of the still for re-distillation. The use of the purifier allows more reflux action and more contact with copper resulting in a light clean spirit.

The stills are the smallest size the customs and excise office will allow so as not to encourage small stills that could be hidden for illicit distillation. But it is not only the size of the stills that is remarkable, but also the design of them. The wash still is small with a conventional onion-shape incorporating a medium-tall head and a downward angle to the lyne arm that allows the heavier flavor components to move into the worm tubs.

The spirit still, however, is very different from its partner. There is virtually no neck or head on the spirit still, but rather a gentle arc rises from the boil ball above the high shoulders of the pot still to resemble the neck of a sleeping bird. This design promotes reflux action and reboiling of the distillate that does not occur in the wash still. The use of a purifier lightens the body of the new-make and enhances the effects of the reflux action. The worm tubs lower the copper and spirit contact but serve to balance the higher degree of exposure to copper that the distillate has undergone in both stills.

The Distillery Cat's Meow

The draff at Edradour, as in most other distilleries, is used for cattle feed, but unlike many other distilleries, farmers still come to the distillery where the draff is shoveled onto their wagons. So much at Edradour is unchanged, and in the local area it is still possible to see men returning to their farms with steaming loads of draff being pulled behind tractors.

Maintaining Tradition, Planning for the Future

Since Andrew Symington assumed the ownership of Edradour, all of the acquired stock has been recasked into sherry casks, bourbon casks, or wine casks. Having made a significant investment in casks, he now matures some of the spirit in first fill sherry. The 10-year-old Edradour forms the base of the distillery's bottlings, but Symington has significantly expanded the expressions he now offers. These include bottlings of a peated Edradour, called Ballechin, cask strength offerings, old expressions, and vintage bottlings. Most significantly, he bottles Edradour in an extensive range of wine finishes, including chardonnay, burgundy, and port, among others. The marriage of Edradour with different wood finishes at different ages and strengths has created very interesting and varied flavor profiles.

The Noser Knows

The new-make spirit at Edradour lends itself to maturing in sherry casks. Consequently, the house style has a medium body and displays flavors of orchard fruits and sherry against a quiet background of spice and nuts. Its wine finishes, most particularly the chardonnay and burgundy, add interesting notes of vanilla and licorice. Although sherry casks seem to partner very well with the Edradour spirit, the limited edition Vintage Edradour, aged in bourbon casks, produces tropical fruit flavors, coconut, and syrupy caramel.

Glengoyne Distillery

➤ Pronounced *glen-GOIN*

➤ Dumgoyne, Near Killern, Glasgow G63 9LB

➤ www.glengoyne.com

➤ Visitors center

Although most people have a favorite distillery (or two), a visit to Glengoyne gives credence to the fact that it is certainly one of the loveliest. Situated in the countryside within striking distance of Glasgow City Center, the distillery entrance lies on the edge of a former drover's trail. Once inside the distillery grounds, however, the seclusion and tranquility of the heavily wooded glen underscores its origins as the hidden site of an illicit still. The distillery is tucked away from the main road, the surrounding fields produce barley, and rainfall from the surrounding Crampsie Hills cascades from a waterfall into the distillery grounds. Its proximity to a large and receptive market in Glasgow provides the final requirement for the location of a successful distillery.

Burnfoot Distillery

Ten years following the Excise Act of 1823, which reduced the cost of a license and lowered the duty on whisky, George Connell built his legal distillery and named it Burnfoot.

During Connell's tenure at Glengoyne, the burgeoning and prosperous city of Glasgow ensured a ready market, and the arrival of the railway ensured the delivery of supplies to the distillery and whisky to the city.

Glengoyne Distillery

In 1876, Lang Brothers Ltd. bought the distillery and renamed it Glenguin and later Glengoyne, a name taken from the Gaelic that translates into "valley of the geese." With their father, the three Lang brothers operated a pub in Glasgow, where they blended and sold their own whisky, as was the custom of the time among publicans. The continued success of their blended whisky business demanded a steady and consistent supply of malt, and the ownership of Glengoyne secured reliable whisky stock, provided independence from other distilleries, and gave them control of their product. Unlike many other distilleries who saw owners come and go, Glengoyne's ownership by Lang Brothers remained constant for nearly a century.

An Extended Family

The Edrington Group, a company that has its roots in the blending company owned by William Robertson since the 1850s, bought Glengoyne Distillery in 1965. Robertson operated as a blender and whisky broker and when he died, his heirs formed the privately controlled Edrington Group, owners of several premium malt distilleries and producers of well-known blends (See Macallan profile). The Edrington Group maintained stewardship of Glengoyne until the independent family-owned Scottish business of Ian Macleod, Ltd acquired the distillery in 2003.

The broad view of almost 180 years of ownership of Glengoyne is quite remarkable within the whisky industry because the distillery has only known four owners— three of them small independent families and the fourth, a small privately owned company. The connection and engagement brought by this proprietary interest seems to have created a loyalty among the employees and a passionate connection to the product. The symbiotic connection has resulted in a release of bottlings chosen by the people who work there.

The Distillery Cat's Meow

"There's always a dram in the tea pot." Until the 1980s, distilleries "drammed the men" twice a day (gave men a large dram of, usually, new-make spirit when they began the day and during their break). For obvious health and safety reasons, this practice was discontinued. At Glengoyne Distillery, the men were drammed with the much more palatable mature spirit. Even so, some of the men preferred not to drink, and they routinely tipped their dram into the teapot on the table in the distillery canteen. If the manager left for the day and forgot to leave the night shift's dram for them, they all knew that it was really "nae bother" because there was "always a dram in the teapot."

While several distilleries release bottlings created by their distillery managers and master distillers, not many release bottlings by the stillmen, the mashmen, or the warehousemen. At Glengoyne Distillery, the owners ask individual employees to choose a cask from the warehouse for bottling and release it under their names. It is a practice that even further connects the employees to the spirit they make and taps into the collective knowledge of the people intimately involved with the spirit on a daily basis.

Their allegiance to the place and the spirit plays out in discussions about the distilling of Glengoyne whisky. The fermentation takes place for a slightly longer time of fifty-four hours in six Oregon pine washbacks before moving to one wash still and two spirit stills for distillation.

The stillmen at Glengoyne also feel passionate about the speed at which they run the stills, preferring a very slow distillation. The lantern-shape of the stills and the tall necks also provide more reflux and keep the spirit at a low and continual boil, encouraging an intensity and complexity of flavors in the new-make. The section of middle cut taken, the shape of the stills, and the slow distillation contribute to the creation of the characteristic green apple and fruit flavors of Glengoyne.

The Sherry Effect

Considering the initial character of the new-make spirit, it seems odd that sherry casks (many of them first fill) are used for maturation. Logically, it would seem that the sherry would overwhelm and mask the original fruit and estery flavors, particularly in older versions that age for long periods of time. But the marriage of the fruit with sherry works amazingly well. Recently, the management at Glengoyne released a bottling aged in bourbon casks, which provides an alternative choice to drinkers who do not like the sherry influence on whisky.

In addition to the recent bourbon expression and the mashman, stillman, and warehouseman bottlings, the distillery also offers limited editions, vintages, rare, and single cask bottlings. It is particularly interesting to taste its 12-, 15-, and 21-year-old core range expressions to appreciate the intensity of the sherry effect at different ages. The management at Glengoyne also capitalizes on its location in the Southern Highlands and its proximity to Glasgow to offer a variety of tours. These not only encompass different whisky tastings and discussions, but also pair the tastings with tours of many surrounding historical sites.

The Noser Knows

Glengoyne single malt is distinguished by a green apple character married with sherry flavors from the casks used for maturation. The resulting whisky has the dried fruits and nutty flavors from sherry casks, but it is always cut and modified by the intense tang of the green apple character.

Glenturret Distillery

➤ Pronounced as spelled

➤ The Hosh, Crieff, Perthshire PH7 4HA

➤ No website

➤ Visitors center

Glenturret welcomes more visitors than any other distillery in Scotland. If you find this figure off-putting because you prefer quiet little distilleries, think again. This is a little gem in a beautiful part of Scotland that should not be missed. Glenturret is small and manageable and situated in a quiet wooded setting. One of its more engaging aspects is the story of Towser, the distillery cat who lived at Glenturret for over twenty years. In exchange for a warm bed and bags of attention, Towser deposited several mice in the stillroom each day, earning her an entry in the *Guinness Book of Records* as the world mousing champion. Brooke, the current distillery cat, is given the prerequisite warm bed and bags of attention, but while she manages to appear with the odd mouse or two, she still has a long way to go to match Towser's record of 28,899 mice.

The Distillery Cat's Meow

A statue of Towser outside the Glenturret distillery memorializes her prowess as a mouser, and probably ensures that the tradition of a distillery cat will continue at Glenturret. In another homage to Towser, the distillery released a special whisky liqueur during the 1990s. The bottle had paw prints in hot wax leading to a stopper in the likeness of Towser.

While Glenturret cannot lay claim to being the smallest distillery, it does capture the title of being the oldest. The distillery site and the immediate area, called the Hosh, housed several illegal stills as early as 1717, and the distillery was established later in 1775. Situated among sheltering hills and near the Turret Burn, providing both a hiding place and a water source, the location was ideal for illicit distilling.

Glenturret Distillery suffered through several owners, bankruptcies, and liquidation, and endured the final insult when it was dismantled in the 1920s. In the late 1950s, James Fairlie, the classic knight in shining armor, bought the distillery and resurrected it. He restored the buildings and installed secondhand equipment in the distillery. Fairlie operated Glenturret for over twenty years, developing its visitors center to showcase the craft of distilling.

Handcrafted Spirit

The whisky-making process at Glenturret is deeply rooted in the heritage of Scottish distilling and bears Fairlie's distinctive commitment to maintaining a traditional distillery. Nothing is done by machines; if it isn't done by hand, it doesn't get done at all. The mash tun is small and has no cover, so it is possible to stand close and feel the heat and smell the mash cooking. After mixing the grist and hot water, the mashman stirs it by hand, using

Whisky Lexicon

A rouser is a paddle with a scoop that resembles a half-moon with a shaft attached to it. Holes in the scoop of the paddle allow the liquid in the mash to pass through and reduce the drag on the rouser. Other distilleries use automated rakes or metal stirrers to turn the mash; but at Glenturret, the operators continue to use wooden rousers to stir the mash by hand.

rousers (no rakes here). The mash then sits, using infusion, and the sugars leach out into the hot water. When the sweet wort is drained off, the men climb into the mash tun and shovel the leftover grist (the draff) out of the tun.

Fermentation of the dark wort then takes place in the eight Douglas fir washbacks that have no switchers to keep the foam from spilling over the tops of the washbacks. The whisky-making at Glenturret seems to reflect a slower and gentler time—even the fermentation takes sixty-eight to eighty hours instead of the more common forty-eight hours. The distillery only runs two shifts a day instead of three, and so the wash is left to rest in the washbacks a little longer, developing fruity compounds during fermentation.

Two Still Designs and a Slow Boil

Both copper stills have a downward angle to the lyne arms and fairly tall, thin necks; the wash still, however, has a boil ball positioned above the high shoulders, but the neck of the spirit still immediately dissolves into its angular shoulders. Quite a bit of reflux occurs in the wash still, and both stills are run very slowly to maintain the distillate at gentle simmer. The straight neck of the spirit still and the slow running of the stills increase the copper contact to produce new-make spirit with floral and fruity notes from the beginning of the middle cut, and some cereal notes from the tail end.

The majority of the spirit is aged on-site in refill Spanish and American oak casks that are still filled using old gas pump-style hoses. Because the distillery has only six dunnage warehouses, a small portion of the spirit is aged off-site. Unfortunately, the majority of Glenturret single malt is sold only at the distillery shop or online to UK residents.

The Noser Knows

Glenturret single malt has a lemon-yellow color and aromas of lemon slices, light solvent, and orchard fruits. With water, the citrus aromas become more vibrant. The malt sweetness of the new-make spirit fades with maturation but still lingers in the background. Warming flavors of pears and apples, lemon sherbet and baked apples with vanilla custard fill the mouth and are enhanced by the addition of water. Some sherry notes and a gently warming tweak of spice appear at the end.

Loch Lomond Distillery

➤ Pronounced as spelled

➤ Alexandria G83 0TL

➤ www.lochlomonddistillery.com

➤ Not open to the public

The site of the Loch Lomond Distillery boasts a history that has its roots firmly planted in the Industrial Revolution. A dye plant, producing Turkey red dye until the turn of the twentieth century, operated next to the River Leven. During World War II, it was used as an armaments factory, and after the war, Barton Brands and Duncan Thomas converted the old boiler houses for the dye works into the present distillery in 1966. It was sold, mothballed, and reopened by Sandy Bulloch (Glen Catrine Bonded Warehouse Ltd.) in 1985. After several attempts, he had the distillery working and producing his own malts for his blends, and he added a grain distillery in 1993 to increase his self-sufficiency.

The Stills

The industrial-style Loch Lomond Distillery produces an interesting portfolio of whiskies from an increasingly interesting array of stills, some of which approximate a Rube Goldberg invention. Loch Lomond houses two traditional pot stills, four rectifying stills with converted columnar necks containing rectifying plates, and two column stills consisting of an analyzer and a rectifier. These three varying types of stills are used differently to produce several different malts. Additionally, the distiller can manipulate the mash and the distillation to produce different spirits.

Traditional Stills

The explanation of these different stills must begin with the most recognizable version of stills—the copper pot still (see chapter 6, *The Art of Distillation*). The two traditional copper pot stills are fat and squat, and they produce less reflux or reboiling of the distillate. The heavier vapors from the boiling wash and low wines go up the heads of the stills and into the condensers with little to impede the journey; there are few obstacles to cause the distillate to fall back into the pot of the still and be redistilled and purified.

Rectifying Stills

The four rectifying stills have tall columns for necks, which house rectifying plates layered at different intervals. The distillate boils in the bottom of the pot and goes up the column as vapor. When it hits the cooler rectifying plates, it condenses and runs down weirs, like little troughs along the side of the neck, and drops into the pot to reboil. If the steam is hot enough, some of the liquid continues up the column and condenses on the next plate. Because different flavor compounds condense at different temperatures, the distiller can decide at which rectifying plate to take the cut, and thus control the flavors of the spirit. Additionally, the alcohol level in the distillate increases as it rises in the column and this allows the distiller to choose the strength of the spirit as well. To add another dimension, tubes that are circulating cool water sit at the top of the neck to condense vapors that manage to rise to the very head of the still, and then drop the spirit back into the pot of the still for redistillation.

Whisky Lexicon

How is a rectifying still different from a traditional pot still? Both stills are copper, but the rectifying still has a tall columnar head rising above the shoulders. The design of the still includes perforated rectifying plates placed horizontally at intervals inside the column. As the distillate vaporizes and rises in the neck, it condenses on the cooler plates and drops back into the pot of the still, allowing repeated distillation and purification of the spirit.

Column Stills

Finally, a pair of column stills also produces malt whisky. At Loch Lomond, both the analyzer and rectifying stills are copper with stainless steel sheaths to insulate them. Typically, the wash enters the top of the rectifier so that the rising steam heats it as it passes to the bottom of the column. It then moves to the top of the analyzer and drops down the still, condensing on the rectifying plates. The collected distillate passes from the bottom of the analyzer into the base of the rectifier. The distillate rises in the rectifier and eventually emerges as a light, pure spirit with a higher alcohol content than one can obtain in a traditional pot still. The distillation runs continuously rather than process in one single batch as it does in a traditional pot still. But column stills traditionally are used to distill grain whisky and not malt whisky. And that creates a problem.

The Scotch Whisky Regulations 2009 define single malt Scotch whisky to mean whisky "produced at a single distillery by batch distillation in pot stills." This legislation effectively forbids the labeling of any whisky made continuously in column stills as single malt whisky.

Consequently, the whisky distilled in the column stills at Loch Lomond Distillery cannot carry the label of single malt, and so it now reserves the spirit from these column stills solely for its blends. But this setback also allows for an opportunity. Some of the malt distilled in the traditional pot stills no longer goes to blending and consequently ages for a longer time in the casks, which might indicate possible future bottlings of older whisky.

Interestingly, a recent expression of Loch Lomond single malt, is actually a bottling of all eight of the single malts produced at the distillery. Ordinarily, this would be considered blended single malt, but because all the malts are produced from one single distillery, the label Single Malt can be used on this bottling. So while the 2009 regulations closed one door to prevent the labeling of whisky made in Loch Lomond's column stills as single malt, another door opened to allow the labeling of its bottling of eight malt whiskies as single malt.

The variation of still design allows Loch Lomond to make multiple whiskies, and its whiskies' character changes from one to another.

The Noser Knows

The flavors found in Inchmurrin single malt, named for an island in Loch Lomond, reflect an emphasis on capturing fresh and fruity flavors to produce a popular light whisky. Glen Douglas remains a close sibling to Inchmurrin but demonstrates greener, more herbal notes. At the other end of the taste spectrum, Croftengea and Craiglodge malt whiskies use both a lightly and a heavily peated mash to produce two variations of smoky whiskies. A visit to the Loch Lomond website lists all the whiskies that it offers at any particular time. It is well worth an occasional visit because the offerings change, and they can include a variety of single cask bottlings under their Distillery Select category.

Royal Brackla Distillery

➤ Pronounced *ROY-al BRAH-k-lah*

➤ Cawdor, Nairn IV12 5QY

➤ No website

➤ No visitors center

William Fraser built Royal Brackla Distillery in 1812 on a site adjacent to Cawdor Castle. Andrew Usher & Co. became partners in the distillery in order to supply the malt for the blends that it sold under the Usher label. Later, the lease for the distillery changed hands several times until it was eventually acquired by Scottish Malt Distillers. Like its sister distillery, Aberfeldy, John Dewar & Sons. Ltd. (Bacardi) bought Brackla in 1998, when United Distillers & Vintners merged with Grand Metropolitan.

The Distillery Cat's Meow

Royal is not just a mindless adjective appended to the name of Brackla Distillery. Rather, Brackla was the first distillery to receive a Royal Warrant of Appointment by King William IV in 1835, indicating that the whisky had come to the attention of the Royal Household and was regarded with favor because of its high standard of quality and taste. Queen Victoria once again awarded the Royal Warrant to Brackla in 1838; and today, it is still only one of two distilleries to have received the recognition (the other is Royal Lochnagar).

The distillery is tucked among agricultural land in a bucolic and tranquil setting, much as early distilleries once were when they were traditionally tied to a farm. Inside the distillery, however, the plant has undergone modernization and automation. The cooling water for the condensers comes from the Cawdor Burn, which is dammed so that the water forms a small lake in front of the warehouses. Both water fowl and trout populate the burn, enhancing the rural scene viewed from the stillroom.

Making Brackla

Royal Brackla was mothballed from 1985 to 1991, and when it reopened the mash room had undergone some refurbishment with a new stainless steel mash tun; computerization of the process was added in 1995. The owners retained the six wooden washbacks, and added two stainless steel washbacks, located outside the tun room. Stewart Christine, the present distillery manager, likens them to "an insulated thermos." Crucially, the additional washbacks allowed the distillery to improve its fermentation time of seventy hours, which Christine notes "is essential to the spirit character of Royal Brackla."

The four stills at Brackla are all of the same design. They have an upward angle to the lyne arm with tall, thick necks disappearing into a curved, pronounced onion-shape. The tall stills and condensers encourage heavy reflux and copper contact, and combine with the long fermentation time to develop the delicate perfumed character of Brackla's new spirit. Royal Brackla is aged in refilled American bourbon barrels, but all of the whisky is aged off-site since other whisky is presently being warehoused at Brackla.

A New Dawn

Dewar offered a 10-year-old bottling of Royal Brackla malt, but that is out of stock and is no longer available. It is worth remembering that Diageo kept all of the Brackla stocks in 1998 and sold only the distillery, but now Dewar is positioned to move forward with Royal Brackla. It has produced spirit at the distillery for thirteen years and now has matured stock. Most significantly, Royal Brackla celebrates its bicentenary in 2012, and the possibility of a commemorative bottling certainly exists. Following that celebration, Royal Brackla is a single malt worth watching to see if the company develops the malt and if it offers any new expressions.

The Noser Knows

I always think of Royal Brackla single malt as a summer garden. It has delicately perfumed notes of floral scents with summer berries. Flavors of vanilla toffee sweetness complement the summer fruits (others detect raisins and orchard fruits as well) with a nicely rounded medium body.

Speyside Distillery

> ➤ Pronounced as spelled

> ➤ Tromie Mills, Kingussie, Inverness-shire PH21 1NS

> ➤ www.speysidedistillers.com

> ➤ No visitors center

Located in a remarkable and isolated setting, Speyside Distillery seems to be an echo from two hundred years ago, when illicit distillers sought remote and quiet areas to hide their stills. What is even more remarkable is that this distillery has no roots in such a checkered past. Indeed, its roots are fairly shallow and the distillery is only in its first growth. It is the work of one man, George Christie, who built the Speyside distillery in 1990.

Christie returned from World War II intent upon a life on the sea, but he began working for a whisky broker and never looked back. He leased warehouses for the maturation of whisky, acted as a whisky agent for other people, and even developed a grain distillery, the North of Scotland. Until his death in spring 2011, he lived near the distillery and made daily visits to Speyside.

The Distillery Cat's Meow

One of the more colorful stories about George Christie concerned his grain distillery, North of Scotland. The property he bought in 1957 had a previous life as a brewery, and Christie needed to raise the roof in order to accommodate the stills necessary to his new venture. When the planning commission looked at his design, it refused to give permission to raise the roof of the building. Not to be deterred and believing the adage "there is more than one way to skin a cat," Christie lowered the floors so that his stills could be properly housed in his new grain distillery.

A Quiet Vision

In addition to operating his grain distillery, Christie bought property in the countryside near Kingussie and began building an elaborate implement shed. The area of Tromie Mills had supported several mills in its history, and it had a good water source nearby in the Tromie River.

In 1989, the implement shed became the likely candidate for housing distillery equipment, and Christie applied for a change of use permit at the local planning commission. Alex Fairlie, a local dry stane dyker (stonewall builder) built the shed-distillery stone by stone over twenty years in his spare time, and Andrew Shand, the current distillery manager, remarked that "after twenty years, we just didn't have the heart to ask him to build some warehouses."

Installation of a stainless steel mash tun, four stainless steel washbacks, and one pair of stills began in March of 1990 and finished by November of that same year. Equipping the distillery happened much faster than the building of it even though the top of the stills were trimmed off because their size would not fit the allotted space. The finished stills have a slight downward angle to the lyne arm but have short necks that join high, plump shoulders. All of the new spirit is tanked off the premises to warehouses for maturing mainly in bourbon casks and a few sherry casks.

This relatively new distillery creates a delicate Speyside malt, using slow and measured old-fashioned methods—the distillery uses a long fermentation to allow esters to develop and takes the middle cut when the distillate runs clear. Traditionally, the distillery has used lightly peated malt, although it has distilled a small amount of heavily peated malt at 50 to 55 ppm for the last five years, which continues to mature in warehouses near Glasgow. Most of the new-make spirit goes primarily for blending with about a quarter of its production reserved for bottling as a single malt.

Speyside distillery bottles Speyside single malt at twelve and fifteen years, and Drumguish NAS (pronounced drum-OO-ish). Recently, Speyside Distillers has also released a sweet black malt called Cu Dubh (Pronounced *coo-DEW*). Although some people have conjectured that the black color comes from spirit caramel, Shand explains that he heavily charred several casks and then allowed the charcoal to remain in the casks when they filled them with new-make spirit.

The Noser Knows

The Speyside malt begins with a delicate nose of ripe pears, cantaloupes, and mangos. The fruit flavors carry through into the mouth punctuated with slight smoky notes paired with caramel and butterscotch sauce. Nicely rounded flavors with a warming finish and full flavors remain on the palate.

Tomatin Distillery

➤ Pronounced *TOE-ma-tin (rhymes with satin)*

➤ Tomatin, Inverness-shire IV13 7YT

➤ www.tomatin.com

➤ Visitors center

At one time almost as many visitors stopped at Tomatin Distillery as those who made a pilgrimage to Glenfiddich or Glenturret, the giants of the visitors center world. Although the number of visitors has fallen, Tomatin still welcomes 25,000 people each year. Much of this phenomenon is probably due to its location, which is on one of the main tourist routes to the Highlands—the distillery is sited 24 kilometers (15 miles) south of Inverness on the A9, with the exit clearly marked. It is also as far from a traditional distillery as one can possibly get. During a major expansion during the early 1970s, Tomatin Distillery underwent a transformation into a malt whisky factory, capable of producing nearly 13 million liters (nearly 3.5 million gallons) of spirit per year.

The modern Tomatin, however, does have its roots in the nineteenth century. The laird's house still occupies its place on the distillery grounds, and drovers, bringing their cattle out of the Highlands, are conjectured to have stopped there for a dram of whisky. Local businessmen established Tomatin Distillery in 1897 during the whisky boom years, and a later group of investors owned the distillery during a time when it suffered some neglect.

Whisky Factory

As with all other distilleries, Tomatin fell silent during the World War II. When the government lifted the restrictions on the use of barley, the company embarked upon a period of expansion and modernization. Over eight years, from 1956 to 1964, the owners expanded the number of stills from two to eleven, and expanded the number of washbacks to twelve. Then in 1974, they doubled these numbers again so that the distillery then had twenty-four washbacks, twenty-three stills, two mills, and two mash tuns. During the whisky recession of the early 1980s, however, Tomatin Distillery suffered a setback because it had filled casks speculatively based on perceived demand. The company went into receivership and closed in 1985, although it managed to fill some casks that year so that there were no gaps in its stocks. It was able to reopen in 1986 with Japanese investment.

Smaller Scale, More Malts

Although Tomatin Distillery carries the moniker of Scotland's Largest Distillery, much of it is not operational. While the sheer mass of all the equipment is overwhelming, the distillery uses only one mash tun, one mill, twelve stainless steel washbacks, and six pairs of stills. Despite the use of stainless steel for both the mash tun and the washbacks, the stills employ a traditional design with tall, medium-thick necks, boil balls, and curving shoulders. The lyne arms lead to external condensers outside the building, where the cold air aids the condensation of the vapors. Significantly, Tomatin employs two coopers in their on-site distillery cooperage, making it one of the few such facilities still remaining in the whisky industry.

The Distillery Cat's Meow

Any reader of literature will recognize that the blended Scotch whiskies Antiquary and Talisman carry the name of two novels written by Sir Walter Scott. J & W Hardie, the original blenders of Antiquary, lived close to Sir Walter Scott in Queensferry, near Edinburgh. Although any personal relationship with Scott remains pure speculation, it would seem that their proximity to the famous author provided inspiration. In 1999, when Tomatin's master blender decided to release a bottling for the millennium, he continued the theme of Scott's novels and named the second blend, Talisman.

The spirit destined for single malts matures in a selection of first-, second-, and third-fill sherry and bourbon casks and ages exclusively on-site. Interestingly, Tomatin also has blending facilities within the distillery grounds, where the company produces its two primary blends, Antiquary and Talisman.

Tomatin offers expressions that are all non-chill filtered with natural color, with the exception of the more commercially available 12-year-old. Both the 12- and 18-year-olds have aged in sherry casks, the 15-year-old has matured in bourbon casks, and the 30-year-old includes a marriage of whiskies aged in both bourbon and sherry casks. Tomatin has also released limited editions and single cask expressions with natural color and non-chill filtering.

The Noser Knows

Tomatin begins with sherry and dark fruits like raisins, dates and figs, on the nose. The heavy fruits seem to dissolve to orchard fruits on the palate, including pears, apples, and quince with a subtle cereal note similar to Cheerios. It is mouth warming with a lingering warm finish. It develops complexity with time and increasing floral notes with additional sips.

Tullibardine Distillery

➤ Pronounced *tul-ly-BAR-din*

➤ Blackford, Perthshire PH4 1QG

➤ www.tullibardine.com

➤ Visitors center

Both the ancient history of the town of Blackford and the more recent history of the Tullibardine Distillery speak to rejuvenation. In the tenth century, the town earned the name of Blackford because of Nordic Queen Helen's tragic drowning while crossing a local ford. Although the local water played a part in the queen's death, it also provided a pure and reliable source of water that enabled the establishment of three breweries and the growth of the town.

The Distillery Cat's Meow

The reputation of the local brewery, on the site of the present distillery, was good enough for King James IV to purchase beer in 1488 following his coronation at Scone. As a reminder of the distillery's heritage, the date of 1488 appears as a recurrent theme throughout the distillery and adjoining shop.

The Vision of Delmé-Evans

By the mid-twentieth century William Delmé-Evans, a Welsh engineer, viewed the pure and abundant water source that had supplied local breweries for centuries as an opportunity to establish a distillery. He opened Tullibardine Distillery in 1947, when whisky production was poised to grow following the wartime restrictions. Rationing, however, still continued after the end of the war in 1945, and Delmé-Evans faced a limited supply of building materials and raw materials for distilling. Indeed, until 1954 distillers were banned from mashing and distilling at the same time in order to prolong the whisky-making process and conserve barley.

Because distilleries at that time still relied upon steam and water as their source of energy, Delmé-Evans designed his distillery to maximize the available water supply to operate the equipment as efficiently as possible. He used lades (aqueducts) to bring water from springs that powered the rummagers in the stills, and also relied upon gravity to deliver the water, located high in the Ochil Hills, to the worm tubs at the distillery. Tullibardine Distillery produced its first new-make spirit in 1949 and operated under Delmé-Evans's ownership until 1953, when poor health forced him to sell it. He went on to design the Isle of Jura, Glenallachie, and Macduff Distilleries, but Tullibardine always held his passion and interest.

The Reawakening and Revival of Tullibardine

For the next half century, the ownership of Tullibardine passed through several hands until it was mothballed in 1995. In 2003, a consortium of four businessmen revived the silent distillery and hired John Black as distillery manager. Black has worked in distilleries for five decades and brought his years of knowledge and experience to bear on the refurbishment and operation of Tullibardine. Initially, the focus was to operate the distillery for fifty-two weeks and to open a visitor and retail center that would welcome people for a "Scottish experience."

The distillery plan allows visitors a clear view of the stainless steel mash tun and washbacks with the four stills situated on a lower level. The stills in particular now use condensers rather than the worm tubs Delmé-Evans had installed, but their design echoes his original innovation. Preheaters resting between the stills and condensers allow the hot vapor from the stills to heat water for the mash tun and also to heat the wash before it enters the stills. The preheaters not only serve to improve energy efficiency, but they also act to improve the distillation. The wash still has a tall, thick head and the spirit still has an extremely short neck allowing little contact with the copper, which helps to remove the sulfur character. The first pass through the copper preheaters and a second pass through the copper condensers provide the desired copper contact that does not occur in the stills.

Tullibardine Malt in the New Millennium

In addition to opening the visitors center during the first year, John Black also restarted production and distilled the first new-make spirit in December 2003. From the start, he wanted to retain the flavor profile of Tullibardine whisky because he wanted continuity between the new-make spirit and the stocks of maturing whisky held in its warehouses. Presently, Black spends most of his time focusing on quality and cask selection

The Noser Knows

The house style of Tullibardine single malt still retains its medium-bodied fruit (citrus, some orchard) and graham cracker character with additional white chocolate and vanilla notes from the bourbon casks used for maturation.

and experimenting with different wood finishes, including whisky aged in Sauterne, rum, oloroso, and Pedro Ximenez sherry casks. His vision holds a view to building a portfolio of single malts, where the wood finishes will complement the age of the whisky.

Much of the production of the spirit at Tullibardine is reserved for bottling as its own single malt, and is aged on-site in first-fill bourbon and sherry casks and some second-fill sherry casks. It remains to be seen what other wood finishes and what limited series of old-age whiskies the owners will release, but with their enthusiasm and sense of adventure, the people who tend to the whisky at Tullibardine have not only resurrected Delmé-Evans's distillery, but also rekindled his passion and innovation.

What You Need to Know

➤ The Central Highlands region denotes a geographical area rather than a style.

➤ The multiplicity of flavor profiles from the Central Highlands distilleries reflects the variety of its geography. Indeed, this region is best seen through the lens of diversity.

➤ Among the twelve Central Highlands distilleries and their whisky styles, one can see a microcosm of the whisky world, encompassing industrial and experimental Loch Lomond, tiny Edradour, and very large Tomatin. It includes Glenturret, one of the oldest, and Speyside, one of the newest, distilleries as well as the resurrected Tullibardine.

➤ The expressions offered from all these distilleries range from the light orchard fruits of Aberfeldy to the berry fruits of Dalwhinnie to the complex and dark fruits of Tomatin.

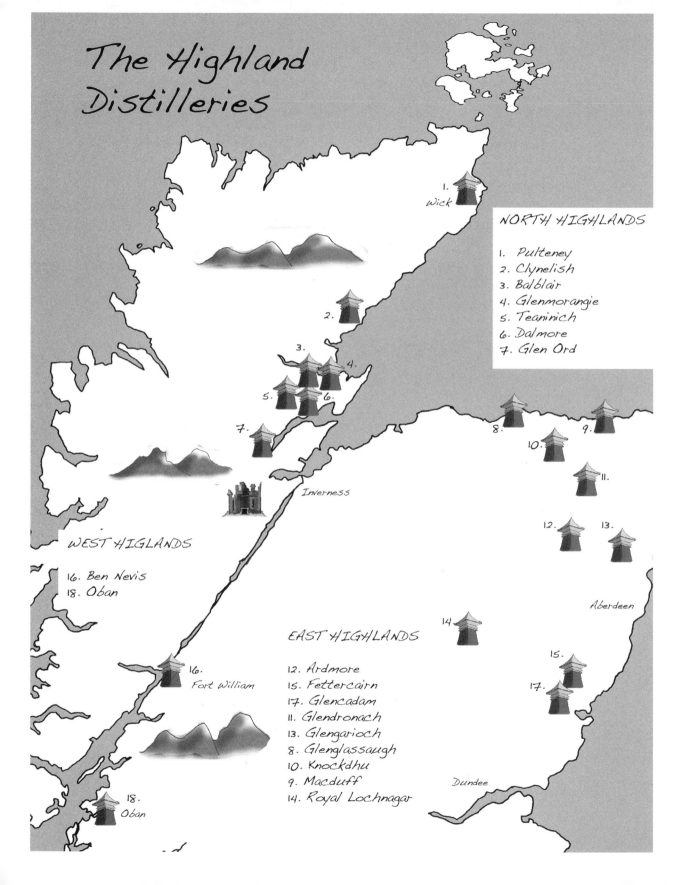

The Highland Distilleries

NORTH HIGHLANDS

1. Pulteney
2. Clynelish
3. Balblair
4. Glenmorangie
5. Teaninich
6. Dalmore
7. Glen Ord

WEST HIGLANDS

16. Ben Nevis
18. Oban

EAST HIGHLANDS

12. Ardmore
15. Fettercairn
17. Glencadam
11. Glendronach
13. Glengarioch
8. Glenglassaugh
10. Knockdhu
9. Macduff
14. Royal Lochnagar

CHAPTER 10

The Northern Highlands

In This Chapter

➤ Is there a coastal character?

➤ A diverse range of flavor profiles

➤ A diverse range of distilleries

The seven Northern Highlands' distilleries are located from the Black Isle, an area known for its fertile farm land and rich black soil, to the northeast tip of Scotland. The distilleries march up the A9 in almost perfect pairs, from the Muir of Ord, just outside of Inverness, to Wick in the far north. They seem to group themselves naturally in pairs—Dalmore and Teaninich, Glenmorangie and Balblair, Clynelish and Brora (now closed), with Glen Ord anchoring the southern post and Pulteney anchoring the northern one. Because they all hug the coast, some of the malts, like Pulteney, share a distinct maritime aspect to their character. But any additional character seems to run the gamut from the dark fruits of Dalmore to the orchard fruits and spiciness of Balblair. Increasing numbers of visitors to the Black Isle have meant that all the Northern distilleries, with the exception of Teaninich, welcome visitors and offer a diverse range of experiences and distilleries. It is worth the detour.

Balblair Distillery

➤ Pronounced as spelled

➤ Edderton, Ross-shire IV19 1LB

➤ www.balblair.com

➤ Visitors center: call for appointment +44-1862 821 273

Ross is a name long associated with Balblair Distillery. John Ross, a local farmer, established the farm distillery in 1790, and generations of the Ross family ran it successfully for more than a century. After the bankruptcy of its second owner, Alexander Cowan, the new distillery sat silent from 1911 to 1948 with all of its mature whisky stocks being sold in 1932 to cover his debts. Although the military requisitioned the buildings for barracks during World War II, the distillery was only used for its intended purpose for less than a third of its time in existence.

The Sleeping Princess Awakes

Much like the sleeping princess, Balblair found its prince in the person of Robert Cumming, a solicitor from Banff, who bought the distillery in 1948 and began production the following year.

Cumming quickly set about the successful operation of the distillery. Within two decades, he increased production and helped Balblair Distillery fulfill its potential

The Distillery Cat's Meow

The present distillery manager, John MacDonald, received a surprise visit from Cumming's daughter, Nan Burnett, in 2009. She had left Balblair as a young person and returned with her grandson. It was the first of several visits and when she returned, she brought memorabilia from her father's tenure at Balblair. Among the gifts she gave to MacDonald were bottles of new-make spirit from 1960, which he used to compare with the new-make of 2010. Burnett remarked that over the years, they had stored bottles of the spirit in the barn and had put it to good use to revive premature lambs—water of life, indeed.

Quiet Pleasures

Visiting Balblair has always seemed like a stolen pleasure. The distillery sits in the countryside near Tain, at the end of a country track, and boasts several horses as its nearest neighbors. Everything about Balblair seems warm—the sandstone buildings, the hospitality, and the tidy working distillery.

Fermentation takes place in six Oregon pine washbacks over a lengthy time of seventy-three hours, allowing fruity esters to develop. The distillery houses three stills, one of which has not worked since 1969. It continues to occupy pride of place, and its riveted copper seams, instead of welded ones, speak to another time in distilling history. The remaining pair of stills are squat and dumpy with thick necks and downward-sloping lyne arms that allow the development of heavier compounds. Indeed, this creates an oily new-make spirit that lends some depth and complexity to the character.

Traditional dunnage warehouses mature all the spirit on-site in mostly first- or second-fill bourbon casks, with a small portion aged in sherry. Balblair continues to manually stencil the cask heads instead of using bar codes, and continues to fill its casks using the original filling head from 1840.

Finally, a Day in the Sun

Until the 1990s, no proprietary bottling of Balblair single malt existed, and mainly independent bottlers made it available. Happily, this is no longer the case, because Inver House (InterBev) decided to showcase it as a single malt with the launch of its vintage editions in 2007.

The Distillery Cat's Meow

The inspiration for the packaging to complement the Balblair Vintage Selection came from the Pictish standing stone, Clach Biorach, which sits in a field several hundred meters from the distillery. The stone dates to 4,000 years ago, and the engravings on its surface of a salmon, the sun, and the moon, date to 2,000 years ago. When the sun rose over the Ardross Hills in line with the stone, it was an indication of the summer solstice. The package for the youngest vintage is a picture of the hills in the morning, the mid-age package carries a picture of the hills in the evening, and the high-age vintage shows a picture of the hills at dusk. When all three boxes are lined up together, a panoramic view from the distillery emerges.

Instead of being restricted by the age of the whisky, the master blender, Stuart Harvey, decided to release the whisky purely by vintage years. This approach allows him to cherry-pick casks and assess them individually for quality. The selection includes three ongoing vintages that include a young vintage, a mid-age vintage, and a high-age vintage. Because the vintage year sells out, the release becomes a limited edition, but it is replaced with a similar (but not necessarily exact) vintage year. Depending on the selected casks, the alcoholic strength may vary, the cask type may vary, and whether the selection is chill filtered or not may vary. Each release has a tailor-made quality about it. And while the single malt will clearly carry the Balblair profile, each vintage carries its own individual and peculiar-tasting profile.

The Noser Knows

Depending on the vintage bottling, Balblair displays a fruitiness that can range from tropical fruits to rich, dark dried fruits with ripe apples in between. These flavors are complemented by coconut, caramel, spice, and wood. Because of the squat, dumpy stills, the spirit has an oiliness that sets it apart from other fruity whiskies and lends it depth and complexity. It holds up well to aging in wood and often has layers of flavors punctuated by a long satisfying finish. This is a sipping whisky with a variety of facets, and its long-overdue availability is welcome.

Clynelish Distillery

➤ Pronounced *KLEIN-leash*

➤ Brora, Sutherland KW9 6LR

➤ www.malts.com

➤ Visitors center

The future Duke of Sutherland built Clynelish Distillery in 1819 to provide an outlet for barley grown by his tenant farmers. It passed through several lessees and owners until the worldwide depression forced its closure in 1931. Although not easily found as a single malt, Clynelish is used extensively in blending, particularly in the Johnnie Walker Black and Gold labels.

Two Distilleries, Two Names, One Site

In 1967-68, Distillers Company Ltd. (DCL) built a completely new distillery on land adjacent to the original Clynelish but kept the same design for the stills and the same water source. The former Clynelish buildings stood unused, and with even its name transferred to the new facilities, it was truly a shell of its former self. It experienced a resurrection only because of plans to demolish and rebuild the Caol Ila Distillery in 1972.

The original Clynelish Distillery reopened in 1969 to produce an Islay malt as a temporary replacement for the Caol Ila spirit. Because it now distilled a very different spirit, DCL gave the original distillery the new name of Brora Distillery.

The Distillery Cat's Meow

Clynelish provides the primary malt for the gold label and also lends its history to the name. Clynemilton Burn provides the water source for Clynelish malt and runs through land that has supported gold panning in the past. Rumors exist that the water contains specks of gold, hence the legend gave rise to the Johnnie Walker Gold brand.

Candlewax

The Clynelish Distillery, built in the 1960s, carried on the tradition of the former distillery, but it is defined by a distinctive waxy (candlewax) character. It is uncertain where the character is developed, but it is thought it might result from an interaction between the distillate and the cast iron chargers. At one point the chargers and pipes were cleaned and flushed and the character of the malt was altered.

The distillery uses stills that employ an elongated boil ball below tall, thick heads that allow for a greater reflux action and copper contact during distillation. The company offers a proprietary bottling of a 14-year-old Clynelish single malt and a Distillers Edition that matures for the last two to three years in oloroso sherry casks. Prior to 2005, Diageo bottled the Rare Malts series, which included an expression of both Clynelish and Brora single malt, and in 2010 it released Clynelish as part of the Managers' Choice.

The Noser Knows

Both the 14-year-old and the Distillers Edition have the characteristic waxiness of Clynelish, with underlying fruit and floral notes; the additional years in the sherry casks of the Distillers Edition bring out robust dried fruit flavors.

Dalmore Distillery

➤ Pronounced as spelled

➤ Alness, Ross-shire IV17 0UT

➤ www.thedalmore.com

➤ Visitors center

At Dalmore, the stone distillery buildings tumble down a small hill and fan out along the water's edge. The entire distillery site is punctuated with green lawns and flowers, as well as ducks and swans that ride the water at high tide.

This area, known as the Black Isle, was capable of easily producing and delivering an adequate amount of barley needed for distilling whisky and providing a good supply of very soft water from the River Averon. Alexander Matheson built the Dalmore Distillery and leased it to two successive families. After the last lessee left the distillery in 1866, Matheson searched for someone who would continue distilling whisky at Dalmore.

The Mackenzie Connection

He found the perfect candidate in a young man, Andrew Mackenzie, the son of Matheson's land agent. Andrew Mackenzie, together with his brother Charles, began repairing buildings and equipment, ordering supplies, making whisky, and selling it to local merchants. The Mackenzie family remained in the whisky business until it was sold to Whyte Mackay (United Spirits) in the early 1970s.

The Distillery Cat's Meow

The Clan Mackenzie has maintained strong ties with the Dalmore distillery—not only through a century's ownership by Andrew Mackenzie, but also through the clan's history.

In 1263 King Alexander III of Scotland went shooting with the chieftain of the Mackenzie clan.

When one of the stags turned and attacked the king, the Mackenzie chieftain intervened to save King Alexander's life. As a result, the king granted the Clan Mackenzie the right to use a twelve-point stag as its family emblem. Today, the figure of the stag graces every bottle of Dalmore whisky.

Remembering its Heritage

Parts of Dalmore's production have been updated, but a look at the tun room and, more specifically, the stillroom is a resounding comment on the distillery's connection to its past. The tun room contains eight Oregon pine washbacks, some so old that they have blackened linings from the lime that was used to disinfect washbacks, a practice abandoned since the 1970s.

The stillroom, which houses eight stills, pays particular homage to Dalmore's nineteenth-century roots. The wash stills have a lantern-glass design with short, thick necks and high shoulders. The top of the still, however, is flat unlike the curving swan neck stills found in other distilleries. The spirit stills, like the wash stills, have high shoulders and use boil balls, but the design of the top half of the still is quite remarkable. The necks are completely enclosed in rounded copper water jackets that flare at the top like an old chemistry beaker. Rivets hold the seams of the jacket and the neck of one has nineteenth-century dovetailed beat welds that date back to 1874. Surrounded by these Victorian giants, people can easily imagine distilling whisky at Dalmore 150 years ago.

The respect for the past is also recognizable in the distillery offices. In 1989, the Roshaugh House located on the Black Isle, was scheduled for demolition. Before the demolition of the gracious interiors of the house could occur, the owners of Dalmore transported and installed much of the carved wooden paneling in the offices at the distillery. Despite a recent upgrade that resulted in painting the wood in one room, the most intricately carved interior remains untouched in another room. It provides an important cultural thread for the people at Dalmore, where strong ties to their heritage exist and where generations pass on skills and institutional memories.

Glen Ord Distillery

➤ Pronounced as spelled

➤ Muir of Ord, Ross-shire IV6 7UJ

➤ www.discovering-distilleries.com

➤ Visitors center

The Mackenzie family had held land on the Black Isle since the thirteenth century, and it took the support of Thomas Mackenzie to build the Glen Ord Distillery in 1838. As the distillery's website notes, he "envisaged an industry where local men could have all-

The Noser Knows

The Dalmore single malt is a rich and luscious malt. It is the color of burnished mahogany and releases sherry and sweet malt aromas. Its character speaks to ripe berry fruits, creamy caramels, vanilla fudge, and bitter orange. It has a medium body with a lingering finish.

year round employment." This vision certainly seems to stem from a sense of social justice, and the local men obviously enjoyed the fruits of reliable and consistent employment. The commitment, however, to local employment also suited the financial needs of Thomas Mackenzie. The arrangement meant that he could immediately use his entire barley crop for distillation, and the men could quickly turn it into ready cash, which would then ensure that they would pay their rents to him on time.

The Singleton Evolves from Multiple Names

When the last owner of Glen Ord died in the 1920s, Scottish Malt Distillers (eventually Diageo) acquired the distillery and has kept it as part of its portfolio. Interestingly, the Glen Ord single malt was released in 1958, but under the name of Ord. Its release arrived relatively early in the marketing history of single malts, but subsequently underwent several name changes. The most recent release in 2006 formed part of a marketing strategy that bottles malt from three different distilleries for three different markets under the over-reaching name of the Singleton. The Singleton of Glen Ord is bottled at twelve years and is sold in the Asian market.

The Noser Knows

Glen Ord begins with a slight peat aroma and lavender and heather florals, followed by flavors of citrus, including lemon zest and orange peel, supported by vanilla sweetness and sherry. The finish is dry and peppery.

Following a refurbishment in 2011, Diageo replaced the old cast iron mash tun with a new stainless steel vessel that continually sprays water from the top as the sweet wort continually drains from the bottom. The wort undergoes a long fermentation of seventy-five hours in Oregon pine washbacks that encourages the development of the citrus and fruit compounds in the spirit. The three pairs of onion-shaped stills with thick necks and downward-slanting lyne arms do not promote reflux and contribute to the full flavors and medium body of the mature malt.

Bourbon casks mature 50 percent of the spirit, and sherry matures the remaining 50 percent. Although the casks are filled off-site, some of the spirit returns to the Glen Ord warehouses for maturation. Even though Diageo has released older ages, limited editions, and a bottling in the Managers' Choice series, the 12-year-old Singleton of Glen Ord remains the primary expression.

Glenmorangie Distillery

➤ Pronounced *glen-MOR-an-gee (rhymes with orangey)*

➤ Tain, Ross-shire IV19 1PZ

➤ www.glenmorangie.com

➤ Visitors center

William Matheson acquired the property in 1840 and applied for a farm distillery license in 1843. MacDonald & Muir, whisky brokers from Leith, became the proprietor in 1918 and held ownership until it sold the property to Louis Vuitton Moët Hennessy in 2004. During its tenure, it quickly acquired Glen Moray in 1920, and later Ardbeg Distillery in 1997, and the Scotch Malt Whisky Society in 2004.

The Gin Stills

Glenmorangie employs a stainless steel mash tun, stainless steel washbacks, and a fairly average fermentation time. Nothing seems particularly distinctive about this distillation process until one looks at the stills and the double-maturation policy used at Glenmorangie.

The owner went one step beyond purchasing previously used whisky stills as other distillers had done. Previously used stills were installed, but they were gin stills instead of whisky stills. The stillroom houses twelve stills that resemble a colony of nesting cranes. Boil balls are small and sharply defined with very tall, thin necks rising above them encouraging a lot of reflux and copper contact and the distillation of only the lightest volatiles.

The Distillery Cat's Meow

The height of the stills at Glenmorangie reach 16 feet, 10¼ inches, which is a figure that people at the distillery equate to the height of a fully grown giraffe. When a new designer window was installed in the stillhouse in autumn of 2010, the subtle lines of a giraffe's shoulders and head appeared on the right side of the glass.

Double Maturation

The design of the stills creates a light, fruity, and floral new-make spirit that takes well to maturation in bourbon casks. Dr. Bill Lumsden and Rachael Barrie oversee the wood policy that includes selecting American oak from the Ozark Mountains in Missouri and directing the double-maturation program that began in 1994 with the Glenmorangie Port Wood Finish. Glenmorangie has been in the forefront of creative finishes, which requires a careful match of the wood finish to the light fruit character of Glenmorangie. As with so much in whisky making, success is dependent on balancing factors that complement, and do not compete with each other.

At present, the core range includes a 10-year-old original Glenmorangie and three non-chill filtered finishes (Quinta Ruban, finished two years in port pipes; Lasanta, finished two years in oloroso sherry casks; and Nectar D'Or, finished in two years in Sauterne casks). The Limited Edition Private Collection offers three non-chill filtered releases to date (Sonnalta PX, finished two years in Pedro Ximenez (PX) casks; Finealta 12-year-old, reminiscent of whisky in the 1900s, when it did its own peated malting; and Astar 10-year-old, matured in selected designer casks from American oak that has air-dried for two years and then held bourbon). And finally, Glenmorangie offers two older whiskies at 18 and 25 years old and Signet, a non-chill filtered malt made from a marriage of whisky distilled from toasted "chocolate" malt and other whiskies matured during the last thirty years.

The Noser Knows

The original Glenmorangie has a delicate rounded style with sweet milk caramel aromas and a light geranium scent. Flavors of blood oranges, ripe satsumas, buttery fudge, and a hint of spice complement the delicate dry finish.

Pulteney Distillery

➤ Pronounced *PULT-knee*

➤ Wick, Caithness KW1 5BA

➤ www.oldpulteney.com

➤ Visitors center

Pulteney Distillery, the most northern distillery on the mainland of Scotland, takes some perseverance to visit, but for people who like history and a distillery with quirky little stills, the reward of seeing Pulteney is worth the effort.

James Henderson who distilled whisky further inland, built the Pulteney Distillery in 1826 in the new Pulteneytown because the road infrastructure in northern Scotland was very poor. The new harbor gave him an access route for the delivery of supplies and for the transport of his whisky to southern markets.

The Distillery Cat's Meow

When the town council of Wick voted for the prohibition of alcohol in 1922, the local publicans tried to marshal opposition to the vote by holding open houses. The turnout was high and enthusiastic, but unfortunately, people drank so much that they were unable to attend the vote to voice their opposition, and the measure passed.

The new harbor also gave rise to a vibrant herring fishing industry, which not only brought as many as 10,000 people to the town during fishing season, but also brought problems for the distillery in the form of prohibition. Malcolm Waring, the distillery manager, remarks, "The men fished at night and returned to the town early in the morning to be paid on a daily basis, and then drank their wages before they returned to the sea in the evening. Meanwhile, the wives and children were left at home with nothing."

The Distillery Cat's Meow

During the two decades that Pulteney Distillery remained closed, it provided the final shelter for the bodies of the sailors who served aboard the HMS *Jervis Bay* prior to their burial in the local cemetery. The only escort ship to a convoy of merchant ships from Halifax, Nova Scotia, the HMS *Jervis Bay* was torpedoed in November 1940, when it intentionally drew fire from the German ship the *Admiral Scheer* in order to allow the convoy time to scatter. Most of the crew died when the *Jervis Bay* sank, and the captain, Edward Fegen, was awarded the Victoria Cross posthumously. The town council eventually sold the distillery in the 1950s with the stipulation that it not be used to distill whisky. The ban was obviously rescinded sometime before it was sold to Hiram Walker and then to Inver House (InterBev), the current owners.

In 1922, the ensuing social problems led the town council, under pressure from the temperance movement, to establish prohibition in Wick that lasted until 1947. Pulteney Distillery continued to produce whisky until 1930, when global economic issues forced its closure. During the years from 1922 to its closure, Pulteney distilled whisky, but no one in town could drink it legally.

Some of the most interesting features in the Pulteney Distillery are the quirky still designs, which provide a lot of reflux in the distillation. The wash still has a boil ball above plump shoulders, but the head of the still is very short and thick with a flat top instead of a graceful curving swan neck. No swan neck exists to connect into the lyne arm, but rather the lyne arm juts directly out of the side of the still head.

The spirit still design is equally strange with a boil ball, also perched above plump shoulders, that leads into a slim, tall head and into a swan neck. But the lyne arm loops down and around in a twisted U-shape with a purifier in the middle of it. The purifier, however, has not been used since the 1960s and now serves to increase the reflux and the contact between the copper and the spirit. The design balances the use of a worm tub at Pulteney, which serves to lower the spirit to copper contact. This results in a heavy, oily, and meaty new-make spirit, but by the time it has matured primarily in bourbon casks and a smaller percentage in sherry casks, the fruity and floral esters emerge and the casks contribute a honey sweetness. It has the distinct briny character of a coastal whisky that may stem from the policy of aging all the spirit, intended for single malt bottling, on-site and mostly in dunnage warehouses.

Whisky Lexicon

Most distilleries reduce the new-make in the spirit receiver to 63.5 percent ABV in order to provide a standard strength that facilitates the exchange of casks among distilleries. Some spirit also matures better at the standard reduction strength. However, a few distilleries, like Pulteney, do not reduce their spirit and fill the casks at receiver strength, which can vary because it is whatever strength the new-make spirit has when it comes from the receiver into the filling room.

The warehousemen continue to fill casks at receiver strength rather than reducing it to the 63.5 percent in standard use, and they still hand stencil the distillery's name and distillation year on the cask ends rather than use the bar coding that so many other distilleries now employ. People at Pulteney Distillery maintain a keen awareness of its heritage and traditions, and the enclosed courtyard is a place better meant for horses and carts than modern trucks. Waring reflects that every bottle of Pulteney seems to contain a "distillation of the people and place that comes out in the whisky."

Inver House offered Pulteney as a single malt in 1997, and today it now reserves at least 60 percent of its production for bottling as a single malt. In addition to offering the 12-year-old Pulteney, Inver House has added several older bottlings, ranging between 17 to 30 years old. Additionally, visitors to the distillery can bottle their own cask strength whisky from two casks. The vintage will obviously change as each cask is emptied, but at present a 1990 and 1995 vintage are provided.

The Noser Knows

The Pulteney whisky is unpeated, but the coastal location adds a slight brine to sweet honey on the nose. It has a syrupy mouthfeel with vanilla bean and fruit compote on the palate, complemented by citrus and banana notes and orange blossom honey with a touch of licorice. It finishes with a lingering taste of oranges, and a warming, but quick, finish.

Teaninich Distillery

➤ Pronounced *tee-ah-NIN-ick*

➤ Alness, Ross-shire IV17 0UT

➤ No website

➤ No visitors center

Teaninich Distillery sits on an industrial estate and exists as a workhorse for blending whisky—a whisky factory, or so I thought. The distillery is innovative and the spirit is robust and tangy. Not meant to be a mainstream brand, the whisky is a good blending malt, and its production proceeds quietly, efficiently, and purposefully.

Captain Hugh Munro, an officer in the 78th Regiment, suffered injuries during the Napoleonic Wars that left him blind. Upon his return to his home in Ross-shire, he threw himself into the rebuilding of Teaninich Castle and the development of his estate, which included the building of Teaninich Distillery in 1817.

During most of the next century, the distillery's ownership stayed in the family, but several tenants saw to the operation of it. Eventually, Robert Innes Cameron became sole owner in 1904 and operated the distillery until his death in 1932. At that time, Scottish Malt Distillers (now Diageo) bought the distillery and retained ownership.

Part A and Part B

The original Teaninich Distillery initially used two pairs of stills, but the smaller of the two pairs was eventually removed in 1946. The whisky boom of the 1950s and 1960s increased the demand for Teaninich single malt for blending and as a result, a newly constructed distillery with six large stills, built in the Waterloo design (see chapter 15, *Caol Ila*), opened next to the old distillery. The owners had never separately named the two distilleries as was done at Brora and Clynelish, so to distinguish between the two operations, because they were technically both Teaninich Distillery, the production team christened the new distillery Part A and the older plant Part B. But Willie MacDougall, the present distillery manager, observed, "It was like having the *Starship Enterprise* sitting in front of a Model T Ford." Consequently, the operation of both plants required a range of skills and experiences and the production workers, who moved between the two distilleries, needed to remain adaptable and multitalented when working both sites.

In the early 1980s, the overproduction and diminishing demand for malt whisky brought about the closure or mothballing of many distilleries. Teaninich Distillery was not immune, and Part B closed in 1984 with Part A following in 1985. The years between 1986 and 1991 saw no production at either site. Part A reopened in 1990—Part B never produced spirit again and was demolished in 1999. Only the concrete pad of its foundation still remains.

Cutting-Edge Distilling

In 2001, the owners replaced the mash tun with a mash filter, a feature that is unique to Teaninich Distillery. The brewing industry tends to use mash filters, but they have not replaced the mash tun in the distilling industry. The extraction is very good compared to the traditional mash tun and brings efficiency to the mashing process.

At Teaninich, the mashman combines the malt and two waters at 64°C (147°F) and 80°C (176°F) respectively (instead of the usual three used at other distilleries) and infuses it for twenty-five minutes. The second water (the sparge) recirculates as the first water of the next mash. He then pumps the wort through a small tunnel in the mash filter, consisting of a long row of large filters. The wort disperses across the filter plates, the air is dispersed to allow an even mix, and the membranes are then inflated. The whole process is like squeezing twenty-four large sponges. The wort drains through the pimpled surface of the filter into the underback (called a buffer tank in this process) and the draff remains behind on the filter.

The Noser Knows

Teaninich has full flavors with a tang like arugula, aromas of freshly mowed grass, and geranium leaves, balanced with a slightly sweet note. The distillery uses a hammer mill rather than the traditional Porteus or Boby grinding mill, and the hammer action releases oil in the husk, contributing to the oily distillery character.

Mashing is a continual process at Teaninich, and everything at the distillery seems to be done on a grand scale. This theme certainly carries through to the six behemoth copper stills. The massive stills at the Teaninich Distillery have large boil balls and short, thick necks that increase the reflux. The design also provides a large surface area for significant copper contact with the spirit, creating a light, grassy new-make style.

The Teaninich spirit is tanked away for filling and aging, primarily in bourbon casks. It has appeared as a release in both the Rare Malts and Managers' Choice range. Any other expressions tend to appear as offerings from independent bottlers.

What You Need to Know

➤ As the term would suggest, *coastal* or *maritime* whiskies come from areas along the coast and bring a salty seaweed component to their character.

➤ All but one (Teaninich) of the Northern Highlands distilleries release proprietary single malts from their distilleries.

➤ The production process and the types of casks used for maturation (particularly at Glenmorangie) play a greater role in the flavor profile than the coastal location.

➤ A coastal location cannot be dismissed entirely because a tang of brine distinguishes the Pulteney malt, which is specifically aged in dunnage warehouses on the site of the distillery on the coast.

CHAPTER 11

The Eastern Highlands

In This Chapter

➤ Speyside neighbors

➤ Speyside with a twist

➤ Aberdeenshire, Deeside: character or region?

The Eastern Highlands borders the eastern edge of Speyside and has rich grain fields, castles, and striking countryside. The Eastern Highlands' distilleries tend to cluster around both the Aberdeenshire region and the more southern Deeside area. Because of its proximity to Speyside, many of the eastern malts, like Knockdhu, borrow the fruity elegant character of its neighbors, but others often provide their own distinctive twist to the Speyside style. Ardmore retains an older traditional character that has more peat than many of its Speyside cousins, but Glen Garioch has consciously excluded peat from its profile. Sherry defines the GlenDronach character, yet the newly revived Glenglassaugh has a maritime profile influenced by its position above the Moray coast. And when one hears reference to the Deeside whiskies, it is more of a geographical placement because Royal Lochnagar, Fettercairn, and Glencadam all exhibit different characters.

Ardmore Distillery

➤ Pronounced *ARD(rhymes with card)-more*

➤ Kennethmont, Huntly AB54 4NH

➤ www.ardmorewhisky.com

➤ Visitors by appointment +44-1464-831-213

Ardmore Distillery lies just east of the town of Huntly, which places it in the Eastern Highlands region. Traditionally it produced a malt used primarily for blending, but recently it has come to the attention of single malt enthusiasts.

Vision of the Future, Lessons from the Past

Ardmore Distillery has undergone changes to upgrade the equipment and improve its efficiency, but it was done with a deliberate intention to preserve the historical memory of the distillery. When it replaced the boiler and steam engine, it removed the ornate boiler plate, painted it, and placed it on display next to the preserved steam engine. Although it removed the Saladin maltings in 1975, it retained the rooms containing the steeps and the malting floor in order to provide options for future use.

Even though the infrastructure demanded changes, the distilling process at Ardmore remains very much manually controlled and reliant on the skills of the mashman and stillman. The distillery retains its original Douglas fir washbacks, but the mashman does not fill them to their full capacities. This provides extra head space so that the fermentation can expand and recede naturally without the need for switchers to disperse the foam.

William Teacher & Sons built the distillery in 1898 because it had to rely on other distilleries to supply whisky for its blends and it wanted to produce its own malt. Building its own distillery near Kennethmont meant that it could control and plan its production. It made Ardmore the fingerprint malt in Teacher's Highland Cream, which contains 45 percent malt whisky in its blend. Using peat from beds in northeast Scotland gives the Ardmore a light smokiness with more wood and carbon flavors than the maritime and iodine flavors that come from Islay peat.

The Noser Knows

In the early twentieth century, Teacher implemented the self-opening cork, which was a cork with a rim on it, and advertised, "Throw Away the Corkscrew." Previously, whisky bottles were closed with a cork that often crumbled or broke when the corkscrew was used to open it. The new self-opening cork was popular and increased the sales of Teacher's whisky when it was introduced.

Changes and Innovation

The Ardmore stills traditionally produced a heavy and full-flavored whisky that complements the east coast peat. The onion-shape design allows the heavier vaporized compounds to rise to the top of the still with little reflux action. These volatiles then continue an unimpeded trip to the condenser because of the short downward angled lay pipe.

Recently, the owners replaced the rummagers and direct coal-fired method of heating the stills with steam heat, but there was concern that the removal of the rummagers and the direct firing would lower the contact of the spirit with the copper and alter the character of the whisky. In order to replicate the copper contact of the former heating system, the stillman uses warm water in the sub-cooler (like a mini-condenser) so that the vapor moves slowly and has more time to interact with the copper. It then moves into the condenser, where the vapor condenses into spirit. This method substitutes the copper activity that happened with direct firing and rummagers. The result is a full-bodied whisky with no sulfur. In order to enhance the robust peaty character of Ardmore, the stillman also ends the middle cut at 60 percent ABV, a point at which more phenols (smoky aromas) occur.

Experimentation with Maturation

Since Beam Global owns Ardmore Distillery, the new-make spirit intended for Ardmore Traditional is matured in first fill bourbon casks and finished in remake quarter casks—a smaller cask that increases the contact between the spirit and the wood and may help to explain the sweet caramel and toffee notes in the single malts. Their recent release of their 100th Anniversary 12-year-old malt whisky received positive reviews and a rating of ninety-two (out of a hundred) by the *Whisky Advocate* Buyer's Guide.

Whisky Lexicon

Pedro Ximenez is a very dark, sweet dessert sherry. Master blenders use the casks that contained the sherry to finish maturing whisky and refer to it on the label as finished in PX sherry casks. Usually, the spirit begins its maturation in some other type of cask (like bourbon) and then finishes in a PX cask for months or years.

The recognition that the Ardmore single malt has garnered has led to different experiments with maturation to determine how the whisky ages in port pipes, in Pedro Ximenez sherry casks (PX), and with triple finishes (i.e., bourbon, quarter casks, and European oak or PX sherry casks).

The Noser Knows

The Traditional Ardmore has some nose prickle because of the higher alcohol content, and it responds well to water, which releases earthy peat notes. It has a creamy mouthfeel with flavors of peat, summer berries, honey, and sweet caramel flavors. It is full-bodied, complex, and layered, with new flavors emerging over time. Light peat notes linger with an uptick of lemon zest at the very end. Notes of licorice emerge with time. The Ardmore single malt has always been well received by blenders and has only recently been appreciated by single malt drinkers. But the experimentation with maturation leads one to hope that future bottlings will be both distinctive and unique.

Fettercairn Distillery

➤ Pronounced *FET-tair-CAIR-n*

➤ Fettercairn AB30 1YB

➤ www.whyteandmackay.com

➤ Visitors center

Several years ago a friend suggested that I read the novels of Lewis Grassic Gibbon for a vivid and accurate portrayal of Scottish rural life at the turn of the twentieth century. The books were powerful, and the descriptions of the land, known as the Mearns, were compelling and intense. Fettercairn Distillery lies in the heart of the Mearns and although the way of life has changed dramatically in the last century, the countryside has not.

The distillery shelters below the Grampian Mountains and was part of the Fasque Estate owned by Sir Alexander Ramsay. Many of the nineteenth-century landowners were well aware that their farming tenants needed farm distilleries, which used the barley grown on the estates, in order to pay their rents. Consequently, as soon as the Excise Act of 1823 made the licensing of distilleries more feasible, Ramsay converted a corn mill at Nethermill to a licensed distillery. The ensuing years saw the owner expand the distillery and adopt the fashionable practice of maturing the new spirit in sherry casks for its "more discerning" customers. During this time, John Gladstone bought the Fasque Estate and frequently entertained his son, William Gladstone, the British Prime Minister.

Fettercairn Distillery suffered a devastating fire in the late nineteenth century and endured a "quiet time" in the early twentieth century, when it was closed. The distillery went into production in 1939 under the management of Joseph Hobbs, and later operated under two other owners. In 2007, United Spirits (Whyte & Mackay), a division of the Indian company United Breweries Group acquired the distillery.

The Distillery Cat's Meow

Whisky enthusiasts traveling toward or from the Deeside area around Banchory sometimes take the rural road between Strachan and Fettercairn on their way to visit Fettercairn Distillery. This was the old smugglers' road that moved illicit whisky between the bothies, housing the illegal stills, and the markets around Deeside. The narrow road winds through the Grampian Mountains with vistas that are unchanged since smugglers first used the road. It is a road to avoid in the wintertime, however, not only because of its narrow and steep inclines, but also because it often closes with the first snow.

Irrigating the Stills

Fettercairn Distillery still maintains its historical ties to the land and remains a very traditional distillery. Although none of the owners have done their own maltings for the last fifty years, the current owner distills a heavily peated new-make spirit (at 55 ppm) for a portion of the year. Although the old malting floor and pagoda chimney may rest unused, they remain unchanged and are a central part of the distillery site today.

The distillery has retained its cast iron mash tun with its old copper cover, its rake, and uses Oregon pine washbacks for fermentation. The four stills are quite compact and plump with short, thick necks and lyne arms angled downward.

Although these stills would appear to produce a heavy spirit, the operators at Fettercairn employ a unique system for increasing the reflux to create a lighter spirit. They irrigate the tops of the stills with cold water, which runs down the outside of the still and collects in

The Noser Knows

The traditional Fettercairn malt has a sweet, tangy nose with oily notes. The flavors include graham cracker sweetness supported by subtle pepper notes, and florals like heather and lavender. It ends with a gently warming finish and a tinge of peat on the palate.

The Distillery Cat's Meow

The Glencadam Distillery is indeed surrounded by spirits, albeit two different kinds, one worldly and the other heavenly. The more earthly (new-make) spirit resides within the distillery's warehouses as it matures in oak casks. While just beyond the distillery's doors, more ethereal spirits reside in the town cemetery that occupies the land

a trough at the shoulders. This cools the heads of the stills so that the vapors condense and drop back into the pot for redistillation. The irrigation system continually draws fresh, cold water so that the stills remain cool and the reflux continues.

Once the spirit has passed through these stocky little stills, it is aged primarily in bourbon casks and the occasional sherry cask. The warehousemen at Fettercairn also continue the practice of identifying each cask with the year, the number, and the name of the distillery marked in paint with brass stencils instead of with barcodes.

United Spirits replaced the Fettercairn 1824 bottling with new Fettercairn Fior carrying no age statement. But 85 percent of the bottling contains 14- and 15-year-old malt; and the remaining portion contains heavily peated malt. The new packaging uses the image of a unicorn, which is found in the family crest of Sir Alexander Ramsay, the original owner. The distillery also offers a Limited Edition single cask at 18 years old with non-chill filtering and natural color. Recently, it released limited editions of very old malts at 24, 30, and 40 years old.

Glencadam Distillery

➤   Pronounced *glen CAD-um*

➤   Brechin, Angus DD9 7PA

➤   www.glencadamdistillery.co.uk

➤   Tours by appointment +44-1356-622 217

The town of Brechin sits north of Dundee and west of Montrose. It is easy to miss the turn for this distillery, but once having located the hidden road on the edge of town, the setting is exquisite. The quiet lane off the main road overlooks the town and church steeple; and as it turns, one sees the town cemetery and its green lawns with Glencadam Distillery settled on a slight rise beside it. It is tidy and trimmed with manicured lawns and well-tended flowers and has a quiet calm about the place.

The Distillery Cat's Meow

Glencadam is associated with the Tenements of Caldhame, which were once plots of land given to the people of the Royal Burgh of Brechin to grow food. Additionally, the water, still in use at the distillery, comes from the Moorans water, which ran into a Victorian reservoir and supplied water to the people of Brechin at one time. Interestingly, a driving force in obtaining the water supply came from David Scott, who also owned the distillery. One wonders if he advocated for the water supply to serve the people of Brechin and then bought the distillery, or if he advocated for the water supply to serve the distillery and secondly to serve the townspeople.

Glencadam was established in 1825, and shortly afterward David Scott purchased it from George Cooper and continued operation from 1827 to 1837. The distillery operated under several different distillers until 1954, when Hiram Walker (later Allied Domecq) bought the distillery and extensively modernized it. Allied closed Glencadam in 2000, but Angus Dundee Distillers reopened the distillery when it purchased it in 2003.

New Tunes on the Old Stills

Because of the expansion and modernization undertaken in the 1950s, much of the distillery reflects a postwar technology. The two stills retain their original nineteenth-century design and are somewhat small with thin, short necks. This design does not promote much reflux or copper contact, but the distinct upward angle of the lyne arms corrects the design by creating more reflux action. This allows some of the heavier elements to boil away, creating a light body and a whisky that lends itself to blending.

Additionally, an external heat exchanger heats the wash by moving it through a steam-fired heat exchanger outside the still. The wash enters the top of the still, pumps to metal plates on the bottom of the still, which diffuse the liquid to the sides and heat the remaining wash in the still. The system is very efficient and continually circulates the wash through the still and maintains a constant copper contact, improving the spirit character.

While all the spirit produced at Glencadam is aged in bourbon casks on the distillery site, almost all of it goes for blending. At one time Glencadam whisky was only available from independent bottlers, but since Angus Dundee Distillers has purchased both Tomintoul and Glencadam Distilleries, it has released several single malt expressions. These include 10-, 15-, and 21-year-old bottlings, as well as a 15-year-old oloroso finish, and a 12-year-old port wine finish.

The Noser Knows

The mature Glencadam has a burst of robust fruit aromas that become a complex syrupy compote of melons, pears, and apples supported by some spice at the end. The Glencadam bottlings are non-chill filtered with natural coloring. Douglas Fitchett, the current distillery manager, notes that "Glencadam single malt has a malty sweetness on the nose that seems to disappear with the older expression. In the older version, the fruits tend to turn toward the dark fruits with the additional notes of marzipan and nuts. And because it is a blending malt, it has the ability to tie flavors together into a balanced taste, which makes it particularly effective with both the oloroso sherry finish and the port wine finish."

GlenDronach Distillery

> ➤ Pronounced *glen-DRAWN-ick*
> ➤ Forgue, By Huntly, Aberdeenshire AB54 6DB
> ➤ www.glendronachdistillery.co.uk
> ➤ Visitors center

GlenDronach means the valley of blackberries (brambles in Scotland), and the day I first visited this distillery the aroma of blackberries was very much in the air. This fertile farming land lies east of Huntly, accessed by quiet rural roads that roam under canopies of trees and open onto views of green hills.

Boynsmill Farm, the original farm established in 1771, probably distilled whisky to use excess barley and to provide some industry during the winter months. Later, William Allardice bought the land in 1775. In 1800, Allardice's son, James, bought the estate and renamed his home Glen House; and in 1826, he joined with businessmen from Aberdeen to obtain a license to distill whisky. The Dronac Burn flowed through Allardice's property, so it not only supplied water to the new distillery, but it also supplied the name for the new whisky (after Allardice had appended the word *Glen* at the beginning of it and the letter *h* to the end of it).

Early in its beginnings, the new distillery survived three fires, with the third fire doing extensive damage to the distillery. GlenDronach continued its roller coaster existence under the operation of several owners, who expanded the distillery, closed it, modernized it, and then reopened it. During a refurbishment in 2005, GlenDronach, one of the last distilleries to direct fire its stills using coal, converted its system to steam heat and removed its rummagers.

Independent Move

In 2008, the BenRiach Distillery Company, Ltd., headed by Billy Walker, bought GlenDronach to complement its earlier purchase of BenRiach. Ownership by this small independent company has enabled it to highlight the single malt produced here in a way that large corporations cannot always do. Its core range reflects a return to GlenDronach's lovely full-bodied sherry character and its extended range speaks to innovation and experimentation.

Glen House, the original house on the distillery grounds, now welcomes people from the whisky industry, and it is still surrounded by farm fields that graze sheep and vegetable beds that include the ubiquitous blackberry. True to its farming heritage, the management decorates Glen House and the visitors center with flowers from the gardens, and uses seasonal vegetables at dinners to entertain guests.

One of the Last Floor Maltings Closes

The distillery has been mindful of its traditional roots and had employed the disappearing practice of malting barley on old stone floors until 2001. But other traditions prevail at GlenDronach, where the mashmen continue to infuse the mash in a cast iron mash tun with a gleaming copper-and-brass cover. Other than a turn of the older traditional rake that settles the mash at the beginning and end of each cycle, the infusion allows the malt to soak in the water without being disturbed by stirring, so that the sugars leach out into the liquid. The GlenDronach mashmen prefer to ferment the sweet wort in four older Oregon pine and five newer Scottish larch washbacks, and use a slightly longer fermentation of at least fifty-six hours.

The Distillery Cat's Meow

Alan Nicol, a former maltman at GlenDronach, is also an avid and experienced gardener. In 1998, he had plans to retire to tend his flowers and vegetables. Instead, the management asked him to stay on as the official Glen House gardener, where he tends the lawn, sets out the cutting flowers and house vegetables (started as seedlings in his own home), and nurtures them into plants for harvesting. One year he disappeared through a hole in the ground where he had been digging and uncovered the former overflow sluice of the old and disused meal mill. The hole revealed a set of stairs that led to a tunnel extending under the garden to the gate at the other end.

Two pairs of stills at GlenDronach have downward-sloping lyne arms and short, thick necks with a boil ball that bulges above high, plump shoulders. The wash stills, however, have slightly taller necks, and the lyne arms dip and curve in an unusual design resembling an elephant's trunk. This unique design, coupled with the removal of the chain mail-like rummagers, results in less copper contact and a full, meaty body.

Sherry and Other Finishes

In addition to the full body of GlenDronach single malt, its sherry character is a defining trait. In 1976, Allied Distillers Ltd. bottled two single malts—one aged in the original oak casks and labeled GlenDronach Original; the other aged in the oloroso sherry casks and labeled GlenDronach Sherry. Since it became increasingly expensive to bottle two different whiskies, Allied Distillers released GlenDronach Traditional, which combined both the original and sherry cask bottlings. Eventually, the company returned to bottling the sherry cask version at 12, 15, and 18 years old because these bottlings best highlighted the characteristics of GlenDronach.

The core range of GlenDronach continues to include bottlings of 12-, 15-, and 18-year-old whiskies, which usually begin their aging in American bourbon barrels, and then finish the second half of their maturation in sherry casks. The spirit is laid down in dunnage warehouses and aged on-site. Additionally, GlenDronach single malt appears bottled at more than thirty years with several different wood finishes, including Sauterne, virgin oak, Moscatel, and tawny port, and limited releases of single casks.

These variations on the core range character of the whisky build on the traditional processes that have persevered for so many years at GlenDronach. While the aromas of peat fires no longer join the smell of sweet blackberries, it is heartening to witness the distillery not only working again, but also prospering.

The Noser Knows

The defining characteristic of GlenDronach single malt is sherry and oak wood. The nose begins with sherry and dissolves to dried fruit, notes of spice, and old leather. Flavors of figs, dates, currents, and prunes in syrup lightened with the tastes of summer berry fruits fill the mouth supported by tastes of vanilla caramels. Rich and full-bodied with a warming, but surprisingly quick finish.

Glen Garioch Distillery

➤ Pronounced *glen GEERIE*

➤ Oldmeldrum, Aberdeenshire AB51 0ES

➤ www.glengarioch.com

➤ Visitors center

Stark moorland turns to agricultural fields at the turn to the Glen Garioch Distillery on the road to Old Meldrum, a small town on the eastern edge of the distillery region. Surprisingly, the distillery sits in the center of the town but quietly blends into the other buildings and is part of the town rather than something distinct and separate.

Blenders used the Glen Garioch whisky in their blends and gave it a popular place in their individual portfolios. And during most of the distillery's life, blended whiskies, particularly Rob Roy and Vat 69, used Glen Garioch whisky for the core of their blends. But water supply problems brought about the distillery's sale in 1970 to Stanley P. Morrison, later Morrison Bowmore Distillers.

Finding Water, Launching a Single Malt

Morrison's ownership brought two significant changes: first, it directed a search for a reliable water source; second, it decided to bottle Glen Garioch as a single malt. Within two years, it located springs of fresh water on a nearby farm that provided Morrison's with a steady water source and allowed it to proceed with plans to offer Glen Garioch as a single malt whisky.

The Distillery Cat's Meow

In 1972, Alec Grant, the father of the present distillery manager, knew of a possible water source for the distillery and went about locating it. Because of his career as a digger driver laying pipes and digging drains, he knew the water existed on the nearby Coutens Farm, despite the fact the spring remained hidden from view.

Morrison already owned Bowmore, the Islay Distillery, and wanted an additional whisky to bottle as a single malt that would represent the Eastern Highlands in its portfolio. In 1984,

Morrison Bowmore bought Auchentoshan Distillery, producing a Lowland whisky, which became the third whisky in its collection.

An interesting part of the distillery's history concerns its relationship with the University of Aberdeen beginning in 1976, which produced the Greenhouse Project. At the time, Scottish tomatoes were disappearing from grocery shelves because they needed to grow and ripen in glass houses. The distillery already used some waste energy to dry barley and to preheat the mash, but it still had additional heat coming from the condensers. An intricate system used the waste heat to warm greenhouses and to bleed CO_2 from the washbacks into the greenhouses at night to ripen tomatoes for the market.

At one point, the distillery had 1.25 acres under glass and annually harvested 2 tons of tomatoes and other hothouse plants with the reclaimed energy. It also installed a similar system at Bowmore Distillery, where the recaptured waste heat warms a community swimming pool nearby. Because people who spearheaded the project were no longer at Glen Garioch and other issues demanded attention, the Greenhouse Project was abandoned in 1993.

The Next Step

In 1994, Suntory Ltd bought Glen Garioch Distillery and closed it the following year. Within two years, Morrison Bowmore Distillers Ltd., now a subsidiary of Suntory, reopened the distillery. Its operation brought the decision to stop peating its malt and produce a completely unpeated single malt whisky. Today, it offers a core range of NAS Founders Reserve and a 12-year-old expression, both non-chill filtered and bottled, at 48 percent ABV to prevent cloudiness. It also bottles limited editions of small batch releases at cask strength. Since 2010, all of its production, aged on-site, goes toward single malt bottling. Part of the company's new direction included the opening of a visitors center in the old cooperage in 2006.

The Noser Knows

The NAS Founders Reserve contains whiskies that are roughly 8 years old and aged in bourbon casks that account for its sweetness, vanilla, and a touch of spice. The 12-year-old contains a marriage of whisky aged in both bourbon casks and oloroso sherry casks. The additional years and sherry casks bring a hint of sherry to the flavors of baked apples with spice and vanilla custard.

Glenglassaugh Distillery

➤ Pronounced *glen-GLAZ-ah*

➤ Portsoy, Aberdeenshire AB45 2SQ

➤ www.glenglassaugh.com

➤ Visitors by appointment +44-1261-842 367

Tucked between Sandend and Portsoy, this distillery commands a stunning view of Scotland's Moray Coast. Only new warehouses and the ruins of an old windmill are visible from the main road, but the rest of the distillery spreads beyond the warehouses to cliffs that frame the beach and the small village of Sandend. A new distillery built in 1959 and new warehouses surround what remains of the old distillery built in 1875 by local businessmen.

An Imagined Footprint

Few of the original buildings remain, but it is very easy to imagine the original design of the distillery and how it might have appeared in the present unchanged landscape. The owners built the distillery of local stone and placed the malt barn at the top of the hill, which descends to the cliffs along the coast. The long first floor of the existing barn appears to have been the malting floor with the steeps at one end. Old photographs show that the distillery buildings tumbled down the hill with the malt kilns next to the barn and the other distillery buildings following afterward. The only other buildings to escape removal are what may have been part of the maltings, now attached to the present malt storage area, a dunnage warehouse (now named Number 1), and the brewer's house that nestles in the curve of a hill at the end of the road.

A Postwar Distillery Design

In order to meet the postwar demand for whisky, the owners, Highland Distilleries, rebuilt Glenglassaugh in 1959, and the design of the new buildings reflected the practicality and modernity of the time. A tunnel connected the old malt storage barns to the newly built distillery and housed a large screw that delivered the grist from the mill room to the mash tun.

Much of the equipment, while employing new technology, continued to have ties to older distilling traditions. All of the milling equipment and the cast iron mash tun, covered by a brass-and-copper canopy,

The Distillery Cat's Meow

The design of the distillery roofs included sequential peaks in the roofline to resemble the waves of the Moray Firth, directly below the distillery.

were made by Porteus, the company responsible for most of the mills used in the whisky industry. Although Highland initially installed Corten steel washbacks, they were eventually replaced with traditional wood, and in the 1970s two new stainless steel washbacks were added.

The new distillery boasted condensers, rather than worms, for use with the pair of copper stills. Ian Buxton quotes Jim Cryle, the manager of Glenglassaugh in the early 1970s, the original stills had "more of a tulip-bulb, straight-sided shape. . . " (Ian Buxton, *Glenglassaugh, a Distillery Reborn*, Neil Wilson Pub Ltd, 2010). Today, the distillery has a pair of stills incorporating a boil ball between the tall, thick neck and the sharply sloping shoulders.

The Noser Knows

The change in the still design at Glenglassaugh occurred because virtually all of Glenglassaugh spirit went to Highland's blends. The water source from the Fordyce Burn had hard water, which proved unsuitable for the blends. Distillers attempted numerous accommodations, including the installation of water softeners. Eventually, they continued to use water from the Fordyce Burn but changed the still design to mitigate the effects of the hard water.

Glenglassaugh Reinvented

Highland's "new" distillery operated for twenty-seven years and completed its last filling in November 1986. In 2006, the Dutch registered investment company, the Scaent Group, engaged primarily in energy interests, investigated the purchase of a distillery to enlarge its investment ventures. It contacted Stuart Nickerson, a consultant in the whisky industry who brought a depth and breadth of knowledge and experience about the production of whisky, to advise them. In February 2008, the newly formed Glenglassaugh Distillery Company Ltd. took ownership of Glenglassaugh Distillery, and under the leadership of Nickerson as managing director, it restored the distillery and restarted production in November 2008.

Glenglassaugh was only occasionally bottled as a single malt for foreign markets, and it was only later that Highland Distilleries bottled a 1974 vintage as part of its Family Silver selection. For the most part, a whisky enthusiast needed to turn to an independent bottler in order to find a bottle of Glenglassaugh single malt. With the reopening of Glenglassaugh in 2008, however, the distillery not only produces spirit for thirty-one weeks a year, but also makes it available to whisky aficionados.

The New Millennium Distillery

Because of more than twenty years of a production gap from 1986 to 2008, the core range presently offered tends to fall at the two ends of the spectrum—either very old malts or very young spirit. The Rare Cask series of over 30- and 40-year-old expressions are single cask bottlings. The Spirit Drinks series, on the other hand, offers unaged new-make spirit, or blushes, consisting of new-make aged for as many as twelve months in wine casks. The Spirit Drinks in particular are intended for cocktails and use with mixers.

The management at Glenglassaugh also has a program for buying casks, particularly octaves made from previously used whisky casks and maturing ideally for five to seven years. The 250 Club offers larger casks, both sherry and bourbon, for maturation up to ten years.

In addition to their present offerings, the owners also cask Glenglassaugh new-make for maturation and will eventually find ideal ages and woods for bottling in the future. Presently, they mature their spirit mostly in first-fill bourbon casks and a small percentage in sherry, and look to experiment with different wood finishes like wine, rum, or port.

The current distillers continue to use hard water because they intend to reserve all their production for single malts and feel that the effects of hard water distillation are part of the flavor profile of Glenglassaugh. Plans include bottling all their spirit/whisky with non-chill filtering and without added color, and reserving all their production for single malts. They do not intend to sell any of their spirit to blenders or independent bottlers.

The Noser Knows

The old expressions of Glenglassaugh have sweet toffee on the nose opening to honey with the addition of water. It has flavors of brown sugar, vanilla beans, and pineapple upside-down cake, cream caramels, and lemon zest with background notes of toasted bread. It takes water well and finishes dry and warming.

The spirit distilled under the new ownership became whisky in November 2011, when the first spirit matured. The Glenglassaugh spirit distilled in the new millennium still needs to form and mature before a distinctive house style emerges. Presently, the mashman uses a cool and long fermentation lasting seventy-five hours in order to produce a tropical fruit character in its new-make. Eventually, maturing in bourbon and sherry casks may contribute some sweetness and sherry notes with perhaps a coastal tang from the nearby Moray Firth.

Knockdhu Distillery

➤ Pronounced *knock-DOO*

➤ Knock, Huntly AB54 7LJ

➤ www.ancnoc.com

➤ Visitors by appointment +44-1466-771 223

I always love to visit Knockdhu Distillery: it is a bit isolated, nestled at the base of the anCnoc hills, and surrounded by farm fields. On arrival during my past visits, one of the two distillery cats always extended the first welcome followed by the quiet hospitality of the staff. It was easy to feel at home at this distillery because people obviously feel a connection to each other and to the place.

On a return visit to gather information for this book, the comfortable and familiar feeling returned as soon as I turned down the single track to The Knock. Two "security" dogs, Tosca and Meg, have replaced the distillery cats, and the welcome was, if anything, more enthusiastic.

A Rose By Any Other Name Would Smell as Sweet

Knockdhu is the name of the distillery; the name of the malt produced there is anCnoc (pronounced *AN-nock*). The locals call the hills surrounding the distillery anCnoc, consequently the name was used to identify the malt so the name *Knockdhu* would not be confused with the malt of a neighboring distillery, Knockando. In 1894, John Morrison, who owned the Knock Estate, opened a distillery that was renowned for its modernity. Not much has changed at the Knockdhu Distillery, and nineteenth-century modernity now provides a view of a traditional distillery, although one with a great deal of future potential.

New Equipment, Old Ways

Much has changed at Knockdhu, but much also remains unchanged, particularly in the areas affecting the distillation of its whisky. The distillery boasts a new destoner, a new stainless steel mash tun, and new mini-condensers in the stills. Additionally, for the last seven years the distillery has produced heavily peated malt at 45 ppm so that the company could be self-sufficient and would not need to buy expensive peated malt in the market. Even where changes have occurred, they were made within the context of their historical tradition.

When the company replaced the mash tun, it could have installed a larger and shallower vessel that would have allowed a faster and more productive mash. Instead, it replaced the old mash tun with a new one having the same measurements and depth so that it can produce a very clear sweet wort and more of the citrus characteristics that define the anCnoc malt. It still maintains six Oregon pine washbacks and uses a slow fermentation. It has also removed the mechanical switchers at the top of each washback, relying on the old method of using a pinch of soap to keep the wash from boiling over the edge of the wooden vessels.

The Worm Turns

The stills use tall, slim heads and a boil ball above very plump, almost pumpkin-like, shoulders so that the reflux action increases and produces the lighter body of anCnoc malt. The lyne arms of the stills attach to a 30-meter (98-foot) worm tub—one of fifteen remaining in the industry. Contrary to logical thought, the long copper worm does not increase the copper contact with the whisky because of a verdigris coating that builds up over time and does not allow direct contact with the metal. While the worm tub at Knockdhu firmly connects the distillery to its nineteenth-century roots, most distilleries have converted to more efficient shell-and-tube condensers. Worm tubs tend to leak, always at inconvenient times, and they are more difficult to keep cool during the summertime when the ambient temperature rises, but their use helps to form some of the character of the spirit.

The Distillery Cat's Meow

One member of the Knockdhu Distillery team, who would gladly see the removal of the worm tub and cooling tank, is Meg, the resident Labradoodle. One summer's day, she mistook some of the algae on the surface of the cooling tower for solid ground and plunged down into the water. Although she comfortably oversees all areas of the distillery, she now refuses to mount the stairs leading to the worm tub.

On-site dunnage warehouses store whisky aging in bourbon casks and first-fill oloroso sherry casks responsible for some of the sweet toffee and butterscotch notes beneath the citrus fruit in the anCnoc. Within the core range of its products, the 12-year-old anCnoc includes whisky from both bourbon and sherry casks, whereas the 16-year-old includes whisky from only bourbon casks. Almost 25 percent of the anCnoc whisky is now aged for bottling as single malt with the hope that perhaps that allocation will increase with the rebuilding of several warehouses. During the harsh winter of 2010, two warehouses collapsed (losing only eighteen casks) and the new warehouses will soon be resurrected, literally, from the granite stones of the old ones.

The Noser Knows

The nose begins a bit prickly because of the higher alcohol content, which also allows this malt to take water very well. It has a creamy mouthfeel with back notes of peat. Water releases the tastes and aromas of candied apples, apple tart with cinnamon and sugar, pineapple upside-down cake, vanilla beans, and baked lemons. It has a warming, lingering finish with an aftertaste of toffee. Some of the vintage bottlings, with non-chill filtering, reflect additional notes of peat and sherry as well.

Macduff Distillery

➤ Pronounced as spelled

➤ Banff, Aberdeenshire AB45 3JT

➤ www.williamlawsons.com

➤ No visitors center

The Distillery Cat's Meow

The original owners built the Macduff distillery in the former orchard of Duff House, the home of the chieftain of the Macduff Clan.

Macduff is a young distillery, built in 1962 by a group of Glasgow businessmen from a design by William Delmé-Evans (see Tullibardine, Glenallachie, and Jura). The distillery was sold to William Lawson Distillers, and later to Bacardi (John Dewar), who bought the distillery and the Glen Deveron malt brand in 1992. Since Macduff's construction occurred in the last fifty years, everything about it continues to look gleaming and new, although the production process is rooted in five hundred years of distillation history and practices.

The Delmé-Evans Design

In 1990, the tun room and still room were renovated, and today they are a model of efficiency. The mash tun and nine washbacks, all made from stainless steel, allow a quick cooling of the distillate, an easier and more efficient cleaning of the equipment, and a more consistent product. Each process clearly leads to the next with all the equipment laid out in sequential and somewhat spacious rooms. Beneath all this modernity however, is an appreciation of the skill required of the stillman, who must move the distillate from two wash stills into three spirit stills, instead of working with the usual set of two pairs.

The stills, themselves, are particularly interesting because of the curious design of the lyne arms and the horizontal condensers similar to the ones at Glenallachie Distillery. At first glance, the stills seem to all be quite similar with short, thick necks and gentle shoulders that seem to puddle where they meet the floor. But the lyne arms that grow out of the necks of the stills and connect to the condensers bend into a lazy L shape, and then join the condensers, which lie on their sides horizontally, like reclining ladies.

Uniquely, Macduff Distillery maintained its own cooperage until the early 2000s for the repair and reconditioning of the sherry and American bourbon casks used for aging the spirit. But the special treasure at Macduff was the solitary cooper who worked in one of the very few distillery-operated cooperages. James Farquhar was in his eighties and worked a full work week doing hard labor in the cooperage. His father was a cooper who trained James who, in turn, trained several of the men who work in the large cooperages that supply the industry. The wrinkles on his face tended to catch the dust and dirt inherent to his job of repairing casks, and he was a bit hard of hearing; but he continued to work by himself. It is a compliment to James Farquhar and his skills that many of the coopers returned to Macduff specifically to visit him and to seek his advice. When Farquhar retired, the cooperage was retired as well.

The Noser Knows

Macduff is the name of the distillery, whereas Glen Deveron is the name of the single malt bottled by the distillery. Any *independent* bottling of the malt, however, carries the name Macduff.

The Noser Knows

The nose begins with a bit of spirit and dissolves to green apples and vanilla reminiscent of baked apples with crème anglaise. Flavors of brown sugar, toffee apples and cinnamon, red candy hearts fill the mouth with complementary tastes of pear and ginger crisp and a syrupy mouthfeel. The finish is gently warming with a smack of green peppercorns and possibly sweet bubble gum.

Royal Lochnagar Distillery

➤ Pronounced *ROY-al-LOCH (as in Bach)-nah-gar (as in car)*

➤ Balmoral, Craithie, Ballater, Aberdeenshire AB35 5TB

➤ www.malts.com

➤ Visitors center

Deeside, the valley formed by the River Dee, known for its salmon fishing, flows through fields of golden barley and winds its path along the base of the Grampian Mountains. It is a land that once produced illegal whisky transported over established drover's roads at night. Like much of Scotland, the area supported a significant number of illicit stills, and so it is surprising that only one of all the original distilleries, Royal Lochnagar, still exists today. The distillery nestles in the foothills above Balmoral Castle and although it has had a fairly long and uninterrupted history since its beginning in 1825, its early years were often difficult and violent.

Shortly after the Excise Act of 1823, James Robertson took out a license for his illicit still, which was promptly burned down by the unlicensed distillers. He built a new distillery near his home in Crathie and named it Lochnagar. But in 1841, it too suffered a devastating fire of mysterious and unknown origins.

The Royal Warrant

John Begg acquired a new distillery in 1845 whose whisky favorably impressed Queen Victoria and Prince Albert when they first arrived at Balmoral Castle in September 1848. Their approval of his whisky brought a Royal Warrant to supply the Queen's Household just a few days after their visit to Lochnagar. Begg's company remained under family ownership until the World War I. At that time, Distillers Company Limited (now Diageo) acquired the distillery, which it still retains today.

The Noser Knows

Royal Lochnagar distillery continues to supply the single malt to Balmoral Castle, particularly when the Royal Family visits on vacation. In 2012, the queen will celebrate her Diamond Jubilee to commemorate her coronation, and it may well be worthwhile watching this distillery's bottlings during the Jubilee year. Since this is the distillery that supplies the queen with her whisky in Scotland, one might expect a special bottling to honor its most famous customer.

Distilling Traditions from Fifty Years Ago

Although the distillery has been modernized and enlarged during the last century, much of Royal Lochnagar remains traditional, and much about the surrounding countryside survives unchanged.

Tenant farmers cultivate the surrounding farms, and the distillery retains a traditional manual operation without much automation. Lochnagar continues distilling as it was done fifty years ago, preserving the practices of another time and the heritage of the industry.

Distilling is not Formulaic

The mash tun reflects a marriage of old and new—the vessel itself is stainless steel, but it has an open top, allowing all the aromas to fill the tun room. The distillery uses only three wooden washbacks made of larch and on average uses a long fermentation. Some people at the distillery muse, with slight humor, that Lochnagar has two-and-a-half washbacks instead of three because one of them is half the size of the other two.

The stillroom houses two small, dumpy stills connected to worm tubs rather than condensers. The downward angle of the lyne arms, the onion-shape stills with short, thick necks, and the worm tubs appear to use a design that would produce a heavy, meaty body. The thick necks, however, encourage a cleansing copper contact, and this is intensified by using warm water to cool the worms. By raising the temperature of the condensing water, the vapor does not quickly condense into a liquid. Instead, the vapor remains in the worm longer and prolongs the copper contact and its purifying effect. As is so often the case in whisky distillation, the character of the final spirit depends not upon a rigid formula, but rather on a balance of all the distilling elements.

Royal Lochnagar bottles its whisky at 12 years old, a Distillers Edition, and a Select Reserve. Each year an evaluation panel arrives at the distillery to choose the best cask on the premises to commemorate Queen Victoria's visit in 1848. Its choice is bottled as Select Reserve in a very limited edition and is available at the distillery and in select markets (most often in the duty-free shops).

The Noser Knows

Royal Lochnagar is a small distillery, so it may take more searching to find a bottle. The single malt produces a nose of solvent and nail polish remover that moves toward fruit flavors. It is alternately malty sweet and sour, reminiscent of a sour cherry pie with a crumb topping. The Distillers Edition has undergone a finish of at least three months in muscat casks, and the most recent tasting notes from the distillery describe it as having "rich fresh fruit aromas, as in a village fruit shop."

What You Need to Know

➤ Deeside and Aberdeenshire define geographical regions to place the location of a distillery, rather than a specific style of whisky.

➤ Several of the distilleries on the eastern edge of Speyside borrow the delicate fruity character of their neighbors but always with their own definition. These can vary from the tropical fruits of Glenglassaugh, the orchard fruits of Macduff, the citrus fruits of anCnoc, or the dark fruits of an old Glencadam.

➤ The addition of smoky notes in Ardmore, or the absence of them in Glen Garioch, the definitive sherry in GlenDronach, the malty sweetness of Fettercairn and Royal Lochnagar, and the maritime notes in Glenglassaugh provide additional variations on the flavor profiles of the Eastern Highlands malts.

CHAPTER 12

The Western Highlands

> **In This Chapter**
>
> ➤ One area, two different malts
> ➤ Is there a coastal effect?

Only two distilleries fall into the Western Highlands area—Oban and Ben Nevis. A clear maritime and seaside aspect has always distinguished Oban malt, but sweet toffee and fruits seem to define the Ben Nevis malt. Both Oban and Fort William (the home of Ben Nevis Distillery) are towns that attract a large number of visitors, particularly in the summertime. But the towns are as dissimilar as their whiskies. Known as the gateway to the Isles, Oban's waterfront overlooks the Firth of Lorn and the island of Kerrera, whereas Fort William holds a reputation among hikers and climbers as the home of Ben Nevis, the highest mountain in Britain. Although this is a sample of just two distilleries from one region, the towns, the malts, and the distilleries are very different.

Ben Nevis Distillery

> ➤ Pronounced *ben-NEV (as in never)-iss*
> ➤ Lochy Bridge, Fort William PH33 6TJ
> ➤ www.bennevisdistillery.com
> ➤ Visitors center

Ben Nevis Distillery is the only surviving distillery in Fort William—one of the distilleries, Nevis, was dismantled and demolished, and the other, Glenlochy, had a checkered history of production and closings. Even more important than Ben Nevis's escape from the same fate of its sister distilleries was its surviving the management of an eccentric owner, Joseph Hobbs.

The Distillery Cat's Meow

When Donald McDonald released Long John's Dew of Ben Nevis in memory of his father, it was probably a blend of the two single malts produced at the McDonald distilleries—Nevis and Ben Nevis. Today it is a blended Scotch whisky composed of many malts and grain whisky.

Prior to Hobbs's ownership, John "Long John" McDonald licensed the Ben Nevis Distillery in 1825, which his son, Donald, acquired and operated. Later, he needed to build a new distillery nearby, which he called Nevis Distillery, in order to meet the growing demand for more production. The control of both distilleries stayed in the hands of the McDonald family until 1944, when Joseph Hobbs acquired ownership of both Ben Nevis and Nevis Distillery.

The Adventures and Misadventures of Joseph Hobbs

Local legend relates the story that Hobbs, a Canadian, turned around the same day he had bought the Nevis Distillery and sold it to the adjacent Glenlochy Distillery so that Glenlochy could expand its warehousing. Sometime between the two transactions, Hobbs had the wall and gates to Nevis carted up the road to Ben Nevis Distillery and installed them there.

Hobbs's escapades continued at Ben Nevis, where he had a grain still installed next to the pot stills so that he could distill all the spirit needed to produce a blend. Additionally, he blended all of the malt whiskies and the grain whiskies together as soon as they had been distilled, and then banged the blends into casks for maturing—a practice he termed blending at birth. Hobbs's blending at birth created a product that had varied results and proved to be inconsistent.

The Nikka Era

Nikka Whisky Distilling Company, a Japanese firm, later bought Ben Nevis in 1989 and ensured the future of the distillery. The association between the Nikka family and Scotland was a strong one and a long one. The chairman and founder of the Nikka Distilling Company had studied at Glasgow University and had worked in Scotland's distilleries during the 1920s. When he returned to Japan, he brought a Scottish wife, Rita Cowan.

Nikka invested extensively in refurbishing the distillery, including removing the concrete washbacks installed by Hobbs and building a visitors center to open the distillery to the public. As the result of renovations carried out by Hobbs and Nikka, the tun room now uses six stainless steel washbacks—four refurbished from the dismantled Glenugie Distillery, and two purpose-built for Ben Nevis.

The Distillery Cat's Meow

Ben Nevis Distillery has five dunnage warehouses and one racked warehouse, which did not always mature whisky. Warehouse #2 is particularly huge, and before it was filled with maturing spirit, it served as the movie set for several films, including *Rob Roy*, *Braveheart*, and *Local Hero*. The present distillery manager, Colin Ross, who then worked at Tormore Distillery, remembers that it had to cease shipments of Tormore spirit to Ben Nevis for aging until the film shooting had finished.

The copper stills remain the heart of the distillery and date to the Hobbs era. Both stills have a slight downward angle to the lyne arm with short, thick necks and sharply angled shoulders, allowing some heavier and fuller flavors to develop in the still. While allowing little reflux action, the still design creates a heavier full-bodied spirit and removes the sulfur notes because of the large surface areas of copper.

The Bottlings

The Nikka Company bottles a 10-year-old at the heart of its core range. But it also released limited editions of a single-cask 25-year-old in 2010 with non-chill filtering and natural color, and a 13-year-old finished in port wood.

A Ben Nevis Traditional with NAS was released in time for the holiday season in December 2011. It is traditional in the sense that this bottling is similar to the style of malt that Long John McDonald would have produced in the nineteenth century. McDonald had his own peats (peat bogs) on the slopes of Ben Nevis Mountain, which he most likely used to malt his barley. Consequently, the Ben Nevis Traditional will follow this practice and will heavily peat its malt, unlike the 10-year-old, which is distilled from unpeated malt.

The Noser Knows

The nose on the Ben Nevis malt begins delicately with aromas of caramel, toffee, and licorice, and opens up over time. It has a medium body with a chewy mouthfeel and includes flavors of baked apples and pears with a hint of spice and salt. It finishes slightly dry with mouth-filling tastes that stay on the palate.

Oban Distillery

➤ Pronounced as spelled

➤ Oban, Argyllshire PA34 5NH

➤ www.malts.com

➤ Visitors center

It is possible to stand within half a block of this distillery and not be able to locate it. Oban distillery, like Pulteney and Tobermory, is a town distillery built in a fishing port and as such was very much a part of the commercial fabric of the harbor. Consequently, the distillery sits a few yards off the crowded main street opposite the north pier on Stafford Street, tucked among all the other buildings concentrated along the teeming harbor.

John and Hugh Stevenson, two brothers, built both the town and the distillery in 1794, making it understandable how both the distillery and town would grow together, eventually encompassing each other. Both brothers were quite prosperous, with John working as a farmer, architect, and builder, while Hugh managed the quarries and whisky distilleries.

The Mesolithic Connection

Eventually J. Walter Higgin bought the distillery in 1883 and began extensive rebuilding and expansion. During this refurbishment, which required excavations into the stone cliffs rising immediately behind the distillery, diggers uncovered caves used by people during the Mesolithic Era. The bones and implements were taken to Edinburgh's National Museum of Antiquities and the caves were sealed.

The distillery changed hands only twice after Higgin's ownership and only experienced relatively short periods of closing. Although it has experienced some modernization, including conversion of the old malt barn into a visitors center, Oban remains a fairly traditional distillery, ringed by the steep rock face that backs it.

The buildings are constructed of nineteenth-century stone punctuated by cliffs on one side and tall wooden gates that open onto the street on the other side. The distillery still uses four wooden washbacks and only one pair of similarly designed stills. Both the wash and spirit stills have sharply nipped lantern-glass shapes and tall, thick necks that allow more reflux and copper contact. However, Oban Distillery uses worm tubs rather than condensers, which limits any additional contact between the spirit and the copper. All of the spirit matures in used bourbon casks with some aged on-site. In addition to being bottled at 14 years old, a limited amount of Oban single malt has been finished in Montilla Fino sherry wood and released as part of the Distillers Edition. Diageo also has released a Managers' Choice expression as well as limited editions and distillery exclusives.

The Noser Knows

The Oban single malt begins with aromas of heather and a delicate iodine nose; water seems to introduce some peat and intensify the iodine and smoke. The iodine continues into the mouth complemented by very subtle fruit and a sweet/salt combination of rich caramels and brine. Lingering flavors of thick toffee define the soft, dry, and warming finish. The finish of the Fino in the Distillers Edition interjects the complexity of sherry to create a pleasant mixture of nicely balanced flavors.

What You Need to Know

➤ All of Oban Distillery's production is reserved for bottling as a single malt.

➤ The west coast location lends a maritime character to Oban.

➤ The Ben Nevis character, however, tends more toward notes of orchard fruits and toffee.

The Speyside Distilleries

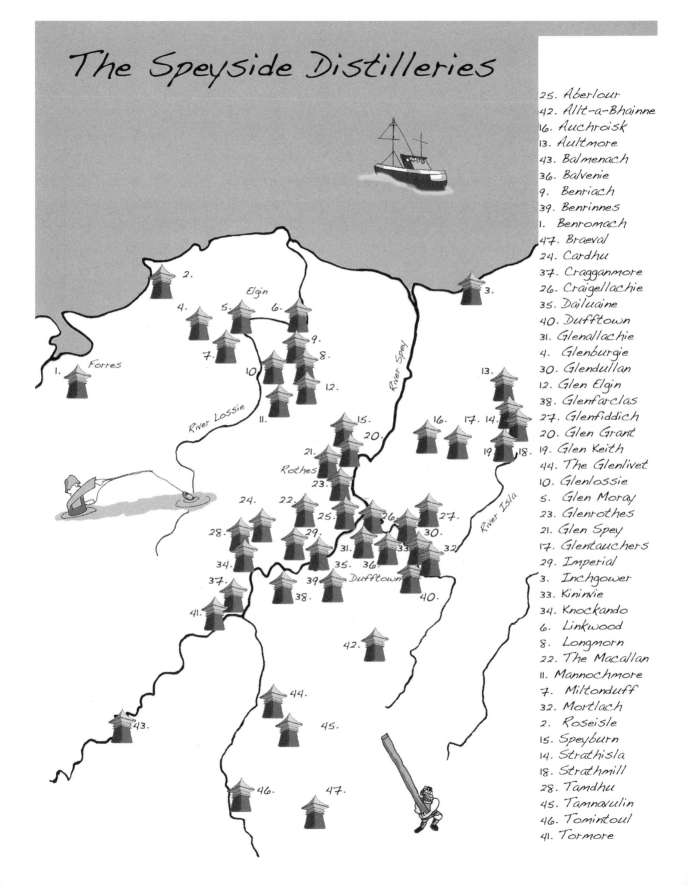

25. Aberlour
42. Allt-a-Bhainne
16. Auchroisk
13. Aultmore
43. Balmenach
36. Balvenie
9. Benriach
39. Benrinnes
1. Benromach
47. Braeval
24. Cardhu
37. Cragganmore
26. Craigellachie
35. Dailuaine
40. Dufftown
31. Glenallachie
4. Glenburgie
30. Glendullan
12. Glen Elgin
38. Glenfarclas
27. Glenfiddich
20. Glen Grant
19. Glen Keith
44. The Glenlivet
10. Glenlossie
5. Glen Moray
23. Glenrothes
21. Glen Spey
17. Glentauchers
29. Imperial
3. Inchgower
33. Kininvie
34. Knockando
6. Linkwood
8. Longmorn
22. The Macallan
11. Mannochmore
7. Miltonduff
32. Mortlach
2. Roseisle
15. Speyburn
14. Strathisla
18. Strathmill
28. Tamdhu
45. Tamnavulin
46. Tomintoul
41. Tormore

CHAPTER 13

 # Speyside

> ## In This Chapter
>
> ➤ What is the Speyside style?
>
> ➤ Speyside with sherry
>
> ➤ The light, clean Speyside
>
> ➤ Speyside with peat (or no peat)

Almost half the operating distilleries sit in the Speyside region in the Highlands, just south of the Moray Firth. Much like the overall Highlands region, Speyside supported the farm industry of distilling, albeit the distillation was illegal. Because the stills were small, the land was rugged, and the magistrates were sympathetic to the distillers, it was easy to hide and transport the stills as well as evade the prosecutors.

In direct contrast to the Lowlands distillers, those in Speyside operated on a small scale, running their stills slowly and developing a style that suited their own or a local preference. When the 1823 Excise Act made it feasible and practical to operate stills legally, a ready market existed for what had become known as the Speyside or Glenlivet style. Visitors to Scotland, fueled by Sir Walter Scott's stories of Scotland and Royal visits to Deeside, found the elegant fruity style of Speyside to be more palatable than the assertive and robust Campbeltown spirit. The new railways that could now provide a ready supply of raw materials and transportation to southern markets coincided with the growing demand for Speyside whisky. Inevitably, the two events fostered a building boom of distilleries along the Spey River Valley.

The period of time between 1860 and 1885 saw a tremendous growth in the number of distilleries as blenders sought to secure malts for their blends by building their own malt distilleries. Much of the building occurred in the Speyside area because the elegant and fruity style of a Speyside or Glenlivet malt had become the fashionable drink.

The whisky industry, especially in Speyside, experienced the resurgence of construction, mergers and acquisitions, and very high production, which reached a fevered pitch in the 1890s. These boom years ended abruptly in 1898 with the Pattison Crash, an event I frequently reference in this section because it forced the closure of many Speyside distilleries.

Robert and Walter Pattison were whisky blenders who built a very large business that included building large offices and homes for themselves, embarking on lavish and expensive advertising campaigns, acquiring shares in distilleries, and, of course, placing large orders with distilleries for their spirit. Distilleries ran at high production rates and extended credit to the Pattisons for the large orders they placed. The Pattisons, however, had built their empire on borrowed money, and eventually the banks refused credit to them. Very quickly, the failure of the Pattisons brought down other people in the industry. Distilleries were left with unpaid bills, and warehouses were full of spirit they couldn't sell. Many of the newly built distilleries managed to operate for a year or to struggle into the twentieth century, but most of them closed. The new century began with a bleak outlook for many of the Speyside distilleries.

The whisky industry did not experience a revival until after World War II, when many distilleries operated at full capacity to meet the growing demand from a prosperous postwar market. The whisky industry, however, seems to suffer from boom and bust cycles, and once again Speyside suffered the closure of a significant number of distilleries when the production of whisky outstripped demand in the 1980s.

The demand is once again high for both Scotch whisky and single malts. Distilleries are once again undergoing expansion and refurbishment and are producing multiple expressions and variations on the traditional Speyside character.

Traditionally, people have associated a delicate fruit with the Speyside style and have often described it as having a pear-drop flavor and aroma, similar to the yellow Lifesaver in the assorted pack. Although an elegant fruit can define the Speyside style, the area produces many other variations—some distilleries like Macallan, Glenrothes, and Aberlour have complemented the fruit with sherry and more robust flavors; others like Benromach introduce some peat; even others like Glen Grant use purifiers to create a light, clean spirit. Today, many distilleries create different expressions by experimenting with different levels of peat and different types of casks to vary the family character of their own malt.

Aberlour Distillery

> ➤ Pronounced *ab-ba-LOAU-ER (rhymes with power)*
> ➤ Aberlour, Banffshire AB38 9PJ

➤ www.aberlour.com

➤ Visitors center

Poor health prevented James Fleming from farming with his family, so he made his way to Aberlour for work and opportunity. Fleming began work as a grain merchant, and later he became a banker. He soon added distilling to his set of skills, when he leased and operated Dailuaine Distillery. Shortly thereafter, he considered the possibility of building his own distillery, and the site he had in mind boasted a reliable water supply and ready access to the railway.

The Distillery Cat's Meow

Aberlour Distillery is located near St. Drostan's Well, named for the nephew of St. Columba, a Christian missionary. He established himself in the area and used the well to baptize newly converted followers. Previous to St. Drostan's arrival, the area had supported and served a druid community that held a reverence for oak trees and water. To commemorate the distillery's connection to its ancient heritage, each bottle of Aberlour has an oak tree on the label.

The Businessman and Philanthropist

Fleming had experience in operating Dailuaine, knowledge about barley, a good water source, and a transportation system near at hand. It was a good business opportunity, and in 1879 he built Aberlour. But he sold Aberlour Distillery in 1892 and died, without children, in 1895. He enjoyed a successful life as a businessman and distiller, and through his philanthropy he reinvested his money in the town and people of Aberlour.

The Distillery Cat's Meow

James Fleming commissioned and financed the building of the Penny Bridge that spans the River Spey in Aberlour. Prior to the building of the bridge, people had to use a ferry to cross from one side to the other. The story of a child who drowned when he fell from the ferry into the river distressed Fleming and motivated him to build the bridge.

The distillery, however, endured an explosion and fire in 1898, Pattison's Crash, two wars, rising excise taxes, and a liquidation, but it managed to persevere until S. Campbell & Sons acquired it in the mid-1940s. Campbell's ownership provided stability and positioned the distillery for growth in the whisky world during the next two to three decades. In 1974, the distillery came under the umbrella of Pernod Ricard (Chivas), but in 2001 there was another adjustment when Pernod Ricard acquired Seagram's Distilleries and Aberlour came into Chivas Brothers portfolio.

Developing a Flavor Profile

During its existence, spanning more than a century, Aberlour whisky has gained a reputation as a high-quality Speyside whisky with its own distinctive flavor profile. The tall, thick onion-shape stills at Aberlour help to develop the full body of the spirit and to remove sulfur notes because of the large areas of copper exposed to the spirit. The new-make spirit ages in both bourbon and sherry casks, and then whiskies from both types of casks are married before bottling. The bourbon has the effect of adding vanilla and red apple flavors, and the sherry contributes its distinctive dark fruit and spice flavors.

The distillery offers bottlings of Aberlour at ten, twelve, and sixteen years. Each bottling has flavors and aromas that become more intense or more prominent depending upon the years spent in the casks. They have also released Aberlour A'bunadh (from the Gaelic meaning "of the origin"), which recreates a whisky the founder, James Fleming, would have distilled. It is bottled at cask strength, with non-chill filtering, and has matured solely in oloroso sherry casks, much as it would have done in the nineteenth century.

The Noser Knows

Aberlour single malt is the perfect Thanksgiving whisky with aromas and flavors that speak to autumn, fallen leaves, and apple cider. The nose of the matured Aberlour has a distinctive sweetness that the distillery people describe as minty-toffee. This is enhanced by a full-bodied sweet-spice balance. It has the flavors of ripened orchard fruits, vanilla ice cream, and pumpkin pie spices. It is a satisfying malt that nicely complements the traditional desserts that follow the Thanksgiving turkey.

Allt-a-Bhainne Distillery

➤ Pronounced *ALT-a-bane*

➤ Glenrinnes, Banffshire AB55 4DI

➤ No website

➤ No visitors center

Because of the relative youth of Allt-a-Bhainne Distillery, many people have the expectation that this distillery will be a stainless steel scion to modernity. At first its twentieth-century architecture seems discordant with the surrounding moors that have witnessed much of Scotland's history. But to dismiss Allt-a-Bhainne out of hand because of impression and expectations would be to miss a place that reflects both modernity and contemporary styling.

The distillery boasts decorative vents on the roofs of the buildings and open ceilings and wood rafters inside. The design of large windows in the distillery continues onto the bridge connecting the production side with the administrative side of the distillery.

A Modern Distillery for the 1970s

Seagram built Allt-a-Bhainne in 1975 and much like its sister distillery Braeval, it was operated to supply a single malt for the company's blends. Pernod Ricard (Chivas) bought the distillery in 2001 and continues to operate it with the same objectives. All of the distillery operations sprawl across large open rooms with the stainless steel mash tun in the center so that a single person can operate the entire distillery. Allt-a-Bhainne uses unpeated malt but occasionally does some peated distillations. The mash tun is fitted with an older rake system for stirring the mash before the wort is transferred into the stainless steel washbacks for a short fermentation of forty-eight hours.

The two pairs of traditional copper stills are very much a study in contrasts. The two wash stills have an onion-shape design with short, thick necks providing little reflux but more copper contact. The spirit stills, however, seem to soar alongside their dumpy sisters. They have tall, thin necks above small and skinny boil balls that promote the reflux action that doesn't occur in the wash stills. No warehouses are located on this site, and all the new-make spirit is tanked to Keith for casking and maturing.

Always a Bridesmaid, Never a Bride

The Allt-a-Bhainne spirit is somewhat unremarkable and clearly meant for blending and to have a role in adding distinction to a blended Scotch whisky. It has never had a proprietary bottling by the distillery, and independent bottlers have offered only a few expressions.

But this unobtrusive blending malt could possibly have its day in the sun of the collectors' world. In the 1960s and 70s, several distilleries produced blending malts that also took on an unassuming secondary role and were not bottled as single malts. Today, these malts, like Ladyburn, Glen Flagler, and Kinclaith, are sought for their rarity rather than their quality.

The Noser Knows

Allt-a-Bhainne has a nose reminiscent of cut lawns in July heat with background notes of new wood. Much about this malt is simple and uncomplicated with barely ripen fruits and herbs on the palate. It has a light and delicate finish. Its long-term future value (outside of the blending halls) may exist for collectors because of its rarity.

Auchroisk Distillery

➤ Pronounced *ar-THRUSK*

➤ Mulben, Morayshire AB55 6XS

➤ No website

➤ No visitors center

Justerini & Brooks (J&B) planned to build a new distillery in eastern Speyside in order to provide an additional malt for its blends. Initially, it identified a pure and reliable water source well known to the local people as Dorie's Well. Before committing to the distillery, it tanked water from Dorie's Well to Glen Spey Distillery in order to make trial distillation runs.

A Change in Plans

In 1971, construction of the distillery began but in 1972, Watney Mann Ltd., a brewing company, bought International Distillers and Vintners, the umbrella company for J&B, and then quickly sold it to Grand Metropolitan a few months later. When Auchroisk finally began production in 1974, it was under the ownership of Grand Metropolitan.

During its early years, the owners used most of the whisky for blending, but some was set aside for deluxe and premium blends. In 1986, the owners released a 12-year-old single malt named Singleton that had aged in bourbon casks for ten years and then matured in sherry casks for its final two years. Many people believe that Grand Metropolitan decided to name the malt whisky Singleton because the name of the distillery was too difficult to pronounce, but the Singleton name was also meant to convey that it was viewed as the single best malt in its class. Later, it dropped the name Singleton and renamed its single malt Auchroisk.

In 1997, Grand Metropolitan merged with Guinness to become Diageo, which revived the Singleton name to label three expressions of different single malt whiskies released in different geographical markets—Singleton Glen Ord (Asia), Glendullan (U.S.), and Dufftown (Europe).

A Distillery for the Late Twentieth Century

The Auchroisk Distillery was one of the new distilleries built during the 1970s and as such has a logical floor plan that flows from one process to the next. In keeping with the modernity of the distillery, the owners installed a stainless steel mash tun and stainless steel washbacks. Four pairs of large copper stills with lantern-glass shapes and tall, thick necks occupy a large and airy stillhouse.

The Distillery Cat's Meow

The Auchroisk Distillery site also has the capability to produce gin as part of a plan to provide continuity if other sources of gin production would stop. Although gin is not presently made at Auchroisk, successful trial runs have been carried out within the last decade.

The Noser Knows

The original bottling of Auchroisk malt whisky under the name of Singleton was made from lightly peated malt, and aged in both bourbon and sherry casks. The result was a medium-bodied, smooth whisky with fruit and sweet flavors and a hint of smoke. Today, the Auchroisk Distillery produces a nutty-style whisky using a cloudy wort, although it has the capability to also produce a grassy style by changing the production process, depending upon the malt it requires for blending. Since Diageo directs all its production into blends, it releases no single malt bottling except for two previous expressions, one in the Flora and Fauna series and one in the Rare Malts series, and a recent one in the Managers' Choice.

The Auchoroisk Distillery occupies a large site, including a filling store for casking not only Auchroisk new-make spirit, but also new-make spirit tanked from other distilleries. The on-site warehouses at Auchroisk also mature spirit from a range of distilleries. Additionally, the complex is used as a disgorging facility, where mature single malt whiskies are married together for use in the creation of blended Scotch whiskies.

The Noser Knows

The original bottling of Auchroisk malt whisky under the name of Singleton was made from lightly peated malt, and aged in both bourbon and sherry casks. The result was a medium–bodied, smooth whisky with fruit and sweet flavors and a hint of smoke. Today, the Auchroisk Distillery produces a nutty-style whisky using a cloudy wort, although it has the capability to also produce a grassy style by changing the production process, depending upon the malt it requires for blending. Since Diageo directs all its production into blends, it releases no single malt bottling except for two previous expressions, one in the Flora and Fauna series and one in the Rare Malts series, and a recent one in the Managers' Choice.

Aultmore Distillery

> ➤ Pronounced *ALT(rhymes with halt)-more*

> ➤ Keith, Banffshire AB55 6QY

> ➤ No website

> ➤ No visitors center

Aultmore, a little village northwest of Keith, is nothing more than a scattering of houses. At first glance, this nineteenth-century distillery appears to be new because the owners modernized it in the 1970s. The recent demolition of some of its nineteenth-century dunnage warehouses has further blurred its ties to another century.

Something Old, Something New

Little of the distillery's history, however, survives alongside its modern reconstruction, but it still pulls its water from the Burn of Auchinderran, about a mile away, as it has for over a century. Once inside the distillery, some of the older machinery still provide an aesthetic pleasure, but recent renovations have unraveled the tenuous hold this distillery has on its history. The six original wooden washbacks made of larch remain in place, but a new stainless steel mash tun replaced the older cast iron one with its copper-and-brass cover. And while the nineteenth-century steam engine, which provided much of the power for the distillery, has not been used since 1969, it still occupies a pride of place.

The Distillery Cat's Meow

At Aultmore Distillery, the industry ran some of the first trials for drying the grains left at the end of mashing and distilling for use as animal feed, a practice now employed by virtually all distilleries.

The stillroom houses four stills with virtually no difference between the wash and spirit stills. Their thick necks directly join the gently sloped shoulders of the stills in a classic onion-shape. The spirit rises to a straight lyne pipe that has no upward or downward angle leading to the condensers. There are no boil balls to encourage redistillation of heavy flavors or elongated necks designed to capture only the lightest vapors. This is a gentle distillation process with heavy copper contact. Former owners released a 12-year-old in the Flora and Fauna range and a 21-year-old in the Rare Malts series. More recently, Bacardi (Dewar's), its present owner, offered a 12-year-old bottling. The final product is a fruity, dry single malt—the end result of marrying whisky that has been aged in a variety of used bourbon, sherry, and plain oak casks.

The Noser Knows

The mature Aultmore has a beginning sweetness and refreshing fruit flavors that develop with time, but flatten with a bit of water. The fruit has tones of lemon, slight citrus notes, and hard candy sweetness—the classic pear drop (i.e., yellow Lifesaver) taste. The fresh finish is nutty and dry.

Balmenach Distillery

➤ Pronounced *bal-MEN-ick*

➤ Cromdale, Moray PH26 3PF

➤ www.inverhouse.com

➤ No visitors center

Balmenach is the Lazarus of the whisky industry. This distillery, set in the Cromdale Hills, was owned by United Distillers (now Diageo), who had closed it in 1993. Sometime after this closure, the decision was made to totally dismantle the distillery. Until that could take place, all the stocks were moved out of the warehouses and the distillery was considered a "spare" site—if parts were needed at any other distillery, they would cannibalize Balmenach.

A White Knight to the Rescue

Fortunately, Inver House moved to buy Balmenach, and United Distillers replaced the parts that were removed from the site before the sale was completed in December 1997. Production began in March 1998, and the warehouses once again stored new-make Balmenach spirit for maturation.

James McGregor established Balmenach distillery in 1824 on a site that supported an illicit still. The family made its money in Malaysia, but at the time of World War I the rubber market in Malaysia collapsed and the family lost many of its investments. It was forced to sell the distillery in 1920, and shortly afterward it was sold to Scottish Malt Distillers (now Diageo). Eventually, the owners decided to demolish Balmenach, but Inver House intervened to rescue it and restart production.

The Revival of a Faded Lady

The distillery occupied a remote location at one time, and today the view of the Cromdale Hills is much as it would have been in the early nineteenth century. Although it is now quite accessible, it continues to sit well off the road but tucked into the Cromdale foothills.

While the original water wheel and the floor maltings no longer exist, much about Balmenach remains quite traditional. The cast iron mash tun dates back to 1968, and six Oregon pine washbacks are used for fermentation. Balmenach is somewhat unique in that it still uses worm tubs rather than condensers and also employs an unusual design for its stills.

If some stills resemble thick-waisted dowagers, the ones at Balmenach resemble gawky debutantes. The spirit stills, in particular, have lyne pipes angled downward with tall, thin necks that slide into sharply defined boil balls. The severely nipped waists below the boil balls then flare out into slim shoulders. The distillation here is a fine balance of push and pull—the boil balls and tall heads encourage the development of light compounds, and the worm tubs and downturned lyne arms promote the creation of heavier elements. The resulting new spirit has a full but elegant body, which then matures in bourbon barrels and some refill sherry casks.

The Distillery Cat's Meow

An engraved collar commemorating Queen Elizabeth's Silver Jubilee in 1977 decorates one of the wash stills at Balmenach Distillery. Almost thirty-five years ago, the owners commissioned the still with the attached memorial, and displayed it in Hyde Park as part of the Jubilee celebration. Afterward, they installed the still at Balmenach, but within a short period of time the collar disappeared into an old storage closet. Some observant and resourceful employees found the discarded collar, shined it up so that the lettering was once again legible, and returned it to its pride of place in time for the Queen's celebration of her Golden Jubilee in 2002. Inver House matched the restoration of the engraved collar with the release of a limited edition bottling of Balmenach 25-year-old.

Although it is a pleasure to see the grand space of the warehouses once again filling with casks of Balmenach spirit, these warehouses were empty when the sale between United Distillers and Inver House occurred. As a result, the owners offer no distillery bottlings, and the only existing expressions include a previous Flora and Fauna bottling and any other bottlings available in the listings from independent bottlers.

The Noser Knows

Balmenach has the color of orange pekoe tea and floral aromas of delicate lavender. Sherry with some wood appears in the mouth with flavors of summer fruits—raspberries and rhubarb with vanilla cream and anisette. It has a full, rounded body with an elegant warm finish. Whisky enthusiasts should look forward to the reappearance of this single malt as stocks in Balmenach's warehouses grow and mature.

Balvenie Distillery

➤ Pronounced *bal (rhymes wih Val)-VEN (rhymes with ten)-ee*

➤ Dufftown, Morayshire AB55 4BB

➤ www.thebalvenie.com

➤ Visitors center

William Grant established the Balvenie Distillery in 1882 and placed it next to the Glenfiddich Distillery that he had built six years previously. The farm adjacent to Glenfiddich became available for sale, and Grant secured the land and water rights with profits from Glenfiddich. In buying the farm and building a second distillery, Grant was able, geographically, to protect his investment at Glenfiddich and also to provide flexibility by producing an additional whisky not committed to blenders. As he did at Glenfiddich, Grant bought used equipment for his new distillery, but this time he bought the old stills from the Lagavulin and Glen Albyn Distilleries.

The Balvenie Rose

In addition to building his distillery, Grant rented the New Balvenie Castle, a mansion house on the property. The name of the house refers to the original Balvenie Castle with its romantic history dating to the thirteenth century. But the romanticism associated with its namesake did not carry over to the New Balvenie Castle, and the house suffered a bit of an ignominious end.

The Distillery Cat's Meow

In the fifteenth century, Margaret Douglas married John Stewart, Earl of Atholl, a kinsman of King James II. James granted Balvenie Castle to the Stewarts for the annual payment of one red rose. William Grant then memorialized the agreement by placing a drawing of a rose on the label of Balvenie whisky.

The Grants used the house for its distillery maltings and stored the grain on the top floor, then dropped it into big steeping tubs on the second floor, and finally spread it out on the ground floor to dry before putting the whole batch into the kiln. The old house suffered these indignities until a new malting barn, built with stones from the first and second floors of the house, replaced it in the 1920s. The ground floor of New Balvenie Castle became Warehouse 24, currently still in use.

Rugged Individualists

Today, Balvenie Distillery is one of the few distilleries that continue to malt its own barley, although the old malting barn can provide only a portion of the malted barley that the whisky distillation at Balvenie demands. But practice dictated that Balvenie whisky was moderately smoky, and the tradition endures at the distillery site today.

The respect for tradition continues to live at the William Grant distilleries, where both coopers and a coppersmith are employed to repair the casks and maintain the copper stills. The stills at Balvenie vary in size but not in shape, which look as if the artist Modigliani designed all of them. They have a standard long neck with a boil ball rising (called a Balvenie ball) above rounded shoulders, but then the entire shape is elongated as if a distillery giant held each end of the still and stretched it out into an elongated variation of a common shape.

The resulting whisky includes several expressions, most of which reflect their aging in sherry casks. The Balvenie Double Wood, similar to the former Balvenie Classic in the flat flagon-shaped bottle, is aged for eleven years in bourbon, and then aged one last year in oloroso sherry casks, which impart a smooth sweetness to the whisky. A second 12-year-old expression is aged in three different types of casks and then bottled in numbered batches. The Single Barrel Balvenie is bottled at 15 years old from a single oak cask chosen by the master blender. The 21-year-old is finished in port pipes, and the 30- and 40-year-olds offer the traditional marriage of different American oak and sherry casks. The Balvenie expressions also include a range of limited editions that include different finishes, different vintage years, and single cask bottlings of rare and old ages.

The Noser Knows

The classic Balvenie character is a combination of luscious berry fruits in syrup enhanced with its distinctive sherry notes. Rich, sweet honey, vanilla, and a touch of allspice completes the rich and full flavors of the mature whisky.

BenRiach Distillery

➤ Pronounced *ben-REE-ick*

➤ by Elgin, Morayshire IV30 8SJ

➤ www.benriachdistillery.co.uk

➤ Visitors by appointment

➤ +44-1343-862 888

This is a traditional distillery, almost old-fashioned, and its well-trimmed hedges defined by roses add to the quiet charm of the place. The time of its completion in 1898, however, could not have been worse because of the failure of Pattison, Elder & Co. a few months after the distillery opened. The demise of Pattison, one of the largest purchasers of whisky, set off a chain reaction that closed many distilleries and caused the failure of companies within the whisky industry. BenRiach did not escape the ripple effect of the Pattison Crash and closed only two years after beginning operations—it remained silent until Glenlivet Distillers Ltd. reopened it in 1965. The distillery operated for more than thirty-five years before its owners, Pernod Ricard (Chivas) closed it in 2002. In more than a century of its existence, the distillery's owners had allowed it to fulfill its purpose for only a third of that time.

The Noser Knows

Seagram offered the only proprietary bottling of BenRiach. In 1994, it released BenRiach 10-year-old as part of its Heritage Collection but limited the bottling of BenRiach to only a few hundred cases each year. Today, the proprietary bottling is difficult to find because it was not only limited, but also short-lived.

Snow White Meets Her Prince

But in 2004, the BenRiach Distillery Co. Ltd., a consortium of South African investors led by Billy Walker who has had more than thirty years' experience in the whisky industry, bought the distillery and renewed its purpose. Within six months, Walker had restarted distillation operations, bottled three different ages of the traditional BenRiach malt whisky, and released a 10-year-old peated version. The peated expression arrived as a bit of a surprise because BenRiach single malt usually reflects a traditional fruity Speyside character. Its explanation lies in its history.

BenRiach Distillery did its own floor maltings on-site until 1998, and the pagoda-shaped chimneys were functional, not merely atmospheric. In 1972, it began producing heavily peated malt for use in blends. Because it was expensive to transport peated malt from Islay, producing it at BenRiach meant a savings in cost and labor. Although the malting floor operated continually, it provided only 4 percent of the required malt, and its operation became no longer viable. The owners made the decision to close the floor maltings in 1998, but stocks of the peated BenRiach still rested in the warehouses.

The stills, where part of the traditional BenRiach character develops, stand the same as they have always stood and are defined by two words—long and thick. The BenRiach stills have elongated onion-shape bottoms, long, thick necks, and long, thick lay pipes. These thick shapes would indicate that there are few obstacles to heavy and robust flavors rising to the lay pipe with little reflux action occurring, but the long distances produced by a drawn-out base and neck allow only the lighter of these elements to move into the condenser. Furthermore, the long and uninterrupted surface of the still design provides large surface areas that increase the copper and spirit contact and its resulting purifying effect.

Finishing School, Latin Smoke, and Age

Presently, the owner's bottlings are non-chill filtered and include a core range of 12-, 16-, and 20-year-old expressions of the old stock of traditional BenRiach single malt. It offers limited bottlings of peated BenRiach malts at different ages all distinguished by a Latin name (e.g., Curiositas, Authenticus, and the Fumoso range). The range also includes editions of BenRiach at older ages and versions with wood finishes, including Madeira, dark rum, tawny port, claret, Burgundy, Rioja, and sherry.

With an eye to the future, Walker pays careful attention to his wood policy and casks his new-make spirit in predominantly first fill bourbon casks and uses sherry casks for re-racking mature whisky. Warehousemen also fill casks with new-make spirit at full strength rather than reducing it to the

The Noser Knows

The traditional BenRiach has a clean sweetness with typical Speyside fruit and floral notes that begin on the nose. These notes follow through into the mouth with tastes of ripe orchard fruits and notes of spice reminiscent of tarte tatin and whipped cream sweetened with vanilla bean and powdered sugar. The flavors are elegant, rounded, and balanced. It has a medium body with a satisfying finish. The peated version delivers full peat-reek at about 35 ppm. Interestingly Stewart Buchanan, the distillery manager, produces a short run of about 25,000 liters (6,504 gallons) of triple-distilled BenRiach at the end of each year, continuing a practice that Chivas began, so that it could produce additional malts for its blends.

standard 63.5 percent. Previous owners had tanked the new-make spirit to other regions for aging, but Walker ages his casks on-site in dunnage warehouses.

Benrinnes Distillery

➤ Pronounced *ben-RIN(rhymes with tin)-ess*

➤ No website

➤ No visitors center

Benrinnes Distillery is a workhorse distillery—it has no visitors center and quietly goes about its business of making spirit that is reserved for blending. It has suffered a flood, a fire, recession, depression, and rebuilding; still it soldiers on, making spirit.

Like many other distilleries, Benrinnes suffered from the recession in the whisky industry at the end of the 1800s, and it experienced several owners over the next half century. By the 1950s it needed significant refurbishment, which resulted in an efficient plant with little connection to its original nineteenth-century character. Its production methods, however, continued steadily during its uneven history, and its unusual variation on triple distillation continued unchanged until the first decade of the twenty-first century.

The Noser Knows

Although Benrinnes had previously employed a variation on triple distillation, it was not the same as the two-and-a-half distillations done at Springbank Distillery. The Benrinnes variation is also different from the variation done at Mortlach Distillery. All three distilleries triple distill a portion of their spirit but in different sequences and amounts. It is similar to three musicians all playing the same fiddle but producing different music.

A Variation on the Distillation Theme

Previously, the wash still distilled the wash and produced low wines, but only a third of the spirit, measuring at about 50 percent alcohol, moved on for distillation in the spirit still. The remaining two-thirds of the spirit, at lower alcohol strength, underwent distillation in a third, intermediate still. Following the intermediate distillation, the resulting spirit was once again divided into the higher-strength distillate, which moved on to the spirit still, while the lower strength returned to the intermediate still. This variation on triple distillation would suggest a high-strength spirit with a light character, but instead, the new-make style is full-bodied, meaty, and sulfury. The distillation at Benrinnes speaks to the fact that whisky making is not formulaic and reflects the knowledge and skill of the distiller.

The use of worm tubs, the low temperature of the cooling water, and the elimination of air rests when cleaning the stills result in little copper contact and more sulfur. Additionally, the puddled onion shape of both the wash and spirit stills creates a heavy and full body. The recent and increased understanding of flavor development during the whisky-making process has allowed distillers "to play different tunes on the same instrument."

During the first decade of the twenty-first century, Benrinnes Distillery abandoned this variation on triple distillation and adopted a straightforward double distillation. The need for additional new-make spirit with a light sulfur character motivated the return to double distillation at Benrinnes. The worm tubs remain in use, the cooling water remains the same, and the shape of the still remains unchanged. But the number of distillations and the addition of air rests when cleaning the stills now produces one more variation on the Benrinnes theme.

The Noser Knows

The only proprietary bottlings of Benrinnes appeared in the Flora and Fauna, the Rare Malts and The Managers' Choice series. These expressions had the full-bodied profile so characteristic of this distillery. The nose includes aromas of molasses, brown sugar, lemon zest, and satsumas. Its maturation in sherry casks produced dried fruit flavors, sherry, honey, Cointreau, and tarte tatin with vanilla ice cream. The malt is creamy and rich with a warm and briefly lingering finish. In ten to fifteen years it will be interesting to taste the matured whisky from the Benrinnes stills that resulted when it varied the distillation process.

Benromach Distillery

> ➤ Pronounced *ben-ROW-mack*

> ➤ Forres, Morayshire IV36 3EB

> ➤ www.benromach.com

> ➤ Visitors center

If ever there were a Cinderella story with a fairy godmother, this is it (complete with a homeless cat). United Distillers not only closed Benromach Distillery, but also dismantled it in 1983. It sat disused and forlorn for ten years, as not a shadow of its former self, but merely a whisper. Much that would have identified this place as a distillery was gone—mash tun, stills, and even the identifying pagoda from its rooftop.

In nearby Elgin, George Urquhart, the chairman of Gordon & MacPhail, had always nurtured a dream to own and run a distillery. And at a time when George Urquhart might have reflected on a long and successful career, he began to look forward. He and his wife decided to buy Benromach Distillery in 1993, and in December 1997 they began refurbishing it so that it could begin production in August 1998.

During the four years between acquiring the distillery and refitting it, George and Katherine Urquhart would visit their distillery and walk the property accompanied by a homeless cat who had taken refuge in the old buildings. The cat acquired the name of Scooby from the Urquharts as well as his own account at the Gordon & MacPhail shop in Elgin, which tended to show charges of fish rather than whisky.

The Distillery Cat's Meow

Scooby lived a long (and luxurious) life before dying of old age. Two cats have replaced his tenure and have adopted his personality and manner (i.e., a sense of complete ownership). They actually live at a neighboring house (no sleeping in a dark lonely distillery at night for them), but return each work day to assume their duties of sleeping in the center of the distillery manager's desk and accompanying visitors around the distillery.

By the summer of 1998, the Benromach Spring once again provided water for production, and a refurbished Boby mill that had begun its life grinding corn for cornflakes now ground the malt for whisky. Local tradesmen installed a new stainless steel mash tun with a copper-and-brass top and rebuilt four new larch washbacks with wood salvaged from the old ones.

From the beginning, the Urquharts had no intention of replicating the old Benromach whisky. Rather, they had a clear idea that they wanted to distill not only a whisky that could mature in ten years, but also one that had sufficient body and weight to withstand an even longer maturation, if desired. They peated their malt to medium specifications so that they could replicate a Speyside whisky as it had existed pre-1960s, when most of the distilleries did their own floor maltings. In the end, they produced an elegant fruity Spey character with more smoke than most Speyside whiskies tend to have today. To help realize their dream, they had Forsyths of Rothes design a wash still with a tall, thick head and high shoulders that would not allow much reflux and that would distill a whisky with a full body and some heaviness. The spirit stills employed the same tall, slim neck but added a boil ball between the neck and the rounded shoulders to create a reflux of the heavier flavor elements.

It is not surprising, given the provenance of Gordon & MacPhail (see chapter 19, *Independent Bottlers)* that the company brought diligence to the wooden casks intended for the maturation of their new-make spirit. But the distillery has moved far beyond the Urquharts' original house profile to vary the distillation process and to experiment with matching the wood and the spirit.

The Benromach bottlings frequently change and tend to be limited editions. Recently they included three different expressions of peated single malt, different vintages, different ages, and different finishes. An organic bottling with all materials certified as organic (including the casks), provided one of its more creative specialty bottlings.

Whisky Lexicon

Gross and tare is a traditional system of determining the bulk content of pure alcohol in a newly filled cask. The bulk content provides a figure that the customs office uses to calculate the duty (tax). Many distilleries have replaced this traditional method with automation, but several of the smaller distilleries like Glengyle and Benromach keep the tradition alive. Using gross and tare, the warehouseman first weighs the cask empty, then weighs it filled and gets a net weight of spirit in the cask. Keith Cruickshank of Benromach notes, "Using a factor (which is dependent on the alcoholic strength) we can then convert from bulk [kilograms] to bulk [liters]. From this we can work out litres of pure alcohol which we declare to HMRC and is duty payable after maturation."

The Benromach Distillery produces only 150,000 liters (39,626 gallons) of spirit each year, which is often what a large distillery will produce in a week. Keith Cruickshank, the distillery manager remarks, "We are not commercialized, but we are quiet and personalized." Benromach is very much a boutique distillery producing a handcrafted product. It still determines the start of the middle cut by using the traditional demisting test, hand stencils the name of the distillery and the distillation year on the heads of the casks, and measures the volume of each cask after filling with the old gross and tare system instead of with automatic gauges. Only two men run the entire distillery, which means the distillery manager does whatever job needs doing, including talking to visitors, filling the casks, acting as mashman or stillman, or choosing the casks.

Whisky Lexicon

During the distillation in the second still, the stillman knows when to end the foreshots and begin diverting the middle cut when the impurities in the foreshots have finished. There are several tests to determine this point, but traditionally the stillman performs the demisting test. He adds water to the new-make spirit and if it remains clear, then he can begin to take the middle cut, but if it turns cloudy, then impurities still remain in the spirit. The impurities in the foreshots are soluble in the spirit at high alcohol strength, but when the strength is lowered by adding water, the impurities become insoluble and the spirit appears cloudy.

The new Benromach Distillery has been reborn with a very keen appreciation of its own past and that of all distilleries. The spirit safe came from Millburn Distillery in Inverness; and its small museum in the converted malt barn exhibits the old mash tun from the Ben Wyvis Distillery, as well as "bits and bobs" that Urquhart acquired over the years. Most telling in this Cinderella story are the signatures on a beam in the filling room of all the men who filled the last cask of Benromach in March 1983. They left the distillery believing that it would never exist as a distillery again. They signed their names so that people would remember that it had played a part in peoples' lives. The Urquharts, in reviving Benromach Distillery, have ensured that the human connection will continue and in bringing closure to their own careers have left a legacy for the future.

The Noser Knows

The Benromach Traditional 10-year-old best reflects the Urquharts' original mission to create a sweet, fruity, and elegant Speyside whisky. It begins with ripe fruit flavors followed by an uptick of lemon zest. The tastes of sweet graham crackers are balanced with smoke and spice. It begins with smoke and ends with smoke and spice on the palate in a long warm finish.

Braeval Distillery

➤ Pronounced *BRAY-val*

➤ Chapeltown, Nr. Ballindalloch, Morayshire AB37 9JS

➤ No website

➤ No visitors center

Seagram built Braeval Distillery in 1973 immediately before the opening of its sister distillery, Allt-a-Bhainne. It originally named the distillery Braes of Glenlivet because it wanted to suggest that the spirit from Braeval was similar to the Glenlivet style. It is also important to note that Seagram did not own the Glenlivet distillery at the time and was probably quite happy to piggyback onto the well-known distillery's reputation. Seagram later acquired the Glenlivet Distillery and in the late 1990s, it changed the name to Braeval Distillery. Braeval was a term previously used in the local area, and Seagram hoped the name change would provide an initiative to stop other people using the Glenlivet name.

The Distillery Cat's Meow

Although Braeval Distillery incorporates a modern design using stone and stucco, the model for this distillery may lie in the history of the surrounding area. During the eighteenth century, the local vicinity housed Scanlan Seminary, the first institution in Scotland for the training of Catholic priests. It was a time in Scottish history when the practice of Catholicism was hidden away in remote areas. In the twentieth century, Braeval Distillery with its arched and closed entrance and its small paned windows with stone lintels seem reminiscent of monastic cells, and Ann Miller of Chivas Brothers contemplates whether the local heritage of Scanlan may have informed the architect of this distillery.

An Outpost in the Early Years

Located in the Cairngorm National Park, Braeval Distillery was viewed as a bit of an outpost because it is not unusual for the area to become isolated by winter snow. In addition to the distillery, Seagram built homes on-site for the distillery workers, who formed their own community around the distillery.

The Noser Knows

Because of the potential for being snowed in, Braeval Distillery has adequate storage space for malted barley and additional numbers of washbacks so that it can continue the whisky-making process despite blowing winds and drifting snow. The problem, however, lies not in the "making" part of the process, but in the pot ales, the by-products of distillation—it is, in essence, the tail that wags the dog. The production workers must dispose of the pot ales, and if they cannot tank them away from the distillery, they cannot continue distilling.

Distilling the Braeval Spirit

From the outset, Braeval Distillery has produced a malt intended only for blending Scotch whisky. It has remained operating since 1973 except for the six years when Pernod Ricard (Chivas) mothballed the distillery after acquiring it in 2001. And like the nearby Allt-a-Bhainne Distillery, Seagram also designed Braeval for its ease of operation so that it would require little manpower.

Because of Braeval's isolation, Seagram installed fifteen stainless steel washbacks so that Braeval could continue distilling if deliveries were interrupted. The stills employ two different designs for both the wash and spirit stills. Two very large wash stills, holding 22,000 liters (5,812 gallons) each, use an onion-shape design with a tall and thick head, which permits little reflux action but allows the heavier components to move into the condenser. The reflux and additional boiling occurs in the spirit still as a result of a tall, thick head above a pronounced and highly convex boil ball. Both still designs promote a high degree of contact between the spirit and the copper, resulting in a light and clean new-make spirit.

The Noser Knows

Expressions of Braeval single malt usually display a characteristic fruity Glenlivet-type profile with additional notes of vanilla custard and sweet caramels.

Neither Braeval nor Allt-a-Bhainne have warehouses for aging spirit on-site, and the exclusion of them from the original building plans was considered innovative at the time. As is the case with all Chivas Brothers' distilleries, the maturation of Braeval spirit in primarily American oak bourbon barrels occurs at a variety of different sites. Pernod Ricard and Seagram have never released a proprietary bottling of Braeval single malt, and any expressions available to the public are offered by independent bottlers.

Cardhu Distillery

➤ Pronounced *car-DOO*

➤ Knockando, Aberlour AB38 7RY

➤ www.malts.com

➤ Visitors center

The history of Cardhu Distillery speaks to the role of women in Scotland's distilling industry, first in the person of Helen Cumming and later in her daughter-in-law, Elizabeth. In 1811, Helen and John Cumming leased their farm, where they worked the land and also distilled illicit spirit. With the passing of the Excise Act in 1823, they licensed their still because it was good business sense and cheaper to legally operate it. They no longer needed to hide their distillation and could openly sell their whisky and use it as a business product.

The Distillery Cat's Meow

The original farm still exists just beyond the entrance of the new distillery that Elizabeth Cumming built in the late nineteenth century. Today, Sandy, Brody, Truffle, Shakira, Diesel, and Scruffy make their home on the original farm. But these new tenants are Highland cattle, and the distillery employee from Cragganmore Distillery, who owns them, keeps them solely as pets.

Whisky Woman

The distillation of the whisky and the management of the distillery, however, fell to Helen because John ran the farm; when he died in the 1840s, she needed the income to raise their sons. Eventually, their son Lewis ran the distillery, but he died in 1872 leaving his wife, Elizabeth, with the farm, the distillery, and several children.

By the 1880s, the whisky business had expanded because of the growth of the blended whisky industry. And at a time when the demand for whisky outstripped the production of it, Elizabeth bought the land from the estate and easily financed it because she had a thriving business. On October 2, 1885, she opened the new distillery, and the small town and community of Cardhu grew and flourished because of it.

During the time between the opening of the new distillery in 1885 and the sale of it in 1893 to one of her clients, John Walker, Elizabeth tripled the sales of Cardhu. But before she completed the sale to John Walker, she ensured that her son John sat on the Board of Directors.

Most significantly, the management and the later building of the new distillery occurred during the tenure of these two women, and consequently they influenced the development of the flavor profile of the Cardhu whisky.

Originally, the size of the stillroom in the distillery dictated the size of the stills, but Elizabeth sold the original stills to William Grant who used them when he built Glenfiddich Distillery. The tall, thick necks of the stills allow the vapor to rise and condense when it contacts the copper in the head of the still, and then drop back into the puddled shoulders at the base to redistill, creating a lighter, cleaner, sweeter whisky.

Although Cardhu mainly goes toward the Johnnie Walker blends, some of it is available as a 12-year-old single malt. Most Cardhu is matured in refill bourbon casks with a small portion aging in refill sherry casks. Expressions of Cardhu were also released in the Rare Malts and Managers' Choice ranges.

The Noser Knows

Cardhu produces a medium-bodied, unpeated, sweet orchard fruit whisky (some berries, too), with the sweetness of honey and vanilla on the palate. It has a quick finish with a hint of spice at the end.

Pure Malt vs Single Malt

Interestingly, in 2002 a shortage of Cardhu existed and Diageo attempted to resolve the problem by bottling a "blend" of single malts, Cardhu and Glendullan, but it used the name Cardhu and labeled it as a pure malt. The whisky world reacted angrily, loudly, and quickly because although it may seem that the difference between the words pure and single malt is small, the difference in the meaning is actually quite big—single meaning that the whisky comes from one distillery, and pure meaning that it is a blend of malt whiskies. In 2009, legislation passed that states if "whisky is a blend of two or more Single Malt Scotch Whiskies from different distilleries" it must be defined as "Blended Malt Scotch Whisky."

Cragganmore Distillery

➤ Pronounced *CRAG-an-more*

➤ Ballindalloch, Banffshire B37 9AB

➤ www.malts.com

➤ Visitors center

Cragganmore Distillery boasts buildings, constructed from the local greenstone, that form a square, open-ended courtyard in a calm, quiet area on the Ballindalloch Estate. The wooden malt bins still occupy the south side of the square, and the stillroom sits to the east. The dramming room, opposite the stillroom, houses furnishings from the time when John Smith, the founder, lived, including an oversized chair that accommodated his large build of over 136 kilograms (300 pounds).

A Family Affair

The footprint of the distillery remains virtually unchanged since John Smith built the original distillery at Ayeon Farm on the Ballindalloch Castle Estate. As an experienced and highly respected distiller, he located a nearby source of water from burns fed by springs on the Cragan Mor, and quickly realized the value of the nearby, and newly opened, Strathspey railway. His drive and ambition ended abruptly when he died at the young age of fifty-three in 1886, leaving a young son, Gordon.

When Gordon came of age, he inherited a distillery that produced a spirit known for its quality.

Gordon Smith updated and reconstructed the distillery in 1901, but retained the original distilling process his father had initiated. He operated the distillery until his death, when his widow, Mary Jane, assumed the management and operation for eleven years before she sold the distillery in 1922. During the tenure of Gordon and Mary Jane Smith and their successors, the still design and production techniques remained very similar to the ones established by the founder, John Smith.

Consistency and Continuity

The distillery maintains John Smith's original still design, which accounts for the body and some of the flavor of Cragganmore whisky. The wash still has a lantern-shape with a tall neck, and the spirit still has a boil ball below a neck ending in a flat top—there is no graceful swan neck on this Cragganmore still. The design is not only quirky (not unlike Pulteney's stills), but it also is clever.

The Distillery Cat's Meow

Cragganmore Distillery continues to use wooden malt bins (a practice since abandoned by most of the industry), because they still function quite well and carry the added bonus of allowing the malt to dry out a bit more than it would in stainless steel.

The Noser Knows

Cragganmore has a medium body and a combination of flavors, including lavender florals balanced with fruit compote in syrup and crème caramel. Although the effect of the casks diminishes the burnt match aroma of the new-make spirit, the matured spirit contains subtle background notes of smoke.

The unusual shape creates more reflux, which Gregor Cattanach, the previous brand manager for Diageo, notes "increases the complexity and richness of the contents of the still." Additionally, the distillery uses worm tubs instead of condensers and keeps the doors closed on the still between distillations to prevent oxidization of the copper. Both of these practices decrease the interaction between the copper and the distillate, which results in the retention of the slight burnt match character of its new-make spirit. These characteristics combine with the sweetness imparted by the refill bourbon casks and the fruity esters captured during a slightly long fermentation to create the complexity of the matured Cragganmore malt.

In addition to the 12-year-old bottling, the core range includes a Distillers Edition that finishes the maturation with a few months in port casks, increasing the fruit flavors in the original expression. Limited bottlings also occur as part of the Managers' Choice and the Special Releases series as well as bottlings intended for the Friends of Classic Malts.

Craigellachie Distillery

- ➤ Pronounced *cray-GELL (rhymes with DELL)-ak-key*
- ➤ Craigellachie, Aberlour AB38 9ST
- ➤ No website
- ➤ No visitors center

Peter Mackie, the head of one of the big five whisky firms of the nineteenth and early twentieth century, spearheaded the building of Craigellachie Distillery. Mackie was larger than life, autocratic, and entrepreneurial. He strutted about in Highland dress, engaged in the business of weaving Highland tweeds, espoused Conservative politics, and pressed his opinions and inventions upon his employees. Besides his well-known interests, quirks, and schemes, he is best remembered for promoting and popularizing the White Horse brand, a blended Scotch whisky developed by his uncle James Logan Mackie.

The Distillery Cat's Meow

In the 1920s, White Horse Distillers Ltd. was the first company to replace corks with screw caps, eliminating the problems of crumbling or failed corks. The new invention was highly successful and highly popular and significantly increased the demand and sales of White Horse.

Very little of the original distillery, built in 1891, remains at the new Craigellachie Distillery. Although it occupies the original site, the distillery was significantly altered in 1964-65, when it underwent an update in the Waterloo design (see chapter 15, *Caol Ila*), and a new stillhouse was built, increasing the number of stills from two to four. Virtually all of the Craigellachie whisky goes into blending, and everything about the distillery production underscores this purpose.

Function Trumps Form

Craigellachie is a work horse of a distillery, and any additions or improvements target efficiency and function rather than any aesthetics. The four large, thick onion-shape stills provide very little reflux and produce a heavy, full whisky. The distillery still uses worm tubs instead of condensers in order to create the heavy, meaty, sulfury spirit required by blenders. Using condensers would increase the copper to spirit contact and would strip some of the sulfur compounds from the spirit and alter the character of the whisky.

Bacardi (John Dewar), the owners, remove all the whisky for warehousing near Glasgow since the dismantling of the last warehouses in 1996. Only one warehouse remains, but it now contains the heat recovery system. The changes to the distillery since Bacardi's ownership in 1998 are very utilitarian improvements, including a new stainless steel mash tun, a new cooling tower, and a heat recovery system. Clearly function defines form with the only nod to tradition found in the wooden washbacks and the behemoth copper stills.

The Noser Knows

The mature Craigellachie whisky has a delicacy about it—oak aromas, a light floral nose of delicate rose petals paired with kiwi, clementines, and old books. Flavors of sherry with earthy notes, cloves, mince pies, and cloves fill the mouth. It finishes quickly and gently, warming with a trace of smoky licorice in the background.

Dailuaine Distillery

➤ Pronounced *dowl-YOU-in*

➤ Carron, Morayshire AB38 7RE

➤ No website

➤ No visitors center

Dailuaine Distillery sits tucked away in a small wooded pocket by the Carron Burn. Its granite buildings sit quietly and somewhat hidden in an area the original owner, William Mackenzie, named the green vale, the English translation of dailuaine. The iconic pagoda chimneys, designed by the architect Charles Doig, were first installed at Dailuaine Distillery. Early photographs of Dailuaine show the original chimneys with rectangular vents under a close-fitting slanted roof, but Doig increased the draft above the malt fires by lifting the roof and curving the tops into a replica of an Asian pagoda. The design improved the efficiency of the kilns, and the pagoda-shaped chimney soon graced the roofs of all the distilleries.

The Little Engine that Could

The distillery also benefited from another nineteenth-century development when the Strathspey Railway arrived directly across the river from the distillery in 1863. It took almost thirty-five years after the arrival of the railway before a small tank locomotive, called a pug, was commissioned to shunt supplies from the railway and return to the station with casks of whisky. In 1939, the distillery bought a replacement pug, christened Dailuaine No.1, which operated until the railway's whisky transportation ended in 1968.

Whisky Lexicon

Following the construction of the Strathspey Railway in 1863, many of the distilleries had short spurs that led from the main line to the distillery. In order to enable the delivery of supplies, most of the distilleries maintained small tank locomotives called pugs to shuttle between the station and the distillery. The pugs delivered coal, peat, barley, and empty casks to the distillery and took away filled casks for transport to southern markets. The main line stopped carrying passengers in 1965, and the whisky trains stopped supplying distilleries in 1968.

Thomas Mackenzie, the son of the founder, took ownership of Dailuaine in 1879 until he died in 1915 with no children to succeed him. Shortly after his death, the distillery was severely damaged by fire in 1917 and did not reopen until 1920, following significant rebuilding and refurbishment. One of the improvements included the installation of electric lighting, supplied by a generator driven by one of four steam engines that provided the power for the distillery. Future improvements had to wait until 1960, when the owners converted the floor maltings to Saladin maltings, installed dark grains plant to process the residues of mashing and distilling, and added two more stills.

The Distillery Cat's Meow

When workers installed two new stills next to the ones already in place at Dailuaine Distillery, they reversed their placement. They located the spirit still where the wash still was meant to be and the wash still in the location meant for the spirit still, resulting in a wash still that was too small and a spirit still that was too large.

Multiple Personalities

Two stills at Dailuaine Distillery vary in size; however, their design remains the same. The wash still has a lantern-shape and a thick medium-tall head, and the spirit still has a classic onion shape with a thick, tall neck that allows little reflux. The still shapes suggest a medium to full-bodied new-make spirit, but actually the people at Dailuaine can also produce spirit with several different characters.

The traditional spirit, indeed, has a full-bodied and robust profile, but it is worth remembering that most of Dailuaine's new-make is casked for blending. Depending on the requirements for blending, the distillers may produce a nutty or grassy/fruity spirit by starting with cloudy or clear worts for fermentation and by varying the fermentation times. Additionally, they can produce a sulfury spirit by reducing the distillate's contact with the copper, which tends to strip out the sulfur character. In order to produce spirit with multiple characters, the mashman and stillman must understand how the stills operate (in both winter and summer temperatures), how they must be run, and how variations affect the spirit. It is far from formulaic and requires experience and skill.

The Noser Knows

Dailuaine has a full, rich nose of dried and dark fruits complemented by notes of sherry and marmalade. Tastes of butterscotch fudge and dark chocolate fill the mouth followed by flavors of sherry, chocolate orange, satsumas, nuts, and cappuccino. It has a medium to full body with a finish of lingering tastes of well-done toast, a kiss of sherry, oranges and dark fruitcake, and a surprisingly quick finish.

Dufftown Distillery

➤ Pronounced as spelled

➤ Dufftown, Banffshire AB55 4BR

➤ www.malts.com

➤ No visitors center

Peter Mackenzie and his partner traveled from Liverpool to purchase a meal mill and a sawmill for conversion to a distillery in 1896. He bought the property from a local farmer John Symon, who profited not only from the sale of the land and buildings, but also from the ensuing agreement to supply the new distillery with barley from one of his farms. Mackenzie had already purchased Blair Athol Distillery, and he was able to keep the ownership and operation of the two distilleries under his family's control for almost forty years.

His blending business suffered when the American market collapsed with Prohibition in 1920, but in 1933, the year that Congress repealed the Eighteenth Amendment, Arthur Bell acquired both of Mackenzie's distilleries. Through a series of mergers in the 1980s and 1990s, Dufftown Distillery became part of Diageo's portfolio of distilleries. Prior to the merger fever, the number of stills grew from two to eight in fewer than ten years so that the Dufftown Distillery became the second largest malt whisky distillery owned by Diageo.

A Blending Malt, but Now the Singleton

The distillery uses stainless steel for its washbacks and has reduced the number of stills to three pairs of large, thick onion-shape stills. The heavy reflux and copper contact produces a light, fruity whisky that usually tends to go toward blending. Bottlings of the single malt have appeared in the traditional Diageo series of Flora and Fauna, Rare Malts, and Managers' Choice, or in the offerings of independent bottlers. However, in 2008 Dufftown became one of the three single malts offered under the Singleton expressions in three markets (the other two are Glen Ord and Glendullan). The Singleton of Dufftown appears in the British and European markets bottled at 12 and 15 years old.

Glenallachie Distillery

➤ Pronounced *glen-AL-ak-key*

➤ Aberlour, Morayshire AB38 9LR

➤ No website

➤ No visitors center

William Delmé-Evans, the distillery architect, designed the Glenallachie Distillery in 1967 after building the Isle of Jura Distillery in 1963 and Tullibardine Distillery in 1949. It is an archetypal 1960s plan with white buildings outside, open spaces and light wood inside. The muted Campbell tartan upholstery, the wrought iron decorations, and large windows opening onto views of the duck pond and the countryside surrounding the peak of Ben Rinnes, speak to the care and the attention that the Glenallachie Distillery receives. All of the production of Glenallachie Distillery goes to blends, specifically the Clan Campbell brand that is mainly available in French markets.

The Noser Knows

The Dufftown malt has spirit on the nose with subtle aromas of solvent and nail polish remover. But the mouthfeel is syrupy and chewy with tastes of fruits in syrup (lycee and plums) supported by flavors of vanilla caramel with a spicy, peppery background. The finish is lingering and dry.

The Distillery Cat's Meow

When the Clan Campbell blend was launched, the Duke of Argyll drew attention to the fact that the brand referred to his clan and his name and subsequently, he became involved in the company. The twelfth Duke of Argyll, Ian Campbell, spoke French fluently and was influential in establishing the Clan Campbell brand in France, which is now the blended whisky's largest market. The use of the muted Campbell tartan throughout the distillery provides a subtle but tangible thread between the Duke of Argyll, the head of the Campbell Clan and the whisky that bears his name.

Scottish and Newcastle Breweries commissioned the building of Glenallachie Distillery in 1967. They produced its first spirit run in 1968 specifically to provide malt for the Mackinlay blends, a subsidiary of Scottish and Newcastle Breweries. In 1985, Invergordon Distillers bought Glenallachie Distillery and its brands, and then proceeded to mothball and close the distillery two years later in 1987.

Campbell Distillers, part of Pernod Ricard (Chivas), purchased Glenallachie in 1989 and began production once again. At the sale of Glenallachie Distillery to Campbell Distillers, all the contents of the distillery were listed in detail. The inventory of the distillery included the ducks in the pond outside, and it was said that Campbell Distillers had bought ducks that cost £3.5 million.

The Noser Knows

Glenallachie Distillery employs typical shell-and-tube condensers, but they are placed behind the stills in a horizontal position rather than the customary vertical placement. In this way, the position of the condensers doesn't block the windows and the view across the countryside and remains true to the aesthetics of Delmé-Evans's original design.

Distilling a Blending Malt

Fermentation takes place in six stainless steel-lined washbacks for a standard fermentation before moving to distillation. The stills at Glenallachie use two different designs in order to produce different results. The wash still has a lantern-shape with a nipped waist that encourages reflux action and a lighter-bodied spirit. The spirit still, however, uses a classic onion shape with a tall, thick head that allows more copper contact with the spirit but little reflux action.

Most of the new-make spirit ages in refill bourbon casks and a few sherry butts. Chivas has produced only one proprietary bottling that it released through its visitors centers in the Cask Strength Limited Edition range. Interestingly, that expression was a 16-year-old malt aged in first-fill sherry casks. Any additional bottlings as a single malt are found in the expressions offered by independent bottlers.

Glenburgie Distillery

> ➤ Pronounced *glen BUR-g-ee*

> ➤ Forres, Morayshire IV36 0QY

> ➤ No website

> ➤ No visitors center

Glenburgie is a whisky that is not bottled by the distillery and only occasionally by independent bottlers. It is a quiet little distillery that does not announce itself or its whisky. There is no reason for its modesty either—it is a whisky that is much sought after by blenders and one that can well stand on its own as a single malt.

The distillery is built on the site of a long-established farm called Kilnflat whose ruins previously rested behind the present distillery; and when the distillery was established in 1810, it was named Kilnflat Distillery. Today, one of the original buildings, built in 1810, which housed the distillery and customs and excise offices on the top floor and warehouse space below the offices, still exists in fairly good condition on the distillery grounds. By 1867, the distillery had fallen into disuse until Charles Hay reclaimed it in 1878 and renamed it Glenburgie. Between 1884 and 1936, the distillery changed hands several times and went into liquidation before Hiram Walker bought it for use in Ballantine's blended whisky.

Lomond Stills at Glenburgie

The year 1958 brought two major changes to Glenburgie. The first was an end to the floor maltings at the distillery and the start of buying its malt from a central maltings. The second change was unique and experimental. The end of World War II had brought an increased demand for Scotch whisky but a shortage of single malts to use for blending. In an effort to create additional single malts, Hiram Walker installed Lomond stills at three sites, including Glenburgie. These stills had thick columnar necks that resembled coffee cans on end, and they housed rectifying plates. These plates could be swiveled or flooded with distillate in order to create different kinds of whisky. One final variable was mounting the lyne arm on a swivel to change its angle, and in so doing change the character of the whisky.

The company named this variation of the whisky, Glencraig, after Bill Craig, the director of Ballantine's Highland Malt Distilleries. Unfortunately, it dismantled and removed these stills in 1981 to make room for two more traditional stills that repeated the design of the two already in place. (See chapter 18, *Lost and Hidden Distilleries*).

After Two Hundred Years— A New Distillery

The Noser Knows

The most significant difference between the stainless steel and the wooden washbacks at the former Glenburgie Distillery were the aromas they both created. The stainless steel vessels were completely covered and the room was heavily vented; there was virtually no aroma in that tun room. The tun room that housed the wooden washbacks, however, was ripe with escaping aromas of apples and fruit—the result of fermentation.

The Noser Knows

Only two proprietary bottlings from the distillery have appeared for a very limited time, otherwise no other expressions are offered, except through independent bottlers. Interestingly, the expression I tasted was an 18-year-old limited in-house bottling. This bottling had aromas of some oak and newly sharpened pencils, as well as vanilla and malty sweetness. The flavors included cream toffees with light fruit undertones of citrus, supported by a surprising spiciness of pepper and cloves in a lingering finish.

The next twenty years saw the ownership of Glenburgie pass to Allied Lyons and then to Pernod Ricard (Chivas). In 2004, the owners demolished the former Glenburgie Distillery and built a new distillery in its place adjacent to the old site. When the distillery came into production in 2005, a new full Lauter mash tun replaced the old rake in the former cast iron mash tun, and twelve stainless steel washbacks replaced the previous configuration of steel and wood. Two additional stills had joined the existing four with a classic onion-shape and a thick head. First fill and refilled bourbon casks continue to mature the new distillate, some of which is aged on-site.

Glendullan Distillery

➤ Pronounced as spelled

➤ Dufftown, Banffshire AB55 4DJ

➤ www.malts.com

➤ No visitors center

The village of Dufftown eventually laid claim to nine distilleries, with Glendullan being the seventh and last one built in the nineteenth century. William Williams & Sons were sole owners of the distillery in 1898 until it merged its interests with two other companies in 1919. Distillers Company Limited acquired the distillery in 1926 and passed it to its subsidiary Scottish Malt Distillers (now Diageo) in 1930, who has owned and operated it since that time.

As with so many other distilleries, the owners chose the distillery site because of its proximity to water and transportation. Glendullan moved water from the River Fiddich to operate a waterwheel, providing power to the distillery, and it also shared a railway spur with Mortlach Distillery for transporting supplies and casks. This arrangement continued well into the twentieth century until the distillery connected to the national electric grid and the local rail service closed.

A New Glendullan

In 1972, the owners designed a new distillery in the Waterloo style (See Caol Ila) adjacent to the existing Glendullan Distillery. The original distillery housed one pair of stills, and the new plant added an additional three pairs of onion-shaped stills. Installing wash stills that are larger than the spirit stills is standard procedure in distilleries, but that standard was intentionally reversed at Glendullan. This enabled the distiller to have a balanced distillation where the contents of two wash stills filled one (larger) spirit still, with nothing left over. This change in a common benchmark, however, gave rise to the standing joke that the architect got the plans wrong and mixed up the wash stills with the spirit stills.

Both the old and new Glendullan distilleries operated in tandem, as they had also done at Linkwood, until the old distillery was closed in 1985. The buildings of the original distillery still stand with their original pagoda roof, but the owners removed the distilling equipment and decommissioned it as a distillery. Today the original Glendullan Distillery has become an engineering center that houses all the Diageo technicians for the Speyside area.

The Noser Knows

The Glendullan has subtle fruits and molasses aromas that expand into full flavors of raisins, citrus peel, cinnamon buns, and sherry. It is nicely balanced with a medium body and dry finish.

Most of Glendullan spirit was reserved for blending with only the occasional bottlings available in the standard Diageo series of Flora and Fauna, Rare Malts, and Managers' Choice, and in the expressions offered by independent bottlers. This changed in 2007 when Diageo released three malts under the Singleton umbrella, including the Singleton Glendullan for the North American market.

Glen Elgin Distillery

➤ Pronounced *glen-L-gin(rhymes with tin)*

➤ Elgin, Morayshire IV30 8SL

➤ www.malts.com

➤ No visitors center

Glen Elgin Distillery sits just off the main road from Elgin to Rothes, but it does not loudly announce its presence. It remains quietly tucked among a gathering of houses—its location, certainly quiet, is almost a best-kept secret, like the single malt produced there.

The Distillery Cat's Meow

Electricity was not installed at Glen Elgin Distillery until 1950. Until that time, lighting in the distillery consisted of paraffin lamps, which required the employment of one man to light and clean them.

A Troubled Beginning

During its early years, the water used for production proved to be a problem. The distillery shared a water source with nearby Coleburn Distillery (now closed) before returning it to the stream for Glen Elgin's use. Because the owners of Glen Elgin needed their own water source, they secured a lease to the Whitewreath Springs.

Even though it had acquired a good and reliable water source, the next fifty years saw the distillery experience a series of liquidations, buyouts, openings, and closures. When the distillery resumed production after World War II, it had undergone few improvements since its construction in 1898 and consequently underwent a needed refurbishment and expansion in the early 1960s.

Moving Forward

The distillery buildings still retain the appeal and appearance of Charles Doig's late Victorian architectural design, but inside the buildings the distillery combines modern advances and traditional procedures. Although the attics surrounding the malt bins retain the old wooden floors and trusses and speak to the workmanship of a previous century, the equipment it houses speaks to the twenty-first century. The old Boby mill continues to grind the barley, but all the screening, destoning, dust extraction, and explosion switches that ensure the safe operation of the mill are state of the art.

The mashmen at Glen Elgin produce a clear wort during mashing and ferment it in traditional Oregon pine washbacks for at least seventy-six hours. The combination of clear wort and a longer fermentation encourages the development of fruity flavors characteristic of a Speyside malt.

The still design includes long, thick heads connecting to downward-sloping lyne arms, which produces little reflux action. As a result, many of the heavier flavor components are allowed to travel unimpeded into the traditional worm tubs. New-make spirit is tanked away and filled off-site in American oak barrels with virtually all of the production going to blends. Maturation does occur on the site of Glen Elgin Distillery, but as with many distilleries the warehouses contain a combination of casks from other distilleries so that the risk of storing the spirit is spread over many locations. Diageo reserves very little of the production of Glen Elgin for single malts, but it is a whisky well worth seeking. It has been bottled as part of the Flora and Fauna and the Managers' Choice range, as a 12-year-old Centenary version and as expressions from independent bottlers.

The Noser Knows

The long fermentation at Glen Elgin encourages the development of the characteristic fruitiness of Speyside whiskies. A lot of cleansing copper contact occurs across the large surface area of the stills, but the long, thick heads and onion-shape of the stills allow little reflux action. Consequently, the heavier flavor components travel unimpeded into the worm tubs and help to promote the full body and robust flavors that complement the fruit and spice flavors in this whisky. It is well regarded by whisky enthusiasts and well worth seeking, particularly through independent bottlings.

Glenfarclas Distillery

➤ Pronounced *glen-FAR-klis*

➤ Ballindalloch, Banffshire AB37 9BD

➤ www.glenfarclas.co.uk

➤ Visitors center

Since 1836, six generations of Grants have distilled whisky at Ballindalloch, and today it is one of the few family-owned distilleries in Scotland. While it was long a favorite dram among drovers beginning their trek to Highland markets, John Grant and his son George began to actively extend the reputation of Glenfarclas single malt beyond the immediate Speyside region.

The family commitment to its whisky remains constant, and the Grants, some of whom still live on the distillery site, are actively involved in its operation on a daily basis. This is a fiercely independent company whose concern is to produce a family whisky rather than answer to shareholders or a parent company.

Big and then Bigger

Glenfarclas means valley of the green grasslands, a name that is still quite appropriate today. For, indeed, the distillery sits well back from the main road near Ballindalloch, amidst green farmlands backed by the imposing form of Ben Rinnes. Everything at Glenfarclas Distillery is big—in the 1970s the Grants doubled the size of the stainless steel mash tun, doubled the number of washbacks to twelve, and increased the number of stills to six.

Whisky making at Glenfarclas begins with very soft water coming from a source in the Ben Rinnes Hills and incorporates a longer fermentation of sixty hours. The six stills have a slight downward angle to the lyne arms with necks that dissolve into very pronounced boil balls to create a lot of reflux. All of the stills are directly fired by gas and use rummagers, significantly increasing the copper contact and removal of sulfur notes from the spirit.

If It Ain't Broke, Don't Fix It

In 1981, the Grants tried using indirect heating with steam coils inside one of the stills but were deeply disappointed with the results, which seemed to take the muscle out of the whisky's character. Similarly, the Grants experimented with using racked warehouses in the 1960s, and once again the family was unhappy with the results. The difference of 4 to 5°C (39 to 41°F) between the ceiling and floor of the racked warehouse negatively affected the maturation of the whisky aged in that warehouse. Consequently, Glenfarclas spirit is aged in twenty-eight earthen floor dunnage warehouses racked three casks high.

The Noser Knows

In 2011, Glenfarclas released a commemorative bottling to celebrate the 175th anniversary of the distillery. The cask selections represented six different decades, and when one added the ages of the casks, the sum equaled 175, the anniversary date. The bottling sold out in a day and a half—another collector's item!

The core range includes 10-, 12-, 15-, 17-, 21-, 25-, 30-, and 40-year-olds, as well as the Glenfarclas 105—the 105 refers to the proof of the expression and equates to 60 percent ABV. All of the expressions except the 40-year-old contain a mixture of whiskies aged in both sherry (60 percent) and bourbon casks (40 percent).

The Noser Knows

Interestingly, first fill bourbon casks are not used at Glenfarclas because the abundance of bourbon lends an oily note to the spirit. Some whisky enthusiasts who adhere to a "first in the bath" view to maturing whisky believe that a first fill in a bourbon or sherry cask must result in a preferable whisky. But as this book has attempted to explain, the type of cask and the number of previous fills must fit the distillery character of the spirit, resulting in a match that is both enhancing and complementary.

In addition to this core range, the Grants bottled limited editions of old and vintage whiskies and a limited edition Chairman's Reserve of four casks from the 1960s. Finally, they have released the Family Casks series of single casks, with natural color and non-chill filtering from consecutive years beginning with 1953 and ending in 1996. As single casks they are, by nature, a limited edition, and as some years sell out, they are replaced with other years.

The Noser Knows

The fermentation time, the distillation in large stills with heavy reflux and copper contact, and the preponderance of sherry casks for maturation creates a tension among distilling components that results in a complex whisky with layers of character.

With the mature Glenfarclas, sherry arrives first on the nose, and becomes more pronounced with water, followed by wood and some spirit. Sweet graham crackers appear in the taste with a touch of citrus giving rise to dark fruits in the background and a nice balance between sherry and allspice. The finish is firm and rounded but does not linger overly long.

Glenfiddich Distillery

➤ Pronounced *glen-FID(rhymes with bid)-ick*

➤ Dufftown, Morayshire AB55 4DH

➤ www.glenfiddich.com

➤ Visitors center

The whisky produced at Glenfiddich Distillery had always been an uncomplicated and straightforward drink, but its recent core range has revealed a new side to an old standard. And almost everyone who drinks Scotch whisky of any sort knows Glenfiddich because it is so ubiquitous—the reasons for which lie in the company's ownership and interesting marketing plans. The distillery, as well as Balvenie, Kininvie, and Girvan Distilleries, has remained completely owned by the Grant family, who remains strongly committed to and involved in the business.

The Pioneering Spirit

The Grant family, the first in the distilling industry to market a single malt outside of Scotland, began selling Glenfiddich whisky in London in 1963. Eventually Glenfiddich began appearing in shops and bars all over the world and consequently, it became the first single malt many people tasted. It also packaged its whisky in distinctive triangular bottles, and the public quickly recognized the shape of the bottle even if the label and name were hidden.

Once the public recognized the Glenfiddich whisky brand, the owners built the first visitors center in 1969. They cleaned and restored the distillery buildings to their original granite and limestone in order to attract visitors and to build a tourist trade. Today they hire local guides to handle the more than 71,000 tourists who annually visit the distillery. Despite their unabashed attempt to attract large numbers of tour buses, I always recommend that visitors tour the Glenfiddich Distillery for an excellent overview of a working distillery and for a sound understanding of the process.

Interestingly, the distillery uses two very different designs for its spirit stills. When I asked the reason, the staff told me that William Grant had bought the stills from another distillery in the nineteenth century and no one had thought to change the design. He and his wife, Elizabeth, saved their money for twenty years to buy stills and distilling equipment from Mrs. Cumming, the owner of Cardhu Distillery (spelled Cardow at the time). With the used Cardow stills, they hand-built their own distillery and took their first whisky off the stills on Christmas Day 1887.

The Distillery Cat's Meow

William Grant & Sons Ltd. continues to employ a team of coppersmiths to maintain the stills and coopers to maintain the casks at its four distilleries. The continual maintenance allows the distilleries to operate without closing for the customary silent season.

Developing the Glenfiddich Profile

At first glance, the shape of the small wash stills—onion-shaped with a thick neck rising from rounded shoulders—indicates that many of the heavier and robust flavors would rise quickly and begin an easy journey through the downward angled lyne arm to the condenser. But whisky distilled at Glenfiddich contains none of these full flavors, and the answer may lie in the two designs of the spirit stills.

One set of spirit stills has a lantern-glass shape, reminiscent of hurricane lamps, with a sharply pinched waist; the second set has a boil ball sitting above the shoulders. Both of these features capture the heavy elements and redistill them until only the lighter vapors rise through the neck. The continual reflux action also allows a great deal of copper contact to lighten and purify the spirit.

The Noser Knows

The expression, called Glenfiddich Snow Phoenix, is the result of making lemonade from lemons—or in this case of making a limited edition single malt from misfortune. In January 2010, the roofs on warehouses at several distilleries in Speyside collapsed under the weight of accumulated snow. Four warehouses at Glenfiddich Distillery also suffered this fate and the casks were exposed to the elements. Teams of production staff moved the casks to other warehouses but not before Brian Kinsman, Glenfiddich's malt master, chose several casks for a special bottling. He selected casks of different ages and casks with different finishes and married them to produce the Glenfiddich Snow Phoenix.

The Noser Knows

The traditional Glenfiddich profile offers flavors of applesauce and pear compote with a touch of vanilla and a dry finish with lingering subtle tastes of licorice. The different expressions, however, allow a variation on this theme depending on the age of the Glenfiddich at bottling and the casks used in maturation and finishing. For instance, the rum casks used to finish the 21 year old expression moves the flavors towards tropical fruits and adds a touch of spice..

A long fermentation and a middle cut that moves toward the fruity esters in the foreshots help to create the orchard fruit and delicate body of the classic Glenfiddich profile. But these flavors are varied by the casks used for maturation. The 15-year-old is matured in three different casks that are then married in a large vat using the Solera system borrowed from sherry bodegas. Once the spirit from sherry, bourbon, and new oak casks marries in the vat, only half the contents are removed for bottling. The vat is then refilled so that some of the previous batch always carries over into the next one. Both sherry and American oak are used to mature the 18-year-old whisky, and the 21-year-old finishes for several months in rum casks. The distillery offers rare bottlings of very old Glenfiddich and limited edition vintage expressions.

Glen Grant Distillery

➤ Pronounced as spelled

➤ Rothes, Morayshire AB38 7BS

➤ www.glengrant.com

➤ Visitors center

In 1840, the brothers John and James Grant constructed Glen Grant Distillery in the village of Rothes, a location that could readily supply them with local barley, peat, and a labor force, as well as access to a nearby seaport.

The "Same, Same, but Different" Brothers

As the success of the distillery grew, the elder brother, John, assumed the role of distiller, philanthropist, and farmer of the adjacent Drumbain Farm until he died, with no heirs, in 1864.

The younger brother, James, adopted a much more public persona and worked to open a railway line from Lossiemouth through Elgin to Rothes, and later pursued a role in politics.

Unlike his older brother, however, James had eleven children, but only his second son, James, showed an interest in distilling and the family business. James had already acquired a share in the business in 1869 before he inherited the distillery when his father died in 1872.

James Grant, the Innovator

James Grant, the son, inherited the distillery during the boom years of the whisky industry and expanded the innovative changes begun by his father and uncle. At the time, bourbon casks were not used and most distilleries produced full-bodied sherried single malt.

James Grant, however, wanted to produce a delicate, clean single malt, so he decided to alter the character of his spirit by adding purifiers to both the wash and spirit stills in order to distill a lighter spirit. Dennis Malcolm, the present distillery manager, remarks that when Grant did this he had "no check. It could be ten years down the road before he knew if there would be any huge difference—it could have been a detrimental difference. It was very bold and brave [to do this], but it worked, and we have this light estery fruity whisky."

The Distillery Gardens

Forty-five years after the founding of Glen Grant Distillery, the founder's son Major James Grant designed and built his home, Glen Grant House, on the grounds surrounding the distillery. He landscaped the house with Victorian woodland gardens and enjoyed walking with his guests along a path through the gardens to a safe he had installed in the rock. Inside the safe he had placed a bottle of (you guessed it) Glen Grant whisky and a copper dog that he used to dip into the cool water of the stream for each glass of whisky. In the early 1990s, Seagram launched its Heritage Program, which included the restoration of the Woodland Gardens and the revival of Grant's dramming tradition, much to the delight of its visitors.

Whisky Lexicon

Through the years, distillery workers regarded the stealing of new-make spirit as a competitive challenge. Among the devices invented to facilitate the smuggling of whisky out of the distillery was the crafting of a **copper dog.** The local coppersmith would fashion a cylindrical container with an attached cord that the worker would fill with stolen spirit and then drop down his roomy trousers—the first smuggled dram usually went to the coppersmith as payment.

Paying Forward to the Grandson

Even though Major James Grant enjoyed significant success in the whisky world, his success did not follow him into his personal life. He married three times and had nine children, but five of his children, including his four sons, predeceased him. With no direct heirs to manage Glen Grant, he offered the position of managing director to his grandson, Douglas Mackessack. He arrived in Rothes in 1929 and worked to learn the distilling trade in the two years before his grandfather's death in 1931.

In the following decade, prior to the outbreak of World War II, Douglas Mackessack developed and expanded markets for the sale of Glen Grant single malt. Before the start of the war, he held a commission as an officer in the Seaforth Highlanders. In June 1940, he was captured during a failed evacuation of St. Valéry-en-Caux and spent five years in a POW camp. Mackessack returned to Rothes and Glen Grant Distillery in 1945.

Mergers and Expansion

The 1950s and 1960s brought a time of expansion and refurbishment to the distillery in order to accommodate the growing appetite for Scotch whisky. During this time, the company underwent two mergers, the reopening of the Glen Grant Number Two Distillery (renaming it Caperdonich), and twice expanded the distillery to bring the number of operating stills to ten.

The Distillery Cat's Meow

Dennis Malcolm, the present master distiller, takes personal pride in the people, the distillery, and the whisky of Glen Grant because he was born at the distillery and began work there as a cooper in 1960. He eventually became distillery manager in 1983, and later general manager in 1992. He retired for a brief time before the Campari Group appointed him as master distiller and returned him to the place where he had begun his life.

The End of the Grant Family Ownership

When the takeover by Seagram occurred in 1978, however, it marked the end of the family ownership in Glen Grant Distillery. In 2001, Pernod Ricard (Chivas) bought Seagram, but in 2006 monopoly regulations required that it sell Glen Grant Distillery to the Campari Group, the present owners.

The Distillery Cat's Meow

When the Campari Group decided to renovate the 1887 Coach House into the new visitors center, it discovered a pipistrelle bat nesting among the rafters. Because it belonged to a protected species, the company delayed construction for six months until the bat had completed its "family" duties and moved out. The final restoration of the Coach House included the addition of two bat houses in the event the bat returned and found new tenants in its previous home. Check it out when you visit Glen Grant.

The Fruits of Glen Grant's Stills

The company bottles almost all of the whisky distilled and matured at Glen Grant as a single malt and reserves only a small portion for blending. A look at the stills explains the subtle and straightforward flavor profile. The wash stills have a distinctive boil ball (described as a German helmet) above puddled shoulders, all leading into a long neck. The spirit stills are similar, but they have exaggerated characteristics found in the wash stills—the neck is longer and the boil ball is stretched out.

And as if this design were not sufficient to increase the reflux and redistillation of the heavier flavor congeners, a purifier encases the lyne arm between the still and the condenser. This has the effect of producing a light and clean spirit. The volatiles that first rise into the neck of the still are condensed in the purifier, and then returned to the still by a pipe that leads back into the base to be redistilled.

The Noser Knows

Glen Grant's tall stills and use of purifiers on both the wash and spirit stills result in a soft and delicate body with what the Glen Grant distillers identify as orchard fruits. And indeed the core range of Glen Grant single malts provide apple and pear flavors with underlying vanilla and almond notes. It offers a clean, light dram with whispered layers of flavor.

The new-make spirit distilled at Glen Grant is filled into American bourbon barrels on-site, and then matured in warehouses at the distillery rather than tanked to other locations for filling and maturation elsewhere. The company bottles Glen Grant single malt at 10 and 16 years old and also releases the Major's Reserve with no age statement. It also has released several limited editions, including a cask strength 1992 Cellar Reserve and a 170th Anniversary bottling. Both releases include whisky aged in not only bourbon casks, but also sherry casks, which impart their distinctive notes of dried fruits and spice.

Glen Keith Distillery (Mothballed)

> ➤ Pronounced as spelled

> ➤ Keith, Banffshire AB55 5BS

> ➤ No website

> ➤ Not open to visitors

The proximity of the Glen Keith Distillery to the Strathisla Distillery makes it possible to walk from one to the other. It sits tucked down behind a solid gray stone wall, but its modern glass front entrance speaks to the fact that this is one of Scotland's newer distilleries, built in 1957. The distillery was never the visitors showcase that one found at Strathisla, but its stillroom is particularly interesting because of the experimental stills there.

The Era of C.S. McBain

The mash tun has a traditional cover, but like the covers designed by C.S. McBain at Strathisla, it has an open space of several inches between the cover and the sides. As noted earlier, he believed the increased air flow was crucial to a good mash and created a better fermentation when the sweet wort from the mash transferred to the nine Oregon pine washbacks. It is interesting to note that Seagram gave McBain some freedom to experiment with the whisky-making process, and it is most obvious in the still room.

One large room contains four stills with a noticeable difference between the wash and spirit stills. Both stills have a long lyne arm, but the wash stills have long, thick necks that end with gently sloped shoulders, whereas the spirit stills have boil balls to increase the reflux action. Both the long lyne arms connecting the top of the stills to the condensers, and the presence of the boil balls suggest that these stills were designed to produce a lighter whisky. Interestingly, McBain initially used triple distillation until 1970 to produce the desired light spirit.

Experimental Stills

Two additional stills that McBain used experimentally are accommodated in a smaller adjacent room. Here, he processed each spirit run with a double distillation rather than the previously used triple distillation. Additionally, he modified the shape of the stills to slightly vary the character of the single malt. At first glance the stills seem to be elongated versions of those in the main still room: the wash still has a long, thick neck and rounded pear-shaped shoulders with no defined waist separating the two. The spirit still, however, has a shorter neck that tapers into a rounded ball.

The Distillery Cat's Meow

One other addition to the stillroom at Glen Keith occurred unexpectedly and rested in a warm box behind the stills. Glen Keith not only was the home to a malt whisky, but also provided a home to an American distillery cat named Passport.

Because the distillery receives shipments of used bourbon casks from America, workers prepared to unload a large container of newly arrived bourbon barrels. On opening the shipment, a small kitten, who had survived the ten-day sea journey, stumbled out on wobbly legs. She then had to endure six months' quarantine in a government kennel since Scotland is a rabies-free country. Following her quarantine, she returned to the distillery workers, who made a bed for her behind the stills where it was warm, cut a cat flap in the door for her convenience, and named her Passport after the blended Scotch whisky produced with Glen Keith single malt. Sadly only the spirit of Passport and the spirit of Glen Keith whisky remain. The cat lived out a contented life at Glen Keith Distillery, the distillery closed, and the stills remain silent.

McBain intended the whisky from these stills to be delicate and fast maturing. This was an important factor if one remembers that this distillery was built and began producing spirit in the late 1950s, when a high demand for Scotch whisky existed. It would take years of aging before the distillers knew exactly the character of the new whisky, and a light, fast maturing whisky would give them that information sooner than a malt that required additional years in the cask. Later, he married the spirit from both the main and the experimental stills to produce the Glen Keith single malt.

The Noser Knows

Glen Keith has a light, dry nose followed by milk caramels, orchard fruits, and vanilla flavors. It is smooth and surprisingly firm-bodied with a very quick finish—a nice, inoffensive whisky.

Seagram mothballed Glen Keith in 1999. When Pernod Ricard (Chivas) acquired the distillery in 2001, it did not reopen it as it had with other distilleries that came into its portfolio. The only distillery bottling at 10 years old appeared as one of four malts offered in Seagram's Heritage series, but no other expressions appeared except through independent bottlers.

The Glenlivet Distillery

➤ Pronounced as spelled

➤ Ballindalloch, Morayshire AB37 9DB

➤ www.theglenlivet.com

➤ Visitors center

Stories about George Smith, the founder of The Glenlivet Distillery, have reached legendary status.

The Glenlivet Distillery we know today was only one distillery (and certainly not the first) that George Smith operated in the early nineteenth century. He assumed the operation of his father's farm still at Upper Drummin, a now-derelict site located above the existing Glenlivet Distillery. It was an ideal site for a distillery because it provided a remote place for the distillation of barley into spirit and provided wide vistas that enabled a system of signaling from house to house whenever excise officers appeared. When the Excise Act of 1823 reduced the tax and licensing fees of stills, legal distillation became a viable proposition. George Smith was the first distiller to file for a license that legalized his stills. The reaction among the other distillers was swift and violent, and Smith slept in his distillery for five years to prevent angry competitors from burning his distillery. Additionally, he armed himself with hair-trigger pistols, given to him by the Laird of Aberlour, and did not hesitate to use them.

The Distillery Cat's Meow

In a very early marketing strategy, Sir Walter Scott, the literary writer, orchestrated a visit of King George IV to Edinburgh in August 1822. During the course of his visit, Scott purposely planned events that included the wearing of the tartan kilt, which served to reestablish the wearing of the kilt and defined a national identity. Of course, the king was also served Glenlivet (a completely illegal whisky) and declared it much to his pleasure. Although the two events might not be a case of cause and effect, the following year did see the passage of the Excise Act, enabling legal licensing of stills.

The Successes and Escapades of George Smith

Often-told stories not only relate his escapades but also provide comment on the man. His distillery remained standing and functioning, and he went on to develop a successful market for his whisky. George Smith's whisky was elegant and fruity, a direct contrast to the more robust sherried versions already in the market. The Glenlivet style of malt became highly popular and defined a specific category of malt whisky. Because of his determination, his strong physical presence, and agility with firearms, he was able to firmly establish his legal distillery and pave the way for others to follow him. Certainly, he was a man for the times, which demanded a forceful personality.

Within twenty years of licensing his distillery, George Smith bought a second farm, leased three others, and also leased a second distillery, Cairngorm Distillery. By 1858, Smith bought one of his leased farms, Minmore, and acquired permission from the

The Distillery Cat's Meow

Why The Glenlivet?

The product of his new Glenlivet Distillery had become such a definitive type of Speyside malt that many competitors appended the name to their own distillery. In order to protect the name of their distillery and their product, Smith's son John Gordon Smith sought relief in the judicial system. In 1884, he reached a legal agreement with the other distillery owners that decided they could use the name Glenlivet if they hyphenated it after their own distillery's name.

The definite article, however, would define Smith's distillery as The Glenlivet because it was the one that had defined the region, the taste, and the style.

Duke of Gordon to build a distillery. He dismantled the distillery at Upper Drummin, and moved it into the sheltered Livet Glen, which also provided room for expansion.

Glenlivet and its American Cousins

The Glenlivet Distillery built on its successes and poised itself to enter the American market immediately following Prohibition. During the thirty years following World War II, the company underwent a number of mergers and expansions. Seagram bought The Glenlivet in 1978 and held it until 2001, when Pernod Ricard (Chivas) acquired ownership of The Glenlivet Distillery. The presence of The Glenlivet single malt in the American market, since its introduction following Prohibition, has increased significantly so that the brand now occupies the number one place in the North American market and the number two place in the world market (behind Glenfiddich). Consequently, Chivas Brothers moved to expand the production facilities by 75 percent in 2010.

Glenlivet and the Big Time

Chivas installed an additional mash tun with a shallow bed that provides a wider surface area to facilitate a faster draining of the wort. It doubled the number of wooden washbacks to sixteen and added three pairs of stills, raising the total number to fourteen (the distillery actually carries a license for fifteen stills, which includes a small still used for demonstration purposes).

The wash stills have a lantern-glass shape below tall, thick necks that lead to downward angled lyne arms. The lyne arms certainly allow some heavier compounds into the condensers, but the tall head and nipped waists ensure the reflux and copper contact necessary to the elegant character of the new-make spirit.

The design of the spirit stills serves to underscore the collection of light fruity esters with very thin and tall heads and lantern-glass shapes. The younger ages of The Glenlivet malt tend to mature in refill bourbon casks while the older ages use more sherry casks for maturation. Other expressions include a marriage of whisky aged in both types of casks.

Chivas has released a wide range of expressions with many of them available in the American market. Its core range includes a 12-year-old aged in bourbon, an 18-year-old aged in sherry casks, and a 15-year-old finished in Limousin oak for up to nine months. It offers limited editions of 21-year-old Archive, Glenlivet XXV, and its Cellar Collection, which includes old malts. It released a 16-year-old cask strength Nadurra (meaning natural) with naturally non-chill filtering and natural color in the U.S. market. Upon completion of the distillery expansion in 2010, Chivas bottled a Glenlivet Founders Reserve at 21 years old; and prior to that, it released a Nadurra Triumph 1991 celebrating the Triumph barley used in its distillation.

Glenlossie Distillery

➤ Pronounced *glen-LOSS-ee*

➤ Elgin, Morayshire IV30 8SS

➤ No website

➤ No visitors center

John Duff, who managed GlenDronach Distillery, built Glenlossie Distillery in 1876 with the support of two partners. The distillery survived the Pattison Crash, a fire in 1929, and closure during two world wars. In the 1960s, it underwent a modernization and expansion, which included the installation of electricity.

The Noser Knows

Classically, The Glenlivet malt has provided a benchmark for the Speyside Glenlivet style. It has a clean, elegant nose with hints of heather rising to flavors of ripe peach pie and vanilla ice cream complemented by tastes of almonds and crumbled macaroons. It is balanced, smooth, and rounded with a long, dry, finish.

Is this One Part Greater than the Whole?

Today, Glenlossie shares a sprawling complex that includes her sister distillery, Mannochmore, a filling store for several surrounding distilleries, extensive warehousing, and an expanded dark grains plant that processes the draff and pot ales for animal feed. At one time the production operators worked six months at Glenlossie and six months at Mannochmore, but increasing demands for new-make spirit now requires that both distilleries operate for forty-six weeks. Presently each distillery has its own set of operators, but they tend to work at both places so that *"cross-skilling"* occurs, allowing operators to gain experience at both distilleries.

The Purifying Effect

The mashman at Glenlossie employs a continuous system for mashing that begins with water at 64°C (147° F) mixing with grist in the mashing machine. Once the mash settles, the operator allows the water to spray constantly onto the mash while steadily increasing the temperature. Meanwhile, he continually drains the wort away and pumps it into the washback.

The large stills have thick necks above plump shoulders in the classic onion-shape design, allowing the lighter components to move into the condensers. The addition of purifiers on the lyne arms of the spirit stills gives the vapor a cold water bath in order to condense some of the volatiles before they enter the condensers, and then returns them through a narrow

The Noser Knows

The Glenlossie single malt has a light body and grassy, floral flavors. The exposure to copper and the use of purifiers creates a fresh-tasting whisky with a touch of oiliness and sweet vanilla notes.

pipe to the pot where they are redistilled. All of the new-make spirit is filled on-site; and some of it is also matured in the extensive warehousing on-site. All of Glenlossie's production goes into blends, and the only bottling of its mature whisky appeared as an offering in the Flora and Fauna series and as a Managers' Choice.

Glen Moray Distillery

➤ Pronounced *glen MURRAY*

➤ Elgin, Moray IV30 1YE

➤ www.glenmoray.com

➤ Visitors center

Glen Moray is very much a working distillery with a small visitors center compared to the other visitors centers in the area. But the tour groups are generally small and the welcome warm. Here, the business is making good whisky without a lot of fanfare.

The quiet road that borders the Glen Moray Distillery was, however, at one time, the main road between Inverness and Aberdeen, and as such saw both the famous and infamous travel on its byways. By 1687, the burgh of Elgin had no fewer than eighty private breweries, all eager to tend to people's thirsts. It comes as no surprise, then, that Glen Moray began its life as the West Brewery in 1828 near Gallow Hill. And Gallow Hill was truly a place name because this is where criminals and witches were "brint to the death, hanged by the craig, or droont" until these practices were ended in 1690.

Proof of the sorry endings to Elgin's criminal population came when some of the warehouse floors needed filling, and excavations began on Gallow Hill to acquire backfill. The digging unearthed several skulls, one of which had a bullet hole with the bullet still lodged in the jaw of the unhappy miscreant. One worker on the site, with a wry sense of humor, gently placed the skulls on the seat of his car so that he could take them all for a ride as he was certain they had never been in a motor car before. After their ride around Elgin, he brought them all back to the distillery, where builders eventually reinterred all of the skulls when they completed work on the warehouses.

Long after the executions had ended and well into its life as a brewery, Glen Moray underwent another and final metamorphosis. By September of 1897, *The Northern Scot*, reported that the owners, R.Thorne and J. Gregory had completed their conversion from the West Brewery to Glen Moray Distillery. Difficult years in the whisky industry began immediately following the conversion to the new distillery, and there were several years when no whisky was produced at Glen Moray. Eventually, the distillery went into receivership and Macdonald and Muir purchased it in 1920.

The Distillery Cat's Meow

Because the original steam engine from Glen Moray had its original parts and had survived unchanged since 1870, it sat in the visitors center at her sister distillery, Glenmorangie. The change in ownership ended this relationship, and it appeared that a piece of Glen Moray's history would reside in another distillery. But Glenmorangie underwent a significant face-lift in 2010, including its visitors center, and returned the steam engine to its home at Glen Moray. The "little engine that could" will soon fire up and operate as a working model to run an old mill inside the Glen Moray Distillery.

Out with the Old, In with the New, Back with the Old

Glen Moray pioneered onward, virtually unchanged, for the next three decades until the company undertook significant expansion in 1958. This included removing the old steam engine that had run the machinery in the distillery, including the mill, the mash tun, and the grain elevators.

Much of the equipment was scrapped in the name of modernization. The wooden washbacks were removed and replaced with ones of stainless steel and the number of stills doubled to two pairs. In 2004, Louis Vuitton Moët

The Distillery Cat's Meow

In 1976, when some of the nineteenth-century brass man doors from the Glen Moray stills ended on the scrap heap with the old spirit safe, Ed Dodson, the distillery manager at that time, put them in the boxes that held the bungs for the barrels. They were beautiful pieces of brass stamped with an 1897 date and the Blair Campbell name. More importantly, they were part of the institutional history of Glen Moray. His foresight meant that they are now displayed next to the replacement stills in the still house.

Hennessey acquired Glen Moray when it bought Ardbeg and Glenmorangie. Within four years it sold the distillery to La Martiniquaise, who wanted the distillery for malt to use in its blend, but who has also undertaken the promotion of Glen Moray as a single malt.

Although much of the equipment at Glen Moray has been modernized, the distillation practices remain traditional. The copper pot stills maintain their original onion-shapes, including a lyne arm angled downward and a short, thick neck that melts into puddled shoulders on the wash stills and angled ones on the spirit stills. The stills run slowly to maintain a heavy copper contact, and the stillman takes a short middle cut in order to capture the fruity esters at the beginning of the run.

New Owner, New Future

If the interior equipment at Glen Moray has changed, the buildings that house it have not. Neither have the old processes changed nor the old warehouses that age the new spirit in bourbon casks on-site. Both the old and the new somehow work well at Glen Moray, because the owners are looking to a possible expansion. They hope not only to supply blenders, who hold the spirit in high regard, but also to continue their promotion of Glen Moray as a single malt.

Presently, La Martiniquaise's core range includes the Glen Moray Classic (NAS), 12- and 16-year-olds, and plans to release a 10-year-old matured (not finished) in Chardonnay casks. It also offers distillery-exclusive bottlings of vintage years, and single casks with both finishes and full maturation in different wine casks. Distillery exclusives are limited editions with non-chill filtering and natural coloring. In both 2010 and 2011, the distillery used peated malt at about 20 ppm to produce a small amount of peated spirit. Although its intention is to use it in its blend, it may appear as a single malt in the next seven to eight years.

The Noser Knows

Glen Moray malt has a clean, grassy, herbal nose. Distinctive toffee sweetness and fruit appear on the palate followed by subtle notes of peat and anise. The body is smooth and creamy with a rounded gentle finish. Since the French owners La Mariniquaise have a long history in the drinks business, it is a possibility that enthusiasts will see Glen Moray matured or finished in different casks like rum and Armagnac.

Glenrothes Distillery

➤ Pronounced *glenROTH-ez*

➤ Rothes, Morayshire AB38 7AA

➤ www.theglenrothes.com

➤ Visitors center

Having a tour of Glenrothes with Ronnie Cox, brand ambassador for Glenrothes, is like having an enjoyable lesson in the history of distilling. Glenrothes lies, unseen, in the center of Rothes, cuddled in a hillside niche alongside the town cemetery. We met and began our conversation in the Rothes cemetery—no pot stills here, no smells of mash or worts, and certainly no whisky.

Instead I was surrounded by headstones and tombs layered in terraces along the hillside, and the names of most of the whisky families in Speyside. Much conversation centers around heritage in distilling traditions and practices, but Cox reflected that the Rothes graveyard also provides "a sense of heritage in the whisky business." Certainly, this cemetery contains a silent history of many distilling families—it was the perfect place to begin a conversation about whisky.

The Devil's Brew and the Church

Fifty-five years after the passing of the Excise Act, which had the effect of legalizing most illicit stills, two bank directors from the Caledonian Bank, a local agricultural bank, joined forces with the owner of Macallan to build Glenrothes Distillery. They wanted to produce a light, more elegant, Speyside malt, which was in fashion at the time and which provided a contrast to the more robust oily spirit produced at Macallan. Banking often has several layers of financial transactions, and this was the case for the Caledonian Bank, which planned to finance the project.

The City of Glasgow Bank had made loans to Caledonian, and when the bank crisis of 1878 caused a run on the Glasgow bank, it called in all loans. Consequently the construction of Glenrothes came to an abrupt end until the bank directors could find additional financing. Redemption arrived in the form of the United Presbyterian Kirk (Church), which invested £600 ($965) and completed the building of the distillery. While the investment may have been a prudent one, it was also an ironic one because the kirk had previously denounced whisky as "the devil's brew."

In 1887, Glenrothes came under the ownership umbrella of Highland Distilleries (now Edrington Group), and its malt quickly became highly regarded as one of the best malts for "top dressing" when making a blended whisky. Because of the high demand for Glenrothes spirit, the owners expanded the still house in 1979 to accommodate five pairs of stills, which were installed in two lines on either side of a large, airy window reminiscent of a cathedral space. The stills have tall, thick heads and boil balls that create reflux action and copper contact, enhanced by the slow, steady running of the spirit stills. The result is a clean, fruity, estery spirit with little sulfur, which matures well in mainly second-fill American and European oak sherry casks.

Whisky Lexicon

A top dressing malt refers to a malt that blenders find very desirable for making a successful blended Scotch whisky. Most blenders do not want an assertive-flavored malt that will overwhelm the blend of grain and other malt whiskies. But a malt used as a top dressing has the ability to marry all of the different flavor components of a blend into a smooth and balanced Scotch whisky and give character to the blend.

The Noser Knows

The Glenrothes single malt has a family profile that includes "good bones" and a classic beauty. It has ripe berry fruits with a touch of bitter orange peel and sweet butterscotch, scented with allspice and a very slight floral back note. All flavors are nicely rounded and balanced with a luscious syrupy mouthfeel and a medium body. It evokes memories of deep summer fruit pies with vanilla bean ice cream.

The Wine Merchant and the Malt

In 1989, Berry Bros. & Rudd, the London wine merchants who have the Cutty Sark brand, needed a malt whisky and approached Edrington to acquire Glenrothes. The ensuing arrangement kept the ownership and operation of the distillery in the hands of Edrington, but left the commercial licensing of the Glenrothes single malt brand in the hands of Berry Bros. & Rudd.

Initially, Berry Bros. & Rudd released Glenrothes at 12 years old as it had been done previously. Relying upon their knowledge as wine merchants, they decided instead to develop a core of different vintage year expressions that would better reflect their belief that maturity of their malt was more important than its age. The result is a range of vintage years from the 1970s, 80s, and 90s, as well as several bottlings of non-vintage Select Reserve expressions, and an occasional single cask bottling at natural strength. The vintage bottlings capture the family profile of Glenrothes single malt with variations of its character and natural color.

Glen Spey Distillery

➤ Pronounced *glen-SPAY*

➤ Rothes, Morayshire AB38 7AU

➤ No website

➤ No visitors center

Polly Macdonald's mother described the distillery her daughter manages as bijou. She was right, as mothers frequently and annoyingly are. And like all bijous, this particular treasure has all the facets and nuances—quirks, even—that make a gem special and unique.

The distinguishing aspects of the Glen Spey Distillery include a unique mill, a distinctive heating system for its stills, and a part-time use of its purifiers.

The Jewel Box Distillery

Unlike most distilleries that use Boby or Porteus mills, Glen Spey Distillery houses a Buhler Miag mill that is one of two extant in Scotland. It began life as a rice mill and is an instrument found more commonly in laboratories. Its one drawback is that an operator cannot "play" with grinding the malt, and it requires a malt with very high friability (an ability to crumble well). Macdonald compares using a malt with high friability to working with "a good crumbly biscuit (i.e., cookie), rather than a chewy one."

The rest of the distilling equipment sits in its own jewel box surroundings with nothing large about it. The mash tun resides immediately beside the stills, which sit slightly below the eight stainless steel washbacks—all steps of the process are in immediate sight and proximity to each other. The Glen Spey Distillery is a water-efficient site because the operation tends to cool water more often than it tends to heat it, resulting in energy and resource

The Distillery Cat's Meow

The first semi-Lauter stirrer, now used in mash tuns throughout the whisky industry, was first installed at Glen Spey and was known as the Glen Spey Gear.

efficiency. The mashing water enters the system warmer than needed and demands the addition of cool water to lower it to the required temperature of 64°C (147°F).

Radiators and Purifiers

The stills also employ a unique system of radiators charged with reclaimed steam from the condensers to heat the distillate. The external condensers are literally sliced into two parts— one part operates like a traditional shell-and-tube condenser, but the corresponding half is a multi-pass condenser. This portion allows five passes of cold water to work in a conventional way to condense the distillate, but when the temperature of the water reaches 94°C (201°F), the water reroutes to a holding tank, then returns under pressure, and flashes steam into the bundle of radiators in the still.

The new-make spirit distilled at Glen Spey has a nutty character that begins with the use of cloudy worts, but the distillery character tends to mature into a light and delicate whisky, influenced by the use of external purifiers on the spirit stills. These enclose the lyne arms in a tank of cool water as they leave the still house, which rapidly condenses the distillate and returns it to the pot via a thin pipe to reboil the heavier elements. Interestingly, however, the purifiers only work from May to September during the warm summer months.

Bound for the Blenders

Very little of Glen Spey appears as a single malt with virtually all of the new-make spirit going to blends. Tankers carry the new-make away from the distillery for filling; and while maturation takes place in three dunnage and two racked warehouses, the warehouses contain a mixture of casks from other distilleries. When Glen Spey appears as a single malt, it is usually offered by independent bottlers, although the distillery's owner, Diageo, has offered a bottling in the Flora and Fauna series and as a Managers' Choice.

The Noser Knows

The new-make spirit distilled at Glen Spey has a nutty character, but the copper contact in the tall, thick necks of the stills and the additional contact provided by the purifiers tend to strip any sulfur notes. The balance of the reflux in the lantern-glass-shaped stills, and the use of the purifiers helps to create the light, floral, almost delicate citrus flavors that one can find in the mature Glen Spey.

Glentauchers Distillery

➤ Pronounced *glen-TOCK-erz*

➤ Mulben by Keith, Banffshire, AB55 3YL

➤ No website

➤ No visitors center

Located between Keith and Craigellachie, Glentauchers Distillery was built in 1987 by W.P. Lowrie, a whisky broker. One of his clients was a young James Buchanan, to whom he gave credit to buy whiskies that became part of the blends which Buchanan later launched. When Lowrie retired in 1906, he sold Glentauchers Distillery to Buchanan. During the twentieth century, the distillery came under the ownership of two other companies before Pernod Ricard (Chivas) acquired the ownership of Glentauchers in 2005.

Always Meant for Blending

Glentauchers sits among farm fields with the buildings arranged around a courtyard. Originally, the water supply was so abundant that it supplied water not only for processing and cooling, but also for driving a turbine that provided electricity and power for the equipment. When Glentauchers reopened after its closure during the World War II, the owners paired steam engines with the turbines to provide power to the distillery, which did not have electricity provided by the national grid until 1958.

Although the floor maltings are long gone at Glentauchers, and stainless steel has replaced the cast iron mash tun, its copper-and-brass cover, and the six wooden larch washbacks still remain in place. Both the wash and spirit stills have a similar onion-shape design—both have a slight downward angle to the lyne arm and thick necks. The spirit distilled at Glentauchers is aged in bourbon casks but is intended for blending. Allied Distillers released only one 15-year-old proprietary bottling in 2000, and whisky enthusiasts need to rely upon independent bottlers for any other expressions.

The Distillery Cat's Meow

Chivas Brothers, the owner of Glentauchers Distillery, have automated all of its distilleries. It made a conscious decision, however, to retain the manual operation at Glentauchers for use as a hands-on training distillery for its employees.

The Noser Knows

Glentauchers has aromas of new-mown grass, herbs, parsley, and cilantro. Flavors appear a bit astringent and mouth filling on the palate but diminish with water and give rise to tastes of baked apples with vanilla. It has a somewhat bitter edge with background notes of licorice, and finishes quickly with faint flavors of anisette.

Imperial Distillery (Mothballed)

> ➤ Pronounced as spelled

> ➤ Carron, Aberlour, Banffshire, AV38 7QP

> ➤ No website

> ➤ Not open to the public

Following its centenary year, Allied Distillers closed Imperial Distillery on a December day in 1998. The closing was made even more poignant when Ronnie Macdonald, the distillery manager at that time, recalled December 19, 1955, a day when his father reopened Imperial after a period of closure.

A Jubilee Distillery

Thomas Mackenzie established Imperial Distillery in 1897, Queen Victoria's Diamond Jubilee year, and the distillery was named appropriately to mark the event. A large golden crown also capped one of the chimneys to celebrate the distillery's name and the queen's Jubilee. Macdonald clearly remembers arriving at the distillery and seeing the golden crown atop the kiln chimney in place of the traditional pagoda design. Shortly afterward, it was removed because of its rusted and dilapidated condition.

The day I last toured Imperial Distillery was one of those glorious early summer days in Scotland, and sunlight emphasized the color of the light red Aberdeen brick used in the construction of Imperial. The little railroad station that served the small community of Carron as well as the distillery remained virtually as it was 100 years ago.

Macdonald remembered taking the train from the station into Aberlour, the golden crown, the original malting barn, and the distillery lit by gas light before it was reopened by his father. It is a pretty place, and now a quiet place because of its closure.

Mackenzie founded Imperial Distillery during the "whisky boom" and built it to help meet the demand for spirit. It must also be remembered that no sooner had it opened than the Pattison Crash occurred; consequently, Imperial Distillery operated only one year before it closed in 1899. Production resumed very briefly at the end of the World War I, but that ended and only maltings were used at Imperial. In 1955, after it had been modernized, Macdonald's father headed the reopening of the distillery to help meet the new demand for Scotch whisky.

The Distillery Cat's Meow

In 2007, copper thieves operated in the Speyside area and targeted closed and mothballed distilleries. Coincidentally, electricians began work at Imperial's warehouses on the day that the thieves decided to loot the distillery. The vigilant electricians noticed several official-looking workers wearing hard hats and yellow fluorescent vests, with a van parked outside the stillhouse. Well aware that Chivas had its own team of maintenance personnel, they phoned the van's registration number into the police. The police captured the thieves nearby and discovered a second unknown van with a collapsed axle caused by the weight of the stolen copper.

Much is unchanged inside the distillery since the 1950s. The cast iron mash tun with a Corten steel lining continued to use the old rake system instead of the newer lauter rake. Six wooden washbacks made of larch now sit empty and silent. The stillroom houses four stills with a different design for the wash and spirit stills. The lantern-glass wash stills have no angle to the lyne arm that tops a broad, thick neck of medium height, allowing for some reflux and copper action. The spirit stills, on the other hand, have a slight downward angle to the lyne arm, allowing some of the heavier

The Noser Knows

Imperial malt whisky has a delicate and lightly citrus nose with some honey-licorice in the background. It has a light body with flavors of fruits (apricots and peaches) in syrup, and clover honey. The finish is warming but quick.

Imperial distillery has operated only 43 of its more than 100 years of existence, and Pernod Ricard (Chivas Brothers) has mothballed it. If it dismantles the distillery, this single malt could become a collector's item, since the distillery has not produced spirit for 14 years.

flavor elements to be vaporized. The neck is still thick but taller, and it melts into an onion-shape with gently rounded shoulders. The new spirit was previously aged in refill sherry casks and bourbon casks, but all have been moved off-site and the warehouses now lie empty and quiet.

Inchgower Distillery

➤ Pronounced *INCH-gow-er (rhymes with power)*

➤ Buckie, Morayshire AB56 5AB

➤ No website

➤ No visitors center

Inchgower Distillery began life in Cullen as Tochineal Distillery in 1824. The common story that circulates about the demise of Tochineal in Cullen and its resurrection as Inchgower Distillery in Buckie surrounds the story of water, or as in this case, the story of not water. Supposedly, the site in Cullen not only had an unreliable water source, but one that dried up completely. At that point, John Wilson deeded the distillery to his son, Alexander, who dismantled the operation at Cullen and moved it piecemeal to Buckie. Eventually Wilson went bankrupt and the city council owned and ran it for many years until Arthur Bell & Sons bought it in the mid-1930s for its blends. Similarly, Diageo, the present owners, operate the distillery solely for blending spirit.

The Distillery Cat's Meow

The local version of the story about Inchgower Distillery's relocation lends more credibility to the real reasons for its reestablishment in Buckie. According to Stephen Woodcock, Inchgower's current distillery manager, "John Wilson built his distillery in Cullen, on land he didn't own. Because the landowner's wife did not like the fact that there was a distillery on their land, the landowner raised the rent to such a point that it was unaffordable." And the high rent, probably compounded by the unreliable water supply, precipitated moving the distillery to another town.

The Original Plan vs the Current Jumble

The character of the original distillery still presides in the elongated courtyard surrounded by the stone whisky-production buildings. They show remarkable stone lintels and coins quarried from local sites that no longer operate. The distillery operated with self-sufficiency—maintaining its own maltings, kiln, cooperage, filling, and maturing stores. Originally, the design of the distillery showed a logical movement from one process to the next—the malt barns formed one side of the courtyard and attached to the kiln; other buildings followed outward from the kiln and housed the mill and mash tun and stills. Each step of the process flowed from one to the other with logic and commonsense. But during the years, repairs and replacements occurred and operators placed new equipment wherever it fit physically, rather than logically. The result is a distillery that certainly works but doesn't necessarily flow as it did when it was first designed.

The malt now takes a tortured journey from its intake: it moves up and down and across empty spaces to reach the grist hopper before filling the mash tun. The stainless steel mash tun uses its stirrers to back-stir the porridge concoction to produce a cloudy wort with solids suspended in it in order to form the required nutty style that develops in the stills.

The onion-shape stills have slim, tall necks with downward lyne arms, and the stillman runs the stills at a high boil, so that the distillate rises rapidly and moves into the condensers quickly. The shape of the stills and lyne arms and the rate of the boil ensure that little copper contact or reflux occurs. Tankers collect new-make spirit for filling at Auchroisk Distillery and maturing elsewhere.

I know of only one distillery release of a 12-year-old Inchgower from at least two decades ago. Other expressions exist in the Flora and Fauna, Rare Malts, and Managers' Choice ranges, as well as offerings from independent bottlers.

Kininvie Distillery

➤ Pronounced *KIN-iv-ee*

➤ Dufftown, Morayshire

➤ No website

➤ No visitors center

Janet Roberts, the eighty-nine-year-old granddaughter of William Grant, dedicated the Kininvie Distillery

The Noser Knows

The 12-year-old bottling of Inchgower has flavors of bubbling brown sugar, molasses, and honey. They are reminiscent of apple tarte tatin or crème brûlée. The mature whisky has the chewy sweetness of Kraft® caramels, and just a whiff of smoke associated with burnt brown sugar.

in 1990. She had previous experience with dedications because at a much younger age she opened the visitors center in 1969. She remembered both William Grant and his wife and the early days of Glenfiddich and Balvenie distilleries, which are very different distilleries from the one she dedicated at the end of the twentieth century.

A Piggyback Distillery

Kininvie Distillery sits modestly on the same property as her two sisters, Glenfiddich and Balvenie. And although Kininvie has its own mash tun and washbacks, they sit next to Balvenie's equipment in a modern addition to the older Balvenie Distillery. Kininvie's stills, however, sit in their own separate still shed, a very functional metal building, which technically constitutes the entire Kininvie Distillery.

Three Bottlings Celebrate a Birthday

Originally, William Grant & Sons wanted to build another distillery that could provide an extra malt to use in its own blends, and has only ever bottled the Kininvie as a single malt on three occasions. In 2006, on the occasion of Janet Roberts's 105th birthday, it did a staff bottling of a 15-year-old Kininvie at 105 proof and called it Hazelwood, the name of her home. When Mrs. Roberts's 107th birthday arrived in 2008, the company released another bottling of Kininvie, also named Hazelwood, at 17 years old and at 107 proof. The placement of the second bottling of Hazelwood in the duty-free shops makes this the only public offering of Kininvie as a single malt. In 2011, Mrs. Roberts celebrated her 110th birthday with a staff bottling of Hazelwood at 110 proof. A remarkable Kininvie to commemorate a remarkable woman!

From the beginning, Kininvie seemed destined to be a good place—with the prescience that only cats seem to have, the Balvenie Distillery cat moved to Kininvie as soon as it was built. Whether the cat found a better home and whether Mrs. Roberts brought longevity to Kininvie (or Kininvie brought it to her), no one will ever know, but good things and Kininvie seem to go hand in hand.

The Noser Knows

A release from William Grant & Sons in 2008 remarks, "The Hazelwood Reserve has matured for 17 years in sherry casks, under the watchful eye of the distillery craftsmen. It has a nutty aroma, with lots of dried fruit and an intense flavor of oaky spice."

Knockando Distillery

➤ Pronounced *no-CAN-doe*

➤ Knockando, Morayshire AB38 7RY

➤ www.malts.com

➤ No visitors center

Locating Knockando Distillery involves finding the hidden turnoff to the narrow, twisting road to the distillery. Built in 1898, well after the legalization of whisky distilling and the need for secret locations, one wonders why John Thompson, the founder, located it in its lovely but obscure setting. The answer lies in its location near to water and the railway.

In addition to securing a reliable supply of water for the distillery, he also obtained land for a siding next to the new railway. He commissioned Charles Doig, the prominent distillery engineer and architect, to design and build Knockando Distillery, which began production in 1899. This followed on the heels of the Pattison Crash in late 1898, which left distilleries with unpaid accounts for whiskies they had overproduced. Although Thompson managed to continue distilling into 1900, the new Knockando Distillery closed less than a year after opening. Knockando came under the ownership of both W&A Gilbey Ltd and later Justerini & Brooks when the two companies merged. Other mergers eventually brought the distillery into the Diageo portfolio.

The Noser Knows

In 1978, J&B launched Knockando as a 12-year-old single malt, releasing it with a vintage year on the label. This gives the assurance that all the malt in the bottle has been distilled in only one year. The drawback, however, is that it contains *only* 12-year-old whisky from a particular vintage year, whereas in other single malt bottlings, 12 years old indicates the age of the *youngest* whisky in the bottle, which can (and often does) contain older malts.

A Variation on the Distillation Theme

The production of the Knockando single malt employs processes that are unique to this distillery. The mashman grinds a fairly fine grist that results in a cloudy wort because of solid particles suspended in the liquid. The solids lend nutty, sulfury flavors to the distillery character in the new-make spirit, but they are balanced and complemented with fruit and a delicate body formed in the distillation. The mashman uses a slightly long fermentation of sixty-six hours to develop fruity esters before he moves it to the wash still.

The first distillation takes place in wash stills with short, thick necks leading into external condensers that allow minimal contact with copper. This combined with boiling the spirit fast to vaporize the volatiles quickly and to limit copper contact preserves the nutty and sulfury style.

On the other hand, the stillman operates the spirit still in a way that is almost diametrically opposed to the operation of the wash stills. In the second distillation, the stillman boils the distillate slowly in a still with a boil ball and a tall, thin neck, which creates reflux allowing the volatiles to condense and reboil. This in turn prolongs the contact between the copper and spirit, suppressing the further development of sulfur notes.

Refill bourbon casks mature the majority of the spirit, with European oak accounting for about 10 percent of the maturation casks. Knockando single malt is bottled at 12 years old, 15 (Richly Matured), 18 (Slow Maturation), and 21 (Master Reserve). The percentage of European oak casks used in aging increases as the number of maturation years rises. In 2010, Diageo also released an expression of Knockando in both the Managers' Choice and Special Release ranges.

The Noser Knows

The bottled Knockando at 12 years old presents fruit and floral flavors with only background notes of nuts, malt, and digestive biscuits (graham crackers). This raises the question about the presence of the forceful sulfur and nutty notes in the original distillery character of the new-make spirit. Where did they go? The cloudy wort and the fast boil with limited reflux and copper contact in the wash still helps to produce this style. The long fermentation and the slow distillation in the spirit still promote more reflux and copper contact and play a part in the production of the fruit and floral notes. These are lighter and more delicate flavors and are masked in the new-make spirit by the stronger sulfur and nutty aromas. Sulfur, however, is one of the first notes to evaporate during maturation, and the bourbon casks help to filter and modify them. Their regression and softening during maturation moves these flavors to the back seat and allows the fruit and floral notes to come forward.

Linkwood Distillery

➤ Pronounced as spelled

➤ Elgin, Moray IV30 3RD

➤ No website

➤ No visitors center

Peter Brown established Linkwood Distillery in 1825, and the ownership stayed in his family for the next seventy-five years. The distillery had only one other owner before Scottish Malt Distillers (now Diageo) acquired it. Clearly, the distillery profited from both a consistent ownership and good management because its success demanded several expansion and refurbishing projects, and it suffered no closures, except during World War II.

The Distillery Cat's Meow

Linkwood Burn, which provides cooling water for the distillery, is dammed into a pond on the distillery property. Attracted by the tranquil setting and the water, swans have long made their home at Linkwood and consequently grace the label of the Flora and Fauna bottling of the single malt. Competition, however, arose in the 1990s in the form of Cooper Park in nearby Elgin, where people lavishly fed the wildlife. Aware that free food was abundantly available only a short distance away, several of the swans took off for Cooper Park.

Because of Linkwood's popularity among blenders, Diageo needed to expand the distillery. But the old site was not large enough to accommodate the expansion. Instead, in 1971 it built a new distillery in the Waterloo design that Diageo favored during the 1960s and early 1970s (See *Caol Ila* profile). The new distillery, known as Linkwood B, sat next to the old site, now named Linkwood A, and both distilleries worked in tandem for several years until Diageo closed Linkwood A in 1985. When demand increased, the production operators could temporarily call the old washbacks into service and move the mash from Linkwood B into the washbacks in Linkwood A and then back again for distillation.

Although the design of the new stills accurately matched the design of the older models, Diageo replaced the worm tubs that were used at the old site with condensers at the new distillery. This change results in a purifying effect caused by additional copper contact in the condensers and in the slow running of the distillation. Most of the spirit is aged in bourbon casks with a portion of them maturing in dunnage warehouses on the distillery site. Although Diageo released a few expressions through the Flora and Fauna series, the Rare Malts range, and the Managers' Choice, most enthusiasts need to rely on independent bottlers for access to this malt.

The Noser Knows

Aromas of perfumed florals with a subtle background of peat define the Linkwood nose. The floral notes continue with notes of heather intermingled with sweet lemonade and citrus flavors. Linkwood has a light, smooth body, nicely balanced with little complexity.

Longmorn Distillery

➤ Pronounced as spelled

➤ By Elgin, Morayshire IV30 2SJ

➤ No website

➤ No visitors center

Longmorn Distillery sits south of Elgin on the road from Craigellachie. Although it was modernized in the 1970s, it maintains a traditional appearance with pagoda-topped chimneys despite the fact that it no longer uses floor maltings that would require them. Longmorn has a very respectable bottling as a single malt, but its value to distillers lies in its reliability and importance as a top dressing in blended whiskies. The Longmorn malt does not push its character forward and overwhelm the blend; instead, it helps to give a blend its character. Ann Miller of Chivas Brothers remarks on Longmorn's track record that reaches back to the nineteenth century, "[Longmorn] was established in December 1894, and we can track the price for which casks of the Longmorn were being bought by brokers. Apparently it went up and up and up, indicating that it was in great demand. Even when it was untested, people appreciated just how good it was."

The Early Years

John Duff built Longmorn Distillery adjacent to its sister distillery, BenRiach, in 1897 and brought his experience and knowledge as a distiller to his newest venture. With the Pattison Crash in 1898, he had to relinquish his distillery shares to the bank. Ownership of Longmorn remained fairly stable, and the distillery underwent an expansion and refurbishment in the early 1970s. In 1978, Seagram took over Longmorn until Pernod

The Distillery Cat's Meow

Longmorn Distillery had a small railway depot at the end of a spur to accommodate whisky trains that brought supplies to the distillery and carried away filled casks. The use of a small pug extended the service to BenRiach, Longmorn's sister distillery. Sadly, both of them fell victim to *Beeching*. In the early 1960s, Dr. Richard Beeching, the chairman of British Railways, issued his first report advocating the closure of small rural lines in an unsuccessful attempt to reverse the financial losses of the railway. This resulted in the closure of half of the railway tracks and two-thirds of the train depots in Britain. The effect on the Speyside countryside and the distilleries was significant. People lost train transport, and the distilleries lost the deliveries brought by the whisky trains. Many of the floor maltings at the distilleries closed as they looked to central maltsters to do the job. The small train spurs and pugs no longer functioned, and they became a casualty of Beeching, or the Beeching axe.

Ricard (Chivas) acquired the Chivas Brothers distilleries in 2001. Under the ownership of both Seagram and Pernod Ricard, much of the distillery production finds its way into the Chivas Regal and Royal Salute blended whiskies.

Making Longmorn

The formation of Longmorn's character begins with fermentation in stainless steel washbacks with a standard forty-eight hours of fermentation. Upon completion of the fermentation, the distillation more fully determines the body of the whisky. Two words—long and thick—define the shape of the Longmorn stills that have elongated onion-shape stills, long, thick necks, and lyne arms. These thick shapes would indicate that there are few obstacles to heavy and robust flavors rising to the lay pipe and little reflux action. But the long distance produced by a drawn-out base and the neck allow an extended time for copper contact with the spirit and its resulting purifying effect. The final and most significant flavor development occurs during maturation in a selection of first fill bourbon casks, refill sherry casks, and refill bourbon casks that help to round and balance the full flavors of the Longmorn whisky.

The Distillery Cat's Meow

A former Longmorn distillery manager tells the story of stolen whisky. During the distillery's centenary year, the company bottled a 25-year-old one-off commemorative bottling of Longmorn whisky. Shortly afterward, a thief burgled the Longmorn Distillery and stole a bottle of its 15-year-old whisky, a lovely full-flavored, balanced whisky, and a loss in itself. Within days of the first break-in, the burglar returned and took only a bottle of the Longmorn limited edition 25-year-old malt.

Although blenders requisition most of Longmorn whisky for blending, Seagram released a proprietary bottling of 15-year-old Longmorn single malt in 1994. Pernod Ricard replaced this expression with a 16-year-old bottling in 2004. Visitors centers for the Chivas distilleries also offer Longmorn in their Cask Strength range, which includes limited edition bottlings at different ages (only available at the centers).

The Noser Knows

The Longmorn single malt has toffee sweetness balanced with violets and lavender. Its flavors include banana and fruit notes, a touch of spice, and a well-rounded profile with a lengthy finish.

The Macallan Distillery

➤ Pronounced *ma-CAL-an*

➤ Craigellachie AB38 9RX

➤ www.themacallan.com

➤ Visitors center

The Distillery Cat's Meow

Jordie Low, the ghillie, was the steward and guide for The Macallan's fishing beat along the River Spey. Jordie Low had worked in the distillery his whole life and was considering retirement so that he could follow his avocation of fishing. Before he left, the managing director approached Jordie to stay on, not at the distillery, but at the river as the ghillie.

He was knowledgeable and kind and patient, and I enjoyed his company and tutoring in the very early hours on a summer's morning. I fished from the center of the river into the deep pools on either side of me with most of the light coming from the working distillery on the top of the hill. In Scotland, the summer dawn comes very early and when the sun appeared, I went home bone-tired and with no fish. Instead, I carry the memory of my adventure with Jordie Low—it was almost as good as catching a fish.

Many distilleries sit in very lovely locations, and The Macallan has one of the loveliest. Agricultural fields lie on either side of the road that leads to The Macallan, and the distillery perches above the Spey River. Mountains rise behind the river and green fields lead down to the water—it must be one of the most beautiful river valleys in Scotland.

The Macallan—a Benchmark

The people working in the distillery show the same attention to detail and depth of knowledge that Jordie Low demonstrated at the river. Distillers and customers consider The Macallan whisky to be one of the best distilled, and the classic standard for full-bodied sherried single malts. The distillery workers are guardians of The Macallan's reputation and heritage but maintain a vision of the future.

In the recent past, The Macallan tied a great deal of its identity to the use of Golden Promise barley, the direct firing of its stills, and the consequent use of rummagers inside the stills. The small stills and sherry casks used for maturation helped to define The Macallan whisky profile. And although whisky making is very much tied to tradition, it also marches forward with an eye to the market place.

The Second Millennium

The use of Golden Promise barley has given way to Minstrel, a new strain of barley with higher yield and higher resistance to mold, and concerns about the safety of direct-fired gas heating gave way to steam heating. But life and whisky making at The Macallan also continues much as it has in the past. The distillery continues to use small, dumpy stills and continues the tradition of maturing most of the new-make in sherry casks. The short stills, with thick necks and downward-sloping lyne arms, allow little reflux action and little copper contact with the spirit.

The Noser Knows

When the distiller at The Macallan changed the stills from direct-fired heating with rummagers to steam heating with no rummagers, he did not make the decision lightly or quickly. Much concern existed that the change in the heating system would alter the classic flavor profile of The Macallan whisky. At first, he converted only one wash still and ran it for twelve months before the final decision was made to change all the stills to indirect firing and to remove the rummagers. The consensus of opinion held that the maturation in sherry casks overcame any marginal differences in the new-make spirit distilled before and after the change was made. The move to steam heating also provided the stillman more temperature control and resulted in a greater degree of consistency in the new-make spirit.

But whisky making is so often a balancing act. And at The Macallan, the stillman runs the stills slowly so that the spirit simmers quietly in the pot, increasing the copper contact and compensating for the small size of the stills. He also takes a very small middle cut that amounts to only 16 percent of the spirit run. Most importantly, he begins and ends the middle cut well toward the heads of the run in order to capture more of the fruit and floral esters found toward the foreshots and to counteract the lack of reflux in the dumpy stills.

The maturation of spirit in sherry casks has most significantly defined the flavor profile of the mature whisky, and The Macallan Distillery takes 65 percent of the sherry casks coming into Scotland. People at The Macallan oversee the harvesting and air-drying of European oak in Northern Spain before the wood is shipped to the South for additional air-drying. Coopers then form the oak into casks and ship them to Spanish bodegas, where they will mature sherry for eighteen months before they are emptied and sent to The Macallan.

During the last decade, management at The Macallan began to harvest American oak from the eastern United States and ship it to Spain, where it is made into casks to mature sherry, as the European oak has done for generations.

In 2005, it launched its Fine Oak range containing whiskies matured in European sherry oak, American sherry oak, and American bourbon oak. Some purists decried the departure from aging The Macallan spirit in anything other than European sherry oak, and some speculation existed that sherry casks were difficult to obtain. Even if it were necessary to ease the demand for sherry casks, it is worth remembering that The Macallan's sherry oak expressions continue the traditional maturation in sherry casks. Other enthusiasts who prefer a wider range of flavors may find an alternative in the Fine Oak range.

The Heritage

Much of The Macallan single malt's reputation rests with one of its earlier owners, Roderick Kemp.

Following its founding in 1824 by Alexander Reid, the distillery passed through the hands of three sets of owners before Kemp took possession in 1892. On his death, a trust took over the management of the distillery for Kemp's heirs, the Shiach and Harbinson families.

The establishment of the trust began one of the more interesting stories of distillery ownership. The trust continued until The Macallan Distillery became a public company (Macallan-Glenlivet Ltd.) in 1967 in order to finance an expansion, although its management remained in the families' hands.

In 1996, Highland Distillers joined with another minority

The Distillery Cat's Meow

The Macallan Distillery had operated two plants known as Still House Number 1 and Still House Number 2, which had closed in the late 1970s. In 2008, the popularity and increased demand for the single malt necessitated recommissioning Still House Number 2 and building additional warehouses.

shareholder to take over The Macallan Distillery. In 1999, the Edrington Group became the majority shareholder when it took over Highland Distillers and effectively moved The Macallan under its protection since it was no longer a public company.

In *Whiskypedia: A Compendium of Scottish Whisky*, Charles MacLean provides the best clarification of the confusing history of the present owners: "Edrington Ltd. was founded in 1961 by the Robertson sisters, as a holding company for their capital interests in Robertson & Baxter, Highland Distilleries, the Clyde Bonding Company and North British Distillery— all of which companies had been founded by their grandfather. Income from the company was channeled into a charitable trust, The Robertson Trust. The reason for this arrangement was to avoid punitive death duties following the death of their father, and to ensure the independence of the companies. Today it is Scotland's leading charitable trust. "

In *Whiskypedia* MacLean goes on to note, "in 1970…93 percent of [the production] went for blending." But today that percentage has almost reversed itself with 90 percent of the production now going for bottling as single malt expressions. The reversal began in the 1980s under the family management of Macallan-Glenlivet when it released its core range of 10-, 12-, 18-, and 25-year-old single malt matured in sherry casks. It later added a 30-year-old to the core range, as well.

The Noser Knows

The Macallan malt has become the gold standard that defines a classic sherried Speyside single malt. It is balanced and full-bodied with dark fruit (figs, dates, plums, raisins) complemented by flavors of sherry and chocolate oranges. The Macallan 18-year-old best showcases the culmination and balance of these definitive flavors, whereas the 25-year-old contains more spice and wood notes, reflecting the effect of additional years in the cask.

In 2005, The Edrington Group released the Fine Oak range and has since added the 1824 Collection, which is available through global trade retail. It has also released the Fine and Rare expression that offers vintage bottlings from the six decades between the 1920s and the 1970s. And finally, a range of expressions, available only at the distillery visitors center, provides an excuse for a visit to Speyside.

Mannochmore Distillery

> ➤ Pronounced *man-NOCK-more*

> ➤ Elgin, Morayshire IV30 8SS

> ➤ No website

> ➤ No visitors center

Scottish Malt Distillers built Mannochmore in 1971 on the same site as its sister distillery, Glenlossie. Similar cohabitation sites also existed at Clynelish with the older Brora, at Teaninich with the older distillery known as B Side, at Linkwood with the older distillery known as Linkwood A, and at Glendullan with the two distilleries operating under the same name. All of the new construction occurred in the late 1960s and early 1970s, and in each of these instances the older distillery was eventually dismantled or closed.

This, however, was not the case at Glenlossie/Mannochmore. Although the newer distillery, Mannochmore, was mothballed from 1985 to 1989, the Glenlossie Distillery was not. During the 1990s the company decided to have one crew of operators work a half year at one distillery and the other half year at the sister distillery instead of closing one of the distilleries and removing it from the company's portfolio. The decision has now paid dividends when it needs more production to meet an increased demand.

A (Relative) Newcomer to the Game

Scottish Malt Distillers designed Mannochmore in the Waterloo design (see *Caol Ila*), and the open plan sweeps from the cast iron mash tun with its copper canopy (soon to be replaced) to the wooden washbacks. The mashman uses a clear wort that he ferments for a long time to encourage the fruity style of Mannochmore single malt. The stills have a similar design to their sisters at Glenlossie and also use a classic onion-shape design. Tall, thick heads rise above puddled shoulders, but these stills do not employ purifiers on the spirit stills as they do at Glenlossie. All of the filling, and some of the maturation, takes place on-site, and virtually all of it goes to blending. The only proprietary bottlings appeared in the Flora and Fauna series, in the Rare Malts series, and as a Managers' Choice.

The Noser Knows

The long fermentation and clear wort encourage the fruity green apple flavors in this clean-tasting, light-bodied malt.

Interestingly, an expression of Mannochmore appeared in the 1990s, labeled Loch Dhu—the black whisky. Spirit caramel coloring provided the deep color but also imparted a sweet treacle taste to the whisky—people either loved it or hated it, and most hated its unusual taste. The bottling is no longer offered, and when it was discontinued, collectors rushed to buy the remaining bottles—more for its anticipated rarity than its taste.

Miltonduff Distillery

> ➤ Pronounced as spelled
> ➤ Miltonduff, Elgin, Morayshire, IV30 8TQ
> ➤ No website
> ➤ No visitors center

The Noser Knows

At one time the Miltonduff Distillery produced both Miltonduff and Mosstowie single malt whiskies. A pair of Lomond stills distilled the Mosstowie whisky that was only intended to provide an additional malt for the Ballantine blended whiskies (See chapter 18, *Lost and Hidden Distilleries*). Increasingly, blenders sought Miltonduff malt for its blends, and the distillery converted the Lomond stills to traditional pot stills in order to meet the demand for Miltonduff.

The Pluscarden Abbey situated east of Elgin lies in the countryside in the Mosstowie area near the town of Miltonduff. Both the area and the town lend their names to the two whiskies produced in the distillery just visible across the fields from the war memorial in the town.

A Large Production Plant

A new focus on increasing the output of Miltonduff called for a modernization of the distillery in the 1970s, including the removal of the floor maltings, pagoda-topped chimneys, and grain towers. Few of the original buildings remain, but in its transformation, Miltonduff has become one of the largest working distilleries.

Despite its modernized exterior, the distillery maintains a traditional copper-covered mash tun with brass trimmings, and the tiny slits in the floor of the mash tun allow a fine milling of the barley. The resulting mash contains more flour, which allows more water to surround the flour and extracts more sugar from the grain. Today, production operators carefully analyze the barley to ensure that the milling produces the required amounts of flour, but stories live on about previous owners who did the analysis completely by touch.

Making a Blending Malt

The stills, however, create the essential body of the new-make. At first glance it appears that these stills would produce a heavy and robust profile—the stills have a round onion-shape, no waists, thick, short necks, and a lay pipe with a downward tilt. This design allows a lot of heavier flavor components to make their way into the condensers, yet Miltonduff whisky has few strong and overwhelming flavors that would be undesirable in a whisky primarily destined for blending.

Instead, the distiller creates the more subtle character of Miltonduff by only

The Noser Knows

Miltonduff begins with a fragrant floral nose with a whiff of smoke. It has a medium body with a nicely balanced palate of light peat, delicate notes of lavender, macaroons, and caramels. Its flavors linger with a slightly dry finish.

covering the bottom of the still with the wash. This technique creates a large boiling area and a longer trip to the lay pipe because of the increased distance between the wash at the bottom of the still and the head of the still. Consequently, the heavier flavor elements continue to boil in the base of the still with only the lighter ones able to complete the trip into the condensers. The slow boil also exposes the distillate to the copper for a longer period of time, and in the process helps to purify the new-make spirit.

Most of the new-make spirit is aged in first fill and refilled bourbon casks, but few expressions of Miltonduff single malt exist. Often Glenburgie and Miltonduff distilleries are viewed as sister distilleries because Pluscarden Abbey provides a backdrop for both distilleries, and the malt from each distillery forms an important part of the Ballantine blends. Interestingly, Allied Distillers, its former owner, released one of the few proprietary bottlings for both Glenburgie and Miltonduff in 2002 at 15 years old.

Mortlach Distillery

➤ Pronounced *MORT-lock*

➤ Dufftown, Morayshire AB55 4AQ

➤ No website

➤ No visitors center

Mortlach single malt is a little-known gem of a whisky. Few people have an opportunity to visit the distillery, and its malt is not readily available. It rates as an excellent example of Highland whiskies, but it often goes unnoticed and underappreciated. Mortlach is a well-kept secret.

The Distillery Cat's Meow

William Grant learned the distilling craft during a long tenure at Mortlach Distillery. Over the course of twenty years, he and his wife saved their money while he built his knowledge of distilling. In 1886, they moved down the road from Mortlach, built Glenfiddich Distillery, and equipped it with secondhand stills from Cardow (now called Cardhu) Distillery.

The distillery, licensed in 1823, was the first one to appear in Dufftown. It suffered through several owners and closures before George Cowie acquired it upon the death of his partner. His son, Dr. Alexander Cowie, assumed the management and during his tenure, he developed the business, expanded the distillery, and built a railway spur from the Dufftown station to service the distillery. When his only son died in World War I, he sold Mortlach to John Walker & Sons Ltd., which eventually became part of Diageo.

The "Wee Witchie" Bewitches

In 1964, the owners built an entirely new distillery in order to meet the demand for Mortlach, but they retained the original stills so that the original character of the spirit would not alter. Indeed, the distillery uses a unique set of stills, an even stranger system of distillation, and worm tubs to create the distinctive heavy character of Mortlach. The stillroom houses three pairs of stills with boil balls and slender heads in common, but each still has a slight variation from its neighbor and all the sizes are different.

The stillman operates the No. 3 pair of large stills like a traditional double distillation as he would in any traditional distillery. He then operates No. 1 and No. 2 pairs of small stills together but takes the tails, the weakest part of the spirit run, and distills them for a third time in the smallest No. 1 spirit still named Wee Witchie. Stillmen call this third distillation the "dummy run" because they take no spirit cut from this distillation in order to increase the alcoholic strength of the spirit. Additionally, the use of worm tubs limits the copper contact so that the final distillery character emerges as a very robust, heavy, and sulfury spirit.

The Noser Knows

Mortlach begins with an explosive nose with very slight aromas of peat and floral notes that appear with the addition of water. Sweet graham cracker flavors join tastes of currents, dates, figs, and citrus zest, with sherry and spice associated with red candy hearts. It lingers long in the mouth and on the palate, and the overall character is full, mouth filling, balanced, and complex.

The distinctive character of Mortlach spirit lends itself to blends and very little Mortlach appears as a single malt. Diageo released expressions of Mortlach in several series including Flora and Fauna, Rare Malts, and the Managers' Choice. Bottlings of Mortlach malt also appear in the expressions offered by independent bottlers, and it is worth the search to find it.

Roseisle Distillery

➤ Pronounced as spelled

➤ Roseisle, Morayshire IV30 5YP

➤ No website

➤ No visitors center

The Noser Knows

The optimistic view of the future of Scotch whisky also drove the sustainable design of the distillery using green technology. The distillery has reduced its CO_2 emission by saving on the use of the fuel needed for producing steam (equivalent to removing 10,000 cars from the road). Additionally, it uses the by-products of distillation in an anaerobic digester, where microbes feed on the waste to produce biogas, a renewable energy source.

The Diageo orchestra reached a full crescendo when it built and opened Roseisle Distillery in 2009. Built adjacent to the Roseisle Maltings, Roseisle Distillery is both Diageo's and the industry's largest plant, with two mash tuns, fourteen stainless steel washbacks, and seven pairs of stills. This distillery has a production capacity of 10 million liters (over 2.6 million gallons) of spirit per annum, with all of it ostensibly earmarked for blends. Diageo notes that "85 percent of Diageo's brand volumes produced in Scotland are sold overseas" and the distillery, it continues, "demonstrates the importance of creating production capacity for the long-term, in particular to meet growing demand from developing markets in Asia and in Latin America."

The opening of the Roseisle Distillery in 2009 begs some comparison with Ailsa Bay, built by William Grant & Sons at Girvan in 2007 because they both carry a similar brief of producing spirit for blends and of implementing "innovative new techniques." But contrasts between the two distilleries also lie within the comparisons—Ailsa Bay's production capacity rests at 6 million liters (1.6 million gallons) per annum in a plant smaller than Roseisle, and Roseisle can produce 10 million liters (over 2.6 million gallons) per annum in a larger plant. Diageo is also a large corporation owning twenty-seven additional malt distilleries, whereas William Grant & Sons is a family business, owning three other malt distilleries. So, a question about Roseisle's future naturally arises, and addressing it is like recognizing the 800-pound gorilla in the room.

The Future—the Low Road?

Both Ailsa Bay and Roseisle distilleries are megalith distilling complexes. Even though this model is not uncommon in the grain whisky industry, it is new to the single malt whisky side. The future of this type of large distillery complex using different methods of distillation and producing multiple styles of malts remains to be seen. One cannot help but wonder if the future of small nineteenth-century malt distilleries, particularly ones producing malts for blending, may be threatened by a huge distillery capable of producing different types of spirits for blending. And one cannot dismiss the collective memory of many people who recall Diageo's closure of sixteen distilleries (with ten of them closed in 1983 and another four in 1985) during a downturn in demand. In an unjust world, these distilling megaliths, producing more cost-effective blending malts, could justify the closing of less-efficient and smaller malt distilleries.

The Future—the High Road?

On the other hand, Diageo took a different approach to slumps in demand following the 1983 closures. In the 1990s, during a brief downturn in demand the company moved operators among different distilleries for a shorter amount of time. In this way, it could continue to produce spirit so that there were no gaps in the inventory, and it could keep the distillery within its portfolio. Perhaps most heartening has been its recent "£100 million three-year investment programme in the development of Scotch."

Assuming the best, whisky enthusiasts will find the future of these huge distilleries an interesting story to follow. In an ideal and just world, they can function the way the Grant Company has indicated it wants to use Ailsa Bay: as a place for trial runs that can improve the distillation at its smaller malt distilleries, and as a distillery that produces blending malts, permitting its premier malt distilleries to produce spirit for sale as single malts.

The Noser Knows

Currently, Roseisle confines itself to the production of two types of spirit for blends. Tom Bruce-Gardyne, in *SMWS Unfiltered,* July 2011, quoted the site operations manager, Gordon Winton, as saying, "We produce a heavy Speyside character, what we call 'nutty,' which is the easiest one for any distillery to make. And we produce a light Speyside style. . . The word is there is no plan for a Roseisle single malt."

Speyburn Distillery

- ➤ Pronounced *SPAY-burn*
- ➤ Rothes, Aberlour AB38 7AG
- ➤ www.speyburn.com
- ➤ No visitors center

I have always loved Speyburn Distillery. It is a beautiful distillery that produces a gentle, fruity Speyside malt, and it holds warm memories of my early education in malts. The distillery stretches along the Rothes Glen with its tall, white buildings in contrast to the dark green fir trees that rise on the hill behind it. Charles Doig, the renowned distillery architect, designed Speyburn to capitalize on the steep geography of the land so that the buildings stretch upward rather than sprawl outward. The sight of it along the floor of the valley never fails to make me smile.

The Old Century

At the time of Speyburn's construction, it included all the modern technology that the nineteenth century could offer. Most notably, John Hopkins, the founder, installed drum maltings that automatically turned the barley in revolving drums and removed the necessity for the intense manual labor of hand-turning the grain. They were the first drums installed in the industry and now are the only ones remaining. Silent since the 1960s, the Victorian malting drums sit quietly in the malt barn with the 1897 Jubilee year marked above the cast iron doors. For more than a hundred years, the production at Speyburn relied on precedence and the knowledge gained from a century of experience.

The Distillery Cat's Meow

John Hopkins constructed his distillery in 1897, the year of Queen Victoria's Diamond Jubilee. He had very definite plans to begin production in November so that his first casks would bear the date of 1897, commemorating the queen's Jubilee. But Mother Nature intervened with a massive snow storm that prevented the beginning of production. With only one week remaining in the year, the production crews began distilling in uncompleted buildings without windows and doors. The coal fires, heavy coats, and hard work kept them warm enough to produce one requisite cask with the 1897 Diamond Jubilee date.

The New Century

The new millennium brought concerns about the cost of maintaining nineteenth-century equipment and the sheer impossibility of finding dies to cast replacement parts. Speyburn became semi-automated in the early 2000s, allowing it freedom to increase production and freedom from long closures caused by break downs. Although they replaced the wooden malt bins with stainless steel and automated the malt intake, milling, and yeast handling, the distillery operators continue to make Speyburn spirit as they always have done in the past.

The mash tun uses a semi-Lauter stirrer rather than the old rake, but the mashman uses it to turn the mash only between the applications of the waters. The remaining time the water sits on the mash to extract the sugars by infusion, much like a cup of boiling water does with a tea bag.

The fermentation occurs in four wooden Douglas fir washbacks during a fairly short, but traditional, forty-eight hours. The distillery has only one pair of onion-shaped stills allowing little reflux action to occur. Notably, Speyburn uses worm tubs rather than condensers, adding a slight sulfur note in the new-make spirit, which disappears in the mature spirit.

Most of Speyburn's spirit is aged in refill bourbon casks with only a small portion aged on-site in two dunnage warehouses. Although the warehouses include several floors, they simply cannot accommodate the volume of spirit produced at Speyburn, so most of the new-make is tanked to other distilleries or to its warehouses in Airdrie.

Traditionally, Speyburn single malt has been available as a 10-year-old bottling, particularly in the United States. More recently, the master distiller has released a 25-year-old bottling named Solera and a no-age statement known as Bradan Orach.

The Noser Knows

I have always thought that Speyburn single malt is a perfect autumn whisky that speaks to mulled apple cider, maple leaves underfoot, and sweet candied apples. The nose recalls herbs complemented by apple and pear notes and some melons. Bobby Anderson, the distillery manager, remarks that "the new-make spirit has a cream-soda note that seems to disappear in the matured whisky." I find that it may be complemented by the vanilla compounds in the American oak casks and appears as flavors reminiscent of candy apples or bubble gum. This is a gently rounded malt with a dry finish.

Strathisla Distillery

➤ Pronounced *strah-THEYE-lah*

➤ Keith, Banffshire AB55 5BS

➤ www.maltwhiskydistilleries.com

➤ Visitors center

In early July, the lupines are in full bloom around the site of the Fons Bulleins Spring at Strathisla Distillery. In the twelfth century, Celtic monks built a brewery here, making this one of the oldest brewing sites in Scotland.

Relocating Glen Grant's Heritage

Under Seagram's ownership, the administrative block was refurbished into a comfortable and welcoming visitors center. In addition, the dramming room, where whisky tastings are held, and the conference room provide a glimpse into some of the most beautiful rooms at Strathisla. When Seagram owned both Glen Grant and Strathisla Distilleries, it relocated the interiors of the old Glen Grant House, the Victorian home of Major Grant, to Strathisla. The home, which stood on the grounds of the Glen Grant Distillery, had fallen into disrepair and was no longer capable of being renovated. Rather than raze the entire building, contractors removed salvageable paneling, fixtures, and mantelpieces to Strathisla, where they recreated the Victorian rooms in order to establish the proper environment for evaluating single malts.

The Distillery Cat's Meow

Strathisla Distillery, first built in 1786, had always been known as the Milton Distillery, and the whisky it produced was known as Strathisla (it is, however, still possible to hear some people use the local name of Milton's Toddie rather than the whisky's proper name). When Seagram acquired the distillery in the 1950s, it permanently changed the name of the distillery to match the name of the malt.

Loopy Lyne Arms

A former distillery manager, C. S. McBain, pioneered the design of the mash tun cover at Strathisla, as well as those at BenRiach and Glen Keith. McBain felt that the free flow of air and the removal of undesirable volatiles were important to obtaining a good mash and a successful fermentation in the Oregon pine washbacks. He, therefore, designed a mash tun with a cover for hygienic purposes, but left a considerable space of several inches open between the cover and the sides of the tun to enhance the circulation of air during the mashing process.

The stillroom contains only four stills—two sets of both a wash and spirit still. At first glance, there seems to be little variation between the two types of stills. Both the wash and spirit stills are dumpy with thick necks and have very short lyne pipes with downward angles. The spirit stills also have boil balls to create additional reflux during the second distillation.

The most interesting peculiarities in the Strathisla stills, however, exist between the pairs of stills (known in the distillery industry as the #1 wash and spirit still and #2 wash and spirit still). The #2 set of stills has a slightly narrower shape with a little bit of a waist. The shorter necks of these stills disappear into two very strange lyne pipes that were built to fit the confines of the stillroom. A rafter unfortunately blocked the point where the lyne pipes should have disappeared into the condensers. To remove the rafter would have brought the distillery crumbling down around the stillmen's ears, so the pipes were looped around the beam—one in a crazy looping C-shape and the other in a slowly curving U-shape. Each set of stills is slightly different, and the combination of the spirit from both sets of stills produces the Strathisla single malt.

The Noser Knows

Strathisla single malt has aromas of sweet caramel, toasted malt, and sherry notes with the addition of water. Flavors of dates, figs, currents, and some sweetness follow with a warm lingering finish. It is a lovely after-dinner whisky, especially at holiday times.

Strathmill Distillery

➤ Pronounced *STRAHTH-mill*

➤ Keith, Banffshire AB55 5DQ

➤ No website

➤ No visitors center

Strathmill started its life as a flour mill in 1891 and began as a distillery under the name of Glenisla. It pulls its water from the Strathmill Spring—a source located within the confines of the distillery. Until the 1990s, this little distillery brought its malted barley directly onto the

The Distillery Cat's Meow

A short access road leads to Strathmill Distillery, where it sits quietly beside the River Isla. This tranquil distillery doesn't advertise itself, but it gained some attention when the entire site was badly flooded in the autumn of 1995 and then again in 2002 after heavy rain storms suddenly swelled rivers and streams in Speyside.

premises by an old railroad line, which although no longer operational, still sits just beyond the stillhouse.

The single mash tun has a modified Lauter rake to stir the mash before it goes into the six stainless steel washbacks. It is a very efficient and straightforward operation, with its most interesting features found in the stillroom, which houses four stills. The two pairs of stills have a quite similar design, sporting tall, moderately thick necks. The stills have very pronounced nipped waists between the boil balls and the high, well-rounded shoulders so that the spirit stills, in particular, seem to resemble large roosting cranes.

As the distillate moves toward the condensers, it goes through a water bath so that the heavier oils are condensed first and redirected through a pipe back into the still for redistillation. The spirit passes through these purifiers for a minimum amount of time so that only the heavier oils return to the still while the lighter ones continue on through to the condenser. This produces a whisky high in flavorful esters with few of the less-desirable and heavier feints.

The distillery reserves most all of its stocks for blending, which is the reason most people are unfamiliar with the Strathmill single malt. Strathmill single malt was released as part of the Flora and Fauna series and recently appeared as a selection in the Managers' Choice series. Any other releases can be found, with some searching, under the label of independent bottlers.

The Noser Knows

Strathmill malt has malty sweet aromas that develop into fruit notes with water. It remains sweet in the mouth, rising to some spice on the palate and ending with a distinctive spicy and sharp note.

Tamdhu Distillery

- ➤ Pronounced *tom-DEW*
- ➤ Knockando, Aberlour, Morayshire IV35 7RR
- ➤ No website
- ➤ No visitors center

In 2010, the Edrington Group closed Tamdhu for economic reasons. In June 2011, Ian Macleod Distillers Ltd. bought the distillery to reopen it in early 2012. Ian Macleod had grown and needed not only more spirit for blends, but also a single malt different from the one produced at Glengoyne, its other distillery.

A Work in Progress

At present, Tamdhu is very much a work in progress while Ian Macleod inventories its inherited stock and makes plans for using Tamdhu spirit and for building the brand. Certainly its success at developing Glengoyne's malt expressions bodes well for Tamdhu.

Tamdhu Distillery was built in 1896 under the direction of William Grant, a director of Highland Distilleries (now the Edrington Group). Grant engaged Charles Doig, the renowned distillery architect, to design the new distillery. The distillery twice experienced a roller coaster ride of increased production, followed by a decrease, and then punctuated by a short-term closure.

The world depression and World War II closed Tamdhu for twenty years between 1928 and 1948. The maltings recommenced operations in 1945 while the distillery underwent refurbishment before it began producing spirit in 1948. In 1950, new Saladin box maltings replaced the floor maltings and eventually supplied the malt for the other distilleries in the Edrington Group.

The Distillery Cat's Meow

The 1970s were good years for Tamdhu Distillery. Master blenders sought the Tamdhu spirit for blending and because the spirit was in demand, the distillery installed two additional stills in 1972 and two more in 1975. The following year, the Edrington Group first released Tamdhu as a single malt and opened a visitors center in the old Knockando train station.

The distillery houses nine Oregon washbacks, and the slightly extended fermentation may account for the initial development of its estery fruit flavors. The three pairs of stills employ a classic onion shape with tall, thick necks and downward-sloping lyne arms. While the design of the still promotes a lot of time with the copper to rid the spirit of sulfur, it does not allow much reflux action. Consequently, the stillman will run the stills slowly to increase the redistillation of the heavier compounds in the pot and allow even more copper contact. Using sherry casks for maturation is under consideration, and depending upon warehouse space, the spirit ages on-site.

Even though the people at Ian Macleod are currently evaluating the future plans for Tamdhu, the distillery is certain to benefit from the attentions of this small, independent family-owned business. It will be worth watching how the company proceeds and the direction it will take, and most encouraging to malt enthusiasts will be the expressions of Tamdhu malt that will emerge as it moves into the future.

The Noser Knows

Tamdhu is a well-rounded Speyside—something of an autumn/spring malt. It has citrus flavors as well as ripe pears and cider with subtle notes of oak and sweet toffee. It is smooth and balanced with a dry, lingering finish.

Tamnavulin Distillery

➤ Pronounced *TAM-nah-VOO-lynn*

➤ Ballandalloch, Banffshire AB37 9JA

➤ www.whyteandmackay.com

➤ No visitors center

Tamnavulin was built a year after Tomintoul Distillery in 1966, and the equipment and technology is from the same time. As the crow flies, Tamnavulin sits diametrically opposite Tomintoul, with hills between the two distilleries. Traveling to the Tamnavulin Distillery in the Livet Valley (Glen Livet) along the river of the same name is as pleasurable as the trip to Tomintoul distillery. Many of the rich grain fields in the Livet River Valley seem to be a mirror reflection of the parallel Avon Valley, but the Ladder Hills to the east seem desolate and lonely.

Whyte & Mackay acquired the distillery in 1993 and then closed it two years later. Several plans existed to resume whisky production at Tamnavulin, but none came to fruition and the distillery remained mothballed for twelve years.

The Distillery Cat's Meow

Tamnavulin Distillery is located in the midst of a small hamlet that once supported a woolen mill. When Whyte & Mackay acquired the distillery in 1993, it gave the mill to the community of Tomnavoulin (spelled slightly differently than the name of the distillery). The mill continued to operate as a visitors center to promote the area, its culture and crafts, as well as its whisky heritage, but eventually this also closed.

All Dressed Up and Nowhere to Go

The interior of Tamnavulin Distillery during its twelve years of closure was an admirable comment about the people who work and live in these river valleys. The distillery was left tidy and ready to resume operation—the place was swept, the equipment was clean—and the whole distillery reflected the pride of the people who had cared for it. When the United Breweries Group of India (United Spirits) acquired Tamnavulin in 2007, it reopened the distillery.

A Face-Lift for Tamnavulin's Stills

Although the distillery is operational, the distillation equipment at Tamnavulin reflects the technology of the 1960s. Almost everything is stainless steel—the mash tun, half of the washbacks, and even the spirit safe. During the last three years, the six pot stills, however, have undergone replacement and some redesign. Once the heads of the stills met sharply angled shoulders, but now the angles are curved and the shoulders are rounded.

The Noser Knows

Because of a long period of time that saw no production of spirit at Tamnavulin, the 12-year-old expression of its whisky is not readily available. Traditionally it had a grassy, herbal character with notes of parsley, lovage, and cilantro with a delicate clean body. Its flavors tended toward a sweet maltiness with a slight trace of peat, ending with a quick, dry finish. It is worth watching how United Spirits develops this whisky—it has slightly altered the still design, it produces both unpeated and peated spirit and will double production next year. Although most of Tamnavulin goes toward blends, it will be interesting to note the flavor profile of any future releases of a single malt.

Purifiers encase the lyne arms, which now angle downward—all designed to create a slightly heavier spirit.

United Spirits uses unpeated malt, but for a short time each year it distills a heavily peated spirit, which is aged in refill bourbon casks. In the past, the distillery has released a 12-year-old bottling, but that is increasingly difficult to find. Because no production occurred at Tamnavulin for twelve years, the owners find themselves with stocks of old whisky or young spirit, but limited whisky stocks for the 12-year-old bottling.

Tomintoul Distillery

➤ Pronounced *TOM-in-towel*

➤ Ballindalloch, Banffshire AB37 9AQ

➤ www.tomintouldistillery.co.uk

➤ Visitors by appointment 44-1807 590 274

During the postwar years, when blended whisky was in great demand, two whisky-broking firms from Glasgow, Hay McLeod Ltd and W. & S. Strong, made a commitment to build a new distillery to meet a perceived need for whisky in the future. Having secured the water sources, the brokers began construction of the distillery in late 1964 and finished building early in the next year. Two years later, the same brokers acquired Fettercairn Distillery as well.

In 1973, a group of investors bought Tomintoul, and the ownership continued to change during the next two decades until Whyte & MacKay acquired the distillery in 1995. Five years later, the ownership passed to Angus Dundee Distillers, which also bought Glencadam Distillery in 2003. In the same year, the owners also built a blending facility and followed the unconventional practice of locating it at Tomintoul Distillery. Angus Dundee exports a significant amount of blended Scotch whisky all over the world, and having its own blending plant gives it control over the quality of its blended whisky.

Postwar Technology

Although this is a very young distillery (the third distillery built after the World War II), much of the equipment reflects the new technology that was available in the 1960s. Both the mash tun and the six washbacks are stainless steel, but contrary to the equipment in the rest of the distillery, some of the stills originally showed the older method of using rivets rather than welded seams. The lyne arm has an upward angle that joins the head of the still and falls into a long, thick neck. Between the rounded shoulders and the neck is a boil ball with strong bold rivets evenly spaced and positioned like a necklace around its base. The design of the two pairs of stills allows good reflux action, and the slow boil increases both the reflux and the copper contact. Tomintoul's stills are quite high at 7 meters (23 feet 2 inches), which keeps the heavier elements in the pot and creates the consistently light spirit so attractive to blenders.

New Age Wood

The new spirit is aged on-site in racked and palletized warehouses and matures primarily in bourbon casks. Since Angus Dundee Distillers is primarily a blender, most of the new-make is reserved for its blends although some is reserved for bottling as single malts. Presently, it offers expressions at 10 and 16 years old, and a 14-year-old that is non-chill filtered, using natural color. Unlike the traditional unpeated Tomintoul malt, the distillery has an NAS heavily peated bottling called Old Ballantruan, named for the distillery's water source. In the past, it has also bottled two limited editions—a 1976 Vintage Edition and a 12-year-old matured in sherry casks.

Because Angus Dundee is a smaller family business, it can experiment with different finishes and allow different casks "to play new tunes" on the traditional flavor character of Tomintoul. To this end, it has released two 12-year-old expressions—one a rosy red-colored malt finished two years in a port cask and the other a dark chocolate brown malt finished two years in an oloroso sherry cask.

The People and the Place

The Distillery Cat's Meow

Robert Fleming's love for the area and for distilling comes from a long and unbroken family history. In the past, many distillers came to the craft because of their family heritage, and Fleming's history spans the entire twentieth century. He has carried the tradition into the new century as a fourth-generation distiller who was raised at Glenlivet Distillery, where his father, grandfather, and great-grandfather had worked.

Robert Fleming, the distillery manager at Tomintoul, makes the point that although this is a "modern distillery," it is still very much a "hands-on" operation. It must be remembered that this is 1960s technology and while it may have seemed relatively new at the time of its construction, there are no twenty-first-century computers driving the equipment. Processes at Tomintoul may take place in stainless steel vessels, but its success still relies on the skills of the people who work there.

The Noser Knows

Tomintoul single malt is known as the gentle dram. It has a light body with grassy and citrus flavors supported by buttery macadamia nuts and honey sweetness with a tinge of white pepper at the finish.

Tormore Distillery

➤ Pronounced *TOUR-more*

➤ Advie, Grantown-on-Spey, Morayshire, PH26 3LR

➤ No website

➤ No visitors center

Traveling east toward Ballindalloch, one sees the Tormore Distillery languishing along a broad curve in the road—it is an architectural pleasure. It was built with local stone and fits the curve of the land so well that it seems to be part of the landscape. Tall windows open the distillery and offices to the maximum amount of Highland air and northern light, a particularly important element during the dark winters when the nights come early and the mornings arrive late. Heavy wooden doors, each labeled strikingly and clearly in bold words, accents the stone and white buildings. A long curling pond (now sporting two decorative fountains) mirrors the main building behind it.

The architectural style of the distillery and its situation in its surroundings are only some of several treasures at Tormore. After commissioning an extraordinary design, which took considerable, thought, planning, and effort, it was pure serendipity that one of the distillery employees possessed creativity as a gardener that dovetailed with the creativity of the architect.

The Distillery Cat's Meow

A restored chiming clock sits above the central buildings at Tormore Distillery and plays "Corn Rigs," "Green Grows the Barley-O," "Coming through the Rye," and "Highland Laddie." The choice reflects some thought and consideration since the music recalls Scotch whisky's association with grain.

Distillery Topiary and More

Beginning with the area around the front entrance, the gardener planted natural heathers then created a garden around the rocky borders of the burn along the road. His experiments with the gardens matched his growing artistic expression. He planned and shaped a topiary garden in a shallow hollow to the west of the distillery. Spurning any formalized placement of his garden shapes, he placed them as a menagerie among other shrubs and plants. Pathways leading toward the hills behind the distillery provide glimpses into natural woodland areas thick with bluebells and little pocket gardens with flowering shrubs and perennials. A Japanese garden provides the final touch where guests are offered a dram of Tormore whisky mixed with a cool measure of fresh water from the burn behind the garden. And finally, meandering paths and crisscrossing bridges continue further into the natural woodland surrounding the distillery. At the least, it is a complement to the fine architecture of the place; at the most, it is one of life's (and Speyside's) quiet treasures.

A Late Twentieth-Century Distillery

The ties to Scotland's culture and surroundings are very much part of the exterior of this distillery. Tormore Distillery has a recent history and youthful traditions that are barely more than a half-century old. This site was developed in 1958, and so it follows that the distillation that occurs at Tormore would very much reflect twentieth-century technology and modernization. Consequently, there were never any floor maltings here; the mash tun and eight washbacks are also stainless steel. One process truly does flow from one level onto another at this distillery. When standing beside the washbacks, it is possible to look back at the mash tun on one side and turn to view the lofty still room. A large Palladian window illuminates and frames eight copper stills—four lined up in straight files on either side of the window. Each onion-shaped still has a medium-tall neck with softly rounded shoulders and purifiers attached at the end of the lyne arm. The purifiers capture the distilled vapor and return it, via a small pipe, to the still so that the distillate can be reboiled and purified even further. The present owners, Pernod Ricard (Chivas) fill the new-make spirit, off-site into primarily refill bourbon casks. It then returns a portion of it to Tormore for maturation, although only a small number of the warehouses are the older dunnage varieties with earthen floors.

The Noser Knows

The mature Tormore has a traditional Speyside fruity nose with flavors of sweet vanilla, oak, and a pleasant honey-licorice note at the end. Flavors linger and hold the anise note with a light, dry finish.

What You Need to Know

> ➤ Speyside defines a geographical region that contains almost half of all the malt distilleries in Scotland.

> ➤ Contrary to other geographical regions, the name Speyside also defines a style of single malt, which is characteristically elegant and fruity like the iconic Glenlivet.

> ➤ The Speyside region boasts malt whiskies that are defined by their sherry character like The Macallan, as well as other whiskies, like Glen Grant that are defined by a light, fruity profile. Still other malts, like Benromach, harken to a pre-1960s' Speyside style that recalls a distinctive touch of smoke.

> ➤ Today, most Speyside whiskies are unpeated or very lighted peated.

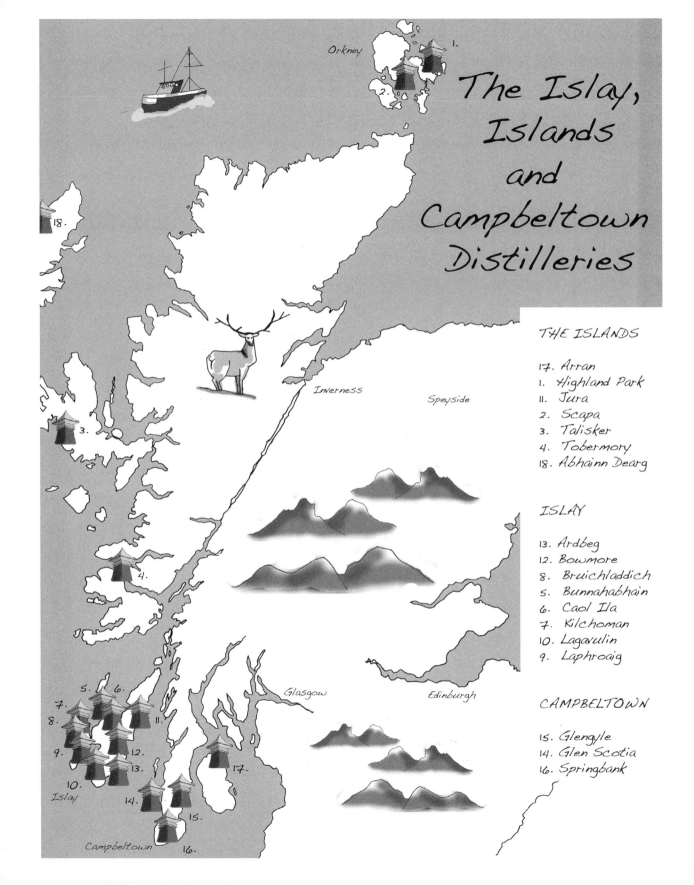

The Islay, Islands and Campbeltown Distilleries

THE ISLANDS

17. Arran
1. Highland Park
11. Jura
2. Scapa
3. Talisker
4. Tobermory
18. Abhainn Dearg

ISLAY

13. Ardbeg
12. Bowmore
8. Bruichladdich
5. Bunnahabhain
6. Caol Ila
7. Kilchoman
10. Lagavulin
9. Laphroaig

CAMPBELTOWN

15. Glengyle
14. Glen Scotia
16. Springbank

Orkney

Inverness

Speyside

Glasgow

Edinburgh

Islay

Campbeltown

CHAPTER 14

The Islands

In This Chapter

➤ Six islands, seven malts

➤ Does island character shape the flavor character?

➤ Two purpose-built distilleries

➤ The new kid on the block

Although the islands are not a designated protected locality and often fall into the Highlands category, the geographical location demands the islands be in a category of their own. The Isle of Arran sits just off the southeast shoulder of Islay, but the other distilling islands stretch northward and encompass the Islands of Jura, Mull, Skye, Lewis, and Orkney.

Because of the self-sufficiency and isolation of the islands, people used only the materials available to them. Consequently, most island malts share a touch of peat and a tinge of maritime saltiness, but vary in their intensity and complementary flavors. Jura and Tobermory both produce a lightly and heavily peated expression of their spirit. Highland Park complements its peated spirit with aging in sherry casks, and both Talisker and Scapa offer different versions of a maritime character. Like the Islay whiskies, a familiar thread seems to connect the island malts, but the diversity among all of them defies the identification of a regional character.

Abhainn Dearg Distillery

➤ Pronounced *AV-EN-jur-ak*

➤ Carnish, Isle of Lewis, Outer Hebrides HS2 9EX

➤ www.abhainndearg.co.uk

➤ Visitors by appointment

➤ +44-1851-672 429

For almost two hundred years, the Outer Hebridean Isle of Lewis has not seen legal distilling. When the licensed Shoeburn Distillery closed in 1840, only illicit stills proliferated. In 2008, Mark "Marko" Tayburn opened Abhainn Dearg Distillery and returned Hebridean whisky to the market place.

A Guardian, Not an Owner

Tayburn's distillery is a variation of the farm distillery that we see at Kilchoman and Daftmill. He is simultaneously building the distillery and the farm that supports it. At present, he grows only 5 tons of the barley he requires for malting, but his plans include producing all the barley needed for distillation. Ultimately he envisions maltings at the distillery with all the barley grown organically and all the ingredients supplied locally in the Outer Hebrides. Marko holds strong convictions that "ours is a fragile environment and that we should want to leave it in a reasonable state as we pass through." His vision of sourcing locally also embraces the practice of recycling locally.

Situated on a former fish farm, the distillery now houses the resurrected fish hatchery that stocks nearby Loch Scaslavat with an eye to making it self-sustaining. He also maintains a herd of Highland cattle that feed on draff and other by-products of the distilling process and works to plant trees to replace the casks he uses for maturation.

Model Stills

The Island of Lewis and the Outer Hebrides are known for the abundance of very soft water, which the mashman puts to good use in the stainless steel mash tun. The wort is moved to wooden washbacks of Douglas fir for a long fermentation of four to five days, helping to develop the fruity compounds that Tayburn wants in his new-make spirit.

Based on the design of a Hebridean illicit still, the pair of stills at Abhainn Dearg Distillery resemble nesting cranes. The prototype that provided the design for the larger production stills sits outside the distillery. The Abhainn Dearg stills have very tall, narrow heads that rise out of wide angular pots, and the downward-slanting lyne arm resembles the long beak of a nesting bird. Everything about the design speaks to creating reflux action, drawing off the lightest compounds, and increasing copper contact—even the spirit safe is made of copper instead of brass. In keeping with former distilling methods, the distillery uses worm tubs to condense the vapors into spirit rather than the more contemporary shell-and-tube condensers.

The Noser Knows

Marko Tayburn ages all of his new-make spirit on-site so that his maturing whisky can reap any climatic benefits of the North Atlantic on one side and the rising mountains on the other. In order for people to have a first-hand experience of both his distillery and the Island of Lewis, Tayburn has started offering on-site whisky courses.

Where Do We Go from Here?

With traditional distilling methods in place, where does the future lie for Abhainn Dearg? Not surprisingly, the single malt from this distillery is a work in progress. Tayburn is very much involved in accessing the developing flavor profile of his spirit as it matures and finding the right combination of age and casks. Presently, he ages the new-make in both American and European oak and is experimenting with different finishes, including sherry, port, Pedro Ximenez, amontillado, oloroso, Rioja, Sauterne, and virgin wood that has had no previous filling. He has already released an 18-month-old spirit aged in bourbon casks named the Spirit of Lewis. But in October 2011, when the spirit reached three years of maturation in oak casks, Tayburn launched his first whisky, named Abhainn Dearg Single Malt Special Edition, a non-chill filtered and natural-colored malt.

The Noser Knows

Tayburn notes that the maturing whisky at Abhainn Dearg is "not heavily peated, with a sweetness. It is light to start and long on the finish." Because of its long fermentation and middle cut toward the heads, which contain fruity esters, one could expect some type of fruit flavor development in the maturing whisky. With only 10,000 liters (2,642 gallons) produced each year, consumers may find only a limited supply of the single malt available. The establishment of farm distilleries like Abhainn Dearg, Kilchoman, and Daftmill provide all of us with the opportunity (and the adventure) of watching a young single malt's character evolve and emerge.

Arran Distillery

➤ Pronounced *AIR-en* (as in the boy's name Aaron)

➤ Lochranza, Isle of Arran KA27 8HJ

➤ www.arranwhisky.com

➤ Visitors center

Arran Island shelters between the mainland of Scotland and the Mull of Kintyre and boasts much of the landscape that visitors often associate with Scotland—bens, glens, and lochs—and since the late 1990s it includes a distillery as well. Indeed, the people at Arran Distillery claim that the island is a bit like Scotland in miniature.

The Return of Distilling to Arran Island

The inauguration of the Isle of Arran Distillery in 1995 marked a return to distilling on the island. Although the island had supported fifty-one distilleries at one time, it took 165 years for the art of whisky making to return to Arran after the closure of the last distillery at Lagg in 1830.

Harold Currie enjoyed a long career in the whisky industry and upon his retirement, he decided to build a distillery. He wanted it on an island near Ayrshire, where he lived, and near a good water source, which he found in the Loch na Davie. Locating his distillery on the Bay of Lochranza brought the additional bonus of abundant rainfall and the possible effect of the sea on the maturing casks.

The Distillery Cat's Meow

The planning and construction of a visitors center began shortly after the distillery opened, but construction stopped because of a pair of nesting golden eagles. Because the birds are a protected species, the construction resumed only after the chicks had fledged the nest. Consequently, the visitors center did not open until 1997. Visitors can still see golden eagles riding the thermals surrounding the distillery.

Decisions, Decisions

The Arran Distillery was built to look like a traditional distillery with whitewashed walls and pagoda roofs (although no malting is done here). Inside, however, the modern design of the distillery floor allows an open view and a natural progression of the distillery production from the stainless steel mash tun to the four wooden washbacks to the stills at the back of the distillery.

From the beginning, Currie wanted to produce a whisky for sale as a single malt, rather than produce malt to sell to other distillers for their blends. He was well aware that the island whiskies, particularly those from Islay, carried a reputation for smoky peaty whiskies, and he consciously chose to make an unpeated, light, and fruity whisky. To this end, the still design uses gently rounded shoulders below tall, slim necks that allow the lightest vapors to move into the condensers. The new-make spirit is aged in small bourbon barrels that allow a faster maturation because of a greater exposure of the whisky to the wood. The warehousemen now also age a small portion of the spirit in sherry casks that allows the distillery to offer additional bottlings.

While the company continues to remain loyal to the original intention of producing a light, fruity whisky, it now also offers limited editions of several different bottlings beyond its core range. Currently, its expressions offer double wood finishes (i.e., whisky aged first in bourbon barrels and then finished for six months in wine casks ranging from a port finish to a Sauterne finish). Additionally, it offers whiskies from single bourbon casks and single sherry casks bottled at cask strength, as well as a medium-peated whisky.

Buy Your Own Cask

In order to finance the distillery in its inaugural year, Currie sold 2,000 shares to Founder's Bond Holders at £450 each (approximately $700 to $750), which entitled the owner to five cases of the distillery's whisky. The owners have expanded on the original idea of bottling casks for investors and allowing people to buy their own cask and mature it in the distillery's warehouses. For those who relish the thought of owning their own cask of whisky, it is worth remembering that in addition to the cost of the cask, an owner must also pay duty, taxes, bottling charges, and a variety of other fees.

The Noser Knows

At heart, the character of Arran malts follows a Speyside profile of elegant fruit. It has a toffee sweetness on the nose, and develops into tropical and orchard fruits on the palate. The addition of water brings forward notes of licorice and vanilla and a touch of wood. It is light-bodied and delicate and finishes with a vanilla bean sweetness.

Highland Park Distillery

➤ Pronounced as spelled

➤ Kirkwall, Orkney KW15 1SU

➤ www.highlandpark.co.uk

➤ Visitors center

Many Orcadians feel that Highland Park Distillery and its single malt belong to Orkney—it is not merely a product of the island. In 1999, the United Nations named Orkney Island a UNESCO World Heritage Site, and some would say that its single malt is as much a part of its heritage as the Neolithic Village at Skara Brae or its long ties to the Viking Norsemen who colonized the Island. The Highland Park Distillery dates to 1798 and is most closely associated with Magnus Eunson, a whisky smuggler and church official. Countless stories exist about his abilities to outwit and charm the excise men who pursued him.

Robert Borwick and his son-in law John Robertson became the official founders of Highland Park Distillery in 1813, when they bought the part of High Park Estate that housed the distillery. The distillery stayed under family control until Borwick's younger son, James, sold it to Stuart & Mackay because he felt that his ownership of a distillery conflicted with his position as a church minister.

By the late nineteenth century, James Grant, a partner in the Stuart & Mackay firm, became the sole owner of Highland Park Distillery and oversaw its improvement and expansion. He held control until 1937, when he sold the distillery to Highland Distilleries, a subsidiary of its best customer, the whisky brokers Robertson & Baxter (now the Edrington Group).

The Highland Park Thumbprint

Blenders had always held Highland Park malt whisky in high regard, consequently the owners reserved all of its production for blended Scotch whisky. This changed in 1979 when they released a proprietary bottling of 12-year-old Highland Park single malt, and they have never looked back. Key to their development and growth during the last thirty years has been their commitment to both Orcadian and distilling tradition.

Floor Maltings on Orkney Island

Highland Park is one of six distilleries that still use floor maltings to produce a portion of the malted barley used in its distillation, which Russell Anderson, the present distillery manager, views as "fundamental to Highland Park." Presently, Highland Park maltmen hand-turn germinating barley on traditional malt floors, and then dry it in kilns over peat fires that impart the characteristic smokiness in the malt whisky's flavor profile. The traditional malting produces a medium to heavily peated malt that provides only 20 percent of the malt requirements for distilling at Highland Park. Central maltsters provide the remaining 80 percent of unpeated malt, and the two types are mixed, resulting in subtle background peat notes rather than very assertive ones.

The Distillery Cat's Meow

All of the peat that provides the smoky notes in Highland Park single malts originates on Orkney from peat bogs located 11 kilometers (7 miles) from the distillery. The peat from Orkney possesses qualities unique to the Island and distinctly different from the peat gathered on Islay or near Aberdeen. Because of Orkney's location and climate, few trees grow on the Island, consequently the top layer of peat contains heather roots, which when combined with cuttings taken from the middle and deepest layers of the peat bog contributes a floral smokiness to the final flavor profile.

Although this step in the production of Highland Park's malt whisky can cause a logistics and financial headache, Russell Anderson, the current distillery manager, observes that they would "lose a thumbprint of Highland Park [malt whisky] if they closed the floor maltings."

Long Fermentation and Slow Stills

In addition to the smoky thumbprint acquired during malting, the long fermentation in Oregon pine washbacks encourages the development of fruity flavors that counterbalance the smoky notes formed during malting. The slow-running distillation in the tall, thick onion-shaped stills develops the whisky's characteristic medium body. Filling takes place at the distillery and most of the maturation takes place in the distillery's warehouses (80 percent are dunnage) into first and second fill sherry casks.

Sherry Casks and Cask Harmonizing

The malting certainly provides a "Highland Park thumbprint," but the use of sherry casks for maturation is equally important to creating the malt whisky's flavor profile. Additionally, the bottlings of Highland Park are done using only natural coloring, and the process of cask harmonizing enables the master blender to maintain the natural color of the malt.

Whisky Lexicon

Once the master blender chooses and combines the casks necessary for a bottling, he returns the whisky to selected casks for harmonizing, or marrying, for several months. In this manner, he can control (and standardize) the color of the whisky by placing the whisky in casks to either deepen or lighten the color without adding any caramel coloring. This harmonizing also allows the whisky to rest, the flavors to marry, and, in some way, the components to stabilize so that the whisky does not turn hazy when water is added.

Among the core range expressions, a percentage of the 12-, 15-, 18-, and 25-year-old bottlings are aged in first fill sherry casks. As the age increases, the percentage of whisky matured in sherry casks for each expression also increases. The older bottlings at 30 and 40 years old usually come from second-fill sherry casks so that the sherry flavors do not overpower the smoke. In addition to its core range, the owners also bottle limited editions and vintage expressions that change as a bottling sells out.

The Noser Knows

The floor malting, fermentation, still design, and sherry casks all contribute to what the people at Highland Park like to describe as Orkney in a glass. At the heart of its single malt is a balance of honey sweetness that doesn't overpower the smoky phenols. As the age of the malt and the percentage of malt aged in sherry casks increases, complementary flavors emerge—vanilla, fudge, licorice, pears, and apples. The older 25- and 30-year-old expressions take on the character that additional years in sherry casks tend to produce—dried fruits (plums, figs, dates) and molasses, dark espresso and chocolate. Overall, Highland Park single malt captures the best components of malt whisky and combines them with complexity, balance, and art.

Jura Distillery

> ➤ Pronounced as spelled

> ➤ Craighouse, Isle of Jura PA60 7XT

> ➤ www.isleofjura.com

> ➤ Visitors center

I don't know which is better—the journey to Jura Distillery or the visit. One boards the ferry at Port Askaig on Islay, whisks across the Sound of Islay, and then bounces off the small boat onto a single-track road that winds through rough grazing land, deep forests, and tiny, very tiny, hamlets. The Isle of Jura provides a home to more than 200 people, 5,500 red deer, a walled garden, a famous author, and, of course, the distillery.

The Distillery Cat's Meow

Jura was home to the author Eric Blair, who wrote *1984* under the pen name George Orwell. He lived and wrote in a home called Barnhill that sat miles beyond the end of the single-track road, and he cherished the seclusion, which the islanders respected. When people came asking for George Orwell, the islanders assumed it was just another person looking to bother the author, so they feigned confusion and a lack of knowledge about someone by that name.

Laird Archibald Campbell established the original distillery in 1810, and it suffered through a series of owners and operators for the next century. In the early twentieth century, the last owners removed the distilling equipment and whisky stocks and allowed the buildings to crumble into ruin.

The existing Jura Distillery in Craighouse reopened in 1963 as part of a 1950s revitalization scheme to attract young people to the island with its promise of employment. William Delmé-Evans, who had designed Tullibardine and later Glenallachie and Macduff Distilleries, turned his talents to reconstructing a new distillery on the former site. This time, however, Delmé-Evans made no attempt to restore the previous buildings or the previous whisky. Instead, he designed his characteristic white buildings and installed large, tall stills to produce a spirit distinctly different from the nearby Islay whiskies.

Making a New Jura Spirit

Unlike its Islay cousins, Jura single malt boasts a light body with honey and vanilla flavors. Most of the whisky's character comes from the distillation and the casking. Willie Cochrane, the distillery manager, remarks that the distillery has undergone a significant change in wood policy since 2000. Currently, the new-make spirit matures in first fill bourbon casks and older maturing whisky has been reracked into new bourbon barrels as well.

The new-make spirit takes the extraction from the first fill bourbon casks very well because its lighter character does not overwhelm the wood flavors with an oily and peaty character. Cochrane notes that the "Jura 10 years old malt went from being the 10th best seller in the UK to the 3rd best seller because they were using really good [bourbon] casks."

The tall lantern-shaped stills, however, help to form the delicate distillery character of the new-make spirit. Cochrane begins with a very lightly peated malt at 2 ppm and uses a longer fermentation of fifty-four hours that will begin to develop fruity compounds. The tall, thick necks of the stills allow only the lightest vapors to move into the lyne arm and the lantern-shape encourages more reflux and copper contact to purify and redistill the spirit.

For one month a year, the stillman uses a heavily peated malt of 60 ppm in order to distill the spirit for the Prophecy bottling. Even though he uses a heavily peated malt, the tall shape of the stills keeps the spirit from becoming oily as it might in a smaller, dumpy still.

The owners release a variety of expressions in their core range that include Origin 10—the original bottling of Jura single malt at 10 years old, and Diurach's Own (i.e., The Islanders' Own Choice), bottled at 16 years old. They also release Superstition, a lightly peated malt, and Prophecy, a heavily peated malt. And, finally, in addition to the core range, they offer limited editions of old whisky, vintage years, cask strength, different finishes, and interesting series (including the Paps and Elements range), usually bottled for the Feis Isle held in May.

The Noser Knows

The Jura malt characteristically has a light, delicate nose matched with a light to medium body. Flavors of milk caramels, vanilla, honey, and elegant citrus notes are complemented with a dry, salty finish. While the core Jura bottlings are not peated, the Superstition and Prophecy expressions have light to heavy peat paired with additional tastes of spice.

Scapa Distillery

➤ Pronounced *SKAP(rhymes with tap)-ah*

➤ Kirkwall, Orkney KW15 1SE

➤ www.scapamalt.com

➤ No visitors center

John Townsend came from Glasgow to Orkney to build Scapa Distillery in 1885 and operated it until it came under the ownership of Scapa Distillery Co. Ltd in 1919. Hiram Walker acquired it in 1954 and installed an experimental Lomond still in 1959. The 1950s saw a significant growth in the demand for blended Scotch whisky, and Hiram Walker needed additional malts for its blends. It not only needed more malt, it also needed the right malts. It installed the Lomond still in order to change the flavor profile of the malt that Scapa Distillery produced at that time, so that it would better suit the Ballantine blend.

Allied bought Hiram Walker in 1986, and Scapa Distillery continued to produce spirit until it suffered through mothballing and sporadic production during the 1990s. Surprisingly, Allied refurbished the distillery in 2004 with an eye to saving all the matured Scapa spirit for sale solely as a single malt. The next year, Pernod Ricard (Chivas) took over Allied Domecq and continued with Allied's plans for Scapa and its whisky. In 2009, it launched Scapa 16-year-old single malt.

The Distillery Cat's Meow

Scapa Distillery overlooks the Scapa Flow where the German navy destroyed its own fleet. Following World War I, the Allies determined that the German High Seas Fleet should surrender. Until they could decide the fate of all the ships, they ordered them to anchor at Scapa Flow off Orkney's main island. In June of the year following the Armistice, the German Admiral von Reuter scuttled the fleet of seventy-four ships rather than have them be under the control of the Allied countries.

Unlike most distilleries in Scotland, Scapa uses hard water for its production because the water on the island filters through sandstone and acquires minerals along the way to the distillery. The long fermentation of 160 hours constitutes one of the more unusual features at Scapa and may contribute some of the estery tangerine flavors in the spirit.

The Lomond wash still contributes the second distinctive feature at the distillery and creates a large degree of reflux action. Looking like an upended coffee can, the head of the still dissolves into angular, sharp-edged shoulders. The lyne arm then emerges, Medusa-like, from the top of the still and coils through a purifier, which contributes to a "light new spirit with the aromas of leather and pineapple." At one time the wash still had rectifying plates to vary the reflux rate of the distillate, but they were removed in 1978 and replaced with the purifier. After the high amount of reflux created in the wash still, it comes as no surprise that the spirit still has a standard onion shape that, in contrast, promotes little reflux. Maturation in refill bourbon casks that are in racked warehouses on-site imparts caramel and honey notes found in the final malt whisky.

The Noser Knows

Scapa's nose begins with wood, spirit, and ozone and develops notes of sweet malt with the addition of water. The aromas expand to flavors of seaweed, oiliness, brine, and old books, supported by vanilla, coconut, and light peat in a medium-bodied malt. It finishes dry with lingering flavors of caramel and butterscotch.

Talisker Distillery

➤ Pronounced *TAL (rhymes with gal)-lis-ker*

➤ Carbost, Isle of Skye IV47 8SR

➤ www.malts.com

➤ Visitors center

The brothers Hugh and Kenneth MacAskill founded the Talisker Distillery on the shores of Loch Harport in 1830. They operated the distillery for thirty-three years until the deaths of both brothers resulted in the transferral of the lease to one of Hugh MacAskill's sons-in-law. He proved an abject failure in managing a distillery and went bankrupt within months. The next leaseholder not only went bankrupt as well, but also served time in prison for fraud.

The ownership eventually transferred to Alexander Grigor Allan and Roderick Kemp, who stabilized and modernized the distillery but took care to retain the flavor profile of the Talisker whisky. In 1916, the majority of the shares in the company transferred to John Dewar and John Walker. Today the distillery falls within the Diageo portfolio.

The Distillery Cat's Meow

The name for Talisker distillery came from Talisker House, owned by the chieftain of the Clan MacLeod. Shortly after procuring the distillery in 1876, Kemp and Allan sought MacLeod's permission to build a pier so that the puffer boats on Loch Harport could bring supplies to the distillery and take away the whisky. The lack of a pier meant that the distillery workers had to float the casks at low tide to a steamer moored in the Loch. It was particularly dangerous in bad weather, and because the men moved the casks at night, it meant that more than one cask went "missing" on a regular basis.

The chieftain refused the distillery owners' request and in exasperation and frustration, Kemp sold out to his partner. Much later, when the old MacLeod died, his successor finally made a concession to build the pier in 1900.

Rebuilding and Replicating

In November 1960, a fire destroyed the still house at Talisker, and it took two years before it reopened in 1962, despite the protestations from local clergy about working on Sunday. The distillery reopened, underwent additional refurbishments, and a visitors center was built.

The Distillery Cat's Meow

In November 1961 following the devastating fire in 1960, Scottish Malt Distillers Ltd., the owners, received a letter signed by ministers from no fewer than three churches admonishing them for undertaking "Sabbath work at Carbost, where the Distillery is being re-built." Although they recognized that God allowed work of necessity and mercy on the Sabbath, they noted, ". . .in our considered opinion there was no necessity for your men to be employed on the Sabbath."

Presently, the distillery uses traditional Oregon pine washbacks with a slightly long fermentation of sixty-seven hours to allow the fruit and floral flavors to begin their formation. Production at Talisker follows fairly standard methods until the process moves into the stillroom with its unconventional number and design of the stills.

The distillery houses a total of five stills because Talisker spirit underwent a triple distillation until the practice ceased in 1928. When it rebuilt the still house following the 1960 fire, it replaced the exact number and design of the previous five stills in order to retain the unique character of Talisker spirit.

Push and Pull Creates a Flavorful Tension

The two wash stills have tall, slim heads rising above a boil ball so that heavy reflux and copper contact can occur. Additionally, the lyne arm loops around in a lazy squared U-shape to create additional reflux so that the vapors are condensed and then returned to the pot through a slim reflux pipe, much as a water jacket or purifier might do in other stills. This design has the effect of creating a light and delicate spirit, but the design of the spirit stills seems to create an entirely different effect.

The three spirit stills are onion-shaped with puddled shoulders, thick heads, and long lyne arms that lead to external worm tubs so that little reflux occurs, and the use of worm tubs, instead of condensers, creates a heavier spirit. Some tension and complexity in the flavor profile results from the balance of lighter components from the wash still and heavier components from the spirit still.

Tankers carry most of the new-make spirit off the Isle of Skye to age in refill bourbon and some refill sherry casks. A small portion of the spirit returns to the island to age in warehouses on the distillery site. Diageo offers a 10- and 18-year-old single malt, and a Distillers Edition that matures ten years in bourbon casks and finishes six to thirty-six months in Amoroso sherry casks. A bottling named 57 Degrees North, referring to the latitude of Talisker Distillery, has aged in bourbon casks, has non-chill filtering, and no age statement (NAS). It also releases Limited Editions of 25- and 30-year-old bottlings, a single cask expression from the Managers' Choice range, and a distillery exclusive.

The Noser Knows

Talisker uses peated malt at 19 to 22 ppm, creating aromas of restrained peat smoke, brine, and iodine followed by faint notes of lemon peel. Mouth-filling flavors of dark fruits and peat moss define the taste followed by notes of vanilla, pears, marmalade, and punctuated by notes of briny seaweed and sea spray. The finish is full and warming with a lingering finish of white pepper and a full body.

Tobermory Distillery

➤ Pronounced *TOE-ber-more-ay*

➤ Tobermory, Isle of Mull, Argyllshire PA75 6NR

➤ www.tobermorymalt.com

➤ Visitors center

In the past, there has been some confusion about the whiskies produced at the Tobermory Distillery. But since Burn Stewart assumed the ownership of Tobermory in 1993, the product line has stabilized and focused. Under previous ownership, Tobermory whisky appeared as a blended malt and a blended Scotch whisky, which are no longer produced. At the present time, Burn Stewart bottles two single malts—an unpeated Tobermory and a heavily peated Ledaig (pronounced in the Gaelic manner, Lay-czech).

The Tobermory Distillery is located directly in the center of the town of Tobermory, the capital of the Isle of Mull, and is indeed landlocked by the other town buildings that surround it. It is very much a part of the town, both geographically and economically. As the town quickly prospered and grew, it expanded by building terraces behind the narrow crescent of shops and houses that ringed the natural harbor.

John Sinclair, a local merchant, realized the commercial potential for a legal distillery and applied for a license in 1797. Not unlike many other distilleries at the time, Tobermory distillery experienced a series of owners during its lifetime, until it was finally closed for a considerable time from 1930 to 1972. Burn Stewart bought it in July 1993 from a Yorkshire property firm that had bought it in 1975.

Necessity is the Mother of Invention

Despite the revolving ownership of Tobermory Distillery, few changes in its fabric have been made so that it remains very much a traditional distillery with no automation. A cast iron mash tun with a copper-and-brass cover, four Douglas fir washbacks, and four copper stills occupy pride of place. The pot stills, in particular, have an unusually designed lyne arm that tilts upward, then turns and continues onward like a flight of stairs with a landing between two sections of steps and risers. Described as having an "S-shaped lyne pipe," the peculiar design was probably an accommodation made to suit the geography of the site. On one side of the distillery lies the harbor, and directly behind the distillery are steep, rocky cliffs. The extra space just didn't exist, so the stills were built to fit the space that was available.

All the components of the pot still work together to initiate the development of the character of Tobermory's single malts. From the minimal boil ball to the thick heads to the quirky S-shaped lyne arm, the stills are designed to promote heavy reflux. This creates a lighter spirit and allows the fruitiness developed in the long fermentation to carry forward through the distillation. In the Ledaig distillation, the still design creates a sweet peatiness rather than an oily one.

Two Single Malts—One Distillery

Creating two very different single malts—the heavily peated Ledaig and the unpeated Tobermory—creates a problem. The two styles of spirit must be kept separate from each other to prevent the flavors of one from crossing over to the other. So that no contamination occurs between the two very different single malts, operators distill Tobermory for six months, and then change to distill Ledaig during the remaining months. Both spirits have separate receiving vessels so that even the residual flavors and aromas of one spirit will not influence the other.

Unfortunately, all of the single malt produced at Tobermory must be tanked off the island to be aged in sherry and bourbon casks at Deanston Distillery near Doune and at Bunnahabhain on Islay. Although the original builders of Tobermory Distillery did, indeed, build warehouses to age their whisky on the site, the previous owners sold the warehouses, which were then converted into housing. And sadly, the same landscape that created the unique stills at Tobermory, prevents any additional warehouses from being built.

The Noser Knows

The lone bottling of Ledaig single malt at 10 years old is poised to change in the near future. Releasing a 15-year-old Ledaig is very much a work in progress. Most notable will be the release of a 40-year-old Ledaig single malt Limited Edition. MacMillan has watched these casks since Burn Stewart bought Tobermory Distillery, when the casks were then aging in the old warehouses. He has recasked them in first fill oloroso sherry casks and returned them to Mull several years ago to prepare them for release in 2013.

Mother of Invention Redux

The lack of warehouses at Tobermory Distillery created a dilemma for Ian MacMillan, Burn Stewart's master blender when he wanted to return some casks to the Isle of Mull for aging. Geography was not on his side, and the possibility of constructing any new warehouses just simply did not exist. MacMillan, however, knew that the distillery had an additional tun room that previously housed old washbacks, now collapsed and long gone. The old tun room became the new warehouse and MacMillan began a program of returning some casks to their spiritual home to finish maturation.

At present, MacMillan has the Ledaig spirit, for the 10-year-old expression as well as the Tobermory spirit destined for 10- and 15-year bottling, shipped off the Island for aging. But the 15-year-old is recasked into first fill oloroso sherry casks and returned to Mull for a final year of maturation, and plans exist to release a 32-year-old Tobermory single malt.

The Noser Knows

Burn Stewart has taken the step of returning to the original method of bottling whisky, so that the Tobermory and Ledaig expressions are offered with natural coloring and non-chill filtering. Ian MacMillan notes that the Tobermory single malt has "aromas and flavors of fruit and gingerbread with a medium sweetness." The additional year in oloroso sherry casks brings additional notes of "sherry fruit cake, softly spicy white pepper and cream toffees" to the Tobermory 15-year-old expression, whereas the Ledaig bottling has "vanilla sweetness yet smoky medicinal notes with a spicy pepper and cloves finish."

What You Need to Know

> ➤ Because of the relative isolation of the islands, the distillers used materials at hand (mostly peat), which accounts for a common thread of light smoke through many of the island malts like Highland Park, Talisker, and Ledaig.

> ➤ The tradition of building distilleries and their warehouses along the coast may contribute to a maritime character in malts like Scapa and Talisker.

> ➤ Other than any custom-made peated expressions, the two purpose-built distilleries, Jura and Arran, consciously make delicate fruity and vanilla whiskies with little peat influence.

> ➤ Having passed its third birthday, Abhainn Dearg released its first "official" whisky in autumn 2011. It will be worth watching how the character of this whisky develops and matures.

CHAPTER 15

 **Islay**

In This Chapter

➤ What defines the Islay character?

➤ Variations on the peat theme

➤ Balancing smokiness with complementary flavors

Atlantic storms often thrash Islay, the southernmost isle of Scotland's western isles, and help to produce the peat fields, soft water, and salt-encrusted warehouses so necessary to producing the island's distinctive single malt Scotch. Indeed, the whiskies produced here are so distinctive that Islay is considered a region separate from the other whisky-distilling areas. The salt and peat and robust characteristics of the Islay whiskies seem to reflect the island's elements.

Accessible only by ferry or plane, Islay developed its whiskies in relative isolation, using only available raw materials. Islay's southern area is a rocky extension of the quartzite granite found on the Isle of Jura, whereas the northern portion is softer, greener farmland that once produced a good portion of the barley that helped to spawn the malt whisky industry. Each of these small areas produces a whisky that takes on the profile of its landscape, resulting in a range of subtle differences from assertive smokiness to soft, silky, Calvados-like dryness.

One excellent time to explore Islay and its whiskies is during the annual Feis Isle (Islay Festival) held in late May, which highlights the distilleries, Islay music, and its signature hospitality. Not only are the distilleries open for tastings and events, but each distillery makes a special bottling available during the festival. It is usually unique, limited, and exclusive to the distilleries during festival time, and possible collector's items.

Ardbeg Distillery

➤ Pronounced as spelled

➤ Nr. Port Ellen, Islay, Argyll, PA42 7EA

➤ www.ardbeg.com

➤ Visitors center

Ardbeg is the last stop on the stretch of road that gives access to three of Islay's eight operating distilleries. Shortly after leaving Lagavulin, the road turns into a distinctly rural lane. The road narrows and the trees crowd closer to the edge until the sight of the pagoda-shaped chimneys rising above the hill provides the first glimpse of Ardbeg.

The first time I visited Ardbeg, the road dropped down to clean and tidy buildings, but they sat next to the rubble of dismantled warehouses. Only the foundation and first floor window sills remained of the owner's house, and the previously used dock had fallen into disrepair. Today, Ardbeg Distillery is a very different place.

Hiram Walker closed the distillery from 1981 to 1989 and its whisky, which was already difficult to obtain became even more so. It had not been truly modernized by the time it became silent and when Allied Distillers acquired it, Ardbeg reopened virtually unchanged. It seemed to close and then reopen on a regular basis, and Ardbeg Distillery sat isolated and ungentrified in somewhat of a time warp. Then Glenmorangie bought the closed distillery in 1997, began its restoration, and rescued this treasure of an old working distillery, renowned for producing one of the smokiest single malts available.

The Distillery Cat's Meow

Duncan Logue, the former brewer at Ardbeg since 1961, remembered when the condenser worm sat in an old worm tub filled with cold water. The distillery used the overflow from the worm tub to power a water wheel that provided some of the distillery's electricity.

Resurrection and Rejuvenation

When Ardbeg Distillery produced spirit in the early 1990s, it was not at full capacity. The distillery only produced a very small amount of new-make spirit, of which only two hundred cases were bottled as a single malt. Under the operation of its new owners, Glenmorangie invested in the plant and increased production.

The old mash tun was replaced by a stainless steel vessel, but it was slipped inside the cast iron shell so that it retained the look and atmosphere of the old one. Additionally, when the old spirit still, which had riveted rather than welded seams, was replaced, faux rivets were added to replicate the original still. The wooden washbacks were kept in place, and now a longer fermentation is used to promote the development of fruity esters. The tiny stillroom continues to house a pair of lantern-glass stills with tall, thick necks that promote reflux and copper contact.

Taming the Peat Beast

For those who like their single malts smoky, this is one of Islay's great whiskies. Smoky flavors (phenols) are measured in parts per million (ppm), and Ardbeg registers one of the highest phenol content at 55 ppm. But the purifier, attached to the spirit still, captures heavier compounds and returns them to the pot for redistillation, creating a cleaner, lighter spirit and providing balance to the high phenol presence.

The peating, the fermenting, and the distilling all contribute to a beautifully balanced and highly complex whisky. The Ardbeg core range includes a non-chill filtered 10-year-old; Supernova, which was released in 2010 and is peated to 100 ppm; Corryvreckan; the non-chill filtered Uigeadail; and Blasda, peated at only 8 ppm.

The Noser Knows

Ardbeg single malt responds well when water is added to release aromas of smoke, creosote, salt, and iodine with an underlying malt sweetness. It is dry in the mouth with "garden peat moss," sweet treacle and fruit, iodine, and some antiseptic. The flavors are balanced, smooth, and rounded with a dry, warm finish that, surprisingly, doesn't linger overly long. Ardbeg is a complex malt revealing layers of flavors, and is a whisky where the sum of its parts is truly greater than its individual components.

Bowmore Distillery

➤ Pronounced as spelled

➤ Bowmore, Islay PA43 7JS

➤ www.bowmore.com

➤ Visitors center

One enters Bowmore, the most centrally located town on Islay, by following the road as it curves around the circular church, which was built in a round design so that no evil spirit could find a corner to hide. The town falls away from the church a very short way to the shores of Loch Indaal. To the left of this convergence of road and water, the Bowmore Distillery nestles into the crook of the coastline with its very distinctive pagoda-topped kilns rising above the shops and houses of Bowmore. The town envelops the distillery buildings, underlining its integral part in the lives, history, and traditions of the people.

Peat and Floor Maltings at Bowmore

Bowmore still does its own floor maltings and kiln drying over peat fires—a practice now ended at most other distilleries. At the distillery site, it malts at least 30 percent of the barley used in the production of Bowmore spirit; a typical mash cycle includes 3 tons of barley malted at the distillery and 5 tons malted at a central maltster.

A distinctive smoky flavor often distinguishes Scotch whisky from other whiskies, and a look inside the kiln at Bowmore provides a visual explanation of the origins of this flavor. Distillery workers spread the grain on the floor above the peat fire for only twelve hours to produce a medium-peated whisky at 25-30 ppm. During that time, the kiln fills with smoke and transfers the peat-reek to the barley.

The Distillery Cat's Meow

The mashman at Bowmore distillery lowers the temperature of the sweet wort to 17°C (63°F) by processing it through a heat exchanger before adding the yeast for fermentation. Interestingly, some of the heat extracted from the cooled liquid is used to heat the public swimming pool located next to the distillery in the former Bowmore Warehouse No. 3.

The materials, used to construct mash tuns vary, but the sample at Bowmore, hand-built in 1947 of hammered copper ribbed with brass, is not only functional but exceptionally beautiful.

The fermentation at Bowmore takes place in Oregon pine washbacks, each labeled with the name of a previous owner. From the tun room, the fermented wash moves into the stillroom, housing four stills. Both pairs of onion-shaped stills have tall, slim necks and upward-tilted lyne arms to produce a light and palatable whisky. Casks, which bear the distillery name and age in stenciled paint rather than in bar code, mature the new spirit in warehouses that rise directly from the shores of Loch Indaal. Warehouse No. 1, dating to 1779, is the oldest building at Bowmore and one of the oldest distillery buildings still used to mature whisky.

Peat, the Sea, and Character

If the peat used at the beginning of the whisky process is part of the distinctive character associated with Islay whisky, the warehouses and their placement may be a final piece of the profile. The wooden casks and the length of time whisky matures in them create variations in each distillery's product.

At the Islay distilleries, one constant is that most of the distilleries' warehouses are situated on the coastline, which may contribute to the salty iodine tang in the Islay malts matured on the island. These warehouses sit directly on the shore, and the sea rises several feet along the walls at high tide and during winter storms often batters the sides of the buildings and crashes over the walls that were built to protect them. At Bowmore, salt crusts the inside walls of the warehouses, and the tide line is clearly marked several feet above the floor.

The Noser Knows

Bowmore Distillery produces bottlings in a wide variety of ages, including some limited edition older bottlings. Some of its most successful ventures were the Black Bowmore, aged in sherry casks, the White Bowmore, aged in bourbon casks, and the Gold Bowmore, aged in a combination of both sherry and bourbon casks. Because the distillery bottled these whiskies at 42, 43, and 44 years respectively in a limited number of bottles, these are expensive and sought after by collectors.

Bowmore Distillery ages most of its new-make spirit in first and second fill bourbon casks with a small portion matured in oloroso and amontillado sherry casks. The core range includes a 12-year-old malt and a 15-year-old malt that matures for twelve years in bourbon casks and then finishes its last three years in sherry casks. Both the 18- and 25-year-old malt marries whisky from both bourbon and sherry casks. The distillery also releases limited editions that include old malts, vintage years, and different finishes, as well as a range for the duty-free stores.

The Noser Knows

The Bowmore malt is spirity and peaty on the nose, and the flavors rise to heather florals with some sweetness, citrus, and a distinctive brine taste, particularly after the second sip. It has a dry, lingering finish and an elegant lightness to it. Edward MacAffer, the present distillery manager, noted that the heavily peated malts of Islay deliver a "punch in the nose, but that Bowmore gives only a light tap on the cheek."

Bruichladdich Distillery

➤ Pronounced *BROOK-laddie*

➤ Loch Indaal, Islay, Argyll PA49 7UN

➤ www.bruichladdich.com

➤ Visitors center

In the small hamlet of Bridgend on Islay, the road turns to the west leading to the Bruichladdich Distillery, which closed in early 1994. In late 2000, a group of private investors headed by Mark Reynier, who had bought and shipped wines since the 1980s, bought the distillery and stocks and reopened the Bruichladdich Distillery in May 2001. It is a fine example of an old, traditional distillery. The whitewashed exterior walls of the distillery overlook the tranquil shore of Loch Indaal, but the interior walls oversee changes that are more revolution than resurrection.

From the beginning, Reynier wanted to run the distillery his way, where "distillation would be about quality, not about yield, volume, or speed." He wanted the people who produced Bruichladdich "to see and watch the progress of what they made, with pride, because they were involved [in its creation]."

The Distillery Cat's Meow

In March 2011, Mark Reynier installed an energy production system to reduce Bruichladdich's carbon footprint. Specially produced microbes feed on the distillery's pot ales (the remaining residue left after the first distillation) and produce methane gas to power the generator, which supplies 100 percent of the distillery's electrical needs.

Avant-Garde in 1881

When Barnett Harvey built the distillery in the late nineteenth century, he commissioned concrete—a new material at that time—for use in its construction. The whitewashed distillery now stands virtually unchanged since then. Because of Islay's relatively remote island location and its new owner's stated mission, Bruichladdich remains one of the industry's most traditional distilleries. Consequently, the distillery provides an infrequent glimpse into distillation the way it was done in the first half of the twentieth century. Many people considered Bruichladdich Distillery somewhat avant-garde in 1881, and it has always produced a fine whisky, so the new owners saw no reason to change equipment and production that always had worked extremely well in the past.

Avant-Garde in 2001

If anything, the distillery has slowed down the production process and incorporated changes to reconnect the distillery to its nineteenth-century heritage. Bruichladdich still uses an old cast iron mash tun with an open top that predates many of the newer covered tuns used by

The Noser Knows

In 2004, Mark Reynier brought the only existing Lomond still from Inverleven Distillery, which was slated for demolition. Allied Distillers installed four Lomond stills during an experimental time when they needed additional malts for their blends—the first appeared as a spirit still at Inverleven in 1955 and had a short columnar "coffee can" neck with three rectifying plates that could be manipulated to increase or decrease the reflux action (See chapter 18, Lost and Hidden Distilleries). The little, dumpy still now resides at Bruichladdich and bears the moniker of "Ugly Betty" and distills gin rather than whisky.

many distilleries. The fermentation process takes twice as long as it did previously. All water —for mashing, condensing, and reducing the final whisky—comes from local sources, all maturation occurs on Islay, and a new bottling plant allows the bottling of the final product on Islay.

The slower fermentation process at Bruichladdich, using less yeast but allowing more time for fermentation, amplifies the fruit flavors in the spirit. Distillation further develops the character of Bruichladdich by using tall, narrow-necked stills to produce a refined, elegant whisky that highlights its subtlety without the medicinal flavors. Additionally, little peat is used during the drying process of the malt, so the resulting classic Bruichladdich whisky has only a slight smoky aroma and flavor.

An Alternative Approach to Whisky Stocks

When Reynier bought 1.2 million liters (317,000 gallons) of whisky stocks in 2000, he faced an inventory of old malts and young malts with a gap of six years when the distillery was not producing. In order to optimize the value of his stocks, he released limited edition bottlings of old malts, and then unleashed Jim McEwan, the highly respected master distiller, to produce selected vintage bottlings.

Additionally, Reynier and McEwan began distilling in 2001 to mature stock for the future. They progressed from producing 100,000 liters (26,000 gallons) per annum in 2001 to producing 750,000 liters (198,000 gallons) per annum in 2010 and in the process decided "to have fun, intentionally not replicating what other distilleries were doing." The result is a staggering number of expressions that require us to make frequent trips to the distillery's website to remain informed about its most recent releases (often with quirky and idiosyncratic names like Waves, Rocks, and Black Art).

Designer Whiskies and Beyond

In addition to the traditional house style, Jim McEwan produces two other peated expressions for those whisky drinkers who do like the smoky flavor: the lightly peated Port Charlotte version and the most heavily peated whisky in production, the Octomore. Reynier also insists that only local Scottish farms, many of them organic, produce the barley provided for the Bruichladdich whisky. Moreover, the barley is stored separately so that the distillery can produce designer whiskies that are specific to the barley production of individual farms.

In additional to the classic Bruichladdich whisky, the distillery offers several designer malts, including those that reflect different vintages, different distillations (i.e., double, triple, and even quadruple), organic and biodynamic distillations, limited editions, single-cask bottlings, and the occasional series, including the Links (golf courses) and Legacy ranges.

The Noser Knows

The traditional Bruichladdich has a touch of iodine on the nose. The aromas approach a mentholated pungency and include slightly charred wood and sweet burnt brown sugar.

The malt has mouth-filling and warming flavors of summer fruits, the light dryness of autumn leaves, and a salt-sweet combination reminiscent of peanut brittle and deep amber caramel sauce. It leaves an increasing dryness and saltiness on the finish, lingering slightly but not overpowering or medicinal.

Many people find that the classic Bruichladdich whisky reflects a delicate and subtle whisky in which the distillation in the tall stills tames the more assertive Islay characteristics. Additionally, the new designer malts, produced in a range of current and new bottlings, offer whisky drinkers a wide variety of ways to approach the Bruichladdich single malt, depending on their preferences.

Bunnahabhain Distillery

➤ Port Askaig, Islay PA46 7RP

➤ www.bunnahabhain.com

➤ Visitors and tours by appointment

➤ +44-1496-840 646

On the outskirts of Port Askaig, a single-track country lane turns off the main road toward the Bunnahabhain Distillery. The leisurely and quiet pace required to travel on the rudimentary road makes the spectacular scenery along the 8-kilometer (5-mile) track even more enjoyable. In this isolated landscape of the inner island, the Bunnahabhain Distillery drops down a cliffside to the Sound of Islay below. It is difficult to determine if the journey or the distillery is more striking.

Entrance to the distillery is under an old arched entrance way and through massive wooden doors flanked by the stone of the distillery walls. The design mimics a French chateau with the buildings surrounding a central courtyard. An external staircase leads up to the distillery manager's office, which commands a singular view across the Sound of Islay. In such a remote and rugged setting, Bunnahabhain produces a surprisingly creamy and delicate whisky, in stark contrast to the whiskies of the eastern coast.

The Distillery Cat's Meow

Lillian MacArthur has provided the administrative support for running Bunnahabhain Distillery for several decades. She has done so with an understated efficiency, competency, and generosity. When I visited Bunnahabhain on a bright winter's day, I left my sunglasses on the desk, and, quite frankly, my schedule and the long bumpy road to the distillery prevented me from retrieving them. I considered them lost.

The next day I arrived at Bowmore Distillery for an interview and was greeted by the receptionist, whom I had never met previously. She looked at me and remarked, "Good morning. Lillian left these for you," and handed my sunglasses to me. Lillian's thoughtful gesture best portrays the Islay character and the kind hospitality one finds among all of its people.

Modernization and an Altered Malt

Bunnahabhain was built in 1881 on land that, even then, was considered to be isolated. But the location of the distillery along the Sound of Islay provided access to a good water supply and a deep harbor, allowing the delivery of supplies and the exportation of whisky for blending. Bunnahabhain remained a blending whisky for almost a century and by the 1960s, the distillery required modernization and expansion.

In 1963, the owners, Highland Distilleries, removed the malt kilns and floor maltings and expanded the distillery. Because Bunnahabhain no longer did its own malting and drying over peat fires, its whisky reflected a less smoky character than it had previously. Presently, the distillery houses a large stainless steel mash tun with a copper top, six Oregon pine washbacks, and two onion-shaped wash stills and two pear-shaped spirit stills.

The Distillery Cat's Meow

Because of Bunnahabhain's remote location, the distillery included not only the traditional housing for the workers, but also a post office, shops, and a school for their children. As recently as the 1990s, the distillery bus continued to travel every Friday to the nearby town of Bowmore to take the spouses of the distillery workers, who all lived on-site, for three hours of shopping.

The Delicacy of Bunnahabhain

The peating of the malt is very low at 1 to 2 ppm, so that the fruity flavors of Bunnahabhain whisky are not overwhelmed by a heavily peated character. The gourd-shaped stills with their high necks and gently rounded shoulders create the delicacy of Bunnahabhain, and the massive surface area of the stills allows more copper contact with the distillate, resulting in a lighter spirit.

Most of this whisky is matured in used bourbon, a portion in used sherry casks, and all whisky is matured on the distillery site. Aging the whisky in warehouses sitting near the Sound of Jura is believed to add a slight brine note to the finished whisky.

When Burn Stewart bought Bunnahabhain from Edrington Group in 2003, it undertook the release of several expressions of Bunnahabhain, including a peated version. Its core range includes bottlings of 12-, 18-, and 25-year-olds and Toiteach, an expression consisting of 10 percent peated malt and 90 percent unpeated Bunnahabhain. It has released two expressions for the duty-free market—Darach Ur, an NAS aged in new oak, and Cruach-Mhona, peated Bunnahabhain at 35 ppm. Burn Stewart also offers some limited editions, particularly during the Islay Festival (Feis Isle), that have included old-age malts, and whiskies matured in sherry and Pedro Ximenez casks.

The Noser Knows

Burn Stewart made a planned decision to release future bottlings of Bunnahabhain using non-chill filtering with natural color, which has improved the flavor intensity and mouthfeel. Bunnahabhain has subtle peat aromas supported by undertones of heather and a smokiness that is not overpowering. The malt has flavors of light caramel sweetness and a slight iodine tang that develops on the second or third sip. It is firm and rounded, and the memory of smoke and brine lightly lingers on the finish.

Caol Ila Distillery

> ➤ Pronounced *cull-EE-la*

> ➤ Nr. Port Askaig, Islay, Argyll PA46 7RL

> ➤ www.malts.com

> ➤ Visitors center

The turnoff for the Caol Ila Distillery appears just before reaching the small town of Port Askaig at the northeastern tip of Islay. The road passes a small collection of houses, curves down a hill, and then turns abruptly left to the entrance of Caol Ila. The old white warehouses bordering the road to the left are reflected in the waters of the Sound of Islay. These old warehouses, remnants of the historic distillery, starkly define the surprisingly modern buildings of the new distillery.

The Waterloo Street Design

Rebuilt in 1974, this distillery fits snugly into the hillside so that it becomes part of the rocky coastline. Forming the centerpiece of this distillery site, the massive glass-fronted facade showcases shining copper stills that appear to rise from the waters of the Sound. Caol Ila is a modern distillery laid out logically for efficiency but with an attention to aesthetics. A gleaming copper cover tops a new stainless steel mash tun installed for ease of cleaning, and draws the eye to the rows of Oregon pine washbacks lined up behind it.

The Distillery Cat's Meow

The Waterloo Street style determined the design of ten distilleries in the decade between 1962 and 1971. Charles MacLean in his book *Whiskypedia* provides the best explanation of this style. He notes that it "was named after the Glasgow address of S.M.D.'s [Scottish Malt Distillers] engineering department. The design was for a six-still distillery and specified that the outside wall of the still house be of glass, with windows that could open, making them light-filled and airy—and in Caol Ila's case providing a stunning view across the Sound of Isla to the Isle of Jura. The mashhouse and tun room were arranged in such a way as to make the best use of gravity, thus saving unnecessary pumps, and the overall plan was both efficient and aesthetically pleasing, while also being pleasant to work in. The design was the brainchild of Dr. Charlie Potts, S.M.D.'s Chief Engineer, and was applied in the following distilleries: Balmenach (1962), Caol Ila (1974), Clynelish (1968), Craigellachie (1965), Glendullan (1972), Glen Ord (1966), Glentauchers (1966), Linkwood (1970), Mannochmore (1971), and Teaninich (1970)." (MacLean, Charles, 2010).

Stills Rising from the Sound of Islay

The glass-fronted stillroom houses six copper giants in a spacious quiet room that seems still in name and nature. It is a direct counterpoint to the whitecaps being whipped by the wind on the Sound of Islay below the glass wall, and one can only imagine the drama of a winter's storm outside this stillhouse.

The onion-shaped stills, topped with thick necks and downward-sloping lyne arms, produce a robust, peaty whisky. But the longer lyne pipe connecting each still to a condenser behind it, and the heavy copper contact create a subtle lightness that distinguishes the Caol Ila whisky from other heavily peated Islay whiskies.

Bourbon casks mature most of Caol Ila's spirit, the majority of which is destined for Johnnie Walker blends. Tankers move all but a very small portion of Caol Ila's production off Islay for filling and maturation.

The bottlings of Caol Ila include a 12- and 18-year-old, a cask strength, a Distillers Edition finished in a Moscatel cask, an exclusive to the Feis Isle, and an unpeated limited edition Special Release.

The Noser Knows

Aromas of smoky peat, seaweed, and a slight oiliness conjure images of dockside piers. Caol Ila has flavors of peat, iodine, salt, and floral notes of heather. This whisky is fairly complex, its complete character unfolding gradually. It ends with a warming finish with peat and smoke lingering on the palate.

Kilchoman Distillery

➤ Pronounced *kil-HO-man*

➤ Isle of Islay PA49 7UT

➤ www.kilchomandistillery.com

➤ Visitors center

Kilchoman Distillery has its roots in the eighteenth century, when distilling was an agricultural activity and whisky was an agricultural product. Although it is Islay's newest distillery, it preserves (or even resurrects) the farm distillery of the eighteenth century, when the entire family distilled whisky in the winter months from surplus barley using ingredients from the farm. In this case, however, the operational farm and distillery are two separate businesses.

The family of Mark French's wife owned the farm for decades when a friend, Anthony Wills, approached him about incorporating a distillery into the farm operation. The farm had a remote location, a good water source, and had the capability to grow the barley for the distillery. Kilchoman Distillery became operational in 2005, producing five barrels of whisky, and released its first bottling in 2009.

Charter Guidelines

From the outset, Kilchoman did not aspire to compete with the big distilling companies, but rather chose to maintain its small rural identity. The distillery employees take pride in producing an "all-Islay" malt whisky that contains barley grown on the surrounding farm, malted and turned by hand on the floor of one of the farm barns, and dried over peat that originates from the Octfad farm in nearby Portnahaven. A converted tractor shed on the Kilchoman farm houses the copper-topped mash tun, the four stainless steel washbacks, and a pair of copper pot stills.

The Noser Knows

The Kilchoman distillery functions as an offshoot of the farm, much as it would have done two centuries ago. The distillery shuts down at night, rather than operate for twenty-four hours, and the entire production staff works at whatever job needs completion, from hand-turning the malt with shovels to bottling the whisky.

In order to provide financing for his new distillery, Anthony Wills knew that he would need to bottle his whisky at a young age, selling a new release after it had matured for the minimum three years in oak. This necessitated creating a light, fruity whisky that would mature quickly in first fill bourbon barrels.

Tony Rozga, Gavin Douglas, and Robin Bignall, the three men who share the duties of resident stillmen and mashmen, ferment the sweet wort slowly at a cool temperature in order to create a fruity whisky with fewer oily notes when it is distilled. The wash and spirit stills are also designed to produce a light whisky by incorporating tall, thick necks and puddled shoulders with the addition of a boil ball in the spirit still. The tall necks and boil ball help to create more reflux action and to provide a large surface area in the still so that the spirit maintains a longer contact with the copper. Additionally, they increase the copper contact by maintaining the condenser water at a warm 25° to 30°C (77° to 86°F) so that the vapors do not condense immediately and remain in the copper condenser for a longer period of time. And when they take the middle cut from the spirit run distillate, they include more of the foreshots, containing fruity and floral esters, at the beginning of the run and fewer feints at the end. John MacLellan, the general manager, remarks that "the resulting three-year-old whisky tastes like a more mature whisky."

Because the farm can produce only 30 percent of the barley required for production, the distillery must buy the additional grain from the Port Ellen maltings. This requires two separate distillations and bottlings—one the all-Islay malt and one more heavily peated, Kilchoman whisky. These two separate operations result in two distinct products. And the people at Kilchoman Distillery are attentive to filling the same kind of casks with each type of whisky, distilled at the same time, so that they can make comparisons in the future.

The Future

Indeed, MacLellan has an eye to the future and is particularly attentive to the wood policy at the distillery, aging all the new-make whisky on Islay in first fill bourbon casks and some sherry casks. By maturing in bourbon barrels that are smaller than hogsheads or butts, he can increase the surface contact of wood to spirit and achieve the benefits of maturation in a shorter period of time. At this time, he feels that Kilchoman malt whisky is good at a young age and should get better, but at present it is difficult to know what the "right" age for Kilchoman whisky will be. As part of his plans for the distillery's future, he reserves some of the maturing whisky so that future releases will include offerings aged for a longer period of time.

MacLellan brings more than two decades of experience to this small and young company and reflects that by the time he leaves the distillery, he "would like people to talk about the 'eight' great Islay distilleries and not the 'seven' great Islay distilleries, and (little) Kilchoman."

Lagavulin Distillery

➤ Pronounced *lag-ah-VOO-lynn*

➤ Nr. Port Ellen, Islay, Argyll PA42 7DZ

➤ www.malts.com

➤ Visitors center

The Noser Knows

The Kilchoman offerings are young but bring a light freshness to the zesty fruit—some citrus, a vanilla sweetness from the bourbon barrels, and a hint of peat.

A mile beyond Laphroaig lies the Lagavulin Distillery overlooking the ruins of Dunyvaig Castle, which rises out of Lagavulin Bay. The White Horse blend uses a significant part of the whisky produced in this tidy little distillery. The very characteristic and meticulously kept white warehouses are punctuated by dark green wooden doors with inscriptions in both English and Gaelic. Everything is fastidiously tended by several of the people who work in the distillery.

Smoke and Stills

Because Diageo uses peated malt at 35 ppm (compared to Ardbeg at 55 ppm), Lagavulin single malt holds a place as one of Islay's smoky whiskies. It is a full, luscious whisky that has a distinctive character shaped by its two pairs of stills. The modified onion-shape and short, thick necks of the stills give testament to the heavier whisky distilled here. The stills have broad, thick waists so that the distillate is not redirected to the center of the pot still where the heavier flavor components would be reconstituted. And all the short lyne pipes connecting the heads of the stills to the condensers have downward angles, ensuring that all the heavy robust flavor compounds will be included in this spirit. In order to retain a meaty sulfur character in the new-make spirit, the stillmen run the stills hard and fast to diminish the copper contact and reflux action.

The result is a very dry, lusty, and almost bitter taste that both Charlie MacLean and Michael Jackson liken to Lapsang Suchong tea. Lagavulin mainly uses bourbon casks to mature its spirit, which seem to round and balance its assertive character. Additionally, the Pedro Ximenez finish in the Distillers Edition bottling provides a fruit and sweetness that complements the other flavors. Currently, Diageo offers Lagavulin at 12 and 16 years old, as well as a distillery exclusive, an exclusive for the Feis Isle, and a limited edition Special Release.

The Noser Knows

Lagavulin malt provides a lush bouquet of heavy smoke, sweet vanilla, and toffee. It appears dry in the mouth with a sweet-salt combination provided by the sherry and brine, supported by flavors of peat and undertones of heather. It is full-flavored with a dry and assertive finish. Lagavulin is a very well-balanced, smooth, and highly complex mixture of varied and contrasting flavors.

Laphroaig Distillery

➤ Pronounced *la-FROYG*

➤ Nr. Port Ellen, Islay, Argyll PA42 7DU

➤ www.laphroaig.com

➤ Visitors center

The southern coast of Islay produces three of Scotland's smokiest whiskies—Laphroaig, Lagavulin, and Ardbeg. Just outside the small town of Port Ellen, past ribbons of green sea grass bordering a rocky coast resides the Laphroaig Distillery. The road into Laphroaig winds through a stand of trees and soon opens onto an expanse of brilliant whitewashed buildings backed by the curving blue line of Loch Laphroaig.

The Distillery Cat's Meow

In the recent past, many distilleries had cats to keep down the rodent population attracted to the grain stored there. Interestingly, Laphroaig didn't keep cats to control the rodents drawn to the grain on the malting floors, since a family of stoats (ermine) happily shouldered that duty when they took up residence beneath the building.

Peat Fields and Peat-Reek

Laphroaig owns and controls its own nearby peat fields and is the only distillery to cut the peat by hand. And unlike most other distilleries, it still does its floor maltings to produce 15 percent of its required malt.

Although the character of the whisky begins with the peat fires and then slowly forms throughout the entire distillation process, it is really the short, thick-necked wash stills that define Laphroaig's heavy, robust flavor. The four spirit stills, however, have a lantern-glass shape that promotes reflux action and refines the distillate from the wash stills.

The Distillery Cat's Meow

Before any feminist movement or political sensitivity existed, Ian Hunter, the sole partner and managing director from 1928 until 1954, hired Bessie Williamson to function as his secretary. She developed a growing interest and understanding of distillation, and soon they both managed the operation of the distillery and promotion of the whisky. Miss Williamson became managing director after Mr. Hunter's death in 1954 and continued in that position until 1972.

The newly distilled Laphroaig matures in first fill bourbon casks, and a portion of it remains on-site in warehouses built along the sea. There is no barrier to protect the warehouses from the pounding surf, particularly during winter storms. At high tide the sea water washes the outside walls of the warehouses and over time may contribute to the dry, briny flavors so typical of Laphroaig. Rather than tame its iodine and briny character, the use of American oak barrels for maturing seeks to complement it with a caramel sweetness imparted from the charred bourbon casks.

The core range of Laphroaig malt includes 10-year-olds, both a benchmark expression and a small batch cask strength edition. People who find the assertive smokiness of Laphroaig too overwhelming should try this malt bottled at 18 years after some of the smoky characteristics have mellowed and smoothed as a result of additional years in the cask.

Laphroaig also offers an NAS Quarter Cask release that seeks to replicate malt that the distillery would have produced a century ago. It is a vatting of 5- to 10-year-old whisky that is reracked into small quarter casks of 125 liters (38 gallons) for a final six to eight months in order to speed maturation. The owners release limited editions of vintage and old bottlings, as well as exclusive offers to the Friends of Laphroaig.

The Noser Knows

This malt has a full, explosive, medicinal, and iodine-like nose with the creosote smell of telephone poles. The peat carries through into the taste with a spirity and chewy oily sweetness enhanced by vanilla and coconut. The flavors open in the mouth with very slight background notes of pears and orchard fruits, punctuated by the dry tang of briny flavors that open in the mouth. Laphroaig has well-balanced flavors that dovetail rather than overtake each other. It ends with a smoky dry (like white wine) maritime finish that stays on the palate, complemented by a full, robust body.

What You Need to Know

➤ Islay malts are defined by the flavors and aromas of peat (phenols).These phenols (peat-reek) can exhibit burnt, smoky, or medicinal characteristics.

➤ The phenols are deposited on the husks of barley as they dry over peat fires. The degree of peatiness depends on the length of time the barley is exposed to peat smoke, not on the amount of peat used on the fires.

➤ The peatiness of Islay whiskies can be assertive or subtle. The smokiness can be mitigated by the use of purifiers (Ardbeg), the level of peating (Bunnahabhain), or the distillation process that develops other balancing flavors.

CHAPTER 16

Campbeltown

In This Chapter

➤ The whisky capital of the world

➤ The survival and flourishing of J & A Mitchell

➤ The revival of Glenglye

➤ Glen Scotia: the comeback kid

Because of high duties and licensing fees, distilling tended to operate illegally in Campbeltown as it had in the Highlands. The raw materials for whisky making were conveniently located nearby, and the government's attempts to collect the taxes and fees on distilling proved to be ineffective and unsuccessful. The Excise Act of 1823 introduced reasonable fees and duty with the resulting effect that Campbeltown could boast having thirty-four licensed distilleries in a little more than fifty years following the implementation of the legislation.

Campbeltown sat among local barley fields, coal mines, and peat bogs, and its location on the coast provided easy delivery of any supplies and dissemination of its spirit to the nearby city of Glasgow. Proximity to raw materials, transportation, and markets created an ideal business opportunity for the people of Campbeltown, and their whiskies became known for their pungent maritime spirit. Indeed, Campbeltown became known as the whisky capital of the world.

Confident that the Glasgow market was assured and insatiable, distillers ran their stills hard and fast. Although this method produces a large volume of new spirit, it also distills a spirit fouled by nasty compounds boiling over into the worm tubs.

Complacency and greed drove some distillers to overproduce their spirit at a time when demand dropped significantly because of the now-inferior quality of whisky. By 1925, only two distilleries remained, and with the ensuing economic depression and Prohibition, the distilling industry in Campbeltown never recovered.

In the last decade, the Mitchell family, owners of Springbank, restored and reopened Glengyle distillery, raising the number of working distilleries to three.

Glengyle Distillery

➤ Pronounced *glen-GILE*

➤ Campbeltown, Argyll PA28 6EX

➤ www.kilkerran.com

➤ Visitors and tours by appointment

➤ +44-1586-552 009

Mitchell's Glengyle Ltd. uses a drawing of the Longrow Church as its logo—the inspiration for it came from a view through the back wall of the distillery. A rectangular opening in the stone framed a striking image of the church and its spire surrounded by trees, and the design for the label of the new distillery became a fait accompli. The church and the logo are dominated by a very tall spire, which prompted the observation that "it was built with distillers' money so that they could be closer to heaven." And a visit to the newly rebuilt Glengyle Distillery is fairly close to a distiller's heaven.

William Mitchell built the original Glengyle Distillery in 1872 because of a quarrel with his brother, John, about sheep. Rather than stay and continue working with him at the Springbank Distillery, William moved down the street and started his own distillery in the shadow of Gallows Hill, but the arrival of difficult economic times and American Prohibition forced the closing of Glengyle in 1925. Seventy-five years later, Hedley Wright, the chairman and owner of Springbank, walked past the buildings of the former Glengyle Distillery and remembered that his great-great-uncle had previously owned it. On a whim, he decided to buy the buildings in 2000 and reopen it as a distillery, placing the design of it into the capable hands of Frank McHardy, the production director at J & A Mitchell. In the years between its previous existence as a distillery and its current resurrection, the buildings had housed a laundry, a small bore rifle range, and a farmers' cooperative—McHardy had a challenge and an opportunity.

A Work in Progress

The distillery is a listed building because of its historic importance, so McHardy kept the buildings, repointed the mortar, and repaired the original roof so that the site retained the look and atmosphere of the original distillery. Inside the buildings, however, he cleared the space and designed the layout of the distillery to incorporate a logical and smooth progression of the distilling process. The updated design incorporated pendant lamps to light the distillery floor and was appropriate to the age of the building and respectful of the integrity of the historic building.

The Distillery Cat's Meow

At the opening of the restored Glengyle Distillery in March 2004, Frank McHardy stood to unveil the dedication plaque at its inauguration. When he uncovered the plaque, he learned for the first time that the site had been named the Frank McHardy Production Building in recognition of his restoration efforts and his vision.

The ground floor of Glengyle houses the malt mill and grist elevator that delivers the grain to the mash tun on the floor above it. A quick trip up the steps to the first floor presents the visitor with a view along the distilling floor that takes in an open and airy space, moving logically and sequentially through each step of distillation. The semi-Lauter stainless steel mash tun sits at one end of the space and four larch washbacks reside nearby, where the very slow fermentation mirrors the fermentation at Springbank Distillery. And, finally, the two copper pot stills sit at the end of the distillery like exclamation points, punctuating the natural progression of the design.

Seventy percent of the equipment at the renovated Glengyle Distillery was new, and the remaining equipment was refurbished. Craigellachie Distillery provided the old Boby mill, but the stills were rescued from

The Distillery Cat's Meow

The name of the distillery is Glengyle, but the name of the whisky is Kilkerran for two well-considered reasons. The Kilkerran website maintains that a blended Highland malt already existed and to use the name Glengyle for its single malt would only result in confusion. Second, "Kilkerran is derived from the Gaelic 'Ceann Loch Cille Chiarain,' which is the name of the original settlement. . .where Campbeltown now stands. Kilkerran is thought to be a suitable name for a new Campbeltown Malt since it was unusual for the old Campbeltown distilleries to be called after a Glen, a custom more usually associated with the Speyside region."

the former Ben Wyvis Distillery and then renovated. Until McHardy rescued them, the stills had resided in the shadows of a shed attached to the Invergordon grain distillery, where they had been since the demise of the Ben Wyvis Distillery in 1977 (See chapter 18, Lost and Hidden Distilleries). McHardy shipped the stills to Campbeltown and modified the angular design by rounding the joints between the neck and shoulders (the ogee) and rounding the base of the stills. He removed the purifier and gave the lyne arms a slight upward tilt.

Bourbon casks are used to mature the new-make spirit, called Kilkerran, and the warehousemen use the very simple but old-fashioned method of gross and tare to determine the contents of the cask (see Benromach). While no casks are aged on-site, all the whisky is matured in Campbeltown; and Cadenheads recently released a new bottling of Kilkerran Work in Progress series, which will follow the whisky's maturation from 5 years to 14 years. It also makes a very limited edition of bottles from the first filling of six different casks (bourbon, oloroso sherry, fino sherry, port, rum, and Madeira) available on the Kilkerran website. These casks were filled at the opening of the restored Glengyle Distillery and will be bottled in 2014.

The Noser Knows

Tangy iodine defines the elegant nose, which becomes more pronounced with water and introduces a citrusy note. The flavors include lemon peel, licorice, lycee, melons, and watermelon with a hint of smoke. The taste is delicately balanced with a smooth, medium body. Its finish is lightly warming with a background note of cigar wrappers.

Glen Scotia Distillery

➤ Pronounced *glen SKO-sha*

➤ Campbeltown, Argyll PA28 6DS

➤ No website

➤ Visitors by appointment

➤ +44-1586-552 288

Campbeltown was once a major distilling center of Scotland until its demise at the time of Prohibition. The distinctive whisky produced at the tip of the Mull of Kintyre had a heavy, oily character that the American market appreciated. The beginning of Prohibition broke many of the ties between the United States and Campbeltown, although reputedly some trade continued, albeit illegally.

The Revolving Door

Stewart, Galbraith & Co. established Scotia Distillery in 1832. During the nineteenth century the distillery experienced stable ownership, which was in marked contrast to the roller coaster ride it experienced during most of the twentieth century. Following the Armistice of World War I, the West Highland Malt Distillers bought the distillery in 1919. For more than seventy-five years, Scotia endured a series of owners and then underwent a name change in 1933, when *Glen* was added to the distillery's name. Loch Lomond Distillery purchased Glen Scotia in 1996, but it operated under the management of a production team from Springbank Distillery for a period of time following Loch Lomond's acquisition. Glen Scotia officially reopened in 2007 and has produced spirit since then.

A New Start in the New Century?

Glen Scotia sits on a slight hill a few blocks from her sister, Springbank Distillery. The distillery seems to be caught in a postwar snapshot, when much of the "new technology" was visited upon distilleries. It still retains its old Boby mill, the old cast iron mash tun continues to use an old rake system to stir the mash, and the washbacks are Corten steel—a material that many distilleries have exchanged for stainless steel.

Everything about the squat, short stills is thick—thick lyne arms with slight downward angles, thick, short necks, and squat, puddled onion-shaped pots. So, much about these stills lends itself to producing a heavy, oily spirit that is matured in used bourbon casks from Loch Lomond Distillery. The aging of all the spirit in warehouses on the distillery site may help to form the iodine tang so distinctive to the seaside Campbeltown whiskies.

The Noser Knows

Glen Scotia malt has a big, peaty nose with additional oily and woody aromas. The oily and peaty notes continue in the mouth, supported by a sweetness (honey?) and subtle tones of hazelnuts and macadamia nuts with the characteristic seaside brine. It has a delicate and soft taste with a full body and a strong finish with a memory of smoke.

The distillery bottles a 12-year-old single malt and a 12-year-old Distillery Select. During the majority of the year, Glen Scotia produces an unpeated spirit, but for two short periods it uses a lightly peated malt at 15.2 ppm to produce a different spirit. The Distillery Select bottling comes from casks chosen for their unique characteristics, and they are non-chill filtered with natural coloring.

Springbank Distillery

➤ Pronounced as spelled

➤ Campbeltown, Argyll PA28 6EX

➤ www.springbankdistillers.com

➤ Visitors and tours by appointment

➤ +44-1586-552 085

J & A Mitchell and Company has its roots firmly planted in the nineteenth century, when two sons of Archibald Mitchell established Springbank Distillery. Their father had operated as an illegal distiller, but John and the younger Archibald procured a license and opened Springbank in 1828. The distillery has remained in the Mitchell family throughout its history, overcoming the Depression, Prohibition, and the demise of most of Campbeltown's distilleries.

The Noser Knows

Springbank Distillery is known for producing a whisky of high quality, and for its employees' obvious commitment to excellence and to the whisky produced here. Their attention to detail extends into the bottling hall as well. Only 10,500 bottles leave the Springbank bottling hall each year, but each bottle is lifted from the line and examined against a back light to evaluate the clarity and color of the bottled whisky.   Then each individual bottle is labeled and packed by hand..

From the time when Campbeltown was regarded as the whisky capital of the world, Springbank has remained steadfast and now stands as one of the three surviving distilleries in Campbeltown. Not only has the family ownership remained unbroken, but the family also has a deep commitment to preserving traditional distilling production.

Whisky Making Completely On-Site

The distilling process at Springbank offers a view into the past because it is the only distillery that still performs 100 percent of the distilling process on-site, including all its malting, fermenting, distilling, warehousing, and bottling. The management at Springbank involves its employees in its decisions and maintains a commitment to small sustainable production. Consequently, it comes as no surprise that bottlings of Springbank do not appear in duty-free shops or supermarkets. People at Springbank maintain a dedication to their heritage by preserving and using traditional methods to complete the whisky-making process.

The Noser Knows

The repercussion of breaking with tradition at Springbank was learned when the method of heating the stills was changed from directly firing the stills to heating them with steam coils. Although it improved the distilling time, it changed the character of the new-make spirit, so the distillery returned to using direct firing to supplement the new steam coils. Since both direct and indirect heating fires the stills, it requires a rummager to swirl along the bottom of the pot, preventing charring and exposing more of the copper to the spirit.

The malting barn, dating to before 1850, houses an unused barley loft and two actively used malting floors. Decorative murals painted by the town's school students underscore the company's loyalty to the town and its people, as does its sense of obligation to buy Scottish barley and grain from area farmers. Peat used during the malting of the grain comes from northeast Scotland because regional peat beds were depleted long ago by the townspeople and distilleries.

Mashing takes place in an old cast iron tun, using four waters instead of the usual three that most distilleries employ. At Springbank, only the third water is returned to provide the first water of the next wash, while the fourth water is used to pump the remaining draff into a tank to await collection by area farmers.

The whisky-making at Springbank does not focus on efficiency and the bottom line but rather on an allegiance to distilling in the way it has always been done at Springbank—not because of any innate stubbornness, but because it produces a high-quality whisky. This adherence to old methods is most obvious during both fermentation and distillation. The fermentation occurs in six larch washbacks and takes between 72 and 110 hours, considered by the industry to be a long time for fermentation. But the extended fermentation time helps to create a fruity new-make spirit.

The original gravity of the Springbank fermentation produces a wash for distillation at 4.5 percent alcohol, considered low compared to most distilleries that end fermentation with a wash at 7 to 8 percent. It would be possible for the production team at Springbank to increase the alcoholic strength of the wash, but this would break with a historic practice that results in the distinctive Springbank whisky.

The Distillery Cat's Meow

Interestingly, the direct-fired still continues to use a bell attached to the rummager arm to indicate that it is working properly. With each turn of the arm, a lever trips a little hand bell and the operators know to listen for the syncopated ring to ensure that the rummager continues to work properly.

Three Spirits, Three Peat Levels, Three Stills

In 1973, J & A Mitchell and Co. began distilling Longrow spirit in addition to the Springbank it already produced. At the time, it bottled a blended whisky requiring an Islay-style malt and rather than depending on the availability of Islay whiskies, it decided to produce its own. None of Longrow was bottled as a single malt until the mid-80s, when it had matured. Almost twenty-five years later in 1997, similar thinking resulted in the distillation of a third whisky at Springbank. As with Longrow, J & A Mitchell revived the name of a former Campbeltown distillery and christened the new whisky Hazelburn.

The Distillery Cat's Meow

The flavor profile for Longrow malt is rooted in a story told to the owner, Hedley Wright, by his uncle William Mitchell. His uncle reminisced about one of the most popular bottlings sold at the Kintyre Show, which was a vatting of Springbank and Ardbeg. Needing an Islay-type malt for his blend, he set out to distill a heavily peated spirit in this style. He then abandoned the idea and sold Longrow as a single malt when it matured.

Even though the production process for all three whiskies is remarkably similar, the length of time the malted barley dries over peat fires and the number of distillations create the differences among the three. The traditional Springbank requires malt to be dried over peat fires for six hours and then undergo distillation two-and-a-half times. A small portion (20 percent) of the low wines distilled in the wash still are moved aside and held in the low wines and feints receiver. Following the usual distillation practice, the remaining 80 percent of the low wines are then distilled a second time in the low wines still. The final step in creating the Springbank new-make spirit occurs when the reserved portion of the low wines from the first still and the spirit from the second still are then combined and distilled in the third still at the distillery. Since only part of the spirit is distilled a third time, this is considered a two-and-one-half distillation and not a triple distillation. This two-and-a-half distillation removes heavier elements in the whisky and raises the alcohol level.

On the other hand, the Longrow spirit requires heavily peated malt that has dried over peat fires for forty-eight hours before it undergoes the traditional double distillation. Interestingly, the spirit still uses a worm tub rather than a condenser, helping to produce a heavier spirit. In the case of the Longrow single malt, it is those heavier and more robust components that help to form the flavor characteristics. Consequently, production workers only distill this heavily peated malt twice.

The production of Hazelburn, however, causes the opposite effect sought in the Longrow. Using unpeated malt, the Hazelburn spirit undergoes a triple distillation, which processes the spirit through each of the three stills. The third distillation removes many of the impurities, resulting in a more delicate and subtle whisky.

Clearly, the manipulation of the amount of peat used in drying and the number of distillations help to create the idiosyncratic differences among these siblings in this single malt family. But the attention to the types and quality of the wood used for maturation completes the formation of each flavor profile. First-fill bourbon casks (50 percent), first-fill sherry casks (30 percent), and refill bourbon casks (20 percent) mature the new-make spirit, which is all aged on-site. True to the company's commitment to retain all the whisky-making processes at the distillery and oversee all its components, the bottling takes place in a hall adjacent to Springbank Distillery.

At present, Springbank Distillery bottles its whisky at four different ages and as a CV expression, with a variety of alcohol strengths. The company has also been a pioneer in producing some unusual bottlings, including malt aged in rum casks and different wine casks. Past bottlings have also included limited editions of whiskies showing unusual quality or character.

In 1965 and 1966, Springbank contracted with a local farmer to grow barley specifically for its distillery. Cut peat from local bogs and coal mined in the area were used to produce a completely regional whisky, which was named West Highland.

Springbank also bottles Longrow at three different ages and a CV expression, as well as Hazelburn at two ages and a Sauterne finish. Because of the independent nature of J & A Mitchell and Co., it is always worthwhile to watch Springbank's website for unusual, surprising, and frequently delightful expressions that can appear serendipitously.

The Noser Knows

Springbank is the iconic Campbeltown single malt that has set the bar high. It has appeared in a wide range of ages, strengths, and finishes, built on a baseline of quality. It is a medium-weight whisky offering soft, ripe fruit flavors with notes of vanilla, sherry, and sweet toffee. It ends with the distinctive maritime tang of Campbeltown. Hazelburn's delicate character reflects berry fruit and peach crumble character with notes of vanilla fudge, whereas its cousin Longrow takes a more assertive approach with a full, thick oiliness and maritime tang punctuated by the aroma of ashes.

What You Need to Know

> ➤ Springbank is known for its diverse and innovative expressions, its independence, and its quality whiskies.

> ➤ The revival of the Glengyle Distillery allows us to watch the evolving and developing character of a new whisky.

> ➤ Glen Scotia's malt is perhaps the closest example we have of an earlier Campbeltown style that was defined by an oily maritime character.

PART FOUR

First a Bottle, Now a Collection

First a Bottle, Now a Collection

You bought your first bottle of single malt, then your second, then a special bottle for your birthday, and now you are looking for an expression not easily found. Part 4 will introduce you to the world of collecting and auction houses. First we'll examine trends, consider collectible malts, and make suggestions for spotting a future rarity.

And now that you have the beginning of a collection (even if it is only two bottles), you really shouldn't stack it under the dining room table. This section will take you through the steps of how to store your collection to maintain its quality and to preserve your collectables as they (hopefully) increase in value.

Next you'll learn about lost and hidden distilleries that once produced single malts that are no longer made. We'll examine their histories to understand their rarity and set you on the hunt for these elusive bottlings.

And, finally, when you have sampled all that your local store may offer or when you really want a malt that is simply not bottled for the consumer or when you want something special and unique, we'll tell you where to look. We'll consider the established independent bottlers with a range of available stocks. With Part 4, you'll move to a new level in your single malt education.

Collecting Whisky

If you are looking for an alternative to investing in the stock or bond market or an additional type of investment, you might consider collecting whisky. Although I am suggesting this very much tongue in cheek, collecting whisky can offer an interesting pastime with some possible very long-term rewards.

Twenty-five years ago I collected old malts before they were given the name of prewar malts, and when they were affordable and available. Over the years, my collection grew, but just as I was considering sending it to auction, the airlines instituted stringent guidelines that made it virtually impossible to transport my collection to Glasgow, where the auctions were held. I had to wait years before other options appeared on the auction scene. So, if you are looking at collecting whisky solely as an investment, I would caution against it. Instead, collecting whisky should be an avocation with the added pleasure of looking for (and finding) unique and special bottlings. It is always possible that the collection will accrue in value, but if it doesn't, the pleasure is in knowing that you can always drink (and enjoy) your failed investment.

Make Me an Offer: What to Collect?

Christie's held the first whisky auction in Glasgow in 1989. It brought an awareness regarding the value of whisky, and suddenly people began to pull strange, unique, and old bottlings out of their drawers, closets, and cellars.

The Distillery Cat's Meow

Prior to the first whisky auctions in 1989, some old malts were available at affordable prices. And while the growth of whisky auctions appeared to bring a corresponding growth in the prices of old whiskies, the auctions also increased and improved the selection and quality of the whiskies offered at the sales.

The heightened appreciation for the potential value of whisky coincided with a time when distilleries began to promote the release of limited edition bottlings. All the right conditions came together at the right time to encourage people to build a collection. It was, indeed, the perfect storm.

Christie's held auctions in Glasgow for several years before the responsibility shifted to McTear's Auctioneers in 2000. Bonhams auction house also joined the market with its first sales in Edinburgh in 2008 and then expanded into the global market with whisky auctions in Hong Kong in 2009 and in New York in 2010. Its entry into the auction of spirits in New York is significant because few American markets for the sale of spirits exist. Fewer than ten states allow the auction of spirits, with New York reversing its Prohibition-era law as recently as 2007.

Trophy Bottles

So what do you buy if the collection bug bites you? Martin Green of Bonhams, author of *Collecting Malt Whisky* and a specialist in whisky auctions since they began two decades ago, recommends beginning with collecting unique bottlings of the top brands (e.g., Macallan, Ardbeg, Springbank, Bowmore, Glenfiddich, Glenlivet, Dalmore, Mortlach, and Talisker) because they tend to sell well.

Collectors could buy the Black Bowmore in 1993 for £150 ($240) and now see it bring over £2,000 ($3,200) at auction. Older versions of these trophy bottles (bottlings done both at an older age—twenty-five years or older—and those done in an earlier year—from the 1950s or earlier) hold a particular attraction for buyers. Most recently, Bonhams in Edinburgh sold a 64-year-old Glenfiddich distilled in 1937 for £25,200 ($40,320). Buyers also look for distillery bottlings (bottlings that come from the distillery and not from independent bottlers).

Independent Bottlers

While distillery bottlings are almost like chateau bottlings in the wine world, collectors really shouldn't dismiss independent bottlings out of hand. Buyers appreciate independent bottlings because they often sell well-known whisky brands in ages that the distilleries themselves do not release. And frequently, some single malts are bottled only by independent bottlers because the distilleries keep their whiskies for blending and seldom release them as a single malt (see chapter 19, *Independent Bottlers*).

Lost Distilleries

Independent bottlings are particularly valuable in the case of closed distilleries like Millburn, Hillside, and Rosebank. Many distilleries closed before the collecting market developed and if any bottlings of their whiskies still exist, they are mainly offered by independent bottlers.

A subset of collecting whiskies from lost distilleries includes hidden distilleries that closed after a rather short life. This includes Lomond, Glencraig, and Mosstowie whiskies distilled during the 1950s and 1960s by Allied Distillers. Allied intended these whiskies for blends, and it produced them in experimental Lomond stills constructed in the corners of larger malt distilleries. At the same time, competing companies also in need of additional malts for their blends, distilled Kinclaith, Ben Wyvis, Ladyburn, Glen Flagler, and Killyloch within their grain distilleries and produced them only for a limited amount of time. Once they no longer needed the whiskies for their blends, they dismantled, or mothballed, the stills that produced them. The whiskies are now collectible because of their rarity more than their quality.

Limited in Numbers

The recent trend of distilleries and independent bottlers releasing single-cask whiskies provides a new dimension to collecting whiskies with limited editions because these editions cease to exist once the bottler sells the bottles from the cask. Single-cask bottlings tend to gain more attention from devoted whisky drinkers, but they are collectible particularly if they have a small output and a high quality.

The best case scenario includes buying a numbered bottle from a limited bottling (e.g.,

Whisky Lexicon

A limited edition can refer to a numbered bottle from a finite bottling, usually from a single cask. Distilleries may use the term also to identify a special bottling done as a one-off occurrence or done for a limited period of time.

if a collector were to buy a bottle numbered 25 out of a total release of 230 bottles). Buying numbered single casks parallels the art world practice of numbering prints in a limited series. And like the art world, distilleries with a reputation for high-quality whiskies tend to sell better.

Special Series

Distilleries sometimes produce a subset to the limited editions in the release of a series. Bruichladdich released a Links series named after famous (mostly Scottish) golf courses and landmarks (like Swilcan Bridge) and paired each bottling with artwork by a known golf artist. And in the 1990s, Diageo produced a Flora and Fauna series of over thirty bottlings from its distilleries, each linked to artistic sketches of the flora and fauna in each distillery's locale.

Whisky Lexicon

A series edition identifies whisky bottled with an eye to a particular theme. Although a series edition can offer a selection of very good or old whisky, some series tend to focus on a theme rather than the quality of the whisky.

But a series really should be complete to have a good value. The emphasis in series collecting is on the appeal of the series, not necessarily on the quality of the whisky (although it is often quite good). And for this reason, the appreciation of the value is unpredictable. On the other hand, collecting means different things to different people, and a very personal interest or taste really needs to drive series collecting.

Celebration Events

What, then, should a collector buy when it comes to limited editions released to commemorate events like the millennium or royal marriages? When Prince Charles married Lady Diana in 1981, Macallan distillery released a Royal Marriage bottling containing whisky from the years they were born. It certainly had an interest among collectors because of the royal marriage, but the value increased because only Macallan and Glenlivet released a commemorative bottling for the marriage. Later, the associated stories of the couple's divorce and the death of Princess Diana added another layer to the premium placed on the bottling.

Collecting event bottlings requires studying what is available on the market at the time of the event. Sometimes the distilleries flood the market with commemorative bottlings at very high prices, and then it is a matter of personal choice as to whether a collector wants to buy it. If a store demands a high price at the time of the event, the chances are low that the prices will rise enough to realize a good return. Some people, however, simply enjoy having a special event bottling, at which point the purchase is personal pleasure, not investment.

The Distillery Cat's Meow

When Prince William, the son of Charles and Diana, married Kate Middleton in April 2011, The Macallan Distillery produced a special Royal Wedding bottling to commemorate the occasion. It sold the bottling only at the Macallan Distillery and offered it only during the week prior to the wedding day. It sold out in two days.

Global Travel Retail, aka Duty-Free

It is worth noting that duty-free shops in airports frequently offer limited edition or series bottling, some of which are specifically produced for the export market. This is especially true of the duty-free shops in Scotland, with the Glasgow airport offering one of the largest selections. This provides good buying opportunities for collecting limited editions, but the specialty bottlings at duty-free shops can command a high price. Even so, these shops present a specific opportunity to the collector, and any bargain offers on the more garden variety single malts allow all travelers to return home with some very nice single malts to enjoy.

The Noser Knows

As ghoulish as it seems, some collectors listen for rumors about the demise or merger of particular distilleries. Once a company decides to close (and possibly dismantle) a distillery, collectors often seek to buy the existing bottles of the distillery's whisky, as happened with Littlemill Distillery when plans for its demolition replaced plans for its revival as a boutique distillery. Additionally, collectors frequently clear store shelves of a whisky or a particular bottling that a working distillery will no longer produce. Stephen McGinty noted that this happened when Diageo ended its production of Loch Dhu, a whisky distinguished by its deep black color.

The Inside Scoop

Collecting opportunities also exist for people who enjoy reading any of the whisky magazines, like *Whisky* magazine and the *Whisky Advocate* that offer current news about distilleries, their releases, and quirky stories about occurrences in the whisky world. These include distillery releases of whisky at an older age, for example a whisky that is usually bottled at 8 or 10 years is bottled for a short time at 15 or 18 years. The value is also enhanced if buyers regard the older bottling as particularly good.

A Good Story

Romantic stories associated with a particular bottling also help to increase the value. Such was the case with bottles of whisky recovered from the SS *Politician*, which sunk in 1941 in the Outer Hebrides. The most recent bottle of this whisky brought to auction at Bonhams commanded a price of £4,200 ($6,720). But herein lies an important caveat. Some sellers embellish or completely fabricate stories, so it is essential that the buyer verify the story. Furthermore, whisky that claims a specific provenance (e.g., a bottle of whisky owned by a famous person) needs to carry verification with it. Whether or not collectors buy the bottle depends on their level of risk taking or their level of romanticism.

Serendipity

Sometimes an occurrence at a distillery or bottling house results in a collectible bottle because of its sheer novelty. Stephen McGinty of McTears Auction House in Glasgow recalls that this happened when a worker at a bottling house accidently mingled an older Ardbeg with a younger Glen Moray. This meant that it could not label the whisky as a single malt, and the age on the bottle had to reflect the age of the younger whisky. After much weeping and gnashing of teeth, someone suggested that they actually taste the accidental result. Of course, the outcome was rather nice, and Ardbeg bottled it as Serendipity, which quickly sold out. Whether it will command a higher price because it is a mingling of both sheer novelty and verifiable romantic story remains to be seen.

Spirited Festivals

And, finally, the explosion of whisky festivals in the last decade has brought a corresponding release of specialty bottling for festival events. Most notably during Feis Ile, the malt and music festival on Islay, the island distilleries offer releases of special bottles that commemorate the festival. Because the expressions are very limited and only sold at the distilleries, they are beginning to command attention at whisky auctions.

Within collectors' circles, other specific and limited bottlings also command buyers' interest. Martin Green notes that local events sponsored by a distillery and for which the distillery will produce a one-off release can be of interest to collectors. These industry-related events can encompass the Manager's Dram, or commemorative retirement bottlings, which are only available to the distillery employees. Although these bottles demand more attention in Scotland, where many people work in the whisky industry and consequently are more familiar with their existence, the global market shows a growing awareness of their unique and limited availability.

The Accidental Investor—What Now?

Some people find themselves with the start of a collection simply because they have bought a special bottle here and there. Others consciously begin collecting as an investment for themselves. Still others lay down whisky on the occasion of a child's birth so that they will have a collection to send to auction when both the whisky and the child mature. If one sees a parallel between collecting whisky and collecting wine, it certainly exists. Techniques for maintaining and storing both whisky and wine share some similarities, but it takes less maintenance to protect a whisky collection than it takes to protect a wine collection.

Keeping Your Collection Safe

First, a whisky collection requires good storage, which includes keeping it at a reasonable ambient temperature that does not fluctuate, and remains at 16° to 19°C (60° and 66°F). This means that collectors should not store their collection in the attic, which can become brutally hot or cold. And certainly no one should store their whisky near a heat source like a furnace or hot water heater because alcohol is highly flammable. Martin Green cautions that "collectors should keep whisky away from sunlight because it can bleach the whisky. And [finally] buyers should preserve the label on the bottle in good condition."

Lying Down or Standing Up

Generally speaking, collecting whisky is a fairly low-maintenance investment. Richard Pike of Bonhams New York recommends storing whisky bottles upright rather than running the risk of some of the elements in the alcohol attacking the cork. Unlike wine, whisky does not age in the bottle, and the interaction between the wine and the porous cork is not required by whisky. But people worry about corks failing in older bottles or a drop in the level of the whisky in the bottle. If a corked bottle has a metal cap holding it in place, there is little danger of it failing. Furthermore, Pike suggests slipping a plastic protective sleeve, like the expandable netting found in wine and spirit shops, over the bottle in order to protect it and the label.

Lowered Expectations

A drop in the level of the whisky tends to be a natural occurrence, with evaporation happening very slowly. Upper shoulder levels are acceptable in an old bottle like a 50-year-old whisky or a Prohibition-era whisky because of normal evaporation over time. However, a 15-year-old whisky should maintain a level into the neck or higher because a drop of the whisky into the shoulder level indicates too much evaporation over a short period of time. Martin Green explains, "Once [the whisky level in the bottle] reaches the shoulder or lower, it will adjust the value. While not worthless, it may reduce the price, [and] if the level has dropped, it will only get worse, so it is wise to sell it."

Going Once, Going Twice

Collecting whisky as an investment takes time and patience before realizing an increase in value. And once a collection is ready to sell, more patience is required because it is hardly liquid, in the investment sense of the word.

Auction houses provide the best conduit to sell whisky because they provide a service to both buyers and sellers. To the buyer, they offer cataloging, opportunities to preview the bottles, and the experience of a specialist; to the seller, they offer inspection, insurance, and marketing to an international client base. This all comes at a price, however, and collectors can expect to pay at least 20 percent of the hammer price to cover insurance, a seller's and/or a buyer's premium, and catalog pictures.

Selling whisky via the Internet to avoid fees really requires a very thorough investigation into the requirements for selling spirits online. This can be particularly difficult in America, given the individual states' byzantine liquor laws. Many states prohibit the sale of liquor online, and the buyer cannot preview the bottles, as they can at an auction house. Additionally, the seller must verify the bottle and take responsibility for shipping a rather fragile, and sometimes rare, item. Much depends on what is permissible on an online auction site and how much risk and difficulty a collector is willing to shoulder.

The Noser Knows

At this time, the best way to sell a collection is through a known auction house with a reputable track record. Although it may charge higher fees, it provides security and safety and a network of buyers. Selling online in America can bring a set of obstacles ranging from navigating different states' liquor laws to ensuring the safe delivery of fragile and rare bottles.

Graduating from Bottles to Casks

The last decade has seen a growing interest among whisky collectors to own their own casks of whisky. Several distilleries, particularly small, independently owned places, have moved to meet this demand and in the process have provided welcome capital for their development. Several distilleries, including Arran, Bruichladdich, Tullibardine, Glenglassaugh, Bladnoch, Glengoyne, and the independent bottler Duncan Taylor offer casks for sale to individual investors. While small details may vary, most distilleries offer a similar general structure.

Generally the purchase price includes insurance and storage in the distillery warehouses for a length of time, usually ten years, and it may be possible for the owner to choose the type of cask for aging the whisky (e.g., bourbon or sherry). Frequently, the distillery sends an annual sample to the owners so that they can decide when they would like their cask bottled. But these terms serve only as general guidelines, and purchasers should contact individual distilleries for details of their cask-owning programs.

The Noser Knows

Buying a cask involves additional costs to the owner when the time arrives to remove the whisky from the cask. At this time, the owner must pay the costs of duty, tax, bottling and labeling, and shipping. If the bottles ship outside Scotland, the owner pays the duty and tax levied by the importing country. Raymond Armstrong provides one of the best explanations that I have seen detailing these fees on his website www.bladnoch.co.uk. Additionally, the website www.whiskywhiskywhisky.com offers a cask calculator to determine the full cost of owning, bottling, and shipping a cask. Although the figures are quoted in GBP, it provides a ballpark figure for estimating costs.

What You Need to Know

➤ Collecting whisky should be first and foremost an avocation embracing the pleasure of the hunt as opposed to being your only investment.

➤ Look for limited editions of the top brands.

➤ Make the acquaintance of independent bottlers and their whiskies.

➤ Store your whisky upright, away from strong light and extreme temperatures.

➤ Have patience. Have fun. Occasionally open a special bottle and share it with friend.

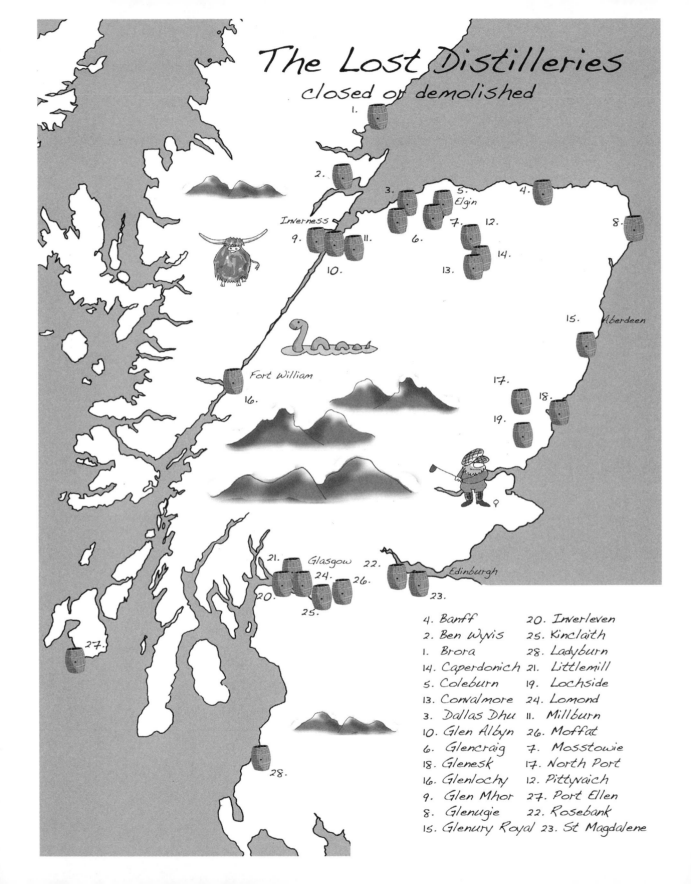

The Lost Distilleries
closed or demolished

4. Banff   20. Inverleven
2. Ben Wyvis   25. Kinclaith
1. Brora   28. Ladyburn
14. Caperdonich   21. Littlemill
5. Coleburn   19. Lochside
13. Convalmore   24. Lomond
3. Dallas Dhu   11. Millburn
10. Glen Albyn   26. Moffat
6. Glencraig   7. Mosstowie
18. Glenesk   17. North Port
16. Glenlochy   12. Pittyvaich
9. Glen Mhor   27. Port Ellen
8. Glenugie   22. Rosebank
15. Glenury Royal 23. St Magdalene

CHAPTER 18

Lost and Hidden Distilleries

In This Chapter

➤ A look at the silent distilleries

➤ The difference between lost and hidden distilleries

➤ Hunting for the lost whiskies

The last three decades saw the dismantling or demolition of twenty distilleries; the 1970s and early 1980s oversaw the dismantling of an additional seven distilleries hidden within larger distilleries. These twenty-seven distilleries, produced thirty different malt whiskies, and only the occasional and rare bottlings remain as evidence of their once-productive existence.

The Lost Distilleries

Fifteen of the twenty dismantled or demolished distilleries share a closure date of 1983 or 1985 when Distillers Company Limited (DCL), now Diageo plc, decommissioned a significant number of its distilleries as a reaction to the recession at that time.

The years following World War II saw a growing demand for Scotch whisky, and the industry responded by refurbishing distilleries and expanding production. Eventually overproduction collided with diminishing demand in the 1970s. The oil crisis of 1973 compounded a difficult situation by triggering a significant rise in the price of raw materials. By the 1980s the recession, several increases of the duty on spirits, and the rising popularity of wine and "white" spirits created "whisky lakes" that burdened distilleries with excessive stock.

Independent bottlers found themselves the happy recipients of surplus casks at discounted prices. Individual distilleries, however, did not fare as well as companies closed distilleries to cut production. And DCL, with the largest proportion of malt distilleries, closed inefficient distilleries, producing malts that other distilleries in its portfolio could replace.

The Hidden Malt Distilleries

Small distilleries tucked within larger grain distilleries also rode the tide of growth and closure that paralleled the larger established distilleries. With the postwar prosperity came production problems caused by a scarcity of single malts needed for making blended Scotch whisky. It was not just a problem of producing more spirit but of producing different types of spirit. The industry responded with innovation and creativity by designing the Lomond still and by building little-known distilleries hidden within larger ones.

Hiram Walker had earlier constructed Inverleven Distillery inside its grain complex at Dumbarton in the late 1930s, but Long John Distilleries revitalized this idea in 1958 when it built Kinclaith Malt Distillery in a corner of its Strathcylde grain distillery. Within five years, Inver House built a malt distillery producing three different malts (Glen Flagler, Killyloch, and Islebrae), inside Moffat Distillery complex near Airdrie, Invergordon Distillers installed pot stills within its grain whisky complex to produce Ben Wyvis, and William Grant & Sons constructed Ladyburn Malt Distillery inside its grain complex at Girvan.

Experimental Stills

Allied Distillers took a different approach to producing additional malts for its blends. It installed four Lomond stills, the creation of Alistair Cunningham, within larger distilleries to create a variety of different malts from one still. The Lomond still, which had a coffee can-shaped columnar neck, contained three rectifying plates that could be manipulated to produce three different spirits. The plates could be flooded with distillate to increase the reflux and purifying action, left dry, or swiveled to a vertical position to negate the reflux action entirely. Additionally, the columnar neck had a telescoping design that allowed the addition of sections to lengthen or shorten the head, and the lyne arm attached to a swivel could be raised or lowered to alter the angle of the pipe.

It mounted the first Lomond still next to the traditional stills at Inverleven to produce Lomond spirit (making this a distillery within a distillery within a distillery). The second and third pair of Lomond stills appeared within Glenburgie and Miltonduff distilleries to produce two entirely different malts, Glencraig and Mosstowie, respectively. These stills operated for almost twenty years, but the same economic conditions that closed so many other distilleries led to the decommissioning or dismantling of the Lomond stills as well.

The Importance

Of course, these silent distilleries hold a place in the institutional history of the whisky-making industry. At the time of their operation, these distilleries produced malts that held little, if any, value for bottling as single malts. Their quality did not distinguish them, and they were intended solely for blends. Certainly, no one foresaw a market for single malts, let alone a collectors' market. Because these whiskies will never again be produced and the existing stocks are extremely limited, they have gained value for their rarity. Some of them like Kinclaith or Glen Flagler became available only through independent bottlers, and others like Ben Wyvis and Lomond are exceedingly rare.

Banff Distillery

The first Banff Distillery opened in 1824 and operated until the owners dissolved their partnership and closed the plant in 1863. The Simpson family then established and operated a second distillery from 1863 until its closure during the Depression in 1932. It remained closed until after World War II, when it reopened until Distillers Company Limited (DCL) closed it in 1983. DCL dismantled and then demolished it in parts until a fire in 1991 destroyed what property remained.

The Distillery Cat's Meow

In summer of 1941, an enemy plane attacked Banff Distillery that housed soldiers in the malt barns. It bombed one warehouse and caused thousands of gallons of whisky either to burn or to leach into the ground. Brian Spiller notes the intoxicating effect on local birds and farm animals in his brief distillery histories: "It is said that ducks and geese dabbling in the Boyndie Burn were recovered on the edge of the sea and that cows were not milked because they could not be got on their feet." (Spiller, Brian. *DCL Distillery Histories Series*, 1982.)

Ben Wyvis Distillery

A year after Moffat distilleries opened in 1965, Frank Thomson, the managing director of Invergordon Distillers, also installed a pair of pot stills inside the Invergordon grain whisky complex. Building the small Ben Wyvis malt distillery within the grain compound made sense because the support system for producing a malt whisky was already in place.

Employees at Invergordon remember that they did the milling and mashing in a remote corner of the grain distillery, and then pumped the sweet wort across the road into six bright red cast iron washbacks. Both the wash and spirit stills had thick necks of medium height with a water jacket at the top of a very short lyne arm. The necks met the shoulders of the stills at sharp angles, creating a unique conical shape, more angular than curvaceous. John Roscrow, the technical manager at Invergordon Distillers remembers that Ben Wyvis malt tended to be heavy because of the thick necks of the stills and the short lyne arm that allowed little reflux action.

By 1977, the small distillery was no longer viewed as an economical operation and was closed. Invergordon kept Ben Wyvis for itself and had no filling customers, people who fill their own casks with new-make spirit and oversee the maturation of it. Consequently, independent bottlers never acquired Ben Wyvis malt and Invergordon never bottled it. Few casks remain, and a ban on drawing samples now exists because of the drips and leaks that can occur during sample taking.

The Distillery Cat's Meow

The mash tun from Ben Wyvis Distillery now resides at Benromach, and the stills have found pride of place at Glengyle, where Frank McHardy modified them slightly before their installation (See chapter 16, Glengyle Distillery).

Brora Distillery

The Duke of Sutherland established the original distillery on this site in 1819 and named it Clynelish Distillery as part of an economic improvement plan to provide an outlet for the farmers' excess barley. Other than brief closures during the Depression and World War II, the distillery operated steadily until DCL built a new distillery in 1967-68 adjacent to the old one. It closed the original distillery and transferred the Clynelish name to the new distillery.

The rebuilding of the Caol Ila Distillery in 1972 brought a brief reprieve for the original distillery. Without the production from Caol Ila, the company found itself in need of a smoky malt whisky for blending to replace the Islay malt until Caol Ila Distillery was rebuilt. The original Clynelish Distillery reopened in 1969 and was later renamed Brora Distillery because it now produced a peaty malt unlike the whisky it had previously distilled. The Brora Distillery closed permanently in 1983 and while the stills remain in the building, DCL removed the mash tun and washbacks.

Caperdonich Distillery (Pronounced *cap-er-DON-ick)*

It was perfectly possible to drive right past this distillery on the main road through the town of Rothes and never know that it quietly sat across the street from its sister distillery, Glen Grant. In 1897, Major James Grant, the owner of Glen Grant Distillery, built another distillery called Glen Grant #2 on the opposite side of the road. The new distillery operated for only three or four years before Grant stopped production in 1901 because of the recession in the whisky industry. He removed all the equipment shortly afterward.

In 1965, the owners decided to refit the vacant distillery buildings with distilling equipment because of a growing demand for blended scotch in the postwar years of the 1950s and 1960s. Once again, the new distillery would use the same raw materials as Glen Grant. But this time the new distillery was given a name of its own because it was clear that the whisky would have its own flavor profile.

It is difficult to find bottles of Caperdonich because virtually all of this spirit went into the Seagram's blends, and only the occasional cask found its way to independent bottlers.

The Distillery Cat's Meow

When I first visited this distillery in the 1980s, the distillery manager at Caperdonich poured a glass of newly distilled spirit, and he then called Glen Grant Distillery. In short time a young man riding a bicycle pedaled over to the distillery office with a sample bottle of new-make spirit from Glen Grant. Even though both distilleries used the same raw materials, differences clearly existed between the two samples.

Seagram also distilled a second "heavily peated Caperdonich" spirit, but none of it made its way to independent bottlers. Pernod Ricard (Chivas) mothballed the distillery in 2002, and then sold the property and buildings to Forsyths of Rothes, the renowned still makers. Forsyths dismantled the distilling equipment, demolished the mash house and stillhouse, and retained the warehouses.

Coleburn Distillery

Whisky blenders from Dundee built Coleburn Distillery in 1896 and began production the following year despite problems and delays in building the excise officer's house and cottages for the distillery workers. The roofs of the closed maltings provide a distinguishing feature at Coleburn—one of the kilns sports the traditional pagoda-shaped chimney, but the other kiln has only a flat roof that looks like a Tuscan bell tower. The flat roof chimney provides a glimpse of the appearance of nineteenth-century distilleries before Charles Doig designed his iconic pagoda-shaped roof. DCL closed the distillery in 1985 and cannibalized the plant for parts until the buildings became unsafe for use. Dale and Mark Winchester have announced plans to renovate Coleburn Distillery for use as a hotel and conference center, but no additional information has been released.

Convalmore Distillery

Convalmore Distillery operated steadily from its opening in 1894 to its closure in 1985, except for brief amounts of time when it required rebuilding after a devastating fire in 1909 and when it billeted soldiers from 1940 to 1944.

William Grant & Sons of Glenfiddich and Balvenie now own the former Convalmore Distillery. It sits in the middle of its property, and it needed to buy the distillery to bridge its two parcels of land. But before the property passed to William Grant & Sons, the previous owners stripped the distillery of all its equipment so that Convalmore whisky, as we know it, is no longer produced. Glenfiddich and Balvenie distilleries now use the building as warehousing, and the working distillery no longer exists.

Dallas Dhu Distillery (Pronounced *dallas-DO*)

Dallas Dhu no longer operates as a distillery but rather exists as a museum under the administration of Scotland's Historic Buildings and Monuments. It is well worth the visit to this distillery- turned-museum because it is possible to see a well-preserved and maintained distillery with Victorian buildings and equipment and methods that were in practice during the 1960s and 1970s. It is heartening to see that this little distillery is now preserved for the future because its history reveals a checkered career of closings, liquidations, and a destructive fire.

It seemed as if history were repeating itself in 1983, when DCL scheduled Dallas Dhu for closure. Luckily this coincided with Scotland's Historic Buildings and Monuments intention to preserve a distillery as part of the nation's heritage. Selected from among several available candidates, Historic Scotland's purchase of Dallas Dhu in 1986 secured its future, not as a working distillery, but as a museum.

Glen Albyn Distillery (Pronounced *glen-AL-binn*)

The Caledonian Canal opened in 1822 and linked Inverness in the northeast with Fort William in the southwest using a series of four lochs. The canal also provided the site for both Glen Albyn and Glen Mhor distilleries because of its ready water supply and transportation link. Glen Albyn was opened in 1840 on the site of a previous brewery and underwent two reconstructions before the plant went silent and sat unused for twenty years. Eventually, the distillery experienced an increased demand for its spirit, requiring the distillery's expansion in 1892.

Glen Albyn continued production into the twentieth century and underwent upgrading and refurbishment in the 1950s and 1960s. The need for significant modernization at the time of the recession in the 1980s brought about its closure and in 1983, DCL dismantled the plant, and it was developed into a grocery store.

Glencraig Distillery

In 1958, Hiram Walker installed a pair of Lomond stills at Glenburgie Distillery in order to produce several different malts for its blends. The little distillery and the spirit it produced was christened Glencraig in honor of Willie Craig, the production manager in North Scotland. The objective was not only to produce several different variations of new-make, but also to maintain a "family" character among all the spirit produced at Glenburgie. By mid-1981, increasing demands for Glenburgie spirit and little space for expansion at the distillery meant that the Lomond stills had to go.

The Glencraig malt was fragrant with the traditional Speyside pear-drop character, but it only appeared in offerings from independent bottlers.

Glenesk Distillery

Founded in 1898, the Glenesk Distillery had suffered through a variety of names and renovations and reinventions. Because of its location in eastern Scotland, which is known for its barley production, it assumed the role of a maltings and in 1968, Scottish Malt Distillers permanently installed modern drum maltings. During its years of operation between 1889 and 1985, it was a malt distillery, served as billets for soldiers during both world wars, suffered the devastation of a fire, and went from a floor maltings to a grain distillery and back to a malt distillery. Additionally, the distillery experienced frequent name changes that matched its revolving door identity. It began life as Highland Esk and before it closed, various owners named it North Esk, Montrose, Hillside, and finally Glenesk, which is the reason it appears on independent bottlers' lists as both Hillside and Glenesk. In 1985, the distillery closed and was later dismantled, although the maltings have continued operating.

Glenlochy Distillery

A consortium of two distillers, one from the Glen Cawdor Distillery and one from Highland Park Distillery with thirteen investors from Inverness, planned and opened this distillery in 1900. It remained opened until grain restrictions during World War I closed the distillery, and then it reopened in 1924 for two years. It experienced a series of openings and closings and survived the ownership of the eccentric Joseph Hobbs, a Canadian, who also owned the nearby Nevis Distillery (for a day) and Ben Nevis Distillery. Scottish Malt Distillers bought it from Hobbs and modernized and refurbished the distillery during the 1960s and 1970s. Its final closure and the subsequent conversion of its remaining buildings into vacation apartments came in 1983.

Glen Mhor Distillery (Pronounced *glen-VAR*)

Glen Mhor's existence occurred as a result of its sister distillery's success. The prosperity of nearby Glen Albyn was attributed to the management of the distillery manager, John Birnie, who was "well qualified for the responsible position he occupies." David Spiller remarks, "Frustrated in his ambition to gain a shareholding in Glen Albyn. . . he acquired a site just across the road from his old shop, and established Glen Mhor Distillery." (Spiller, David. *DCL Distillery Histories Series,* 1982.) Birnie expanded the distillery and continued to receive supplies by sea until the outbreak of World War II. From 1972 onward, Glen Mhor and Glen Albyn distilleries operated in tandem until they closed in 1983.

Glenugie Distillery

Glenugie Distillery began life sometime between 1831 and 1834 under the name Invernettie and was located near Peterhead on the east coast of Scotland. It was refurbished as a brewery, and then rebuilt as a distillery in 1875. Unfortunately, the distillery experienced a series of openings and closures under a variety of owners and operators until Schenley Industries (later Long John International) acquired it in 1956 and refurbished and updated the distillery.

Sometime during the changes in ownership, the distillery added a purifier in the lyne arm to increase the reflux action. Almost twenty years later, Whitbread & Company acquired Glenugie and closed it in 1983. Two North Sea oil companies later demolished the buildings after purchasing the distillery.

Glenury Royal Distillery

Records show that Captain Robert Barclay owned Glenury Distillery in 1833 and was the person responsible for acquiring the use of *Royal* as part of the distillery's name. Only two other distilleries have that privilege—Royal Lochnagar and Royal Brackla.

This distillery only had three other owners in its lifetime, including the idiosyncratic Joseph Hobbs. Distillers Company Limited purchased Glenury in 1953 and undertook the construction, expansion, and refurbishment of the distillery in the 1960s. After Glenury's closure in 1985, it was sold and any existing buildings were converted into apartments.

Inverleven (and Lomond) Distillery

Inverleven was a small malt distillery operated within the large grain complex at Dumbarton. This little historical gem with its mash tun, washbacks, and pair of stills also housed the first experimental Lomond still, which was tucked among the distillation equipment in the Inverleven stillroom. This was a double hidden treasure!

Hiram Walker built the huge grain distillery at Dumbarton before World War II, and installed a small malt distillery with a pair of onion-shaped stills so that the company could produce the Inverleven spirit and increase the number of single malts available for blending.

In the late 1950s, Tom Scott, the managing director at Hiram Walker, installed a Lomond still, but only placed one spirit still in the Inverleven stillhouse because of space limitations. The wash still distilled all the wash, then a portion of it moved to the Inverleven spirit still, and the remaining portion moved into the Lomond spirit still. The spirit from the Lomond still was named Lomond in order to distinguish it from the Inverleven spirit.

By installing the Lomond still, it was possible to produce an additional single malt that was different from the malt produced by the Inverleven stills. Eventually, production operators removed the rectifying plates from the Lomond still because the spirit it produced was too different from the family profile of the Lowlands spirit from the Inverleven stills. Hiram Walker decommissioned the Lomond still in the 1980s and the Inverleven stills in 1991. Soon afterward, the distilling equipment was dismantled and moved.

Independent bottlers occasionally offer an expression of Inverleven single malt, but I am aware of only one bottling of the Lomond single malt that appeared in the Scotch Malt Whisky Society's Christmas list of 1992.

The Distillery Cat's Meow

Mark Reynier of Bruichladdich Distillery resurrected both the Inverleven stills and the Lomond still by dismantling them and transporting them to Bruichladdich. The Lomond still has undergone a polish and makeover and now sits proudly on display in the stillroom but is used to distill gin. The Inverleven stills also made the move to Islay to await their renewal as the stills in the proposed Port Charlotte distillery.

Kinclaith Distillery

With the growth in the sales of Scotch whisky in the 1950s, four distilling companies decided to build small malt distilleries within their large grain distilleries in order to produce additional malts for their blends.

Long John Distilleries was the first to realize this idea in 1958 when it built Kinclaith malt distillery in a corner of its sprawling Strathclyde grain distillery near Glasgow. It gutted an old warehouse within the grain complex in order to construct a purpose-built malt distillery with its own mill room, mash tun, six washbacks, and two stills, both fitted with purifiers between the necks and condensers. Of the four experimental distilleries, Kinclaith was the only one housed in a separate building with its own set of distilling equipment. In 1976-77, the company dismantled the stills producing Kinclaith malt whisky to provide ground for the growth of the grain distillation.

Ladyburn Distillery

In 1966, William Grant & Sons followed Invergordon Distillers and constructed the Ladyburn malt distillery within its large grain complex at Girvan. The decision to add Ladyburn to the Girvan compound made it possible for William Grant & Sons to produce a Lowland malt needed for its blend Standfast and allowed the company to be self-sufficient.

Brewers processed a separate mash through six stainless steel washbacks and then through two pairs of stills. The wash stills used a standard onion-shape, and the spirit stills incorporated a boil ball above the gently sloping shoulders, creating more reflux and a light Lowland character in the whisky. John McDougall, who worked at the distillery, recalls Ladyburn as a very passable spirit—light, mellow, and soft, but definitely not a Speyside.

Ladyburn operated for ten years until the company dismantled the little distillery in 1976 because it was cheaper to buy malt whisky on the open market.

Littlemill Distillery

Littlemill Distillery is reputed to date to 1772, and Alfred Barnard mentions in 1887 that "the distillery is a very old work, having been built about the year 1800." Barnard also mentions the use of three pot stills because the distillery used triple distillation until the 1930s.

Clearly, Matthew Clark & Co. operated it from 1817 to 1818. From then onward, Littlemill experienced the management of a long series of owners, including a Jane McGregor from 1825 to 1839. In the early 1990s, the Glen Catrine Bonded Warehouse Ltd. acquired the distillery when it bought stocks from the former Gibson International. There was much consideration about turning it into a visitors center or boutique distillery, but it became obvious that it would take too much work and capital to redo it. Glen Catrine removed the distillery equipment in 1996, converted some buildings into apartments, and eventually demolished the remaining buildings following a fire.

Lochside Distillery

When Lochside began its life in 1781 as a brewery, it was known as Clayshades, which referred to the clay area to the south and west of the present site. Sometime during its early life, the name changed to Lochside as evidenced by title deeds in 1830 that refer to the brewery by that name. James Deuchar acquired the brewery in 1833 and quickly commissioned Charles Doig, the distillery architect, to rebuild the brewery to reflect the Brauhaus design used in the breweries of Germany and Belgium.

In 1957, Macnab Distilleries Ltd., a registered company owned by several investors including Joseph Hobbs, purchased Lochside. Hobbs's interest in Lochside was in its potential as a grain distillery, which was its sole product until 1961. Afterward, distillation of both grain and malt whisky took place at Lochside simultaneously for use in blending.

The Distillery Cat's Meow

Interestingly, for the first half of the twentieth century, the brewery transported beer by ship from the Montrose dockside to the Newcastle dockside on vessels called Beeries. This practice continued until 1956, when Scottish and Newcastle Breweries bought Lochside and promptly closed it and moved all its operations to Edinburgh.

Lochside was closed between 1971 and 1973 until Destilerías y Crianza del Whisky (DYC) acquired the distillery in order to improve the quality of its Spanish blends by using Scottish malt whisky. Then Allied Domecq purchased Lochside in 1992, closed the distillery, and moved the last of the mature whisky out of the warehouses in 1996. By 1999, Allied had demolished the bottling plant and warehouses on one side of the road and had scheduled the dismantling and demolition of the distillery buildings. Following a fire in 2005, the entire site was cleared and scheduled for redevelopment.

Millburn Distillery

Records indicate that a Millburn Distillery Co. operated very near to the center of Inverness as early as 1837. But by 1853, it was operating as a flour mill in tandem with five other mills that operated along the Mill Burn. The owner, David Rose, commissioned and opened a new distillery on the site in 1876, which remained under family control until 1892. In the next three decades, it came under the management of only two other owners and managed to rebound after a fire in 1922. Distillers Company Limited (DCL) acquired Millburn in 1937 and after its closure during World War II, it reopened and operated from 1945 until 1985. Following its decommissioning as a distillery, the property was sold and the buildings now house a restaurant and pub.

Moffat Distilleries (produced Killyloch, Glen Flagler, and Islebrae malts)

In a move to become self-sufficient, Inver House, a subsidiary of Publicker Industries of Philadelphia, USA, constructed a malt and grain complex at Airdrie in 1964, named Moffat Distilleries (sometimes known as Garnheath). The malt distillery located the milling, mashing, and distillation processes in the stillhouse and situated the fermentation area in a remote location 69 meters (75 yards) away. Six copper stills dominated the stillroom, making this the largest of the malt distilleries built within a grain complex. Each still had a purifier at the head of a thick tapered neck that joined the shoulders at sharp angles rather than sloping in gentle curves.

Because of his desire for independence, the owner, Sy Neuman, used these stills to produce three different whiskies—Killyloch, Glen Flagler, and Islebrae. Each whisky used the same mash, but since it had its own maltings, the distiller could vary the intensity of peat used in the production of each individual whisky.

George McClements, retired production director at Moffat Distilleries, and Eddie Drummond, the blender at Inver House, recall that they distilled Killyloch as a Lowland malt, using little peat in the drying process. They used a medium peating to produce Glen Flagler with a Speyside character and reserved the heaviest peating for Islebrae to yield an Islay style. McClements remembers that Neuman had easy access to bourbon casks and used the American barrels to age the Killyloch, but he used hogsheads treated with sherry to age the Glen Flagler. The malt distillery at Airdrie operated for almost twenty years until 1982, and the grain distillery continued production until 1986.

The Distillery Cat's Meow

Interestingly, the intended name for Killyloch was Lillyloch, the name of the water source for the distillery, but the stencil for painting the name on the casks arrived with a misspelling. Since the whisky was only meant for the obscurity of the blending hall, the misspelling remained unchanged.

Mosstowie Distillery

Like Glenburgie, Miltonduff Distillery housed a pair of Lomond stills to produce a different malt called Mosstowie. The new spirit was grassy and herbal with sweet sherry flavors balanced with spicy notes. After the initial trials at Inverleven Distillery, a pair of Lomond stills was installed both at Glenburgie and later, in 1964, at Miltonduff so that the experimentation could continue. In addition to manipulating the rectifying plates to vary the reflux, the coffee can-shaped head could have additional sections either removed or added in order to lengthen or shorten the head of the still. Miltonduff went one step further and sprayed the outside of the still with cold water to encourage additional reflux action. Like Glencraig, the Mosstowie stills were reconfigured into traditionally shaped stills in 1981, when demand increased for the Miltonduff spirit.

North Port Distillery

North Port Distillery originally operated under the name Townhead and later Brechin, the name of the city where it was located. Consequently, the name North Port-Brechin sometimes appears on the labels of this distillery's single malt. David Guthrie established the distillery in 1920, and it remained under family control until Distillers Company Limited (DCL) purchased it in 1922. Between DCL's purchase and the end of World War II, the distillery operated for fewer than ten years. It reopened when the war ended and produced spirit for blends until 1983, when the owners closed it and then later demolished the buildings.

Pittyvaich Distillery (Pronounced *PEH-ty-vake*)

No long tradition of illicit stills, nineteenth-century buildings, or Victorian owners exists for Pittyvaich Distillery because Arthur Bell & Sons built it in 1975 next door to its sibling distillery Dufftown. Both were operated in tandem to produce malts for its Bell's blends. It closed in 1993 and later was demolished.

Port Ellen Distillery

The somewhat protected shores around Loch Indaal and the Sound of Islay seem relatively tame compared to the dramatic rocky southeastern shore where four of Islay's smokiest whiskies were produced. Port Ellen Distillery is an old distillery, established in the early nineteenth century on the southern coast so that its owners could easily transport its spirit.

Port Ellen Distillery was founded in 1825, but it truly reached its stride when John Ramsay acquired it in 1836. The distillery remained under the family's control until his son sold Port Ellen to subsidiaries of Distillers Company Limited (DCL) in the early 1920s. It operated for almost a hundred years before it closed in 1929. Enlarged and modernized and sporting large areas of glass, the new facility reopened in 1967. Large drum maltings were built adjacent to the distillery in 1973 and although the maltings remain open, the distillery closed in 1983 and underwent dismantling in the 1990s.

Rosebank Distillery

Rosebank Distillery sat on the banks of the Forth and Clyde Canal in Falkirk, which afforded it easy delivery of supplies and dispatching of filled casks to the markets in Glasgow and Edinburgh. The distillery underwent expansion and rebuilding, which proved challenging because the main road formed one of the distillery's property lines, and, as such, limited additional building. Rosebank single malt was triple distilled and was always regarded as a very good whisky with an elegant and full-flavored profile that was closer to a Highland whisky than a Lowland.

The distillery remained under the control of the Rankine family and because of its careful management coupled with the demand for Rosebank's spirit, the distillery managed to survive the Pattison Crash of the late nineteenth century. In 1914, five Lowland distilleries formed the Scottish Malt Distillers Ltd. to concentrate their resources, which enabled them to weather the recession in the whisky industry.

Rosebank remained opened during most of the twentieth century, including the war years of 1939 to 1945, but was closed in 1993. Some of the buildings were converted and others redeveloped. Although most of the distilling equipment remained in place, it recently suffered vandalism and theft by copper thieves.

Recent plans for a new distillery in Falkirk that would replicate the Rosebank style and also provide retail shops, a restaurant, and conference facility received planning permission in 2010.

St. Magdalene Distillery

Linlithgow, the location of St. Magdalene Distillery, provided ideal transportation facilities and copious water supplies because of its proximity to the railway and the main road between Stirling and Edinburgh, and its location on the Edinburgh & Glasgow Union Canal.

> **The Noser Knows**
>
> Single malt from the St. Magdalene Distillery also appeared under the name of Linlithgow. Some bottlings carry the name St. Magdalene; others have Linlithgow as the name on the label.

The licensed distiller, Adam Dawson, operated the distillery, which continued under the family's management until 1912, when it went into liquidation. Distillers Company Limited (DCL) purchased the distillery at that time. In 1914, St. Magdalene became part of the amalgamation of five Lowland distilleries under the umbrella organization of the Scottish Malt Distillers Ltd.

St. Magdalene reopened after the World War II, but closed in 1983 and was sold for redevelopment.

What You Need to Know

➤ Hidden distilleries sat tucked in corners of larger established distilleries.

➤ Lost and hidden distilleries are gone forever.

➤ The malts from these distilleries are collectors' items.

CHAPTER 19

Independent Bottlers

In This Chapter

➤ The unusual role of independent bottlers

➤ A look at the long-established bottlers

➤ What niche do they fill?

Independent bottlers fill casks with a distiller's spirit and then sell it under their own label. I know this seems incredible that one business would allow another business to sell its product under another person's label. You may find this difficult to understand, but it is a completely legitimate business rooted in whisky history and personal relationships. Independent bottlers fill a very important role of providing malt whiskies unavailable from distilleries or unavailable at old ages. They are independent guardians of maturing stocks of malt, and in the process they offer broad and deep choices of single malts to the consumer.

Bottlers as Blenders

Initially, distilling spirit was essentially a product of farming until local grocers and merchants proposed selling it in their shops. During the nineteenth century, they not only bottled the product of individual distillers, but also began to blend several malts together.

The invention of the continuous still in about 1829 resulted in the production of a colorless, somewhat tasteless, inexpensive spirit. It seemed to be a spirit that no one would like, but the grocers and independent bottlers saw a swan in the ugly duckling. They could use the inexpensive grain spirit as a base, add several single malts to give it character, color, and taste, and the development of blended Scotch whisky raced onto the Victorian scene.

In order to have the required number of malts necessary for some of their blended Scotch whisky, they needed to secure and store a sufficient number of casks from different distilleries. To this end, they sent their own casks to the distilleries and filled them with new-make or young spirit and held the casks either in their own or the distillery's warehouses until they required them.

The Noser Knows

Sending casks for filling enabled independent bottlers and blenders to control the types and quality of the casks used for aging, the length of maturation time, and the number of casks they held. Not surprisingly, some of the older independent bottlers built enviable stocks of matured whisky.

Frequently, distilleries licensed the independent bottler to bottle and sell their single malts. At other times, the bottler, faced with a surplus of stocks or an old cask, would release a bottling of a particular distillery's malt. The independent bottler filled an important role by providing malt whisky that distilleries did not bottle and by offering a breadth and depth of choices unavailable from the distilleries. The distilleries, more intent upon distilling and producing malts for blends, seemed comfortable with the symbiotic relationship with independent bottlers. It was a market built very much on personal relationships and led to the long-established independent bottlers like Gordon & MacPhail, Douglas Laing, Duncan Taylor, and Cadenhead.

Reciprocal Trades and Whisky Brokers

Whisky brokers emerged to answer a need for companies to acquire different malts for their blends as the blended Scotch whisky industry grew. Primarily, brokers moved required casks from the distilleries to the blenders and arranged reciprocal trades between one distillery and another. They were the movers of whisky. And in their role, they fulfilled an individual's request for a cask to celebrate a milestone and a distillery's need for a buyer to purchase excess stock or the unused blending malts from other distilleries. An open market developed wherein the broker could move casks of whiskies for sale as parcels to individuals, other distilleries, and independent bottlers who looked to fill gaps in their inventories.

Legal Protection and "Teaspooning" Protection

Opportunity can also bring unintended (or unforeseen) consequences. The late 1980s saw an emerging market in single malt whiskies that had not existed previously, and with it came the development and establishment of brands that now needed protection to ensure their quality. This led some distilleries to seek legal protection to prevent other businesses from buying their casks on the open market and labeling them as their own (particularly if the cask did not maintain the same quality as their proprietary bottling). Others have engaged in "teaspooning" by adding a drop of another malt to each cask so that their casks now are technically blended malt and cannot be sold as single malt from their distillery.

One Man's Trash is Another Man's Treasure

The whisky recession during the 1980s provided an opportunity for both independent bottlers and whisky brokers, and, in the end, the customer as well. Overproduction in the 60s and 70s met a decreased demand as these whiskies came into maturity. The industry's reaction was to close distilleries, decrease production, and sell surplus stock to raise cash. Large numbers of casks, many of them containing old whiskies and many of them from distilleries that would never produce again, came onto the open market. Brokers had business, independent bottlers and their customers had significant choices, investors could collect defunct distilleries' stock, and the sheer volume provided an opportunity for the emergence of new independent bottlers like Murray-McDavid and Signatory.

The distillers saw their excess stocks as a problem; others saw it as an opportunity. Historically, however, the whisky industry has experienced cycles of boom or bust, and the pendulum has swung from the recession days of the 1980s to the growth market of the new millennium. As a result, distilleries are consolidating and holding stocks, and few casks are finding their way to the open market.

The Future?

Certainly, independent bottlers have served several important functions by making unbottled malts available to the consumer, collecting and maturing the stocks of lost distilleries, and purchasing excess whisky stocks during the recession years of the whisky industry. Independent bottlers, who have historically filled and matured casks in their own bonded warehouses, have stocks available during times when there is a shortage of casks for sale. But the last decade has seen a significant growth of newly arrived independent bottlers who do not have large stocks and who rely on buying individual casks to bottle. These bottlers may have difficulty finding quality casks. Without really knowing the source of their stocks, consumers have difficulty predicting the quality of their single cask bottlings.

Whisky Lexicon

Vatting (marrying) refers to mixing several casks from one distillery (bottling single malts) or mixing several casks from different distilleries (bottling blended malts). The term *blending* is usually reserved to define mixing grain and malt whiskies to make blended Scotch whisky.

I am not certain why so many independent bottlers have appeared on the scene in the last decade, particularly since distilleries are holding stocks for their own use. Consequently, rather than bottle just single casks, a few bottlers have taken the step toward vatting several different malts to offer blended malts or vatting several casks from one distillery to offer small batch bottlings in order to ensure some harmony and balance in their products.

The list of independent bottlers that follows begins with long-standing and well-established bottlers. The shorter list that ends this chapter includes small, and often new, bottlers who seem to offer primarily single-cask bottlings. Both Murray-McDavid, which releases small batch whisky bottlings, and Compass Box, which releases blended malt and grain whisky (although with interesting twists), seem to be the exception to the trend of single cask bottlings. The field of independent bottlers may look very different in ten years, but it will be an interesting ten years with new trends and developments to watch.

William Cadenhead Ltd. (Pronounced *CAD* (rhymes with Tad)-*in-head*)

www.wmcadenhead.com

J & A Mitchell & Co. Ltd. bought the 130-year-old William Cadenhead Ltd. in 1972, acquiring only the premises and name because Christie's had auctioned the stocks that were in the warehouses. During the time prior to the auction and sale, Cadenhead stockpiled a large number of bottles, labels, and cartons. In the 1960s, a shortage of glass bottles existed, and J & A Mitchell needed to bottle casks of whiskies that the owner had bought as an investment. Interestingly, the motivation for buying William Cadenhead was not the whisky stocks that Mitchell might need as independent bottlers (they were sold at auction), but rather the bottles, cartons, and labels that were to be had.

The Cadenhead's Edinburgh shop opened in the early 1980s and offered a unique range of single malt whiskies that were not available to the public. At the time, it had no idea it would include a single-cask range, but the decision followed quite naturally. If it continued to bottle single malts using non-chill filtering with natural color, it would need to raise the ABV of the whisky to prevent the whisky from becoming cloudy. Consequently, the Cadenhead single malts became exclusively single-cask expressions, now bottled at cask strength in clear glass.

The Distillery Cat's Meow

The first bottlings of Cadenhead's single malts initially appeared in a squat, dark bottle known as a Haig Amber Dump. The shape of the Cadenhead bottles was reminiscent of the shape of the Haig Blended Scotch whisky bottles, and they were indeed a very dark amber color and most certainly dumpy in shape. The whisky was bottled at 46 percent alcohol, but it was not chill filtered, unlike most other malts at the time; the dark color of the glass served to cover any cloudiness that might occur. The Haig Amber Dump bottles occasionally appear at auctions and indicate Cadenhead's original bottlings.

Cadenhead made the conscious decision to sell directly to the consumer through its shops and in the process educate customers about natural-cask strength malts. The Cadenhead shops not only offered single malts that were difficult to obtain, but also provided knowledge about the benefits of no filtering and natural color well before it became a mainstream practice in the industry.

Presently, Cadenhead offers a range of expressions, including single casks, both at cask strength and reduced strength, older-aged single casks, casks from closed distilleries, and blended malt whisky. It offers bottlings of world whiskies from other countries, as well as bottlings of rum and gin. While not all of its bottlings are cask strength, all are non-chill filtered with natural color.

Gordon & MacPhail

www.gordonandmacphail.com

James Gordon and John Alexander MacPhail began as grocers on South Street in Elgin in 1895. In the early years of the store's existence, they took on an apprentice, John Urquhart, who aided Gordon in the selection and buying of casks of whiskies and then the subsequent blending of them.

Stocks—A Depth and Breadth

When Urquhart became the senior partner, he developed the whisky-brokering aspect of the business and undertook the licensed bottling of single malts for several distilleries. Most significantly, he continued and increased the practice of filling his own casks at most distilleries, and then holding them for long periods of time in his own warehouses. By the 1950s, Urquhart's children joined him in the business, and by this time the family owned a large range of maturing malt from most of the existing distilleries.

In the 1960s Urquhart's son George released the Connoisseur's Choice range of single malts that were unavailable anywhere else. Consequently, Gordon & MacPhail became the one source where a customer not only could buy malt whisky, but also could find a quality bottle from all the distilleries. Within the last five decades, the range of whiskies increased, the third and fourth generations joined the firm, and the family bought and reopened Benromach Distillery.

History in a Cask

Presently, Gordon & MacPhail matures 7,500 casks in its warehouses, representing a silent history lesson of Scotch whisky. Its warehouses mature 70-year-old whiskies with cask heads bearing the names of distilleries and a progression of their owners in stenciled paint. In 2010, it celebrated the legacy of both the family and whisky generations by releasing its Generation series beginning with a very limited edition of a 1938 Mortlach and a 1940 Glenlivet.

The Noser Knows

True to its legacy as a grocer, Gordon & MacPhail conducts business at its original location on South Street in Elgin. Granted the food side of the store has diminished, but the whisky side has increased, and the Whisky Room offers more than eight hundred malts from 1938 to the present decade.

Gordon & MacPhail seems to act less like owners and more like guardians who believe that its heritage and knowledge needs to be handed to the next generation. In addition to the Connoisseur's Choice and Regional Malts, the store also offers rare and old vintages, a

Private Collection chosen by the directors, and the Secret Stills series. Although most of its bottlings appear at 43 percent ABV, Gordon & MacPhail does offer a range of Cask Strength malts bottled with non-chill filtering and natural color.

Douglas Laing and Co.

www.douglaslaingwhisky.com

The philosophy of the independent bottler Douglas Laing seems to be "good business is good fun." One look at the website underscores the self-deprecating humor of the two brothers, Fred and Stewart, who own the company. They emphasize personal service and offer some good single casks, as well.

Their father, Douglas Laing, established his Glasgow company in 1948 and set up a filling program, which meant that he contracted with a distillery to fill casks with its new-make spirit and then left it to age. He then used the aged whisky with grain whisky to produce a line of blended whiskies, which was really the backbone of his company.

The Noser Knows

The Laing brothers offer expressions of their whiskies in small 200 ml bottles so that customers can sample a cask offering before committing their money for a larger bottle. Fred Laing recommends retaining the small bottles when they are empty to use for decanting small amounts of single malt that remain in larger 750 ml bottles to prevent its degradation from exposure to air.

New Opportunities

Laing and his sons set about developing the Pacific Rim market, until the Asian market suffered a decline in the 1990s. In this adversity, however, the brothers saw an opportunity, and shifted their focus from blends to single-cask bottlings. The growing interest in single malt whiskies created a market for something beyond the original distillery bottling. Independent bottlers like the Laing brothers held casks of whisky from distilleries not usually bottled, as well as casks that now held older vintages.

In the late 1990s, they released their series of Old Malt Casks, which were limited bottlings of a single-cask, non-chill filtered whisky. Interestingly, rather than bottle this series at cask strength, they reduced the whisky to 50 percent, which they labeled as golden strength. However, if Fred and Steward Laing pull a cask from their inventory that they deem extraordinarily rare or of fine quality; they will bottle it under a limited edition Old Rare label issued at cask strength.

The Laing brothers also release small batch single malt in the Provenance series, as well as two blended malts: the Clan Denny expression, which blends malts in small batches from a specific geographical area, creating a regional style (i.e., Speyside, Islay, etc.), and the Big Peat label, which marries four smoky malts from only Islay distilleries. A visit to their website lists all their current offerings including blends and grain whiskies.

The Scotch Malt Whisky Society

www.smws.com

The Scotch Malt Whisky Society (SMWS) is an independent bottler of unique single casks, and it offers some incredible venues in which to enjoy a dram from the casks it has chosen. These single casks of whiskies represent all the whisky regions, appear in a range of ages, and span a whole spectrum of tastes. They are all non-chill filtered with natural color.

The Noser Knows

The SMWS practice of using numbers on the labels rather than names to designate the distillery is easily deciphered. The SMWS logo sits above two numbers, such as 19.8. The first number references the distillery of the whisky's origin, and the second number indicates the number of casks the SMWS has bottled from that distillery (a bottle of 19.8 translates into the eighth cask bottled by the society from distillery number 19). Brief tasting notes appear below the number and give the whisky drinker an idea of the flavors and aromas of each malt.

The tasting notes on the label offer novices a way to access the flavors and aromas awaiting them, and then to expand upon them with their own assessments. These notes originate with the society's tasting panel, comprised of independent experts who write the tasting notes in very quirky language—a trademark of SMWS tasting notes.

In addition to making unusual and quality whiskies available to their members, the SMWS offers an environment in which to enjoy them. Initially, it began with a members' room in Leith, the port area of Edinburgh. This offers a comfortable clubby room with an open fire, a small dining room, and lots of its single malts available by the dram. It later opened additional members' facilities in London and another in center city Edinburgh. Inclusive, rather than exclusive, the members' rooms are approachable for different people regardless of age or gender or profession, and they offer a quiet refuge or a place of conviviality and entertainment.

The society also supports eleven international chapters beyond its British base, including an American chapter operated by Alan Shayne. Members of the American chapter www.smwsa.com receive the tasting panel's notes; they read *Unfiltered*, the whisky information magazine, and attend tasting events held in twenty to twenty-five major cities.

Unique to the United States market, the SMWS America holds a whisky Extravaganza, in fourteen cities that showcases approximately one hundred Scotch Whiskies, the significant majority being single malts. True, the Scotch Malt Whisky Society of America presently does not offer the members' rooms that the British chapter does, but plans are in place to open a members' room in New York in 2012. Additionally, an American membership means that all the society venues are open to any member traveling to Edinburgh or London.

Signatory Vintage Malt Whisky Company

In 1988, when Andrew Symington was in his twenties he was the assistant manager at Prestonfields, a hotel in Edinburgh used by the whisky industry for hospitality. Inspired by the opportunities in the industry, he bought his first cask of whisky at a time when distilleries looked to sell their surplus stock because of the whisky recession. Both the number and choice of whisky casks for sale made it a good time to buy casks, so Andrew and his brother, Brian, seized the opportunity when it arrived.

The Distillery Cat's Meow

Originally, the Symingtons named the company Signatory and used a quill pen as their logo because they planned to have a celebrity sign each bottling. This proved impractical, and they eventually dropped the quill pen from their label but kept the name.

Building the Brand and Securing the Future

Signatory developed a reputation for quality bottlings of very rare malts often from little-known distilleries like Killyloch and Glen Flagler. But within the next two decades, the whisky industry rebounded from the 1980s recession and a growing interest in single malts meant that distilleries needed to husband their stocks. Surplus whisky no longer existed and few casks were available for sale. Symington realized he needed "to create an infrastructure to secure the future of Signatory."

To this end he bought Edradour Distillery in 2002, which also ensured the continuation of the production and maturation of Edradour malt, invested heavily in maturing casks to ensure stock for Signatory, invested in a bottling facility to provide extra capacity, and moved the Signatory offices to Edradour in 2007. The growing inventory of maturing Edradour and his investment in additional casks from other distilleries meant that he was no longer dependent on the variable availability of surplus casks of whisky.

Presently, Signatory bottlings focus on its Cask Strength collection, but it offers a non-chill filtered selection at 43 percent ABV, as well. From the beginning, Symington established himself as a premium independent bottler and his decisions in the last decade should help to secure his reputation for bringing good casks to the consumer.

Duncan Taylor Ltd.

www.duncantaylor.com

Euan Shand has had ownership of Duncan Taylor since 2002, but the company has long-established roots, which were planted in Glasgow in 1938. In the beginning, the company operated as a merchant and broker of whisky casks, but today Duncan Taylor operates solely as an independent bottler offering bottlings of casks from its warehouse under its own labels.

The New York Connection

In 1961, Abe Rosenberg of New York bought the company as something of a pet investment. Rosenberg, who built the J&B brand in America, was well established in the drinks business and acquired hundreds of casks of malt whisky, many from premium distilleries, and stored them for his own use. Shand, who once trained as a cooper, observed, "Coming from a coopering background, I couldn't believe the quality—his casks were the best. He sourced his wood very well, and bought second-fill casks so that the strong sherry and tannins had leached out [in the first use]."

New Ownership

Euan Shand began life at GlenDronach Distillery, where his father was manager, and when he began his career as a cooper, he started his training there. After gaining experience with several other companies, he returned to his roots within the whisky industry. Because of this experience and his knowledge of casks and wood policy, Euan Shand decided to acquire the Duncan Taylor Company in 2002, following Abe Rosenberg's death.

Within months of his purchase, Shand moved the company to Huntly in eastern Speyside, which allowed him to centralize the bonded warehouse, the shop, and bottling facility in one location. The company takes pride in doing everything itself from tracking the provenance of its casks from the day they are bought to designing the labels and filling the bottles.

The Noser Knows

Most notable, Duncan Taylor has casks for sale in both the quarter and octave size, which provide 75 to 150 bottles. This offers malt enthusiasts the opportunity to buy their own cask, have it filled with whisky that is at least three years old, and mature it in Duncan Taylor's bonded warehouse. After an appropriate maturation period, the people at Duncan Taylor will bottle and ship it to the owner.

No longer brokering whisky casks to other independent bottlers, Duncan Taylor offers only expressions of its own brands with natural color and non-chill filtering. Although it offers a blend bottled at different ages, the vast majority of its expressions are single-cask bottlings. These include whiskies bottled at a minimum of forty years in the Peerless range as well as whiskies ranging between 16 to 40 years old in the Rare Auld line. It also bottles heavily peated malt whisky, malt whiskies from closed and dismantled distilleries, and some malts at reduced strengths.

Adelphi (Pronounced *ah-DELL-fee*)

www.adelphidistillery.com

At the end of the nineteenth century, Archibald Walker added Adelphi Distillery to the two he owned in Ireland and England; a century later, his great-grandson, Jamie Walker, revived the name of his ancestor's distillery to introduce his new independent bottling company. In 1993, Walker set out to offer bottles of malt from high-quality single casks. In 2004, he sold the company to Keith Falconer and Donald Houston, who had approached Walker simply to buy a cask of whisky.

Under the tutelage of Charles MacLean, Adelphi continues to adhere to quality cask selection and offers single cask bottlings with natural color and non-chill filtering. Additionally, it released a blended Scotch whisky with a label that has a drawing from a nineteenth-century *Punch* cartoon of a dancing Scot as he celebrates the removal of taxes on maturing whisky. The little "dancey man" became and still remains the iconic mascot of the company.

Blackadder International

www.blackadder.com

Robin Tucek and John Lamond, coauthors of *The Whisky File*, established their company to bottle single casks with natural color and non-chill filtering. Most bottlings are reduced in strength, but some selections are bottled at cask strength. The Raw Casks series goes one step beyond non-chill filtering by leaving sediment from the casks in the bottle. While an argument exists for retaining the elements lost to chill filtering, the benefits from leaving bits and pieces in the bottle remains unclear. Blackadder also bottles under the labels of Aberdeen Distillers, Clydesdale Original, and Caledonian Connections.

Compass Box Whisky Company

www.compassboxwhisky.com

First, it must be clear that Compass Box does not bottle single malt whisky; instead it bottles innovative blended malt, blended grain, and blended Scotch whisky. However, its releases are interesting and merit some exploration.

John Glaser worked in both the wine and whisky industries before establishing Compass Box in 2000. By its own description it is a "specialist Scotch whiskymaker." Glaser's bottlings are usually blended malts that begin maturation in one type of cask and then undergo a second maturation in an innovative manipulation of another cask, often involving the introduction of different oak heads on the cask. Compass Box also offers bottlings in both the Signature range and the Limited Edition range, including different styles of whisky, blended grain whisky, blended Scotch whisky, and one single-cask expression in the Canto Cask offering. One can expect traditional whiskies with a different twist from Compass Box.

Dewar Rattray

www.adrattray.com

This company actually opened in 1868 as importers of wines and blenders of Scotch whisky. The original Dewar-Rattray sold the company in the 1920s. In 2004, Tim Morrison, fourth-generation descendent of Andrew Dewar, resurrected the company. Looking to bottle a range of styles from different regions, the company offers bottlings of single casks with non-chill filtering and natural coloring. Available bottlings in America seem confined to California.

Hart Brothers

www.hartbrothers.co.uk

Hart Brothers began as wholesalers and blenders in 1964. Later, Iain and Donald Hart brought their brother, Alistair, into the business to find casks for independent bottling. They offer a few blends, but their list primarily offers single casks that include some bottlings from lost distilleries. They release their malts at reduced strength with natural coloring and non-chill filtering. A limited selection of their releases is available in the United States.

James MacArthur

www.james-macarthur.co.uk

Established in 1984, James MacArthur offers single casks with natural coloring and non-chill filtering. Its releases have limited availability in the United States.

Ian Macleod Distillers Ltd.

www.ianmacleod.com

In 1933, Leonard J. Russell's family business operated primarily as whisky brokers. Thirty years later, the family bought the Ian Macleod brand and acquired the Isle of Skye blended Scotch whisky, necessitating its move into blending and bottling.

The Macleod Company bought whisky stock five years ahead,and this stock, once intended for blends, became the inventory to launch its single malt range. In 2003, the Russell family purchased the Glengoyne Distillery in order to secure stocks of single malts for its blends and for trading casks with other distilleries. The company then became Ian Macleod Distillers Ltd., built the Glengoyne single malt brand, and focused on developing a range of expressions. In June 2011, it acquired the Tamdhu Distillery in Speyside.

Whisky Lexicon

Single-cask bottlings are just that—the malt comes from one single cask with a limited number of bottles. **A** small batch includes several, often select, casks from one distillery and can provide a larger number of bottles.

The Ian Macleod range of malts does both small batch and single cask bottlings and offers an extensive list of whiskies with natural color and non-chill filtering. The Chieftain bottlings are meant to be "fit for a king" (or chieftain) and offer small batch premium brand single malts at different strengths from varied types of casks and at different ages and vintages. The Dun Bheagan range has both small batch and single-cask offerings and the Regional Malts selection showcases small batch malts from five whisky regions (Islay, Highlands, Speyside, Lowlands, and the Islands).

Known to many enthusiasts is the As We Get It range of cask strength single malts from unnamed distilleries. For those who like the peat of Islay, Smokehead is an unnamed, heavily peated single malt. The gentler version is Six Isles Island Blended Malt, which offers a blend of six malts from Islay and the other islands (i.e., Jura, Arran, Mull, Skye, and Orkney). The Islay contributes a robust smoke, which the other Island malts soften and balance.

Murray McDavid

www.murray-mcdavid.com

Mark Reynier with Simon Coughlin and Gordon Wright established Murray McDavid as independent bottlers in 1995, borrowing the names of Reynier's two grandparents as the name of the company. Reynier notes that the company was formed because of a "frustration with single casks" and the perception of its "heroic individuality." He will readily admit that single casks can be extraordinary, some can be quite good, others are good, but a portion can be bad.

Recognizing that all single casks of whiskies are different, the company uses the small batch approach by marrying four to seven casks of the same age and from the same distillery, rather than bottling single casks. This allows Murray McDavid "to put together different styles [of casks] to get something more interesting."

Reynier's interest in malt whisky expanded into new territory when he acquired Bruichladdich Distillery in 2000, which also became home to Murray McDavid's independent bottling operations. Currently, it offers a range of small batch vintage bottlings of casks chosen by Jim McEwan, Bruichladdich's master distiller. They are aged and bottled on Islay and are non-chill filtered with natural color.

Scott's Selection

www.speysidedistillers.co.uk

Initially George Christie, owner of Speyside Distillery, asked Robert Scott, master blender, to choose casks for independent bottling. Scott, now retired, makes selections with Andrew Shand, the current Speyside distillery manager, of both malt and grain single casks with natural color and non-chill filtering. These are offered at cask strength and reduced strength, and a range of blended Scotch whisky is also offered.

Vintage Malt Whisky Company

www.vintagemaltwhisky.com

Brian Crook founded his company in 1992 and promotes the personal service of his family-owned business. Somewhat confusingly, he bottles two single malts under his own brand names from "secret" distilleries. Finlaggan is a single Islay malt and Tantallan is a single Speyside malt and Glenalmond is a blend of Highland malts. He also offers single-cask bottlings under the Cooper's Choice range but the labels carry the distillery name (no secret distilleries).

Whisky Words: A Glossary of Whisky Terminology

ABV (alcohol by volume): the percentage of alcohol in a bottle expressed as a percentage of the entire volume.

acrospire: the green shoot that begins to grow during the first steps in the malting process. When the acrospire has filled three-quarters of the husk, it is time to kiln (dry) the barley to stop its continued growth.

Amylase: an enzyme that begins the conversion of starch to sugar (maltose).

angels' share: the amount of spirit lost to evaporation during the time it matures in oak casks. Evaporation accounts for the loss of approximately 2 percent of the cask's contents for approximately the first twelve years and then 1 percent afterward.

blend: to mix grain and malt whiskies to make blended Scotch whisky.

boil ball: a convex bulge between the shoulders and the head of a still that creates reflux action in the still. The more convex the shape, the greater the reflux.

cask strength (natural strength): the alcoholic strength at which whisky is bottled directly from the cask after maturation. It undergoes no reduction by water to 40 or 43 percent ABV as many other whiskies do. A cask strength bottling usually registers in a range from 50 to 61 percent ABV. It is different from new-make spirit that has not lost any of its volume or strength due to the evaporation loss of the angels' share.

column still: a pair of columnar stills consisting of an analyzer and a rectifier. Typically, the wash enters the top of the rectifier so that the rising steam heats it as it passes to the bottom of the column. It then moves to the top of the analyzer and drops down the still, condensing on the rectifying plates. Then the collected distillate passes from the bottom of the analyzer into the base of the rectifier. The distillate rises in the rectifier and eventually emerges as a light, pure spirit with an alcohol content higher than spirit distilled in a traditional pot still.

congener: a chemical compound developed during the whisky-making process that produces the flavors and aromas in both new-make spirit and matured whisky. Its formation tends to occur most commonly during malting, fermenting, and distilling, with the most significant flavor development happening during maturation in oak casks.

charging the still: filling a still with wash or low wine prior to distillation.

clearic (spike): also called spirit or new-make; the distillate as it comes off the last still. The alcoholic strength is usually about 68 to 70 percent ABV and is usually reduced with water to 63.5 percent when it is filled into casks.

condensers: a series of copper tubes, usually in the shell and tube design, that contain cool water and are inside a tall column that causes the hot vapor to condense into a liquid.

Cytase: an enzyme that breaks down the walls of the starch cells in grain kernels and makes the starch accessible.

Diastase: an enzyme that makes the starch soluble so that warm water can extract it.

direct firing: heating the bottom of the still until it runs hot enough to heat the wash inside the pot (similar to lighting a gas burner on a stove).

distillery character (spirit character): the flavor profile developed during distillation and evident in new-make spirit. Maturation develops and enhances this profile over time in a cask, when the whisky takes on its mature character.

double distillation: the standard distillation used in the whisky-making process. The wash is processed through two stills—the first distillation occurring in the wash still; the second distillation occuring in the spirit still.

draff: the husks that remain in the mash tun after the wort is drained. It is dried and used as cattle feed because of its high-protein content.

dramming the men: a practice carried out at all distilleries until the late 1970s that consisted of providing a large glass of new-spirit, which has a high alcohol strength, to distillery workers when they reported to work, finished work, and during their break. Additional drams were doled out to workers when they did particularly dirty work. For obvious reasons, The Office of Health and Safety stopped this practice.

drum malting: a machine with a revolving drum that turned grain while air, pumped through tubes running the length of the drum, maintained moisture in the barley.

dunnage warehouse: the traditional stone-built warehouse with earthen floors and low ceilings in which warehousemen stack maturing spirit three casks high.

endosperm: the part of a barley kernel that holds starch, which acts as food for the growing plant. The first enzymes activated in the malting process make the starch accessible and make it soluble. During both the malting and mashing processes, the starch converts to fermentable sugars.

esters: the fruity and floral flavors that many distillers want to capture as key components to the flavor profiles of many whiskies. Esters develop during fermentation as a byproduct, particularly if the mashman uses long fermentations. They tend to appear early in distillation and show toward the end of the foreshots and the beginning of the middle cut.

feints (tails): the last part of the distillation run, which has too many impurities and is diverted for redistillation in the spirit still. Phenols tend to appear at the beginning of the feints and some distillers who want to capture a smoky character will move the middle cut toward the tail end of the spirit run.

fermentation: the addition of yeast to sugary wort to produce alcohol, carbon dioxide, and esters. Fermentation also activates enzymes in the yeast that promote the conversion of sugar into alcohol.

filling program: a program that allows independent bottlers or other distilleries to send casks to specific distilleries for them to fill with new-make spirit. Filling programs allow the buyer to control the types of casks and the length of time used for maturation.

foreshots (heads): the first part of the distillation run, which has too many impurities and is not casked for aging. The stillman will divert the foreshots into the low wines and feints receiver to hold until he distills them once again in the spirit still. The beginning of the foreshots often contains some of the undesirable remnants of the end of the previous distillation; whereas the end of the foreshots contains the first appearance of the desirable fruity esters.

friability: the "crumbly" factor of the malted barley that distillery operators consider when adjusting their mills to produce the grind they desire.

green malt: the condition of barley after it has steeped in water in order to trigger germination. At this stage the barley kernel has about a 45 percent moisture content, and the green shoot has grown to fill three-quarters of the husk.

grist: malted barley after it has been ground in mills. It consists of approximately 70 percent grits, 20 percent husks, and 10 percent flour.

gross and tare: a traditional way of determining the bulk content of pure alcohol in a newly filled cask in order to calculate the duty owed. It was the method used before the introduction of automatic gauges. The warehouseman first weighs the cask empty to ascertain its tare weight, then weighs it filled to determine its gross weight. Quite simply, the tare is subtracted from the gross to ascertain a net weight of spirit in the cask. Keith Cruickshank of Benromach notes, "Using a factor (which is dependent on the alcoholic strength) we can then convert from bulk [kilograms] to bulk [liters]. From this we can work out litres of pure alcohol which we declare to HMRC [customs] and is duty payable after maturation."

heat exchanger: used in distilleries to pass hot liquid through pipes or plates containing cold liquid for cooling, or passing cold liquid through hot pipes and plates for preheating and conservation of energy.

hydrometer: an instrument used to measure the specific gravity of the distillate to determine its alcoholic strength.

indirect firing: heating using steam coils or pans within the still until the wash runs hot enough to heat the still (similar to using an electric tea kettle).

intermediate spirit receiver (ISR): a vessel for holding the middle cut of the distillate before it moves to the spirit vat in the filling room.

kilning: the process used to dry barley after it has been steeped in water to start the germination process. Drying barley with warm air or peat fires (to give it a smoky taste and aroma) stops the germination process and prevents the plant from using the starch for food. Instead, the kilning preserves the starch for conversion to fermentable sugars.

Lauter mash tun: a model of a mash tun first used in the brewing industry. It has feet that slice through the mash to prevent it from clumping, and its ability to move forward and backward and move the feet up and down makes it a more efficient model than the traditional rakes.

Lomond still: a still designed by Alistair Cunningham in the 1950s to produce additional malts for the Ballantine blends. It had angular shoulders and a "coffee can" head that held horizontal rectifying plates. By flooding the plates with distillate, leaving them dry, or swiveling them to a vertical position, the stillman could vary the reflux action, which varied the style of new-make spirit. Additionally, the stillman could raise or lower the lyne arm in order to affect the body of the spirit. He could also add or remove sections to the head of the still in order to lengthen or shorten it.

low wines: the resulting distillate from the first distillation in the wash still. The low wines join the foreshots and feints from the previous second distillation, and then move into the spirit still.

low wines and feints receiver: a vessel that holds the low wines from the first distillation as well as the undesirable heads and tails from the second distillation.

lyne arm (lye pipe): a pipe that connects the head of a still to a condenser or worm. Whether it has an upward or downward tilt influences the body of the new-make spirit.

malt (malted barley): the barley that has undergone the malting process.

malt culm: the dried root left on a kernel of barley after drying. It is removed and pressed into pellets with other culms for animal feed.

malting: a process that forces the barley to germinate in order to trigger the production of enzymes that make the starch accessible and begin its conversion to fermentable sugars.

maltman (maltster): the operator responsible for processing the barley through steeping, germinating, and kilning in order to produce malted barley necessary for Scotch whisky making.

Maltase: an enzyme that breaks down sugar, maltose, to form glucose, a simple sugar.

Maltose: sugar formed by the breakdown of starch.

mash: a porridge-like concoction made from adding hot water to grist in a mashing machine.

mashing: the process that activates enzymes to complete the conversion of starch to sugar, which was started during malting. It begins by adding hot water to grist, and then extracting the sugar with a total of three (sometimes four) water baths.

mashing machine: a small machine in which the grist and hot water are combined before it is poured into a mash tun.

mashman: the person who oversees the storage of malted barley when it is delivered, as well as milling, mashing, and fermenting.

mash tun: a large metal vessel that stirs mash with a rake or with blades.

middle cut (heart): the center portion of the run, which is the desirable spirit directed for maturation. The stillman can move the middle cut either forward or backward during the spirit run, in other words he can take it earlier in the distillation run in order to capture more esters, or he can take it later to capture more phenols.

Morton's Refrigerator: a common piece of equipment in dairies and distilleries that was used to cool the wort after mashing. Only Edradour Distillery still retains an operational refrigerator, which is a reproduction of the 1934 original

neat: the drinking of whisky as it is poured from the bottle without diluting it with water or mixers.

new-make: see *clearic*.

peat: the compacted, partially decomposed plant debris found in bogs, which contributes to the smoky *(phenols)* character of malt whisky.

peat–reek: the pungent smoky aroma in single malts that have a high level or high intensity of phenols.

phenols: chemical compounds responsible for the smoky, medicinal, iodine, or burnt character of some malts, particularly Islay malts. The husks of malted barley absorb phenols when they are dried over peat fires for a designated amount of time. The intensity of phenols are measured in parts per million (ppm).

pot ales (burnt ales): any solids left in the wash still after the first distillation, which are converted into syrup and usually used as cattle feed.

pot still: the traditional copper still used in the distillation of malt whisky. Unlike the column still, the pot still has a determinate size, with a pot-shaped bottom and a head that rises from the shoulders. The head then ends in a swan neck, where it attaches to a lyne arm.

rectifying still: a still with a tall columnar head rising above its shoulders. The design of the still includes perforated rectifying plates placed horizontally at intervals inside the column. As the distillate vaporizes and rises in the neck, it condenses on the cooler plates and drops back into the pot of the still, allowing repeated distillation and purification of the spirit.

reflux: the action that occurs when vapors condense before they reach the lyne arm and drop back into the pot still to reboil. The redistillation allows a greater separation of the volatile components that rise in the vapor and the nonvolatile components that stay behind in the pot.

Heavy reflux action allows the distillate to stay in contact with the copper longer, creating a cleaner spirit.

rummager: links of metal, which resemble medieval chain mail. It is used in a still that directly heats the bottom of the still (like a gas flame) to prevent solids from sticking to the bottom of the still and burning. It also serves an additional purpose of exposing more copper to the distillate.

Saladin box: a machine of revolving tines that moved along a long box to turn grain while air circulated through the wet barley.

Scotch Whisky Regulations of 2009: UK legislation enacted in November 2009 at the urging of the Scotch Whisky Association (SWA) to regulate many aspects of Scotch whisky production, labeling, and exportation.

steeping, germinating, and kilning vessel (SGKV): a large container that performs all three processes at central maltsters.

shoogle (shake) box: usually a rather nicely crafted box with several layers of increasingly fine mesh that evaluates a sample of grist. A worker shakes the box (hence the name shoogle), and the mesh separates the grist into its three parts to verify that the proper balance of flour to grits to husks has been milled.

sight glass: a glass porthole in the head of a wash still used to help the stillman monitor the boiling of the distillate.

small batch: the mixing of a very small number of casks from one distillery that share distinctive characteristics and similar ages.

sparge: the last water of the mashing process, which is very low in dissolved sugar so the mashman diverts it for use as the first water of the next mash.

spent cask: a cask that has been filled so many times that the effects of the wood and the original fill are used up (spent).

spent lees: the residue remaining in a spirit still which is processed as waste.

spirit: see *clearic*.

spirit safe: a brass and glass case locked by the excise officer, which allows the stillman to monitor the distillate without touching it. By using external handles he can divert the first and last part of the spirit run for redistillation and channel the middle (and desirable) part for casking.

spirit still (low wines still): the last (and usually second) still used in distillation. It is usually the smaller of the two stills.

spirit vat: a vat that holds new-make spirit in the filling room in preparation for filling into casks.

standing and shooks: the way in which American bourbon barrels are shipped to Scotland. Scottish distilleries can buy them and ship them *standing*, or they can break the barrel into numbered staves and tie them together and ship only the bundles, which are known as *shooks*.

steeping: the first step in the malting process in which barley soaks in water and then alternately rests with an infusion of warm air. This process raises the moisture content of the barley to 45 percent and triggers germination in the kernels.

stillman: oversees the distillation process. This includes pumping the fermented washbacks, charging and operating the stills, and taking the cuts during the spirit run.

switcher: revolving propellers at the top of the washbacks used to keep the fermenting wash from foaming over the top of the washback.

top dressing: a malt that blenders find desirable for making a successful blended Scotch whisky because it can marry all of the different flavor components in a blend into a smooth and balanced Scotch whisky with character.

triple distillation: the addition of an intermediate still between the wash and spirit stills. Distilling in three stills instead of two raises the alcohol strength of the new-make and produces a light, clean spirit.

underback: a large tank for the storage of the sweet wort after it has drained from the mash tun and before it is poured into washbacks for fermentation.

vatting (marrying): mixing several casks from one distillery (for bottling single malts) or mixing several casks from different distilleries (for bottling blended malts).

wash: the result of the fermentation of the sugary wort in vessels called washbacks. It smells and tastes like apple cider at about 8 percent ABV.

wash charger: a vessel that contains the wash until it holds sufficient liters to charge (fill) the wash still.

wash still: the first still used in distillation; it raises the alcohol strength of the distillate to about 23 percent. It is usually the larger of the stills and has a sight glass in its neck.

washback: the fermenting vessel used in distilling to convert the wort to wash with the addition of yeast.

weir: a narrow trough that runs along the sides of the interior neck of a still with rectifying plates to ensure that the spirit drops back into the pot. As the distillate condenses on the rectifying plates, the spirit rolls off the plates into the weirs and travels downward into the pot of the still.

worm: a spiraling copper pipe that is immersed in cold water in a worm tub and is built outside of the stillroom. The hot vapor enters the top of the worm, where it is widest, and condenses back into a liquid as it descends the ever-decreasing diameter of the worm.

wort: the sweet, sugary liquid, which also contains vital enzymes, that is the end product of the mashing process.

Zymase: an enzyme in yeast that helps promote the conversion of sugar into alcohol.

APPENDIX B

Alphabetical Distillery Locator

APPENDIX B

INDEX

M

V

W

Z